Screening a Lynching

Screening a Lynching

The Leo Frank Case on Film and Television

MATTHEW H. BERNSTEIN

The University of Georgia Press

Athens & London

Designed by Erin Kirk New
Set in 10 on 14 Sabon
Printed and bound by Thomson-Shore

The paper in this book meets the guidelines for
permanence and durability of the Committee on
Production Guidelines for Book Longevity of the
Council on Library Resources.

Printed in the United States of America

13   12   11   10   09   C   5   4   3   2   1
13   12   11   10   09   P   5   4   3   2   1

Library of Congress Cataloging-in-Publication Data

Bernstein, Matthew.
Screening a lynching : the Leo Frank case on film and television /
Matthew H. Bernstein.
         p. cm.
Includes bibliographical references and index.
ISBN-13: 978-0-8203-2752-5 (hardcover : alk. paper)
ISBN-10: 0-8203-2752-2 (hardcover : alk. paper)
ISBN-13: 978-0-8203-3239-0 (pbk. : alk. paper)
ISBN-10: 0-8203-3239-9 (pbk. : alk. paper)
1. Frank, Leo, 1884–1915—In motion pictures. 2. Frank, Leo, 1884–
1915—On television. I. Title.
PN1995.9.F795B47   2009
791.43'75—dc22   2008024046

British Library Cataloging-in-Publication Data available

The film and television illustrations that appear in this volume are from the
author's collection.

Images from *Murder in Harlem* appear courtesy of the G. William Jones Film
and Video Collection, Hamon Arts Library, Southern Methodist University.

Images from *They Won't Forget* © Warner Bros. Pictures.

Images from *Profiles in Courage: Governor John M. Slaton* courtesy of
Steven Saudek.

Images from *The Murder of Mary Phagan* © 1988 Orion Pictures
Corporation. All rights reserved. Courtesy of MGM CLIP+STILL.

To the memory of my father,
Harold P. Bernstein

HORATIO: I saw him once. He was a goodly king.
HAMLET: He was a man, take him for all in all.
    I shall not look upon his like again.

—*Hamlet*, act 1, scene 2

Contents

Preface

THIS BOOK grew out of an interdisciplinary research project I began more than ten years ago with Professor Dana F. White of Emory University, an urban historian and authority on Atlanta history. In researching the history of Atlanta's film culture, we focused on films about the South and about race relations. Two 1930s films about the Mary Phagan–Leo Frank case were an obvious point of interest. Yet Atlanta's film censor at the time cut one in half and banned the other; they are not part of Atlanta's film history.

As I began examining the production histories of Oscar Micheaux's *Murder in Harlem* and Warner Bros.'s *They Won't Forget*, I became fascinated with the ways in which the filmmakers dramatized the case. What first intrigued me was the filmmakers' intricate knowledge of the trial and its aftermath. Watching these films with Leonard Dinnerstein's *The Leo Frank Case* (first published in 1968) in hand, I felt almost as though directors Micheaux and Mervyn LeRoy had jumped into the future and read that book while making their films in the 1930s. I was equally fascinated by the ways in which these films shaped the disturbing history they dramatized into sellable stories. In short, I joined the ranks of the many Americans who are fascinated with the case itself. The case was made even more fascinating by the publication in 2003 of Steve Oney's incredibly detailed account of it, *And the Dead Shall Rise*.

What follows are close examinations of the Phagan-Frank case juxtaposed with the two 1930s films and with two television treatments of it, the 1964 *Profiles in Courage* episode "Governor John M. Slaton" and the 1988 miniseries *The Murder of Mary Phagan*. I did not undertake primary research into the case itself looking for overlooked clues; nor did I try to formulate a new interpretation of the case. Instead, I sought to discover how filmmakers and television creators researched and understood the case and why their productions took the form they ultimately did—writing, of course, from the perspective of what we know today. As George Stevens Jr., the producer and cowriter of *The Murder of Mary Phagan*, put it to me, I was "walking the cat backward." This book is the result of that reverse promenade.

Acknowledgments

I had a great deal of help as I delved into the history of the four dramatizations of the Phagan-Frank case. No historian of film or television can work without the aid of archivists and librarians, and I have many debts. At UCLA's Young Research Library, I had the expert assistance of Octavio Olvera of the Department of Special Collections (for materials from the George P. Johnson Collection relating to Oscar Micheaux and race filmmaking), and Julie Graham and Lauren Buisson of the Arts Library Special Collections (for a script draft of part 1 of *The Murder of Mary Phagan*). At the Margaret Herrick Library of the Academy of Motion Picture Arts and Sciences, Barbara Hall of Special Collections was extraordinarily helpful in providing the relevant materials from the Motion Picture Producers and Distributors Association Production Code Administration files, as well as press books for Warner Bros. and MGM films. At the Warner Bros. Archive at USC, Head Curator Haden Guest and his staff facilitated my research into the making of *They Won't Forget*; Haden's successor, Sandra Lee Joy, was incredibly helpful with last-minute document requests. At USC's Cinema-Television Library, the indefatigable Ned Comstock made available materials on Fritz Lang's *Fury* and an extensive set of clippings on *The Murder of Mary Phagan*. At the Wisconsin Center for Film and Theatre Research, Harry Miller and Maxine Fleckner-Ducey and their staff were extremely helpful. At the Wesleyan Cinema Archives, Joan Miller and Leith Johnson graciously guided me through materials in the Robert Saudek Collection. I also thank Stephen Plotkin at the John F. Kennedy Presidential Library in Boston for helping me examine President Kennedy's papers and those of his special counsel, Theodore C. Sorenson. I thank Shannon Fifer of Warner Bros. Studio's Legal Department and Steve Saudek for permission to quote from and use materials in the Warner Bros. Archives and the Robert Saudek Collection, respectively.

For help with images, I am in the debt of Professor Jane Gaines of Duke University; Beth McLain, Research Manager, and Betsy Rix, Manager of Reprographic Services, at the Kenan Research Center of the Atlanta History Center; Sandra Berman, Curator, and Ruth Einstein, Special Projects Coordinator, of the Breman Jewish Museum of Atlanta; Gail DeLoach, Visual Materials Reference Librarian at the Georgia Archives; Peter Roberts, Photographic Collections Archivist at Georgia State University Special Collections; Steven Saks at the New York Public Library's Photographic Services and Permissions Division; Kristine Krueger of the Margaret Herrick Library of the Academy of Motion Picture Arts and Sciences; Amy Turner and the G. William Jones Film and Video Collection, Hamon Arts Library, Southern Methodist University; Barry Dagestino of MGM's Clip+Stills Department; and again Ned Comstock at the USC Cinema-Television Library. I am deeply grateful to them all.

I am also indebted to several members of the creative team behind *The Murder of Mary Phagan* for granting me interviews on their work: producer-writer George Stevens Jr., cowriter Jeffrey Lane, production designer Veronica Hadfield, and cinematographer Nic Knowland, as well as Charles Dutton. Their recall of a project nearly twenty years into the past was truly remarkable and aided me enormously in reconstructing that miniseries's history in the absence of archival sources. Likewise, I thank Steve Saudek for graciously sharing with me a draft of the portion of his father's memoirs on *Profiles in Courage*, and Theodore C. Sorenson, Mary V. Ahern, and Don M. Mankiewicz for sharing their recollections of the series and the Slaton episode with me.

For other assistance of various kinds, I am grateful to Shona Barrett of the British Film Institute's National Film and Television Archive in London; Professor Jeanine Basinger of Wesleyan University's Cinema Department and Archives; Angela Gordon of the Endeavor Talent Agency; Dottie McCarthy at the Kennedy Center in Washington, D.C.; Genevieve McGillicuddy, Brand Manager, and Scott McGee, Writer/Producer, at Turner Classic Movies' On-Air/Creative Division; Lee Tsiantis, Corporate Legal Manager in the Turner Entertainment Group; opera experts Rabbi

Phil Krantz and Cecelia Shannon; and Dr. Robert W. Gern. Kathy Fuller-Seely helped me sort out the Richmond locations. Miles Alexander, an Atlanta attorney, shared his invaluable Leo Frank case files with me, and this account is much richer for it. For legal advice, I thank James D. Peterson of Godfrey & Kahn S.C. I thank Professors Richard Neupert and Gaylyn Studlar for general encouragement and friendly support.

One of the great pleasures of this project was sharing research and ideas with others. This includes Jessica Rosner of Kino International, who sent me a portion of her Wesleyan University senior college thesis on Warner Bros.'s 1930s message movies. I have also received considerable advice, feedback, encouragement, and shared resources from Professors Marc Auslander and Ellen Schattschneider of Brandeis University; film historian Kevin Brownlow; Professor Jane Gaines of Duke University; Rutgers University Press editor Leslie Mitchner; and film biographer extraordinaire Patrick McGilligan, whose full biography of Oscar Micheaux was published as I completed this project. For much needed guidance on researching television history, I am deeply indebted to Professor Michele Hilmes of the University of Wisconsin and especially to Professor Jason Mittell of Middlebury College. For information on *Profiles in Courage*, I was guided by the pioneering research and advice of Professor Daniel Marcus of Goucher College and the suggestions of Patrick Loughney of the Eastman House Film Archive. I am also very grateful to Professor Amy Wood of Southern Illinois University for sharing with me some chapters from her extraordinary forthcoming book on images of lynching, including films. I also owe a considerable debt to Leonard Dinnerstein and Steve Oney, whose books on the Phagan-Frank case were of invaluable aid. Steve also provided excellent feedback on the manuscript and corrected several errors of fact.

For opportunities to present portions of this project, I am grateful to my colleagues Professor Rudolph Byrd of African American Studies at Emory University and Miriam Petty, who enabled me to present an early version of chapter 2 at the Emory International Conference on Lynching in fall 2003; Professors Thomas Doherty and Stephen Whitfield of the American Studies Program at Brandeis University, as well as the Jewish Studies and Film Studies Programs at Brandeis University, where I presented an abridged version of chapter 2; and Professors Barbara Klinger, Gregory Waller, and James Naremore of Indiana University's Department of Communication and Culture for the chance to present an abridged version of chapter 3.

This book is a spin-off of the "Segregated Cinema in a Southern City" project with Dana F. White. We have received considerable support from the University Research Committee of Emory University, which provided us first with a seed grant to develop an overview of our project and then subsequent grants to aid us in completing the project's research. The URC grant allowed us to apply for and be awarded a National Endowment for the Humanities Collaborative Research Grant from 1997 to 2000, which also greatly aided us in our work. This project was again supported by the University Research Committee of Emory University in 2008 with generous funds for this volume's illustration program and marketing.

More specifically, this volume began in earnest during a senior fellowship at Emory University Center for Humanistic Inquiry for the 2002–2003 year. I am grateful to its director, Professor Martine Brownley, Associate Director Keith Anthony, and Senior Secretary Carol Burnside for providing such a first-rate, welcoming, and stimulating space to pursue research. I am also grateful to Dean Robert A. Paul and my former chair, Professor David A. Cook, for providing the means to accept the fellowship.

One result of that fellowship was the publication of "Oscar Micheaux and Leo Frank: Cinematic Injustice across the Color Line," in *Film Quarterly* 57, no. 4 (2004). I am grateful to then-editor Ann Martin and the editorial board for their excellent feedback on the piece and for nominating it for the Katherine Singer Kovacs Essay Award given by the Society for Cinema and Media Studies. I am indebted to the SCMS Essay Award committee for selecting this article for that singular honor in 2005. I also thank Derek Jenkins and Paul Reyes of the *Oxford American* for their assistance in publishing a much abbreviated version of chapter 2.

I am grateful to the extraordinarily capable support of our staff in the Emory Film Studies Department, Academic Department Administrator Annie Hall (yes, her real name) and Cecelia Shannon, department secretary, for their perennial good cheer and manifold assistance as I prepared this manuscript. I also appreciate the general support of my faculty colleagues, David A. Cook, Nina K. Martin, Karla Oeler, and Eddy von Mueller.

At the University of Georgia Press, Andrew Berzanskis and Courtney Denney have been far more patient than any editor has a right to be. Their constant encouragement was a boon to this project. I also thank Regan Huff and Nancy Grayson. I am grateful for all their hard work and invaluable advice on behalf of this project. One could not ask for a more adept copy editor than Mindy Conner. Bob Schwarz provided a thorough index.

Four individuals were especially helpful to me as this project took shape. Professor Dana F. White persuaded me, over my objections, that there might be scholarly interest in this topic and encouraged me to publish a version of chapter 1. He granted me leave from our collaboration to finish this project, gave me a valuable reading of a first draft, and helped me understand Oscar Micheaux's relationship to the Leo Frank case. David B. Pratt gave me a copy of Leonard Dinnerstein's book, performed dogged research, read a first complete draft with minute precision, and gave me invaluable criticisms of my arguments and evidence on virtually every page. Dave actually helped me see what my argument could be; I am grateful for his advice as well as his friendship. Professor Tom Doherty of Brandeis University provided a sympathetic, insightful reading of the manuscript for the University of Georgia Press. A first-rate film and television historian himself, Tom offered innumerable suggestions for making the book a more compelling and accurate read, and even suggested the title. Susan Carini provided astute, expert copyediting as I revised the manuscript; her eagle eye, sagacious judgment, and lively prose writing style improved every page of the typescript.

The support of my family has been essential to the research and realization of this project. I thank my mother, Elayne P. Bernstein, who suggested to me to a career in education; my brother Gene Bernstein, who showed me the path to becoming a university professor; my brother Jay Bernstein, whose imagination, energy, and enviable intensity have always been an inspiration; my sister, Linda Rubin, and her husband, Tony, who have housed me too many times to count as I pursued research in the Los Angeles archives. I also thank Pamela Bernstein, Jill Bernstein, Helen Bernstein, Sol Schwartz, Robert W. Bond Jr., and the late Alice F. Bond, who passed away as I was completing this project.

As always, I cannot express my profound debt to Natalie Bernstein for her love, support, and encouragement over the course of our life together. She and our sons, Justin and Adam, budding scholars in their own right, remain our greatest source of joy and our favorite movie-watching companions.

I lost my father, Harold P. Bernstein, while I was writing this book. I will always cherish the example he set for me—his keen intelligence, his constant striving in all his endeavors, his unfailing optimism and humor, and his humility. I dedicate this book to his memory.

Screening a Lynching

Leo Frank's body remained hanging for hours while onlookers took photographs and ripped off pieces of his clothing for souvenirs. (Courtesy of Vanishing Georgia Collection, Georgia Archives.)

Introduction

IN AUGUST 1915, in the woods outside Marietta, Georgia, a mob of angry white southerners lynched a man for rape and murder. Neither the event—a well-planned act of vigilante violence—nor the inspiration—the alleged violation and murder of a white woman—was particularly unusual at that time and place in American history. What *was* unusual was the race of the man at the end of the rope. He was white. Stranger still, his fate was sealed not by his crime but by his religion. He was Jewish.

The victims—I overtly use the plural here—were Leo Frank and Mary Phagan. As the title of Mervin LeRoy's 1937 film about the matter prophesied of all those who learn of the case, "They won't forget." And indeed, few have. In some ways, though, the better question is: Why do so many still remember? Mary Phagan's murder was one of thousands of crimes committed in 1913, and the lynching of Leo Frank in 1915 was just one of an estimated 288 such acts perpetrated against white Americans between 1882 and 1930. And this number pales in comparison with the estimated 2,500 black lynchings between 1880 and 1930—nearly one per week during a fifty-year span, all without the benefit of a trial and "at the hands of persons unknown."[1]

For many Americans, the Phagan-Frank case has been an obsession out of proportion to its status as a discrete historical event in a rough-and-tumble time. All manner of artists—songwriters, novelists, journalists, playwrights, and filmmakers—have considered it worthy subject matter.[2] This volume looks at the two surviving theatrical films and the two television programs (shot on 35 mm film) depicting what befell Phagan

The most frequently published photograph of Mary Phagan, the victim. (Courtesy of the Kenan Research Center at the Atlanta History Center.)

and Frank. Why do filmmakers return to this ground? Has the passing of decades done anything to rewrite the moral ledger recording victims and perpetrators? The fullest answer resides in the case itself.

It began the night following Confederate Memorial Day on Saturday, April 26, 1913. White, thirteen-year-old Mary Phagan was found beaten and strangled in the basement of the Atlanta, Georgia, National Pencil Company factory, which Leo Frank supervised and of which he was part owner.

Several early suspects surfaced, including the factory's black night watchman, Newt Lee, who discovered Phagan's body around three a.m. and called the police. Two "murder notes" lay beside her body, apparently written by Phagan and alleging that "that negro hire down here" was guilty. The Atlanta Police Department's detectives grilled Lee abusively for days to extract a confession. (Though the murder notes were widely perceived as implicating Lee, they had actually been intended to accuse William Nolle, the factory's boiler operator.) Yet various other men seemed to have an ominous connection with Phagan, however casual.

After several fruitless days with Lee, police turned their suspicion to the twenty-nine–year-old factory superintendent, Leo Frank, who by his own admission was the last person to see Phagan alive. Ironically, she had been laid off earlier in the month when the supply of metal used to make the pencil tips ran low and had returned to the factory on Confederate

Leo Frank. (Courtesy of the Kenan Research Center at the Atlanta History Center.)

Memorial Day to collect the $1.20 in wages still owed her. Frank was working on factory accounts that afternoon and dispensed Phagan's pay to her. Spurred by some unusual behavior on Frank's part before the discovery of Phagan's body, and by Frank's nervousness when the police came to question him, the Atlanta law officers "lost" evidence that might have exonerated him. The police force of the time was corrupt and extremely anxious to solve the case after mishandling several other Atlanta murders. The overzealous work of police and press convinced the majority of Atlantans that Frank was guilty even before the trial began.

The prosecution, led by forty-two-year-old Fulton County Public Solicitor Hugh M. Dorsey, built on the pretrial and in-court testimony of young female factory workers who claimed that Frank had been physically attentive to them as they worked and had offered them money for sex. The glue binding all the hearsay "evidence" was the perjured testimony of black janitor Jim Conley. An early suspect, Conley had provided two affidavits with distinctly different contents, then offered the hungry Atlanta police a third that gave a satisfyingly full account of the murder.

Conley claimed that Frank had accidentally killed Phagan in a storage room near his second-floor office while struggling to have sex with her— as Frank allegedly had done or tried to do with other factory girls. Conley told the police that Frank had strangled the girl so she could not accuse him of sexual assault and then had called Conley upstairs and compelled

A rare photo of Jim Conley, the prosecution's chief witness against Leo Frank. (Courtesy of the New York Times Company Records, Adolph Ochs Papers, Manuscripts and Archives Division, the New York Public Library.)

him to transport her body via the elevator to the basement. Frank then dictated to him the mysterious murder notes the police found by Phagan's body purporting to identify the murderer as William Nolle or Newt Lee and instructed Conley to burn Phagan's body. Conley claimed that he performed, reluctantly, all but the last of Frank's demands. The three loosely stitched affidavits notwithstanding, Conley proved amazingly invulnerable to extensive cross-examination by Frank's accomplished lead defense attorneys, Luther Rosser and Reuben Arnold.

That Phagan might have died fighting to preserve her virginity from Frank ignited the fury of many Georgians, who saw the young woman as a symbol of southern innocence and martyrdom. The presiding judge, Leonard Roan, and the jury could not ignore the increasingly vocal crowds inside and outside the courtroom, and Roan was too intimidated by popular sentiment in Atlanta and across the state to try to silence them. Frank's attorneys finally moved for a mistrial late in the proceedings, but Roan dismissed the motion. After failing to break down Conley on the stand, Frank's attorneys took a huge risk by basing their defense on Frank's upstanding reputation among Atlanta's German Jewish elite and the business community. This move left Frank vulnerable to Dorsey's demonization of him as a lecherous northern capitalist exploiting young female laborers who, like Mary Phagan, were the daughters of rural families who could no longer survive by farming.[3] That Frank was Jewish provided Dorsey

The *Atlanta Constitution* published this drawing of Hugh Dorsey questioning star witness Jim Conley during the trial on August 5, 1913. Dorsey is quoted as asking Conley to demonstrate how he found the strangling cord around Mary Phagan's neck. (Courtesy of the *Atlanta Constitution* and the Cuba Archives of the Breman Museum.)

Hugh Dorsey (standing at left) questions Newt Lee (seated at right) during the trial in a makeshift courtroom in City Hall. Leo and Lucille Frank are seated at center right (Lucille is behind and just to the left of Leo). Judge Leonard Roan presides. (Courtesy of Special Collections and Archives, Georgia State University Library.)

with an additional, if unstated, prejudice that—combined with Frank's northern upbringing and managerial status—confirmed widespread belief in his guilt.

The monthlong trial had many unusual aspects. One was that a white jury convicted a white man on the basis of the inconsistent testimony of a black witness only seven years after Atlanta's infamous race riot in which white Atlantans killed or injured an estimated forty black citizens. As the prosecution exploited prejudices against northerners, upper-middle-class managers, and Jews, Frank's defense team tried to activate racist bigotry against Conley, alleging that Dorsey had coached Conley (which was undoubtedly true). Frank's lawyers and Frank himself excoriated Conley as "a dirty, filthy, black, drunken, lying nigger" and "black brute."[4] Their views were echoed in papers around the country favorable to Frank, but their comments had no impact on the jurors at the original trial. In fact,

Leo Frank sits in his usual posture during the trial. Lucille Frank sits behind him. (Courtesy of the Cuba Archives of the Breman Museum.)

renowned as they were, Frank's attorneys badly mishandled the case. They were powerless to undermine the prosecution's witnesses and an aroused public opinion that demanded vengeance for Phagan's death beyond the conviction and execution of a southern black male. This was one key reason why the Atlanta police acted against Frank, the jury chose to convict him, and his lynchers carried out his execution when at least one perfectly serviceable black suspect was available.

Frank was convicted in late August 1913. After the verdict, several appeals to the state appellate and supreme courts failed, as did two appeals to the U.S. Supreme Court (despite dissenting opinions by Justices Oliver Wendell Holmes Jr. and Charles Evan Hughes). It was not until the ruling in *Moore et al. v. Dempsey* in 1923, long after Frank's murder, that the Court finally acknowledged that defendants are entitled to safeguards against mob intimidation to ensure due process.

The *Atlanta Constitution* ran this layout of the attorneys involved in Leo Frank's trial on July 27, 1913. The full figure is Luther Z. Rosser, Frank's lead defense attorney. The remaining faces are (clockwise from top left): Solicitor General Hugh M. Dorsey; Reuben Arnold, Rosser's assistant; Assistant Solicitor General E. A. Stephens; and Frank A. Hooper, Dorsey's assistant. (Courtesy of the *Atlanta Constitution* and the Cuba Archives of the Breman Museum.)

Frank's appeals were accompanied by a groundswell of national support mobilized by wealthy, northern, Jewish businessmen and by prominent publications such as *Collier's* and William Randolph Hearst's papers, including the *Atlanta Georgian*. Even *New York Times* publisher Adolph Ochs directed his paper to follow the Frank appeals closely as new evidence came to light. Thus, the Frank case became a nationwide cause célèbre.

Dorsey vigorously opposed the judicial appeals, and many Georgians supported his efforts to see Frank executed. The most prominent and effective of these was publisher Tom Watson, a former politician whose greatest moment on the national political stage came when he ran for vice president alongside William Jennings Bryan on a Populist ticket in 1896. The fifty-seven-year-old Watson's weekly publication, the *Jeffersonian*, and his self-referential monthly, *Watson's Magazine*, characterized Frank

Tom Watson railed against Leo Frank and his appeal efforts in his publications and encouraged Leo Frank's lynching. (Courtesy of the Kenan Research Center at the Atlanta History Center.)

as a rich Jew who considered himself above the law. Many Georgians believed that folks in other states—particularly those north of the Mason-Dixon line—had no business meddling in Georgia's affairs.

After a final appeal to the Georgia Prison Commission proved futile, the matter came down to the usual two players in such a drama: the accused man and his governor. In June 1915 Frank petitioned the outgoing governor, John M. Slaton, to commute his death sentence to life in prison. Slaton had been a very popular governor and had ambitions to run for the U.S. Senate. The governor spent twelve of his final days in office sifting through evidence in the case, holding hearings, reading the trial transcript, and paying two visits to the pencil factory. Slaton also received more than 100,000 petitions in support of Frank's life (including one each from the state legislatures of Tennessee and Texas) and petitions urging him to ensure that Frank's death sentence was carried out.

Governor John M. Slaton, who
commuted Leo Frank's death
sentence to life in prison in
the final days of his term,
circa 1911–12. (Courtesy of the
Vanishing Georgia Collection,
Georgia Archives.)

The governor had the chance to consider evidence that had come to
light or was better understood since the original trial, such as similarities between the mysterious murder notes found by Phagan's body and
Conley's writing in some letters sent to another woman. Another piece
of information came from the trial's presiding judge, Leonard S. Roan,
who shortly before his death from jaw cancer stated his firm belief that
Frank was innocent. Yet another fact had not been properly considered at
the trial: Conley had admitted defecating in the pencil factory's elevator
shaft on the morning of the day Phagan was murdered. Given that the
police had mashed the excrement when they took the factory elevator to
the basement to retrieve Phagan's body early Sunday morning—that is,
Conley's feces were intact until that moment—Conley must have committed perjury when he claimed that he and Frank had used the elevator to
convey Phagan's dead body to the basement on the preceding Saturday afternoon. For all these reasons and many more, Slaton, just days before his
term ended and Frank was scheduled to be executed, commuted Frank's

sentence to life imprisonment on the grounds that reasonable doubt existed as to Frank's guilt.

Mobs massed in response to the announcement. Georgians marched on and entered Slaton's office, the state capitol, Atlanta's City Hall, and even marched to Slaton's suburban Buckhead home. They were aroused in good part by Tom Watson's fiery calls in the *Jeffersonian* to correct what was perceived as Slaton's hijacking of the judicial system. Accusations swirled that Slaton had been bribed by wealthy, northern, Jewish interests (such as those financing Frank's appeals); that he had a conflict of interest in the case owing to the fact that his law firm had merged with that of Frank's defense attorney Luther Rosser; or both. Slaton called out the state militia to protect himself and restore order; one protestor even tried to strike Slaton with a lead pipe as he left City Hall after the inauguration of his successor, Nat Harris. Slaton's promising political career was over. Dorsey was elected governor in 1916, Watson to the U.S. Senate in 1920.

Meanwhile, Leo Frank was nearly killed in July 1915 by a pathological fellow inmate at Milledgeville State Prison, where he was taken for his own safety after the governor's decision. Nearing recovery from the deep wound this attack had inflicted, Frank awoke on the night of August 16 to find himself being abducted by twenty-five "Knights of Mary Phagan" whose stealthy and smooth invasion of the penitentiary was, according to historian Steve Oney, tolerated by prison officials sympathetic to their aim.[5] After driving through the night, this group lynched Frank the following morning near Mary Phagan's birthplace in Marietta, several miles north of Atlanta. Frank's body hung for hours as crowds posed for photographs next to it and tore off pieces of his clothing for souvenirs. No one was ever tried for the crime. We now know that leading figures in Marietta—including an ex-governor, the son of a U.S. senator, two newly elected state legislators, and an active judge—planned the abduction and lynching. Supervising the execution were several sons of prominent citizens, successful Marietta businessmen, a chain-gang supervisor, and an attorney. Those who actually abducted and lynched Leo Frank included sheriff's deputies. Only one of the lynch mob was a relative of Mary Phagan.[6] As for Frank's family, Lucille Frank never remarried and maintained her husband's innocence until her death in 1957.

Although the original jury had breezed to its verdict, Governor Slaton's more studied deliberation uncovered many ambiguities in the case. Some emerged as the investigation was under way, some as the trial proceeded, and others as the appeals process made its way through the

Leo and Lucille Frank in Atlanta's Grant Park in happier times. (Courtesy of the Cuba Archives of the Breman Museum.)

judicial system. Revelations continue to this day. Setting aside Conley's three conflicting affidavits, numerous witnesses offered evidence against Frank, recanted their statements, and then recanted their recantations. For example, the teenager George Epps claimed that he was friendly with Mary Phagan, that he rode the streetcar into town with her on the day of her murder, and that Mary had shared with him her fear of Frank's sexual overtures. After the trial, he admitted to lying. A few days after that, however, he insisted that his testimony was the truth. Other witnesses traveling such a crooked path included the Franks' cook, Minola Knight; her husband; and several factory girls who testified against Frank initially. To Frank's supporters, they appeared to have recanted their testimony out of fear or conscience and then reversed course again because of police coercion. Those convinced of Frank's guilt viewed these recantations as evidence of coercion and moneyed influence on the part of Frank's defense team.

One witness well disposed to Frank—thirteen-year-old office boy Alonzo Mann—gave only muted testimony favorable to Frank during the trial. In

1982 Mann, aged eighty-three, confessed that he had seen Conley carrying Phagan's limp body in the factory lobby. Conley had threatened him with death if he ever spoke of it, and Mann's nervous parents encouraged their son to keep his silence during the two-year period—1913–15—that marked Frank's trial and appeals. Mann passed numerous lie-detector tests in 1982. His testimony led to a 1986 Georgia state pardon that stopped short of exonerating Frank for Mary Phagan's murder but acknowledged that Georgia had not conducted a fair trial and, further, had failed to protect Frank from his lynchers.[7]

The Phagan-Frank case reflected and was shaped by many interlocking cultural tensions of the period. Mary Phagan came from a family of tenant farmers forced to move into the city to seek factory and mill work. The working conditions she and others found were what we today would call sweatshops. Such circumstances inflamed southern populists' resentment of industrialization, modernization, and child labor outside the protective supervision of the family.[8] Sending a child of Phagan's age to work in an urban factory was a source of understandable anxiety to her mother and stepfather; however, her family needed her pitiful earnings to make ends meet.

Gender played a role as well. The unfounded charge that Frank had attempted to rape Phagan played on commonly held fears about what vulnerable daughters faced when they left the safety of the family for the viper's nest of the city and factory.[9] No wonder so many working-class Atlantans and Georgians cheered Hugh Dorsey as he prosecuted Leo Frank. No wonder they listened to Tom Watson, the only prominent voice in the state who articulated their resentment of the demeaning conditions under which their children worked and expressed their outrage in response to Slaton's pardon.

Watson's editorials portrayed Frank as an agent and beneficiary of the changes sweeping the South at that time. Frank's status as a northern "carpetbagger" roused sectionalist sentiment against him. His position as superintendent of the factory stirred class resentments. His Jewishness encouraged Watson and other enemies to demonize him as a lecherous pervert whose whiteness hid his rapacious intent and whose affluence emboldened him to leave one of the South's flowers dead in a basement and think he could get away with it. Watson was not alone in condemning Frank in terms typically applied to black Americans, comparing Frank to a black rapist, and denouncing Jews' struggles to be identified as white. The defense's racist condemnation of Conley seemed but another act of cowardice to place at Frank's door. No airtight proof of his guilt was necessary.[10]

Why was the testimony of a black man, especially one so challenged when it came to telling the truth, allowed to have such an impact in this case? White supremacist assumptions informed the prosecution's handling of Jim Conley on the stand. Dorsey and his associates believed that Conley's testimony was truthful, even if many features of it were suspect. Conley had a criminal record and had served time on a chain gang. In his first affidavit, he denied being present at the factory on the day of the murder. In the two subsequent ones he headed straight into the maelstrom, elaborating in greater and greater detail how Frank killed Phagan and got Conley to help him dispose of the body. Conley ultimately asserted that he witnessed Frank engage in perverse (that is, noncoital) sexual activities with female employees after hours.

Conley's more elaborate testimony bore the hallmarks of a suspect/accessory goaded into providing amazing detail when his original story was "not good enough." White Atlantans of the day believed that, like a child, a black person who felt threatened would initially lie before ultimately revealing the truth. Following this line of thinking, Conley's last affidavit was the key to Frank's conviction. White opinion also held that a black man could not have lied so elaborately and steadfastly as Conley did on the stand without breaking down, especially under extensive cross-examination by some of the best white attorneys in the state. Just as Frank's Jewishness had condemned him, cultural stereotypes of blackness replaced the hard evidence so lacking in the case. It would be decades before such stereotypes were overturned, before white Atlantans could recognize, as Atlanta attorney Allen Lumpkin Henson put it in his 1959 memoir, that "Conley had been in the Criminal Courts most of his adult life. He knew better than to talk to anyone except his lawyer when the heat was on him, and was wise enough to go to any length to unload on someone else." Here, Henson attributes a level of intelligence and cunning to Conley that few Atlanta whites in 1913 were willing or able to do.[11]

The national and local impact of the case was considerable. Writing in 1968, Leonard Dinnerstein called it "one of the most infamous outbursts of anti-Semitic feeling in the United States."[12] Dinnerstein's characterization is overwhelmingly the predominant interpretation of the Frank case and for good reason. Yet a handful of students of the case argue that Frank's Jewishness, introduced by Frank's attorneys and Frank's sympathizers, became an issue only as the trial proceeded, and then only as a subtext, albeit a potent one, of Dorsey's prosecution and the witnesses' testimony.[13] This has always been a decidedly minority interpretation of what befell Leo Frank, but it is worth noting several contemporary observers of the case agreed with it, as did a few of the filmmakers discussed in this volume.

What befell Atlanta's Jews in the trial's aftermath is certainly not in doubt. Jewish schoolchildren were cursed and stoned as they walked to school, and stores owned by Jews were vandalized.[14] Acting on their horror at what some called an "American Dreyfus case," Jewish leaders of B'nai B'rith—the Jewish fraternal organization whose Atlanta chapter Frank had led—formed the Anti-Defamation League in 1913 to combat anti-Semitism and prejudice of all kinds. Simultaneously, however, the Atlanta Jewish community became even more resolved to assimilate into the city's cultural life and not to mention the Frank case publicly. Atlanta resident Tony Montag recalled that his father, Louis Adolf Montag—nephew of the pencil factory's owner, Sig Montag—always refused to discuss the Leo Frank case. Oscar-winning screenwriter Alfred Uhry (*Driving Miss Daisy*, 1989) has similar memories. In explaining how he came to write the book for the 1998 Tony Award–winning musical about Leo Frank, *Parade*, Uhry said: "Southern extended families are prone to telling stories and so are Jewish ones. Mine was both, so I got a double dose. I grew up hearing about the quirks of distant relatives, in-laws, and a whole network of people I didn't know. They all came with stories attached. But nobody mentioned Leo Frank. Some of the family even walked out of the room if the name came up. I found this confusing, because I knew that my Great Uncle Selig had been his employer, and Lucille Frank was my grandmother's friend."[15]

If the Frank case gave Atlanta's Jews reason enough to be fearful, equally ominous developments were on the horizon. On Thanksgiving Day 1915, just three months after Frank's lynching, an estimated fifteen "Knights of Mary Phagan" joined traveling Methodist minister Colonel William J. Simmons in a ceremony at Stone Mountain, ten miles east of Atlanta, to revive the Ku Klux Klan (KKK); the burning cross they lit on the mountain-side was visible for miles in every direction. These men anointed Atlanta the national capital of the Invisible Empire—a designation that would endure for decades.

The Phagan-Frank case remains a powerful issue in the minds of Georgians. Many people in Marietta and some in Atlanta believe that Frank was guilty. As recently as 2000, Thomas Watson's great-grandson,

Tom Watson Brown, told an Atlanta reporter that Frank was lynched not because he was Jewish but because Governor Slaton either was influenced by his Jewish law partner, Luther Rosser (Frank's lead defense attorney at the trial), bribed by wealthy Jews to commute Frank's death sentence, or both.[16]

Yet far more people believe in Frank's innocence. At least as early as 1915, prior to the lynching, national publications cast Frank as a victim of circumstance. This view has come to prevail. In 1947 Hugh Dorsey pleaded with a Georgia judge to write a new history of the case, saying: "Not a single year has passed but that some publisher has sent people down here to write about it. None of them has been fair to me or to the State."[17] And indeed, today's legal standards regarding circumstantial evidence do raise reasonable doubt as to Frank's guilt. For the record, I share that view and believe Frank was innocent of Mary Phagan's murder, if not of the other allegations against him.

But despite strong feeling on both sides, Frank's innocence has never been definitively proven; Steve Oney, author of the most comprehensive and detailed account of the case written to date, agrees. The publication of Oney's volume in 2003 attests that the Phagan-Frank case is still a compelling story. Many of the social forces informing the case—including sectionalism, class antagonism, anti-Semitism, and sensationalism—are still active today. Though the power of these forces has diminished, America still struggles with racial hostilities (black and white, black and Jewish, white and Jewish), employee-management hostilities, an inadequate minimum wage, exploitative child labor, sexual predation, media exploitation, the death penalty, the miscarriage of justice, and violent crime. Although quite different in its specifics, the Phagan-Frank case was the O. J. Simpson trial of its day: the trial riveted Atlantans, and Frank's appeals fascinated Americans nationwide. The fact that this story of a northerner resented in the South begins with a murder on Confederate Memorial Day, a holiday that pointedly defies the national Memorial Day held to mourn all those who died in the Civil War, is just one of the case's many dramatic ironies.

Several story lines and subplots attached to the case link it to the movie screen. Phagan herself was an inveterate movie fan; an afternoon at the "flickers" was one of her preferred amusements. In late 1913, scandalous motion pictures such as *Traffic in Souls* and *Inside of the White Slave Traffic* were depicting the nightmare of so-called white slavery—the abduction into prostitution of innocent young country girls who had moved to the city looking for employment. In fact, the day Phagan failed to return home, her worried parents speculated that she had been kidnapped by just such a ring. Jim Conley was also a movie fan. In his first affidavit, he claimed to have gone to the movies the Friday before the murder; being something of a critic, apparently, he added that he had left because he had not found the fare worthwhile. In any event, by 1913 the movies were a favorite pastime of Atlantans on both sides of the color line.[18]

The same Supreme Court that rejected Leo Frank's appeals in 1915 had earlier that year denied that movies were a medium for the communication of ideas and therefore were not entitled to First Amendment protection. The Supreme Court's decision gave state and city censors around the United States the power to ban controversial films, and indeed, two theatrical films about the Frank case were banned in Atlanta. Even the man who commuted Frank's sentence to life imprisonment had a connection with the movies. During the 1930s, former Georgia governor John M. Slaton was a practicing attorney, but he was also a member of Atlanta's Film Board of Review, which oversaw the work of city censor Mrs. Alonzo Richardson.

There are other connections between the case and the movies. Steve Oney notes that Frank's lynchers were spurred on by Frank's screen debut. Writer-director Hal Reid—the father of heartthrob Wallace Reid—had booked his sympathetic fifteen-minute documentary, *Leo M. Frank and Governor Slaton*, into several large New York City movie theaters. The very existence of Reid's film, coupled with its showing in theaters owned by Jewish vaudeville and film theater magnate Marcus Loew, outraged Mary Phagan's self-appointed avengers.

Reid's film has not survived. Descriptions of it indicate that it showed footage of Frank talking with Reid himself and with Warden Smith of the Georgia state prison. According to Frank's mother, Rae Frank, the rushes included a shot in which Smith directed Frank to look out a window at something and another shot of Frank reading a book. There were also shots of Rae, and of Governor and Mrs. Slaton in their home and car. Reid had even deputized a cameraman to shoot footage of Frank's wife, Lucille, then vacationing in Athens, Georgia, with her uncles; Lucille was instructed to "talk and show animation" for the silent camera.[19]

Reid's short documentary was a prototype of the films to come that would assume and dramatize Frank's innocence. Made with the Frank family's cooperation and encouragement, it lacked—in Oney's estima-

This ad for Hal Reid's short documentary film featuring Leo Frank and Governor Slaton appeared in the film industry trade paper *Motion Picture News* on July 31, 1915.

tion—any "mention of troubling facts or of Slaton's conflict of interest. In other words, this was just the movie its subject had wanted—and exactly the one New Yorkers wanted to see."[20] The city had embraced this son of Brooklyn.[21] Reid's distributor, Circle Film Corporation, capitalized on the continuous press coverage of the Frank case by boasting to theater managers in the trade paper *Motion Picture News* that this film was "the Feature that has had *Millions of Dollars* of 'Front Page Publicity.'" Featuring small profile photos of Frank and Slaton, the ad went on to claim that *Leo M. Frank and Governor Slaton* was "the Only Genuine and Authentic Motion Pictures of the Principal Characters in Our Nation's Greatest Legal Conflict. Posed with Their Permission and to Be Used in Connection with an Authentic and Celebrated Legal Case." The same issue of *Motion Picture News* also reported that Frank and the other principals had given Reid their permission to be filmed when "it was pointed out to them that they would greatly aid in this campaign. They had up to that time refused countless offers made to them by various motion picture companies, who had in mind a purely commercial proposition." Reid personally introduced at least one New York screening of his film.[22]

Reid, a staunch opponent of capital punishment, was not done with his work on Frank's behalf, however. Both *Variety* and *Motion Picture News* mentioned Reid's plans to combine his documentary with fictional footage to re-create "an authentic and celebrated legal case."[23] Premiering in November 1915, Reid's next film used the general outline of Frank's plight and a southern setting: it depicts a newcomer to the Kentucky hills who is executed for the murder of his brother after the two have been seen arguing. The film reveals that the brother was actually killed by a murderous tramp, but the authorities learn this fact too late. The melodrama of coincidence and circumstantial evidence, already a fundamental principle of reporting on Leo Frank's plight, was easily transferable to the movies.

Two newsreels flickered onto screens ahead of Reid's magnum opus. *Pathé News* number 67, as the film was termed, was released on August 21, less than a week after Frank's murder. The *Atlanta Constitution* reported that it featured footage "of the crowds at the scene of the lynching and at the Greenberg & Bond undertaking establishment," but not "scenes of Frank's body hanging by the rope to tree [*sic*] near Marietta." Nonetheless, in cautious Atlanta, the mayor and censorship board instructed the Georgia Theatre manager to cut out the portions of the newsreel concerning Frank because "prominent officials and citizens" had complained "that their being run would be a lack of consideration for the feelings of many people in Atlanta."[24]

Film historian Kevin Brownlow reports that the theater manager promoted the film—on the one day he could show it complete—by driving a truck around town "with a set [of] chimes playing and a sign splashed along the sides: 'Leo M. Frank lynched. Actual scenes of the lynching at The Georgian today.'" A second film, a Gaumont News release distributed as the *Mutual Weekly*, appeared five days later. It showed Frank's body hanging and Marietta Judge Newton Augustus Morris, much later revealed to be one of the lynching's planners, at the site asking the crowd to allow the return of Frank's body to Atlanta. George K. Rolands's 1915 five-reel film titled *The Frank Case*, which does not survive and about which little is known, was banned by the National Board of Review and the New York City license commissioner because it advocated Frank's acquittal and was released while his case was still being appealed.[25]

The case's connection to the movies extends to films that did not concern the Phagan-Frank affair itself. Visiting Metropolitan Opera star Geraldine Farrar, an Atlanta favorite, spoke of her complete belief in Frank's innocence just months before her screen debut in Cecil B. DeMille's *Carmen* in November 1915. Some of the men who lynched Leo Frank, and all of the men who gathered on Stone Mountain to reenergize the Ku Klux Klan, were among the cheering moviegoers who stomped and rebel-yelled at the Atlanta premiere of D. W. Griffith's racist epic *The Birth of a Nation* in early December 1915. The film was the cinematic culmination of various commemorations of the fiftieth anniversary of the Civil War. With Leo Frank's punishment fresh in their minds, KKK members no doubt especially approved the climactic sequences in which their celluloid brethren lynch "black renegade" Gus to avenge the fatal "attempted rape" of Little Sister. The Klan goes on to "triumph" over armed blacks holding white northern *and* southern families hostage. Griffith's film not only apotheosized the KKK but also provided a powerful justification for extrajudicial justice in the form of lynching, regardless of the color of the "guilty" party. The KKK paraded down Peachtree Street—Atlanta's main thoroughfare—during the film's first run. After that, Atlanta KKK meetings regularly screened the film as a recruitment tool.[26]

The tensions between blacks and Jews that informed the Frank trial played out in the films and film-related commentary of the 1910s as well. It was likely the *Mutual Weekly* newsreel that provoked the black *Indianapolis Freeman* to editorialize about the link between the Frank lynching, the film footage of same, and the controversy surrounding Griffith's film. Writing of blacks' and Jews' shared history of oppression the *Freeman* concluded that "it is difficult to understand . . . why Jews should have anything to do with pictures that are so distasteful to the Negroes and so harmful." Certain Jewish publications did recognize that Jews had to fight against lynching or face joining blacks as its regular victims.[27] Certainly, the demonization of Frank (and of Conley by Frank's legal team) during the trial followed the line of thinking about racial inferiority taken by Griffith's film. And at the heart of both dramas was a white woman wronged.

The case's connections to the movies extend even further forward in time. William Schley Howard, who represented Frank's appeals before the Georgia Prisons and Parole Board and Governor John M. Slaton, later represented Robert E. Burns, the Georgia chain gang escapee who returned to Georgia to serve out his sentence and was immortalized in Warner Bros.'s *I Am a Fugitive from a Chain Gang* (1932). Leo Frank's fate also made a lasting impression on Hollywood director Vincent Sherman—né Abraham Orovitz—a Jewish native of Vienna, Georgia, best known for directing Humphrey Bogart in *All through the Night* (1942), Bette Davis and Miriam Hopkins in *Old Acquaintance* (1943), and Rita Hayworth in *Affair in Trinidad* (1952). Nearly eighty years after Frank's lynching, Sherman recalled the case in his memoir as one of the rare instances of anti-Semitism he encountered in Georgia; he remembered helping his Russian immigrant father collect money for Frank's appeals. As Sherman was establishing his Hollywood credentials, another Frank link was added to the chain. John Wood—the driver of the car that raced to Atlanta carrying Frank's body before a pursuing mob could destroy it completely—would be elected to Congress in the 1940s and would serve on the 1947 House Committee on Un-American Activities, whose hearings led to the infamous blacklisting of suspected and actual Communist Party members working in the film industry.[28]

All in all, considering the Phagan-Frank case's sensational details; its unanswered questions; and the troubling issues of race, class, sectional, and religious prejudice it raises, filmmakers' interest is not surprising. For all its uncomfortable truths and perturbing uncertainties, the case fits into many different genres of visual storytelling. It is a murder mystery, a detective story, and a tale of cynical and sensational journalism. It has courtroom drama and features an extraordinary sacrifice by a politician. It involves a devoted married couple torn apart by external events. It features the perturbing qualities and multiple ironies of a "wrong man" story such as those portrayed in several Alfred Hitchcock films and Errol Morris's *Thin Blue Line* (1988). It has the fury of mob violence and is pervaded by the ugliest emotions and thoughts known to human nature. These elements make the case irresistible material for a dramatic narrative film.[29]

The Phagan-Frank case is an unhappy chapter in American history with many volumes devoted to exploring and explaining it. Yet no book has examined the feature films and television programs it spawned. This book fills that gap. In chronological order, it examines two feature-length, theatrically released films of the 1930s: Oscar Micheaux's *Murder in Harlem* (1936) and Mervyn LeRoy's *They Won't Forget* (1937) for Warner Bros.; and two television programs broadcast on NBC, the *Profiles in Courage* episode "John M. Slaton" (1964), produced by Robert Saudek Associates, and the two-part miniseries *The Murder of Mary Phagan* (1988), produced and cowritten by George Stevens Jr. What each screen version retains, discards, alters, and amplifies reflects each storyteller's interpretation of the case and simultaneously attests to the constraints of budget, censorship, and format that each creative team faced. Moreover, each work provides fascinating answers to the questions of how films have represented history.

Critics and historians have long recognized and often decried the fact that films and television docudramas and shows about historical events frequently—and sometimes gleefully—deviate from historical accounts in the name of dramatic cogency or in the service of the filmmaker's ideological assumptions or cultural beliefs. This phenomenon has been a topic of scholarly investigation since the early 1990s, galvanized by the controversies surrounding such films as Alan Parker's *Mississippi Burning* (1988) and especially Oliver Stone's *JFK* (1991). Docudramas must restage events that occurred far from the camera. They are often accused of simplifying history, inventing scenes that never took place, and not signaling to viewers the difference between established historical facts and fictionalized events. Such charges can be leveled at each of the screen treatments of the Frank case discussed here, for they are all hybrids of historical reconstruction and creative embellishment of actual events.

Yet written history has no lock on historical accuracy, and many historians—including Robert Rosenstone and Hayden White—recognize the commonalities between their own methods, if not their mission, and those of literary and visual storytellers. Just as a historian interprets available facts to construct a story according to certain storytelling conventions, so does a filmmaker shape the historical record to tell a tale. Just as a historian interrogates the historical record, the visual storyteller advances an interpretation of a historical event to show how and why it unfolded as it did. In fact, film scholar Dudley Andrew has even suggested that historical films are comparable to literary or theatrical adaptations in film and television: "The debt owed to the traces of the past by the historian is analogous to the onus felt by the filmmaker to respect some text from the cultural storehouse. And so why not treat historical films as adaptations, particularly now that so many historians, following on Hayden White's *Metahistory*, consider their work to be largely that of re-creation, re-presentation, and textual elaboration?"[30]

Following this logic, we can note that the 1940 Hollywood film version of *Pride and Prejudice* starring Laurence Olivier and Greer Garson offers an interpretation of Jane Austen's classic novel distinctly different from the 2005 adaptation starring Keira Knightley. We can acknowledge that literary adaptations feature source materials (novels, plays, and so on) that typically do not change over time, unlike historical accounts of events. But even as different interpretations of historical events are published, the idealized facts of the case—however visual storytellers discover them—enable each version to allude to a floating authoritative account of events (what actually happened) even if they have not been, and could never be, set down in a published account. This gives each version even greater power and resonance than one based on a fictional work. Finally, these four texts treat the same historical event from different vantage points and time frames. The three major English-language films about the sinking of the *Titanic* (*Titanic*, 1953; *A Night to Remember*, 1958; and the 1997 blockbuster *Titanic*), for example, stress different aspects of the same event, fabricate subplots for entertainment purposes, and take advantage of different kinds of special effects technologies. The same adaptation dynamic—changing knowledge of events and a mix of documented events and fictionalized elements—can be found in the four screen treatments of the Phagan-Frank case I consider in this volume.

All four dramatizations are based on extensive research into the history and interpretations of the case available to the filmmakers at the time of production. These interpretations and the genre conventions prevalent at the time led the storytellers to retain certain details and discard others as they dramatized the case.[31] All the films strongly imply that Frank was innocent, or at least that his guilt was highly uncertain. But there are significant differences among the four versions as well, in part because the historical record and the interpretations of the case available to filmmakers changed over time. Neither film version identifies the Leo Frank character as Jewish; both television treatments do. No filmmakers before George Stevens Jr. were aware of Alonzo Mann's encounter with Jim Conley in the National Pencil Company factory lobby. Mann's statements enabled Stevens to suggest more strongly than any previous storyteller that Jim Conley fooled the jury and the press and was hiding something. Further, the miniseries's representation of its black characters reflects the post–civil rights era context in which it was filmed. Stevens's *The Murder of Mary Phagan* is the only white-produced account of the case that equals black director Oscar Micheaux's more multifaceted 1935 portrayal of Conley and black America.

These four visualizations of the case show how the very elements that made the Phagan-Frank story irresistible to visual storytellers often proved too complex, contradictory, or ambiguous to be given their due. The case was a traumatic event in American history, and this is another reason storytellers keep returning to it. Any representation of trauma—and of history more generally—is an attempt to process and comprehend what is disturbing in human experience. The most recent and dramatic example of this dynamic is the appearance of television and theatrical films such as *United 93* four years after the terrorist attacks on America of September 11, 2001. Yet whether the trauma in question is personal or national in scale, its representation is informed by ruptures and gaps in the telling; its depiction always pushes against the limits of what can be represented—as critics and theorists of traumatic representation would have it, the portrayal of trauma involves dramatizing what cannot be expressed.[32] While this characterizes films that are fragmented and incoherent, this dynamic also applies to films that feature a strong, steady story line. The murder of Mary Phagan and the lynching of Leo Frank raise the question of how such horrific acts can be visualized onscreen. Even though lynching photographs were circulated proudly to friends and family by participants and witnesses in the early decades of the twentieth century, lynching could be shown only indirectly or momentarily, if at all, in film and television before 1988. Psychic mechanisms create this effect in the individual who has experienced trauma; various regulation agencies and institutions in the mass media create it in films and television shows.

This raises an intriguing artistic, historic, and ultimately ethical question. Why tell a historical story if you cannot tell it accurately? A quick answer is that these visual storytellers thought audiences would be interested in seeing it—that they would buy tickets at the box office or devote an evening's television viewing to the story of how an actual lynching came about. The fuller answer is that each creative team was determined to tell the story as accurately as its research, budget, and other constraints allowed. The storytellers also believed that whatever the obstacles they might face in telling the story, they could still portray the most important and most disturbing dimensions of the Phagan-Frank case with power and authenticity. I believe they succeeded.

To demonstrate why I think so, and how these storytellers did so, I devote one chapter in this volume to each screen dramatization of the Phagan-Frank case. Each chapter analyzes how the filmmakers researched and understood the case, and then made creative choices to dramatize that understanding. In certain instances, those choices were dictated not only by the creative team's interpretation, but also by the circumstances in which they worked and the representational conventions they had absorbed. Those conditions and conventions were in turn a function of the times. The fact that each version treats the same historical phenomenon provides an unusual opportunity to consider the dynamics of historical representation on the screen over time.

Cinematic Justice across the Color Line

Oscar Micheaux and Leo Frank

This white man's got something up his sleeve. —LEM HAWKINS

JIM CONLEY'S TESTIMONY against his wealthier, white, northern factory supervisor has always been a tricky aspect of the Phagan-Frank case to dramatize on-screen. We can infer from their descriptions in the trade press that none of Hal Reid's dramatizations of the Phagan-Frank case in the 1910s—or any of the other anti–capital punishment films of the time—gave any prominence to Jim Conley, the prosecution's chief witness against Leo Frank. They likely gave no role to the racial aspects of the case either.

The passage of time would hardly be liberating. Indeed, in the 1930s, Hollywood's feature film on the case would have to tiptoe around the issue of the Conley character's role in the conviction of a man who very likely was innocent. The television series *Profiles in Courage*'s episode on Governor John M. Slaton mentions Conley but never even acknowledges that he was black. In the white-produced treatments of the case, only the 1988 miniseries *The Murder of Mary Phagan*—made more than seventy years after Frank's lynching—could give the Conley character his due.

The miniseries was preceded in this achievement by the first and second feature-length (that is, sixty minutes or longer) treatments of the Phagan-Frank case, which by contrast focus a great deal of attention on the Conley character. Both of these films were produced and directed by Oscar Micheaux (1884–1951), the most prominent and successful of the "race" filmmakers who worked outside the mainstream American film industry to create movies for black audiences.[1] The second and only surviving film of the two, *Murder in Harlem*, dramatizes the case from a black standpoint and provides several distinct twists to the Phagan-Frank story line that were not in the historical record. At the same time, both of Micheaux's films omit some of the case's most harrowing aspects.

Born in 1884 in Metropolis, Illinois, to former slaves, Micheaux was an unlikely filmmaker. He left home in 1901 to strike out on his own, working as a Pullman porter and at other menial jobs before he began homesteading in South Dakota. Though his formal education was minimal, Micheaux began writing autobiographical novels. In 1912 he self-published his first book, *The Conquest: The Story of a Negro Pioneer*, which covered his early days as a struggling homesteader, his interracial romance with a Scottish girl on a neighboring homestead, and his marriage to the daughter of a black minister. Other novels followed in rapid succession: *The Forged Note: A Romance of the Darker Races* (1915) and *The Homesteader* (1917). Micheaux sold copies personally to his South Dakota neighbors and by subscription via ads in the black press.

Micheaux entered filmmaking in 1918 when he refused to sell the film rights to *The Homesteader* to race filmmakers who would not let him collaborate on the project. Micheaux raised money by going door to door to interested individual investors, taught himself filmmaking, established a film company, and produced *The Homesteader* himself in 1919. He would go on to become the most prolific race filmmaker in American film history, full author of forty-plus films that spanned the silent and sound eras. *The Betrayal*, his last film—adapted from his last novel, *The Wind from Nowhere* (1945)—appeared in 1948.

Micheaux had plenty of competition. Fellow black directors were provoked by D. W. Griffith's racist epic *The Birth of a Nation* and were otherwise keen to capitalize on America's fascination with movies. All of them, Micheaux included, faced an uphill battle, one that crucially influenced the final form of *Murder in Harlem*. Funds for production were in low supply, and Micheaux could often afford only inexperienced actors and poor equipment. Patrick McGilligan reported that the budget for *The Homesteader* was $15,000, while Griffith spent an estimated $100,000 to make *The Birth of a Nation*.[2]

If the struggle for funds did not exhaust or defeat a race filmmaker, his efforts to ensure his films' distribution might. Just as race filmmaking was gaining critical mass, the Hollywood studio system was consoli-

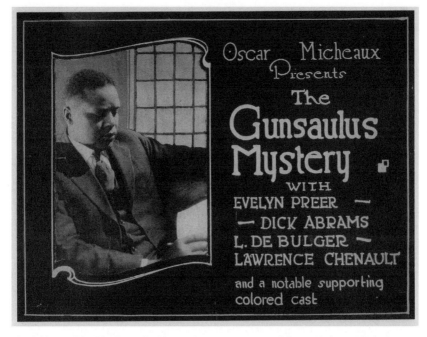

This lobby card for *The Gunsaulus Mystery* features a portrait of Oscar Micheaux. Only three years after making his first film, Micheaux was already an expert at promoting himself. (Courtesy Professor Jane Gaines and the Oscar Micheaux Society.)

dating its organization and ensuring its dominance of the American film market—a phenomenon that continues today. In Micheaux's time, the Hollywood studios made well-financed films with polished production values and popular movie stars. Black theater managers were able to book these films, which meant that Micheaux and his cohort struggled to obtain favorable booking terms for their films on a theater-by-theater basis for limited runs. Nevertheless, Micheaux outlasted all his race filmmaker competitors.[3] He even survived the costly transition to sound. Amid all his successes, though, his late 1940s exit from filmmaking witnessed two cruel ironies. First, in 1948, the year Micheaux finished *The Betrayal*, the Supreme Court compelled the major Hollywood studios to give up their ownership of the most profitable first-run theaters. In principle, this action meant that race films—like other independent and non-Hollywood fiction feature films—could get better play dates in theaters and, at the end of the day, more income. But the race filmmakers had essentially taken their last bow by this time.

Second, in 1949, three studios and one independent filmmaker released four films on race relations. Two of them (*Pinky* and *Lost Boundaries*) portrayed black characters who pass as white—a very controversial subject matter Micheaux had explored in his heyday. Such films were highly convoluted treatments of race relations designed to give minimum offense to white (and especially southern) film audiences, but they offered black performers star turns and black audiences relevant subject matter that made race films superfluous. The stardom of Sidney Poitier in the 1950s and 1960s was emblematic of these filmmaking trends. With Poitier and other black actors performing leading or important, dignified roles in white-produced films, the affirmative function of race films became obsolete.

In his prime, however, Micheaux operated in the interstices of the American film industry, making films in Chicago or New York on shoestring budgets with modest camera, editing, and sound technology. His casts were typically a mix of amateur actors and seasoned stage performers drawn from the Harlem Theater Lafayette Players. His *Body and Soul* (1925) was the first film to star Paul Robeson. Micheaux's films featured an idiosyncratic style that emulated Hollywood's in certain ways and was indifferent to it in others.[4] He operated on his own, outside even the Harlem Renaissance, whose members paid him scant attention.

Posthumously, however, Micheaux has received a great deal of attention from film scholars and the American film industry. The Directors' Guild of America gave him a special Lifetime Achievement award in 1986, and he was given a star on Hollywood Boulevard's Walk of Fame in 1987. The Producers' Guild named an award after him, appropriately given to filmmakers who overcome great odds to make films.

Ironically, although Micheaux's sidewalk star remains, few of his films survive. Those that do reveal a driven artist with a distinctive worldview derived from Micheaux's experiences as a homesteader and his perception that black Americans struggled against overwhelming social prejudice and professional restrictions and had yet to reach their great potential. His perspective reflected the view—articulated by Booker T. Washington and supported in many particulars by W. E. B. DuBois—that blacks needed to nurture pride in their race, strengthen their community, acquire practical skills, develop self-reliance, find fulfillment in work and worthy companions, and develop their own business enterprises.[5]

Micheaux's films thus addressed issues of major concern to black Americans of the period. He sought to inspire viewers with professional, middle-class heroes and did not hesitate to portray the lazy, corrupt, or gullible within the black community. Duplicitous preachers, gamblers, and blacks who betray their race by insinuating themselves with whites all appeared in one film or another. His depiction of underhanded characters earned him criticism in the black press for airing dirty laundry. Yet Micheaux insisted on the need to dramatize how such people compromised the possibility of racial uplift for all. "Film was a storytelling medium" for Micheaux, notes his biographer, Patrick McGilligan, "but . . . it was also a pulpit. He wanted to show life the way he alone saw it. He was determined to bear witness, to *testify*."[6] This logic informed the various characters he created in his two films about Leo Frank.

Micheaux's film paragons faced considerable obstacles in white-dominated society. In *Body and Soul*, for example, a black preacher so dominates one of his congregants that she lets him make advances to, and ultimately rape, her daughter. While many characters in Micheaux's films suffer the heartbreaking consequences of passing as white, he consistently showed black heroes who could prevail without trying to be white. *Within Our Gates*, his earliest surviving film, follows the efforts of Sylvia—a single, southern black woman who raises money in the North for the school where she teaches—and her budding courtship with a northern black doctor. Its climax is a twenty-minute flashback in which we learn from extremely powerful and direct imagery that her innocent adoptive parents were lynched for the murder of their white landowner (actually committed by a white tenant farmer) and that Sylvia herself was nearly raped by her own white father. Micheaux unflinchingly depicted the mob violence that informed lynchings and race riots during his time. His willingness to dramatize unpleasant realities and controversial subjects brought him into conflict with white city and state censors around the country.

Clearly, Micheaux learned much from other filmmakers of the day, both black and white. *Within Our Gates*, for instance, uses cross-cutting and the near rape of Sylvia at the hands of her real white father to reverse the hateful racism embodied in D. W. Griffith's *Birth of a Nation* by Gus's attempted rape of Little Sister. Although censors cut the portion of Griffith's film portraying the lynching of Gus, *Within Our Gates* shows the lynching of Sylvia's parents with an unprecedented explicitness that created controversy wherever the film was shown. As if its agenda were not ambitious enough, Micheaux's film also made a plea for tolerance and black pride in the wake of the post–World War I race riots that threatened blacks throughout the country.[7]

Ever in pursuit of rich source material to treat the topics of miscegenation, concubinage, and intraracial conflict, Micheaux drew on diverse sources, including novels (his own but also those of others such as Charles Chesnutt), plays, and news headlines. Examining Micheaux's sources and unconventional adaptations of others' works, Micheaux scholar Corey Creekmur argues that "the comfortable identification of one text as an 'original' and another, or others, as 'derived' adaptations frequently oversimplifies the actual multimedia and multidirectional circulation of texts . . . that at moments might be better described as translation, allusion, deformation, parody, homage, copyright infringement, 'signifying,' or . . . masquerade." Micheaux's "incessant refashioning of his own and others' 'source' materials," Creekmur adds, was *radically* unoriginal."[8] Micheaux's novels and films thus display an exuberant bricolage and creative playfulness drawn from whatever personal experiences and story lines he felt would amount to a compelling narrative compatible with his views on the place and conduct of blacks in America.

It should thus come as no surprise that Micheaux turned to the Phagan-Frank case for the plotlines of two of his films: the silent *Gunsaulus Mystery* (1921) and the sound-era *Lem Hawkins' Confession* (1935), which was recut as *Murder in Harlem* and rereleased in 1936.[9] In this instance of Micheaux's "radically unoriginal" cinema, the filmmaker took a public controversy and used it as a foundation for his preferred plot elements and character types.

The Phagan-Frank case would have appealed to Micheaux as dramatic material for many reasons, both practical and thematic. Pragmatically speaking, the fact that the crime, the trial, and their aftermath were all in the public record meant no copyright issues or costs, always important for a race filmmaker with a minimal budget. As the Circle Film Corporation's ads for Hal Reid's films in the 1910s had noted, the Phagan-Frank case had received sensational press coverage nationwide, so Micheaux was also tapping into public interest—a fact ads for *The Gunsaulus Mystery* explicitly mentioned. A similar consideration encouraged Micheaux to adapt Charles Chesnutt's *The House behind the Cedars*, based on an actual miscegenation case reported in both black and white newspapers, in which a wealthy white family sought to annul their son's marriage to a poor black woman. In fact, Micheaux had written Chesnutt that he was looking for "stories of the South—strange murder cases, mystery with dynamic climaxes—but [wanted to] avoid race conflict as much as possible." That did not mean that he wanted "all colored" stories. Rather, he wanted tales portraying the races as they lived "in relation to each other in every day life."[10] Certainly, the Phagan-Frank case fulfilled that prescription for drama.

Such stories juxtaposing blacks' lives with whites' inspired Micheaux to dream of expanding his audience beyond African Americans. Indeed, just before shooting *Lem Hawkins' Confession* Micheaux visited Atlanta twice—in the spring and summer of 1934—and informed the local black *Daily World* that, based on the universal "success" in 1933 of the white-produced and -distributed *Emperor Jones* (starring Paul Robeson but with a mixed-race cast), "all-Negro films" would soon be "acceptable in all parts of the country."[11]

Most of all, however, Micheaux would have been drawn to the Phagan-Frank case because it was a genuinely fascinating story with mysterious and unresolved details as well as both sexual and racial aspects. The black-white dimensions of the case rendered a ready-made story line consistent with the kinds of controversial subjects—such as lynching, miscegenation, mixed blood, and passing—that Micheaux's films had addressed and would continue to depict.

Micheaux's abiding fascination with the case—evidenced in his two films about it and his many allusions to it in his novels—testifies to the electrifying effect Jim Conley and his testimony in the Phagan-Frank case had on African Americans of the time. Like other Micheaux characters, Conley and Newt Lee were, in the director's view, unjustly suspected. Micheaux was often drawn to stories of a falsely accused and ultimately exonerated black suspect accused simply because she or he was black. Jean-Baptiste in *The Homesteader* novel and the later film *The Exile* (1931) is one example; Sylvia Landry's father in *Within Our Gates*, suspected of murdering his landowner until it is ultimately revealed that a white tenant farmer did the deed, is another. When Micheaux's camera rolled, a racial tide often turned. In that respect, his films stand in dramatic opposition to the other screen versions of the Phagan-Frank case.

The Gunsaulus Mystery

The advertising for *The Gunsaulus Mystery* played on the audience's familiarity with the Phagan-Frank case. One ad, for example, asked: "Was Leo M. Frank Guilty?" It continued: "Do you recall the strange and tragic case of Leo M. Frank, charged with the murder of little Mary Phagan;

tried, convicted and sentenced to be hanged on the testimony (so claimed) of Jim Conley . . . who testified that the defendant led a double life?" The film's advertising also boasted of Micheaux's firsthand knowledge of the case: Oscar Micheaux, "the well-know[n] Race author and motion picture producer, was in the court room during this most sensational trial."[12] Although Micheaux's attendance at the trial—and even his presence in Atlanta in 1913—are difficult to verify, he clearly knew the details of the case and the prosecution's brief against Frank, which, after all, had been trumpeted in the city papers, black and white, on a daily, sometimes hourly, basis.

Micheaux drew on those details both for his film and for his 1915 novel *The Forged Note: A Romance of the Darker Races.* A chapter of the latter titled "A Jew; a Gentile; Murder—and Some More" recounts thinly disguised aspects of the Phagan-Frank case. Micheaux set the novel in "Attalia" and had the case prosecuted by one "Doray [Dorsey] the solicitor" and publicized by a "Big Noise" "whose editor [Watson] had once run for president, on a ticket [Populist] we cannot recall." He even included a Conley character, here named Dawkins. The novel's hero, Sydney Wyeth, represents film's first "race detective."[13] Micheaux's book also includes actual case details whereby a series of witnesses recant their affidavits indicting Frank but then reaffirm them.

Micheaux was determined to make this film. As early as 1919, four years after Frank's lynching, he had proposed a film to be titled *Circumstantial Evidence,* likely drawing on his novel's sketch and perhaps inspired in part by Hal Reid's fictional films and documentary footage. In early 1920, he announced in the *Chicago Defender* his plans to make a film called *The Mark of Cain* and to publish a novel by the same name when the film premiered; his mid-1930s sound version of the Frank case had the latter name as an alternate title. A decade later, in 1945, Micheaux returned to the Phagan-Frank story line in his novel *The Case of Dorothy Stanfield.* He used the name of the black night watchman, Newt Lee, for a minister in *The Wind from Nowhere.*[14] Clearly, the Phagan-Frank case was a "story well" that Micheaux returned to as both novelist and filmmaker.

Plot descriptions in black newspapers gave the setting of *The Gunsaulus Mystery* as New York City. Micheaux even included location shooting: the film opens with shots of the city skyline "by water" as well as nighttime views of Broadway to set the scene. The film focuses on West Indian author-lawyer Sidney Wyeth (also the protagonist's name in Micheaux's

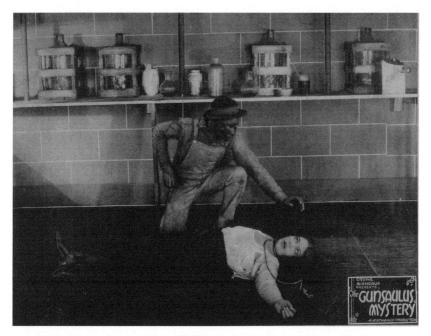

The night watchman discovers the body of Myrtle Stanfield in this lobby card for *The Gunsaulus Mystery.* (Courtesy Professor Jane Gaines and the Oscar Micheaux Society.)

novel *The Forged Note*), who is hired to defend Arthur Gilpin, a black night watchman at a factory. Gilpin has been charged with the murder of a white woman, Myrtle Gunsaulus (where or how Micheaux came up with this unusual name for the victim is unclear). The police find murder notes and strands of Gunsaulus's hair near her body. Arthur's sister Ida May is Sidney's former girlfriend, and she hires Sidney to take the case. The character Sidney Wyeth is probably based in part on the two black detectives working for Burns in *The Forged Note*.[15] Sidney is also clearly a Micheaux stand-in, an autobiographical figure; he sells novels door to door, in Sidney's case to finance law school.

Sidney establishes that the woman's killer was a white man. The guilty factory supervisor, Anthony Brisbane (Lawrence Chenault), is convicted on the testimony of black janitor Lem Hawkins (Louis De Bulger). On the stand, Hawkins describes Brisbane as a Jekyll/Hyde type—a respectable manager at work and a sexual pervert in secret—who killed Myrtle to hide his attempted rape of her, made Lem help him hide the body, and then tried to blame Hawkins for the murder itself.[16] Having successfully defended Ida May's brother, Wyeth publishes a novel that mentions why he broke off his relationship with her: he thought she was a criminal. She reads his novel, comes to him to clear up this misunderstanding, and the film ends happily with the couple reunited.[17]

Lem Hawkins clearly represents Jim Conley, and ads for the film in the black press continued to emphasize the connection between the film and the Phagan-Frank case. One such ad for the film's weeklong run at the Chicago Vendome Theater described *The Gunsaulus Mystery* as a "melodramatic photoplay showing the part being taken by our people in the progressiveness of the race," a phrase alluding to Wyeth's upstanding composure. A May 1921 ad in the *Baltimore Afro-American* claimed, "The evidence shows that Leo Frank committed the crime and got a COLORED MAN to help him dispose of the body. And then tried to blame the crime on the COLORED MAN."[18] A *Chicago Defender* article about *The Gunsaulus Mystery* also mentioned the Frank case connection and similarly noted with pride that Frank was convicted on the testimony of "one of our folks."

Reviews of *The Gunsaulus Mystery* published after its April 18, 1921, premiere at the Lafayette Theater in Harlem regarded it as a winner. The *Chicago Whip*'s reviewer reported that "Mr. Micheaux this time has surpassed all of his previous efforts in the production of this picture." A *Chicago Defender* review hailed Micheaux's film as "highly dramatic with bits of comedy" (likely the Conley character) that made it Micheaux's best film yet. Novelist Charles Chesnutt was among the film's fans and wrote Micheaux to say that it gave him confidence in the filmmaker's future adaptation of Chesnutt's work. In Atlanta, Micheaux's decision to promote the film's Phagan-Frank case connection provoked the city's film censor to order *The Gunsaulus Mystery* shipped out of town—an action that merited a brief item even in the white newspapers. Atlanta's censor had banned the film because "it was simply a rehearsal of the Frank case from beginning to end." The censor conceded "that it was a very well produced picture, and might do to show in other cities where public sentiment had not been aroused to such an extent, but that in Atlanta, where everyone was so familiar with all the details of the case, it simply would not do."[19]

Lem Hawkins' Confession and *Murder in Harlem*

Although it is unfortunate that *The Gunsaulus Mystery* does not survive, Micheaux remade his films constantly (for example, his silent *The*

Homesteader and *The House behind the Cedars* became *The Exile* [1931] and *Veiled Aristocrats* [1932], respectively). True to form, he returned to the Phagan-Frank case in the sound era, writing and directing *Lem Hawkins' Confession* in 1935 and recutting and rereleasing it as *Murder in Harlem*—the only version that survives—the following year. For this sound dramatization, shot at Micheaux's studio in Fort Lee, New Jersey, Micheaux maintained the silent film's New York setting and romantic plot, and again altered the names of most of the principal characters. Roughly half the running time of *Murder in Harlem* reenacts the Phagan-Frank case.[20]

Murder in Harlem begins as black night watchman Arthur Vance (played by Lorenzo McClain)—the Newt Lee character—discovers the body of white employee Myrtle Stanfield in the National Chemical Laboratory basement; the parallels to the National Pencil Company factory in Atlanta are obvious. Arthur looks directly at the camera (a taboo in Hollywood films other than musicals and comedies) in panic. The white laboratory supervisor, Anthony Brisbane (the Leo Frank character, played by Lafayette Players and Micheaux film veteran Andrew Bishop), appears to be hiding something. As was alleged of Frank, Brisbane does not answer his phone when Vance tries to reach him to report finding the body.[21] Vance then calls the police. On arriving at the factory, the black detectives (one of them played by Micheaux himself) discover ambiguous notes next to Myrtle's body that contain material identical with that in one of the two notes found next to Phagan's body. In the actual case, one note read: "He said he wood love me land down play like the night witch did it but that long tall black negro did buy his slef [*sic*]." In Micheaux's film, one note reads: "He tell me lay down like night witch." A second one reads: "The tall Negro did this. He will try to lay it on the night."

The police take Arthur Vance into custody. The booking officer at the jail is visibly alarmed when he learns that the victim is a white woman. The police plan to keep Arthur in a secret cell; their concern for his safety implies that he could be the target of a lynch mob. A newspaper story reveals that Myrtle Stanfield, like Mary Phagan, received a major blow to her head but died from strangulation. To anyone familiar with the specifics of the Phagan-Frank case, the source of the murder mystery plot in *Murder in Harlem* would be unmistakable.

After these opening scenes, *Murder in Harlem* detours from the Phagan-Frank case to develop its romantic plot. A flashback to three years earlier introduces author Henry Glory (Clarence Brooks) and shows his efforts

The opening scene from *Murder in Harlem*. Chemical plant night watchman Arthur Vance discovers Myrtle Stanfield's body in the basement. (Unless otherwise indicated, the images throughout are from the author's private collection.)

Vance's panic registers when he looks at the camera.

Two black policemen, the one on the right played by Micheaux himself, read the mysterious murder notes—with text verbatim from one of the actual notes—found next to Myrtle's body as Vance looks on.

to sell his novel door to door to finance his law school education. His first customer laughingly suggests that he will find an avid female reader in another building. When Glory arrives there, the first woman he sees is holding a book, but she is hardly the studious type. She is brassy and casually dismisses a boyfriend, claiming that she wants to read. But then, across the hallway, Henry meets the very proper Claudia Vance (Dorothy van Engle), who lives with her mother (Alice B. Russell, Micheaux's wife), and a spark flares between the two. When Henry later returns to see Claudia, hoodlums who are friends of Claudia's neighbor mistake him for someone else and rob him. Henry assumes Claudia set him up for this as-

In chemical plant supervisor Anthony Brisbane's flashback, Arthur Vance acts suspicious, smokes a cigarette, and follows Myrtle Stanfield into the back room after she has collected her pay from Brisbane.

sault, and their relationship ends because of the misunderstanding. After the flashback, back in the present, Claudia comes to Henry's law office to ask him to defend her brother Arthur, the night watchman.

Glory and Vance interview Arthur in jail and get his version of events: he is innocent. Arthur recounts in a flashback that Anthony Brisbane had given him time off earlier that day. This version of events matches Newt Lee's affidavits to Atlanta police and his testimony at the trial that Frank had asked him to come in early on Confederate Memorial Day and then told him to come back two hours later because Frank had not finished his work. The police and prosecutor Hugh Dorsey believed that Frank had sent Lee away to delay his finding of Phagan's body.

The subsequent preliminary hearing and trial scenes offer competing black versus white versions of how Myrtle Stanfield was killed, continuing to rely—as Micheaux's films frequently do—on character flashbacks. A well-groomed Brisbane alleges at the hearing, and we see in a flashback, that Stanfield had come to his office to collect $1.50 in pay (recall that Mary Phagan had come to the pencil factory to pick up $1.20). Then, according to Brisbane, Arthur Vance, smoking a cigarette and acting suspicious, entered the stockroom to retrieve some shoes after Stanfield had entered it to check on a new shipment. Brisbane claims that when he entered the room later, Myrtle was dead. (By contrast, Leo Frank never saw Mary Phagan's body and claimed complete ignorance of her demise.) Brisbane actively works to frame Vance in his testimony. Subsequently, Myrtle Stanfield's tearful mother testifies in court that Myrtle and her boyfriend, George Epps, had gone to the plant that day to collect her salary because Brisbane had insisted that Myrtle collect it personally. (Phagan's mother was one of Dorsey's first witnesses; she broke down on the stand, as Dorsey intended.)

This point-of-view shot shows the magazine George Epps looked at in Myrtle Stanfield's home.

George looks up at the camera before Myrtle and her mother return to the room, obviously titillated by what he has been reading.

With the appearance of Epps, Micheaux adds another striking detail from the Phagan-Frank case to his script: George Epps was the young Atlantan who rode the trolley with Phagan into the city on the day she died. The real Epps claimed that Mary Phagan and he had planned to see the parade and a movie after she picked up her wages; Epps further claimed that Phagan spoke to him of Frank's advances and ogling.[22] Epps subsequently retracted and then reasserted these claims. In Micheaux's film, Epps looks at cheesecake photos of scantily clad women (it is unclear whether this is a magazine article or an advertisement) while he waits to accompany Stanfield to the factory, then quickly puts down the magazine when he hears her coming. Later, after leaving Myrtle at the factory, Epps returns to Stanfield's house and nervously asks her mother if Myrtle has returned home, informing her that he did not see Myrtle again after she entered the factory. Later in the film, we learn that Epps is extremely jealous of Brisbane's relationship with Myrtle.

After a trial session one day, Claudia Vance overhears Brisbane telling plant worker Lem Hawkins (Alec Lovejoy), the Jim Conley character, to "stay away from liquor and keep your mouth shut." Hawkins is well known to be a heavy drinker (as Conley was), and Brisbane fears he might talk if he gets drunk. Two days later, in what J. Ronald Green has identified as her neighbor's "buffet flat" nightclub, the Catbird's Seat, Claudia Vance flirts with Hawkins at length, acting like a sophisticated, hard-drinking party girl. She gets Hawkins drunk and tricks him into admitting that he knows that Arthur Vance is innocent. After she informs Glory of this news, he calls Hawkins to the stand.

At this point, *Murder in Harlem* dramatizes Lem Hawkins's testimony in flashback, and his story closely follows Jim Conley's assertions at the actual Leo Frank trial. Hawkins relates that Brisbane paid him a quarter to keep watch in the factory stairwell. Up in his office, Brisbane gave Stanfield her pay and then followed her when she went into the stockroom and attempted to rape her. In this flashback sequence, Hawkins sneaks over to the stockroom door, looks through the keyhole, and watches Brisbane's assault on Stanfield. While Brisbane is attacking Stanfield (he tries to kiss her before the camera cuts away), another woman comes for a tryst in his office, and Hawkins hurries back to his post in the stairwell. (A shot of Brisbane's office clock—not strictly necessary to the drama of the film as such—recalls the importance of the time in Hugh Dorsey's prosecution of Frank.)

In his affidavits and at Frank's trial, Conley claimed that Frank paid him to act as a lookout. He also claimed to have seen Frank performing oral sex on factory employees in his office—which he did, Frank allegedly told Conley, because he was "not 'built' like other men." In fact, Conley claimed at the trial that Frank regularly held rendezvous with factory girls in his office while Conley served as a lookout. He also claimed that a second woman came to Frank's office the day of Phagan's murder. Many female employees affirmed Conley's claims that Frank acted improperly with them—and propositioned some of them.

As Hawkins's flashback continues, a disheveled Brisbane appears at the top of the stairs, summons Hawkins, and explains to him that he accidentally knocked Stanfield unconscious when she resisted his advances in the other room. Brisbane sends Hawkins in to revive her, and Hawkins finds her dead. Micheaux heightens the moment by having Hawkins look directly at the camera at this moment of panic. A surviving still from *The Gunsaulus Mystery* indicates that Micheaux staged exactly the same scene with his character Arthur Vance. The black character's discovery of a "raped and murdered white woman," notes Ronald J. Green, is "the worst possible state of affairs, the beginning of an almost automatic lynching scenario."[23]

The flashback goes on with Hawkins helping Brisbane move Myrtle's body to the basement (this action occurs offscreen in the film). The two men return to Brisbane's office, where Brisbane dictates the notes intended to frame Arthur Vance (who is a "tall Negro," whereas Hawkins is short). He also orders Hawkins to burn her corpse so no evidence will remain. He gives Hawkins $250 as payment to do this—and then takes it back.

During his extended flashback sequence, Lem Hawkins sits on the stairwell keeping watch for Brisbane as Stanfield comes up the stairs to get her pay.

Brisbane teases Stanfield by repeatedly offering her pay and then withdrawing it when she reaches for it.

As Hawkins's flashback continues, Brisbane follows Stanfield into the back room.

Hawkins, having left his lookout post in the stairwell, spies on Brisbane and Stanfield through a keyhole.

Hawkins recounts that Mildred Bates came to Brisbane's office and waited ten minutes while Brisbane was busy with Stanfield in the back room.

This shot of the clock alludes to the importance of time in the prosecution's case against Leo Frank as well as showing that Bates waited ten minutes for Brisbane.

Brisbane, appearing disheveled, gestures to Hawkins to come up to his office.

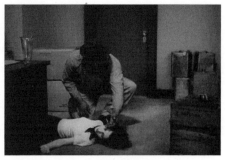

Hawkins finds Stanfield lying dead on the storeroom floor.

Hawkins looks at the camera in panic.

Jim Conley's third affidavit to the Atlanta police claimed that Frank had killed Phagan in a room across from his office, a claim to which Dorsey tied the alleged discovery of Mary Phagan's blood and hair on a lathe (these identifications were quietly refuted after the trial, too late to help Frank). Frank then forced Conley to help him move the body, dictated to Conley the puzzling notes found beside her, and offered him $200 to dispose of the body before withdrawing this cash offer.[24] In the film, Hawkins pleads pathetically with Brisbane to forgo burning the body and passes out drunk at a bar across the street. Vance discovers the body in the basement that night, as we saw in the film's opening scene. Thus ends Lem Hawkins's confession in the film trial—spectacular testimony through which the black janitor indicts his white employer.

Clearly, Micheaux used the general outline of Jim Conley's testimony in this portion of *Murder in Harlem*. Yet he also went further, using specific verbiage from the trial in the film's dialogue. During Lem's testimony flashback, for example, Brisbane explains Myrtle's fate to him:

Brisbane: Did you see that little girl who came up here a while ago?

Hawkins: Yas suh, uh, I seen one come up here and she done come back down. And then I seen a . . . a . . . another one come up, but she ain't come back down yet.

Brisbane: Well, the one that didn't come back down, came into my office and then went into the stock room where I followed her. I . . . I wanted to make love to the little girl, but she refused me. We got to scuffling and she got her fingers in my face and eyes, and I . . . I had to hit her to make her turn loose. I . . . I don't know how hard I hit her, but she . . . she fell down and hit herself against something and got hurt. I don't know how bad she's hurt. I want you to go back there and bring her here so we can put her somewhere. Hurry up, Lem! Hurry up! There's money in it for you!

Lem: Yas suh.

At Frank's trial, Conley described a conversation with Frank the day Phagan was murdered:

After I got to the top of the steps, he asked me, "Did you see that little girl who passed here just a while ago?" and I told him I saw one come along there and she come back again, and then I saw another one come along there and she hasn't come back down, and he says, "Well, that one you say didn't come back down, she came into my office awhile ago and wanted to know something about her work in my office and I went back there to see if the little girl's work had come, and I wanted to be with the little girl, and she refused me, and I struck her and I guess I struck her too hard and she fell and hit her head against something, and I don't know how bad she got hurt." . . . He asked me if I wouldn't go back there and bring her up so that he could put her somewhere, and he said to hurry, that there would be money in it for me.[25]

Micheaux also used Conley's testimony to show how Brisbane confided in Hawkins. Moreover, he staged Conley's descriptions of another woman visiting Frank's office while Frank was busy with Phagan and then Frank calling Conley up the stairs to describe what he had done to Phagan and to get Conley's help. Micheaux even had Glory question Hawkins as to why his current testimony differs from that Hawkins had offered previously, much as Conley was questioned about his different affidavits.

Both of Micheaux's films about the Frank case reflect the consensus of many black newspapers at the time of the trial that Conley's testimony was true and that Leo Frank was a duplicitous, lecherous murderer. For obvious reasons, the black press followed the Phagan-Frank case closely: a black witness was crucial in the prosecution's case, and the lynching noose dangled over his head even as he testified against Frank. In general, the black press understandably resented the fact that—in historian Eugene Levy's words—"such large amounts of money and effort were being spent to save the life of one accused Jew when blacks were continuing to be lynched for crimes far less serious than murder, and long before they ever reached trial." The black press was further inflamed when Frank's legal team attempted to accuse Conley of the murder. Their consensus was, Levy notes, that "whites were again looking for a black scapegoat." This feeling was especially clear in newspaper comments as Frank began the appeals process. The *Chicago Defender* dismissed the charges against Conley as an accessory to the murder as "ridiculous" and "a plan to vent spite on Mr. Conley by some of Frank's race hating friends"—a view of Conley and Frank completely in agreement with the tone of Micheaux's later ads in that same newspaper for *The Gunsaulus Mystery*. Even the *Crisis*, the official publication of the NAACP (a group cofounded and led by Jewish and black Americans—including Julius Rosenthal, one of Frank's most generous supporters), fully endorsed Frank's conviction. In its September 1913 report on the trial, the journal commented: "Atlanta tried to lynch a Negro for the alleged murder of a young white girl, and the police inquisition nearly killed the man. A white degenerate has now been indicted for the crime, which he committed under the most revolting circumstances."[26]

Frank's appeals kept the issue alive. Black newspapers expressed their resentment of Frank's support by wealthy Jews, the prominent newspaper advocacy in his defense, and his impressive legal team. The *Chicago Defender* commented that "there seems to be absolutely no question of his [Frank's] guilt." Further, the attempt to convict Conley demonstrated that "money and influence, with the emphasis on the former, can work wonders." As Frank pursued his appeals, the *Chicago Defender* cheered his setbacks: "Every effort has been made to fasten the crime on Conley, for no other reason apparently than he happened to have a dark skin, a badge that in some sections of the country is sufficient to convict alone. . . . We have enough to carry our own burden without having crimes of others laid upon us."

Similar sentiments appeared on the editorial pages of the *Philadelphia Tribune* and other black papers. The *New York Age* had "no desire to see Frank executed or even imprisoned for life. Our contention all along has been against the organized effort to free the convicted man on the ground that the principal testimony for the State was given by a Negro. This effort went to the extent of declaring that the Negro in the case must be the guilty man, for the simple reason that he was a Negro. It was this phase of the case that *The Age* fought." The black newspapers did not romanticize Conley, but they did believe him. Moreover, they reasoned quite accurately that if one bit of evidence had emerged to cast suspicion on Conley, he would have been indicted, if not lynched, immediately.[27] The fact that a white southern jury believed Conley only confirmed the truth of his testimony.

One significant exception to this view in the black press was Atlanta's own *Independent*, which labeled Conley "a discreditable Negro" and asserted that regardless of Frank's guilt, he certainly had not received a fair trial:

> Under ordinary circumstances the public conscience is such that it is impossible to convict a white man upon the evidence of a Negro unsupported, and it is easily within the perview [sic] of reason that [a] native white man would not have been convicted upon the evidence of a discreditable Negro like Jim Conley. In our opinion, Jim Conley is unworthy of belief, it matters not if he told the truth, as any liar will do sometimes. His evidence is not sufficient to take the life of an individual. . . . If there is any doubt in our minds as to the guilt or innocence of the accused he is entitled to that doubt, and the law does not demand conviction unless the jury is morally certain of guilt. . . . And no reasonable man could believe, who heard the demands of the mob and its tramp through the streets, the ovation given the prosecuting attorney inside and outside of the court room, and the jeers and hisses flung at the jury as they passed through the streets while deliberating the case, but what public sentiment did not have more to do with the making of the verdict than the evidence. . . . Frank denies his guilt, disavows the confession, and is only contradicted by a man who swears that he perjured himself in giving evidence in the Frank case three times before he swore to the truth. . . . And *The Independent* joins the *Atlanta Journal* and that part of the clergy and the enlightened sentiment in demanding for Frank a new trial, not because he is a Jew; but because he is an American, because he is a man and entitled to a fair and impartial trial by a jury of his peers at a time when public sentiment is normal.[28]

Lem Hawkins personifies the *Independent*'s characterization of Conley as a "discreditable Negro," even as the film presents Hawkins as telling the truth. Brisbane is likewise consistent with the prevalent views of Frank in the black press: that he was an immoral, manipulative white employer who abused his social and economic power over a white female and two black male employees and tried to evade the consequences of his actions. His treatment of Myrtle Stanfield is utterly reprehensible. Brisbane as portrayed by Bishop is single and burly rather than married, thin, and short, as Frank was. Yet, as was alleged of Frank, he attempts to gain sexual favors by using his power as the women's supervisor (one flashback scene visualizes that power casually by showing Brisbane's office full of typing secretaries). When Stanfield comes for her pay, Brisbane repeatedly teases her by pulling away the envelope. Stanfield's vulnerability as a female factory worker is duly noted but not emphasized.

Brisbane's treatment of the black characters is just as bad. He calls Hawkins upstairs when he needs help. He berates Hawkins for not spelling the murder notes correctly and has him rewrite them (as Conley alleged Frank had done). He tells Hawkins that Vance, the night watchman, should have been lynched "by now" and generalizes that "Negroes spill their guts when they see a cop." When Hawkins balks at burning the body, Brisbane expresses his sense of class entitlement with the comment, "Somebody's going to hang for this job—why should it be me? I've got wealthy people in Boston." In the actual case, Conley's first affidavit alleged that Frank had told him that he "had some wealthy people in Brooklyn and then he held his head up and looking out of the corner of his eyes said, 'Why should I hang?'"[29] Brisbane, in short, is Frank as the black community would have recalled him in the 1930s and as the black press saw him at the time of the trial.

At such moments and several others (for example, when Vance and Hawkins each look directly into the camera on finding Stanfield's body), Micheaux's film makes it clear that black suspects in the case could face lynching, even though the film's setting is ostensibly Harlem, not the South or Midwest. The first reference to a black suspect's fate occurs when Vance is booked for the crime at the police station and the police discuss getting him to a safe place when they learn the murder victim was white. It comes up again when Brisbane discusses with Hawkins the plan to frame Vance for the murder; and again when Hawkins himself expresses his fears to the camera after helping Brisbane with Stanfield's body, saying, "The white folks gonna lynch me sure."

Those fears were powerful—and realistic—in the mid-1930s, when lynchings still occurred with sickening regularity. Moreover, Micheaux's film was shot and exhibited while the Scottsboro Nine were still on trial. These nine young black men—accused of assault and rape in late March 1931 and nearly all convicted and sentenced to death within weeks of their arrest—were brutalized by the Alabama courts. Only the Supreme Court's rulings in 1931 and 1935 enabled them to receive second trials, during the course of which one of the alleged white rape victims conceded that none of the black defendants had raped her at all. Bribery of the alleged rape victim, the absence of blacks on county juries, and many other forms of injustice transpired in Alabama. The Scottsboro trials were an obvious point of reference for any cinematic depiction of southern injustice in the 1930s.

Adding to the lurid high drama of the Frank case as portrayed in *Murder in Harlem* is a final twist. After Hawkins has testified in court, Claudia Vance brings Neil, a teenaged pal of Stanfield's boyfriend, George Epps, to Glory's office. Neil leads Vance and Glory to George's distraught mother (Lafayette Theater veteran Laura Bowman), who informs them that her son was adopted. Then, via yet another flashback, Mrs. Epps tells Vance and Glory that her son had confessed to her that he murdered Stanfield in a jealous rage. Rather than leaving Stanfield at the factory's entrance, as he had claimed, Epps had followed her into the plant and had witnessed Brisbane's advances. From his vantage point, Stanfield's resistance had looked to Epps like a loving embrace. When he entered the room after Brisbane had knocked Stanfield to the floor, he interpreted her unconsciousness as make-believe, a way of taunting him with her infidelity, and killed her. (Micheaux likely used Epps's real name for his cinematic killer on the assumption that Epps either would not know that the film existed or would have lacked the resources to sue the filmmaker.) Epps wanted to kill Brisbane as well but had to flee when Hawkins entered the stockroom. By an amazing coincidence—the kind that turns up only in the movies—Epps killed Stanfield in the *very* few minutes between the time Brisbane left her unconscious and the time Hawkins found her dead, leaving Brisbane, Hawkins, and the audience to assume that Brisbane was the murderer. Mrs. Epps sadly admits that her son bears "the mark of Cain" (the alternate title for the film).

Epps does not go unpunished for his crime. A newspaper headline informs us that he was shot while trying to help two inmates escape from

George Epps's mother reveals to Vance and Glory that her son murdered Myrtle Stanfield.

In Mrs. Epps's flashback, George Epps (in the background, left) thinks he sees Myrtle embracing Brisbane, but she is actually trying to resist him.

George strangles the unconscious Myrtle because he believes her unfaithful.

the state penitentiary. In an opaque allusion to the infamous Leopold-Loeb case of 1924, sensationalized as "the crime of the century," Neil had told Claudia and Henry that George wanted to help two boys escape from prison. The boys remain unnamed because the uncredited actor playing Neil seems to have forgotten his lines at this point. (The real Epps was placed in a Georgia state reformatory after the trial.) After Arthur is cleared, Henry publishes *A Fool's Errand*, a novel about his shaky romantic history with Claudia. After she reads it, particularly a passage in which Henry describes his heartbreak at her deceptiveness, Claudia invites Henry to come to her apartment so she can explain the misunderstanding. In the end, they declare their love for one another, Henry promises to take her away from the neighborhood, and they kiss and laugh together as the book-loving Catbird and her boyfriend continue to bicker across the hall.[30]

Murder in Harlem is a fascinating mix of docudrama and fictional elements. Even as Micheaux appropriated numerous details from the Phagan-Frank case for the film, he also diverged from it to create a more conventional romantic plot between Henry and Claudia and injected formulaic elements to entertain the audience beyond the murder mystery story line. Among the most striking aspects of the film when it is viewed today is Micheaux's creation of an intrepid heroine. Claudia Vance, Arthur's sister, intervenes decisively in the case at several points. Vance reasons during the trial that someone must know that Brisbane is lying. She discovers the Brisbane-Hawkins connection after the court session one day, overhears Hawkins assure the Catbird that he will attend her party, accosts Hawkins at the Catbird's Seat, gets him drunk, and gets him to admit that "that poor jug" Arthur Vance is "just being railroaded." No such effective amateur investigative work transpired in the Phagan-Frank case, though Conley's common-law wife was tapped to provide an alibi for his whereabouts during the time of Phagan's murder.

The nightclub scene—where Vance gets Hawkins to indicate that he knows a great deal about Myrtle's demise—also has no basis in the actual Phagan-Frank case, although Micheaux might have been referring to a startling post-trial development. During Frank's various appeals, Conley became obsessed with Annie Maude Carter, a woman he met at the state prison while serving his sentence for being an accessory to Frank's crime. Conley wrote Carter "love letters" but also, Carter claimed in an affidavit, confessed to her that he killed Mary Phagan. Yet Micheaux never displayed any interest in—or even knowledge of—the post-trial part of the Phagan-Frank story. In any case, Micheaux used the scene in the Catbird's Seat for many ends: to show Claudia's competence; to reveal Lem to be a foolish slob; and to insert several cabaret singing and dancing performances, a feature of nearly all of his sound films, which he calculated would appeal especially to southern black audiences.[31] Finally, Vance provides the other major break in the case: we would not know who really killed Stanfield if Vance had not found Epps's pal Neil.

Claudia Vance thus takes her place beside Micheaux's many other admirable heroines (such as Sylvia in *Within Our Gates*) as an informed, plucky, and courageous woman. She saves her brother's life far more dramatically than the learned Henry Glory does. At one point, she even orders Glory to sit down at his desk while she tells him something he does not know, and Henry dutifully obeys. Micheaux scholar J. Ronald Green

Claudia Vance thinks someone else must know whether Brisbane was telling the truth on the stand. She solves the case virtually singlehandedly.

Vance flirts with Lem Hawkins at the Catbird Seat to learn what he knows about the murder.

Vance brings George Epps's friend Neil to Glory's office, and Neil reveals that Mrs. Epps can tell them what they want to know.

goes so far as to assert that "Glory is not much more than a professional consultant and implementer of [Vance's] insights and plans."[32]

Both Claudia and Henry are typical of characters in Micheaux's other films—positive representatives of black Americans who embody Micheaux's belief in racial uplift. Glory is a barely disguised double for Micheaux: "Of course you're going to order one," Henry tells a customer for his novel, "if for no other reason than it is a colored author." Their shared interest in reading and writing bespeaks their educated and refined qualities and of course has implications for racial uplift and voting rights. Moreover, Glory and Vance discuss the "dicty" (that is, high-class, snobbish) people who would not read Glory's book if they knew the author was black. They also joke about the preponderance of unemployed but suitably married

The Catbird holds a book while she argues with one of her hoodlum boyfriends.

Henry Glory shows his newly published book to Claudia Vance and her mother.

"colored professional men" in Washington, D.C. Vance jokes that Glory could join them and marry a schoolteacher to support him after he completes his law degree. Green points out that "their laughter is a sign of mutual understanding and respect; they both see themselves as strivers, as productive citizens, not as leisure class, not as the dicty 'black bourgeoisie' that E. Franklin Frazer later made famous for its politically conservative inertness."[33] Compared with the gangsters who hang out in Vance's building and the Catbird herself (actress-singer Bee Freeman, a veteran of the *Shuffle Along* review, plays her as a hands-on-hips, Mae West type), Glory and Vance appear solidly middle class and unpretentious. It is a judgment solidified in the film's final sequence: Micheaux cuts back and forth between the reunited couple, who happily embrace, and the neighboring couple, who continue their physical fight.

If the Glory-Vance romance seems an awkward addition to the Phagan-Frank narrative, Micheaux at least creates parallels between the two story lines by basing their romance on two instances of mistaken identities and false suspicions. Glory's first book customer laughingly directs him to a woman who loves reading; the customer means the Catbird, but Glory finds Vance, who lives across the hall from her. Then Glory is mugged by accident when the Catbird's criminal associates attack the wrong man (their intended mark was white). The Stanfield-Brisbane murder mystery story line also has a few mistaken identities—Brisbane is incorrectly thought to be Stanfield's killer; and to deflect attention from himself, Brisbane tries to frame Arthur Vance. We know he would not hestitate to frame Hawkins if he found it necessary.

Henry Glory interrogates Lem Hawkins on the stand. The entire film is structured around the contrast between the upstanding Glory and the reprobate Hawkins.

Brisbane meets Hawkins outside the factory to give him instructions. Micheaux may have deliberately chosen a backdrop that imitates the well-known photo of Frank seen in the introduction.

The professional, dignified Henry Glory—described by Claudia as "a strange and unusual man with a definite direction"—is a sharp contrast with Hawkins, the spineless, lower-class, alcoholic slob who does Brisbane's bidding. Clarence Brooks gives Glory an air of dignity and refinement, while Alec Lovejoy's Hawkins is a buffoon.[34] Green's insightful analysis of Hawkins describes him as "one of the less-than-admirable black characters who is caught in the machinations of white intrigue." Hawkins embodies a minstrelsy caricature, "the worst characteristics of the world of race entertainment." At the Catbird's Seat, where Vance tricks Hawkins into revealing what he knows about Myrtle's murder, Lovejoy performs a great vaudevillian turn as he paws at Vance, gets progressively drunker, and tells her she is a "girl that knows class when she sees it." (Lovejoy's performance in this scene is comparable in its vaudevillian antics and voice modulations to Bert Lahr's Cowardly Lion in *The Wizard of Oz*.) Other customers in the room subject Hawkins to a "cutting gaze"— "the middle-class look of disdain upon lower-class behavior"—as do courtroom spectators when Glory badgers Hawkins on the witness stand, evoking repeated laughter from the audience.[35] Hawkins may be literate like Glory, but he does nothing with these essential skills beyond aiding, albeit reluctantly, his employer in framing a fellow black employee.

It is illuminating to consider Green's analysis of how Micheaux rendered personal vice and virtue in *Murder in Harlem*'s black male characters. Hawkins's minstrelsy caricature continues during his flashback testimony, as he subserviently embodies the "slave mentality" that some black newspapers ascribed to Jim Conley and which Conley encouraged. Hawkins

Hawkins does a brief dance after Brisbane pays him a quarter to stand lookout for him.

Brisbane dictates to Hakwins the murder notes that will frame Arthur Vance.

happily agrees to follow Brisbane's orders—taking Brisbane's quarter as payment for keeping watch on the plant stairway, he comments, "Sure is a good white man," and does a shuffle in what Green aptly describes as "a white man's living juke box."[36] His attempt to spy on Brisbane and Stanfield in the stockroom turns comical when he hurries back to his post in the stairway as another female employee approaches (to the accompaniment of music that resembles Charles Gounod's "Funeral March of a Marionette," the theme music of *Alfred Hitchcock Presents*). Hawkins turns infantile when Brisbane wants him to help move Stanfield's body and when Brisbane threatens to call the police if Hawkins refuses to burn her body. When Brisbane takes back the $250 bribe, Hawkins starts crying, bawling, "Is that the way you do business?" Green notes that all these scenes are played "for laughs, in spite of the distinctly unhilarious predicament Hawkins finds himself in—being implicated in the rape and murder of a white woman."[37] In each of his scenes, Hawkins implicitly affirms Glory's upstanding nature.

Yet, Green also notes a striking inconsistency in Hawkins's behavior during the scene in which Brisbane dictates the murder notes to him. Hawkins drops the minstrel caricature and turns temporarily shrewd and serious. The turning point seems to be the sobering experience of helping Brisbane carry Myrtle's body to the basement, although this occurs offscreen. In Brisbane's office, the dissatisfied boss dictates the notes to Hawkins several times (as Conley alleged Frank had done), and Hawkins debates his phonetic spelling of "Negro," thinking Brisbane means for him actually to write "nigger": "I think you mean an 'i' here instead of an 'e' and two 'g's instead of one."

This scene is particularly significant when considered in light of the murder notes in the Phagan-Frank case and what was construed from them at Frank's trial. Discovered next to Mary Phagan's body, the notes were written on factory letterhead and composed as if written by Mary Phagan before she died ("he play with me while I make water"). Both sides in the case agreed that she could not have written them. Conley claimed at first not to be able to read and spell but subsequently admitted he could when Leo Frank so informed the authorities. Conley eventually claimed that Frank dictated the notes to him after the two had carried Phagan's body to the basement—the very scenario played out in Micheaux's film. Conley was certainly aware that if he admitted he could write, he risked being accused of being the sole author of the notes and of having committed the murder; if the conclusion was affirmative to the two previous points, could lynching be far behind?

The authorship of the notes was a crucial aspect of the Phagan-Frank case, part of the prosecution's insistence that Conley was an "old faithful darky" who was just following his master's orders in the writing of the notes. Historian Jeffrey Melnick discusses this aspect of the trial: "Drawing on the conventions of the minstrel show and the plantation-school novel, Dorsey insisted that Conley be understood within the category of 'old Negro.' In turn, it fell to Frank's supporters to contend that Conley was a new kind of African American—anarchic, degraded, and dangerous . . . who loafed, got drunk, and attacked white women."[38] Melnick goes on to compare these competing versions of Jim Conley with the depiction of the "Sambo" type in minstrel playlets. Sambo would win the lottery, for example, and be derided by his fellow bootblacks for pretending to be more educated than he was (as when Sambo read a newspaper upside down).[39] Following such logic, Hugh Dorsey argued in court that no southern black male would have been stupid enough to linger around a dead white woman's body or able to write the notes. Dorsey demonstrated that even if Conley could write, he was incapable of spelling words correctly. He then questioned whether Conley would have written "negro" or "nigger" in the murder notes—the precise words Hawkins queries Brisbane about in the note-writing scene in the film.[40]

Given all the other details Micheaux took from the Phagan-Frank case, the fact that he replicated the debate about Conley's literacy may not be surprising; but the relative significance of these details in the case and in the film is worth a closer look. It can be no accident that Micheaux layered his portrayal of the Jim Conley character in so many ways in this

"This white man's got something up his sleeve," Hawkins says to the camera while Brisbane is out of the room.

scene in *Murder in Harlem*. When Hawkins turns serious while Brisbane dictates the murder notes, he tells him, "I understands why," meaning that he knows his boss hopes to frame Vance with them as Stanfield's murderer. Perhaps this line is meant for the edification of audience members who were not familiar with the details of the Phagan-Frank case murder notes. Brisbane replies, "You understands too damn much."[41] Hawkins does indeed; as proof, he mutters to himself, "This white man's got something up his sleeve." As if to counter the reasoning of Frank's jury and Dorsey's argument that no black man could be intelligent enough to plant the notes by Mary Phagan's body to incriminate Frank, Micheaux shows that even this black buffoon is plenty intelligent. He speaks seriously to the camera of what Brisbane is up to, confides that he will try to leave the office with the $250, and then puts on his subservient act with a big smile when Brisbane returns. If Hawkins's behavior presents black dissembling in the presence of white social authority, it also alludes to Jim Conley's trickster shrewdness. Conley was, after all, able to transform police suspicion to trust and to redirect the white lynch mob toward Leo Frank.

Hawkins also in this scene counters the Frank defense team's characterization of Conley as a drunkard and a beast. Hawkins gets drunk in the film, and he belches constantly in the bar where he repairs after aiding Brisbane in his flashback, but he in no way embodies a lecherous black brute (though in flirting with Claudia he is being unfaithful to his "lady"). In short, Hawkins's note-writing scene with Brisbane builds on the same interplay between old and new conceptions of African American males—that is, obedient figure and shrewd trickster—that informed the trial's debate about Conley's true nature. It was very likely for all these reasons that Micheaux chose to dramatize Hawkins's shift from minstrel buffoon to literate, perceptive employee in the note-writing scene in *Murder in Harlem*. Patrick McGilligan reports that the scene evoked "extreme disgust," rather than laughs, from one critic in the *New York Amsterdam News*.[42] That might well have been Micheaux's intent.

If the parallels between Micheaux's film and the Phagan-Frank case help us to appreciate how Micheaux chose to represent the case, the same is true of the divergences—the ways in which Micheaux altered the case, particularly the final twist in the story, the guilt of George Epps. This twist did not exist in *The Gunsaulus Mystery* or in Micheaux's early novels.[43]

Did Micheaux change his mind about Frank's guilt in the intervening two decades? That the murderer is ultimately revealed to be Epps, a minor figure in the actual case, once again exemplifies Micheaux's propensity to play with the details of the works—fictional or factual—on which he based his films.[44] For *Murder in Harlem* to shift the blame for Myrtle Stanfield's murder from her sleazy factory supervisor to her sexually obsessed, juvenile delinquent, lower-class boyfriend implicates multiple classes (upper, middle, and low) of white society in her death. Epps here becomes the white counterpart to the Catbird and her gangster boyfriends. On the other hand, changing the identity of the girl's true murderer may have been a simple, practical way of adding a new angle to the Phagan-Frank story Micheaux had told so often before; or perhaps it reflected his awareness that censorship trouble might have ensued if he reproduced the case intact.

Strikingly, Micheaux eliminated any overt reference to Jewishness from the film; neither Brisbane nor Epps is so identified. Perhaps anyone in Micheaux's 1930s audience familiar with the trial would have made that association without being told. Patrick McGilligan suspects that Harlem Theater owner Franklin Schiffman's earlier lawsuits against Micheaux for breach of contract must have made the Phagan-Frank case and its guilty Jewish factory supervisor a very appealing subject to Micheaux. After all, Micheaux's film indicts the Frank character for mendacity, lechery, and perjury—but not murder. Micheaux may have been trying to avoid the censor's scissors, or he may have wanted to avoid insulting the Jewish film producers and backers for some of his sound films. *Murder in Harlem* was financed by Jews—specifically Alfred N. Sack and Lester Sack of Texas— who may have insisted that Micheaux omit the Jewish angle.[45]

Micheaux's depiction of Brisbane also raises the issue of whether Micheaux was anti-Semitic and what role that might have played in his decision to leave Frank's Jewish identity out of the film. His biographer Betti VanEpps-Taylor describes letters in which Micheaux complains about Jewish "race" filmmakers and deduces from it "a bitter anti-Semitism that he always denied." Green and McGilligan have argued otherwise, drawing on Micheaux's favorable depiction of Jews and his other comments about them in his novels. They contend that Micheaux resented Jewish filmmakers because they were competition, not because they were Jewish. For example, Sidney Wyeth—revived as a film producer in Micheaux's 1940s novel *The Case of Mrs. Wingate*—refuses to make anti-Semitic films for the Nazis in spite of the fact that some Jewish producers have treated him ill.[46] Only Brisbane's lust for Stanfield and Epps's fascination with scantily clad women hint at the kind of sexual obsession implicitly linked to Frank's Jewishness in the actual trial.

Whatever Micheaux's reason for eliminating the Jewish angle from *Murder in Harlem*, its omission prevents the film from explicitly exploring the intriguing convergences and tensions between the black and Jewish communities during the case. Brisbane is a WASP with "wealthy people in Boston." Equally significant, by setting the film in Harlem—a northern mecca for black America in the 1910s and 1920s—Micheaux eliminated the element of North-South conflict that informed and so influenced the outcome of Leo Frank's trial. The film thus narrows the case's central tensions to those of race and class—across and on both sides of the color line (employer-employee, lawyer-janitor). (There is not even a hint of solidarity between the black employees Vance and Hawkins.) All in all, *Murder in Harlem* reflects contemporary black newspapers' consensus that the murder of Mary Phagan was in both inspiration and execution entirely white people's business.

Perhaps the most surprising element in Micheaux's film is the fact that justice is achieved, although only after great effort both in the courtroom and outside it (with Epps's demise). Although we do not see Brisbane's punishment for perjury, he has been exposed as a liar. Intentionally or not, *Murder in Harlem* expresses faith in the American judicial system, particularly when the defendant is represented by a "smart" black attorney (as Brisbane calls him) such as Henry Glory and when a lowlife such as Lem Hawkins agrees to tell the truth.[47]

The fact that justice does reign in the end might also explain why lynching plays no part in Micheaux's film beyond the perennial threat to the black suspects. Given Micheaux's harrowing depiction of this practice in *Within Our Gates*, his decision to omit the actual trial's violent denouement might seem surprising if not disappointing. Is lynching an atrocity only when its victims are black or innocent? Presumably, Micheaux could not make a film in which "justice" was served by a lynching, even if the white boss was guilty of murder. Leo Frank's lynching is twice removed from *Murder in Harlem*: not only do we *not* see the killer lynched, but the Leo Frank character, Brisbane, is not even the actual killer.[48]

Murder in Harlem also shares with other Micheaux films the suggestion, through its repeated and sometimes contradictory flashbacks, that uncovering what really happened requires persistence and intelligence to see beyond the "white truths" printed in newspapers or offered in trial testimony. It is worth noting in this connection that the newspaper headlines in *Murder in Harlem* are not the instruments of a sensationalizing press, as they will be in subsequent depictions of the case. They merely forward the narrative, giving us information that would be too costly, elaborate, or time-consuming to show—such as Epps being shot as he attempts to help friends make a prison break. Micheaux, Melnick notes, made the "fascinating move" of suggesting "that none of the principals in the action has enough information to be a trustworthy witness at the trial that follows." As a result, Henry Glory must, to paraphrase Corey Creekmur, accumulate and coordinate the "black and white narratives."[49] And that he can do only with Claudia Vance's help.

In any case, *Murder in Harlem* displays Micheaux's creativity in multifaceted form, starting with the fact that he took a nationally known murder mystery and dramatized it—up until its final minutes—in accordance with the prevailing view of black Americans (that Frank was guilty). He added certain cinematic conventions—the romantic plot, bits of character comedy, the amazing coincidence revealed late in the story, and the musical performances at the Catbird's Seat. He reasserted his gender and racial politics by adding the characters of the protofeminist heroine; the aspiring, novel-writing, middle-class attorney; and the "disreputable" Lem Hawkins. Rather than being just a message movie or an exploration of the Phagan-Frank case, the film assumes the outlines of a subtextual exploitation film,[50] one whose basis has until recently been opaque to contemporary viewers and scholars.

If Micheaux's allusions, deformations, and parodies of the Phagan-Frank case in *Murder in Harlem* have encouraged scholars to deemphasize the links between the case and the film, that connection was recognized clearly in Atlanta in 1935 when *Lem Hawkins' Confession* was booked into a segregated black theater. Advertising taglines in the black *Atlanta*

Daily World referenced the film's multiple flashbacks ("the truth at last"), its generic identity as a murder mystery, and its basis on "the mysterious Stanfield Murder Case" (Micheaux would publish a novel with that name in 1946). The *Daily World* advised readers—correctly—that "few of the audience will dare guess its solution" and briefly noted that "the picture is based on authentic news reports of an actual murder case, which strangely enough, occurred in Atlanta."[51]

Like her predecessor in 1923, Atlanta's city censor in 1935, Mrs. Zella Richardson, needed no such prompting to recognize the film's source. She accordingly ordered that *Lem Hawkins' Confession* be cut so that "all objectionable allusions [to the Leo Frank case were] deleted, and all scenes which would make the picture local, taken out."[52] This meant cutting the film in half.

Thus, the Micheaux film was suppressed, like his previous account of the Phagan-Frank case (and like *They Won't Forget*), in the very city where it transpired. Nor was the film well received in the cities where it was allowed to play (including Los Angeles, the first time a Micheaux film had played in Hollywood's home city).[53] *Murder in Harlem* was criticized for continuity errors, poor lighting and camerawork, lousy makeup (which made Dorothy van Engle look like "a coal miner"), and hackneyed and confusing plotting. One newswire critic complained of "stilted language, absence of action and stiffback performances." Although Alec Lovejoy, Bea Freeman, and Andrew Bishop earned great praise for their acting, Clarence Brooks and Dorothy Van Engle were accused of speaking "as if they are afraid they will split a verb . . . the air of artificiality smells up the entire show." Yet *Murder in Harlem* remains in many ways one of Micheaux's more accomplished and compelling surviving sound films, full of dramatic flourishes and striking camera movements.[54] The film's poor reception is all the more surprising given the resonance of the film's plot with the ongoing trials of the Scottsboro Nine.

Oscar Micheaux would continue to reference the Phagan-Frank case as he went on writing novels and producing films—even though he never produced another film about it. His 1945 book *The Case of Mrs. Wingate* has the wife of a "wealthy textile magnate" in Atlanta confess to black hero Kermit Early that her husband "is not a . . . *normal man*" and express her regret that she can never have children. Her confession provokes a lengthy flashback in which the narrator presents Jim Conley's account of Leo Frank's guilt—including his (oral) rape of Mary Phagan while she was unconscious—and the aftermath of the case. Conley (Micheaux characterized him, much like Lem Hawkins, as "a simple ignorant Negro") averred that Frank had confessed to him that he was not built like other men, which was taken to mean that he derived pleasure from oral rather than genital sex. During the appeals process of the actual case, there was some speculation that Conley conceived this detail from vague knowledge of the Jewish practice of circumcision and from the fact that the Franks had no children.[55] In Micheaux's book, Mrs. Wingate uses the confession of her husband's sexual inadequacy to inaugurate a seduction of Kermit Early, a move that makes the latter extremely uncomfortable ("This is still down South," he tells her, "even if we are in Atlanta"). A sign of the times, Micheaux's 1945 novel was far more sexually explicit than his earlier novels and films had been. In fact, the frontispiece of the original edition of the novel depicts the scene of Mrs. Wingate's confession about her husband to Kermit.

One year after Micheaux released *Murder in Harlem*, Warner Bros. released a film on the same subject, *They Won't Forget*. The two films differ dramatically in several ways. Like Micheaux's film, *They Won't Forget* would face significant censorship in Atlanta; unlike Micheaux's film, it was made within identifiable constraints in Hollywood.

2

The Phagan-Frank Case as 1930s
Hollywood Message Movie

They Won't Forget

We know how it's gonna end. —SHATTUCK CLAY

CRITIC WILLIAM JOHNSON suggests in the influential *Film Comment* that *They Won't Forget* "may be the most shocking movie ever produced by a major Hollywood studio."[1] This assessment is all the more striking because it was rendered in 1996, nearly sixty years after the film's premiere. Countless Hollywood films made since 1937 have shocked audiences— especially after film censorship ended in the early 1960s. Yet this veiled treatment of the Phagan-Frank case still retains extraordinary power as a portrait of southern sectionalism and mob violence. How it achieved that power is the subject of this chapter.

That *They Won't Forget* was made at all in 1930s Hollywood is remarkable and yet in some ways unsurprising. American audiences of the 1930s may not have chosen to see such a topical film in overwhelming numbers, but those who did likely connected strongly with its depiction of personal upheaval and the absence of justice in American society. In 1937 Americans were still struggling through the Great Depression—a catastrophic failure of capitalism and, at least initially, the U.S. government. More to the point, by 1937 movie fans had already seen a number of films like *They Won't Forget*.

No Hollywood studio made more social consciousness movies in the 1930s than Warner Bros.[2] The most celebrated of those early in the decade was *I Am a Fugitive from a Chain Gang* (1932), whose director was none other than *They Won't Forget*'s Mervyn LeRoy. Both films were based on true events in Georgia. In fact, the state was one of Warner Bros.'s favorite punching bags—a rich source for tales of southern barbarity that fit nicely into the national perception of the South as embodying all that was backward and uncivilized about the United States. Warner Bros. likely would not have hit Georgia so hard and so often if the studio's first-run theaters had been located in the South.

Regardless, by addressing lynching, *They Won't Forget* became one of the most controversial message movies of the decade. While publications by the NAACP and other organizations often featured lynching photos as part of their antilynching campaigns in the 1930s, only one other Hollywood film had dared to focus on the subject. MGM's acclaimed *Fury*, directed by German émigré Fritz Lang (also known for *Metropolis* [1927] and *M* [1931]), was released in the summer of 1936, precisely one year before Warner Bros.'s film.[3] Like *I Am a Fugitive from a Chain Gang* before them, both antilynching films focused on white victims of social injustice fueled by personal prejudice. *Fury* played it safer, sidestepping lawsuits and some measure of controversy by setting its story west of Chicago. *They Won't Forget*, in closely following the Phagan-Frank case, took as its setting the unspecified South. "Georgia" is never uttered in the course of the film—as was the case in *Fugitive*.

Social problem films were relatively rare exceptions to the industry's publicly repeated policy of producing only "harmless entertainment." A *Fortune* profile of Warner Bros. noted that "most Warner executives are quick to disown the role of crusader for social justice; they protest that their only purpose in treating these 'controversial' themes is a harmless passion for gold. . . . But except for MGM with its one brave picture *Fury*, Warner is the only major studio that seems to know or care what is going on in America besides pearl-handled gunplay, sexual dalliance, and the giving of topcoats to comedy butlers."[4]

This publicized profit policy was essential to the studio's ongoing success in the 1930s. Overtly political films would have diminished Warner Bros.'s income and likely provoked calls for federal movie censorship—something that had never existed in America although it often loomed on the horizon. A dismantling of the major studio oligopoly that dominated the film industry (and kept Oscar Micheaux and his ilk on the margins of the business) might follow. Hence, even Warner Bros. generally produced westerns, adventures, costume movies, adaptations, musicals, and biographies; topical films such as *They Won't Forget* were comparatively rare.

Like Oscar Micheaux, Mervyn LeRoy and screenwriters Aben Kandel and Robert Rossen deployed many screen conventions to tell their version of the Phagan-Frank case, often drawing on the social problem and newspaper film genres. But the key template for their film's basic storyline and characters was the well-received 1936 fictionalization of the case, Ward Greene's *Death in the Deep South.*[5] In closely following Greene's novel, LeRoy and his team came smack up against the Production Code Administration (PCA), a division of the Motion Picture Producers and Distributors Association. This entity was empowered by the major studios with two crucial functions: to anticipate what details of Hollywood movies might incite anger and controversy, and to help filmmakers find ways to avoid offending anyone. When Warner Bros. made *They Won't Forget*, the PCA helped the studio to transform a historical atrocity into a morally acceptable, sellable narrative—the very compelling film, in fact, that William Johnson praised in 1996.

They Won't Forget focuses on the aftermath of the murder of an extraordinarily pretty fifteen-year-old victim (the voluptuous Lana Turner in her first featured role) named Mary Clay. The murder, like Mary Phagan's, occurs on Confederate Memorial Day in a southern town barely identified as "Flodden." Clay's body is found early the following morning in the basement of the Buxton Business College. Clay had returned to the building after her class to retrieve her compact before meeting her boyfriend to attend the parade. Black janitor–elevator operator Tump Redwine (Clinton Rosemond) finds her body in the elevator shaft in the middle of the night and immediately calls the police. As a narrative figure, Redwine combines the actual night watchman who found Phagan's body, Newt Lee, and Jim Conley, who testified decisively against Frank.

As Lee did, Redwine becomes an early suspect along with a few other men, among them the elderly head of the business school, Carlisle Buxton (E. Alyn Warren), and Mary's boyfriend, Joe Turner (Elisha Cook Jr.), who is clearly modeled on Mary Phagan's boastful trolley-car acquaintance, George Epps.[6] Ambitious prosecutor Andy Griffin (Claude Rains) takes charges of the investigation. He quickly dismisses Joe Turner as a suspect, given that Turner was not in the building when the murder happened. (Joe, true to Elisha Cook Jr.'s screen type, is a figure of ridicule: he brags to his friends about being a friend of Griffin after we have seen him cower in terror during Griffin's questioning.) Griffin also rules out the business school's head, Mr. Buxton, because prosecuting him would hurt Griffin's political career. Griffin—closely modeled on Atlanta Public

Solicitor Hugh M. Dorsey—is looking for "something big to put me on top" and states outright when he takes charge of the case that he is "after bigger prey" than a black man such as Tump Redwine.

Griffin eventually focuses on newly arrived northerner Robert Hale (Edward Norris), a happily married twenty-four-year-old who has no local friends and little money. Hale differs in this from the well-established factory supervisor Frank, who had lived in Atlanta for five years at the time of the murder and was firmly entrenched in Atlanta's Jewish community.[7] Hale, who teaches shorthand to Mary Clay and other girls at the business school, was in the building (grading papers, he claims) when Clay returned to retrieve her makeup kit from her classroom desk, much as Frank was working on accounts in the pencil factory and gave Mary Phagan her pay.

Mary Clay's classmate and pal Imogene Mayfield (Linda Perry) clearly envies what she imagines is Hale's romantic interest in Mary. Imogene later tells reporter Bill Brock (Allyn Joslyn) that Clay and Hale "were crazy about each other." (Even though Hale stops and leans over Clay's desk to correct her shorthand in the classroom scene—to Clay's delight—the film offers no indication that Hale is sexually attracted to her.) Imogene's suggestion that Hale and Clay were in love faintly echoes the accusations that Frank lusted after Mary Phagan, knew her by name, and brushed up against her in a flirtatious manner.

Griffin is aided in his quest to convict Hale by the restless, wisecracking reporter Bill Brock, who like Griffin is bored and looking—by any means available—for his own big break. (Brock anticipates the callous, restless reporter Chuck Tatum [Kirk Douglas] stuck in a small town in Billy Wilder's 1951 *Ace in the Hole*.) Brock and his competitors stand in for the three opportunistic newspapers (the *Atlanta Constitution*, the *Atlanta Journal*, and the *Atlanta Georgian*) that used the Phagan-Frank case to build up their circulation with multiple extras and uncorroborated claims that inspired the frenzy that engulfed Atlanta. It is, in fact, Brock who suggests to Griffin that Hale is his man, pointing out that Hale was in the building at the time of Clay's murder and repeating Imogene's allegation that Hale and Clay were "crazy about each other."

At Griffin's direction, the police go to Hale's apartment building to take him in for questioning. In a coincidence possible only in a Hollywood film, they enter the hallway just as Hale is about to leave the building carrying a draft of a telegram accepting a job in Chicago. Hale had returned home on the afternoon of Confederate Memorial Day and described to his wife how Professor Buxton humiliated him in front of his female students. He did not feel accepted in the South, he said, and wanted to move back to the North. While Hale is talking to the police, a delivery boy brings Hale his suit and explains that the cleaners could not take out a bloodstain. Hale claims the blood is his own and got there when his barber cut him while shaving him. The detectives take Hale in for questioning so abruptly that he barely has time to tell Sybil about it. Like Frank, whose shaking hands impressed Atlanta police, Hale nervously smokes many cigarettes and fidgets while under interrogation in Griffin's office.[8]

Meanwhile, the press follows up on Hale's arrest. *They Won't Forget* is especially notable for depicting Brock and his competitors as vultures without a shred of compassion or consideration. In one of the film's most memorable scenes, Brock and company invade the Hales' apartment the afternoon Robert is arrested, thoughtlessly inform Sybil about the arrest, and photograph her as she faints in reaction rather than trying to break her fall. Assuring the hapless Sybil that "the press is a powerful influence for justice," the journalists rummage through her personal effects in her bedroom and take a honeymoon photo from her night table. In the living room, female columnist Dolly Holly deceives the friendless Sybil into revealing that her husband feels uneasy in the South and is planning to take a job up North. After promising to keep this revelation a secret, she and her colleagues plaster it on their front pages and help to inflame local opinion against Robert. In a local bar-restaurant, Griffin listens as local men discuss the case and respond with hostility to the news that Hale dislikes the South.

Although she wants to see her husband, the police will not allow Sybil to communicate with Robert for a considerable time after his arrest. This echoes Lucille Frank's perceived delay in visiting her husband in jail, which the prosecution and press interpreted as a sign of her belief in his guilt. When Sybil is finally allowed to see her husband in the city jail, the camera shoots their embrace through the bars as Sybil asserts, "It's good to be together." Unlike the optimistic and oblivious Frank, Robert Hale knows that he will not live long.

The national press picks up on the story and further sensationalizes the case. (In fact, the case received nationwide coverage only during the appeals process). As the screen shows a montage of teletypes printing out the story over a map of the United States, newspaper editors tell their reporters to emphasize the North-South angle of the trial and to "keep selling prejudice." When Brock calls Griffin to tell him that a celebrated northern attorney is coming to defend Hale, he yells into the phone: "The war's started! . . . What war? The Civil War all over again! The *New York Independent* is hollerin' about Southern prejudices. What are we doin'? We're hollerin' about Northern prejudices. It's gettin' to be some story." The fact that a man's life is at stake is lost in the hullabaloo.

Nurtured by Griffin and Brock, sectionalism is further inflamed when a northern investigator arrives to help the defendant, much as William J. Burns, hailed as the "World's Greatest Detective," arrived in Atlanta during Frank's appeals. The detective, named Pindar in the film (played by Granville Bates), immediately recognizes that public sentiment is against Frank and that "the real trial is going on right now." He is also clever enough to catch the town barber, Jim Timberlake (Clifford Soubier), in a lie about how well he remembers cutting Robert while shaving him on the day of Phagan's murder. The townsfolk ostracize Pindar, and he is beaten offscreen by Mary Clay's friends and brothers. William J. Burns actually was slapped, chased down by a mob, and nearly lynched in Marietta — Phagan's hometown — when his car broke down there during his investigation on Frank's behalf. He was abused mostly for being a Yankee working in Frank's support, but he was already extremely unpopular for his earlier union-busting investigations of Atlanta factory workers.[9]

Michael Gleason (Otto Kruger), a showy New Yorker who is reputed to be the greatest lawyer in the country, is hired as Hale's trial attorney. When he arrives at the train station and is nearly stoned by the locals, he seems unfazed, almost as if he enjoys it. In fact, Leo Frank's lawyers in his initial trial were Atlantans Luther Rosser and Reuben Arnold, by reputation the best attorneys in the state; northern attorneys — most prominently Louis Marshall — came into the picture only during the appeals process. The role of northerners in leading these appeals at hearings and in fundraising to finance them further inflamed Georgians' resentment of Frank's efforts to exonerate himself.

The attempted attack against Gleason at the train station brings the town's leading banker, publisher, and merchant to Griffin's office to complain that the city has become a "powder keg." They plead with him to make sure he is prosecuting the guilty party. Griffin points out their hypocrisy: their offers of rewards for major leads in the case and their inflammatory statements in the papers — all to make money and promote themselves — had stirred up the sectionalism and sensationalism in the first place. "You should've thought of all these things before, gentlemen, but you didn't," Griffin tells them. "Now you're frightened. It's grown too big

In this publicity still for *They Won't Forget*, defense attorney Michael Gleason squares off with Andy Griffin as Professor Buxton sits in the witness chair. (Courtesy of the Academy of Motion Picture Arts and Sciences.)

for you. Well, it's not grown too big for me. You started it, my aristocratic friends, but I'll finish it." Griffin's accusations here corroborate the conclusions of historians that southern elites at that time were generally more concerned about social stability than social justice.[10] Flodden's rage for vengeance is most vividly embodied in Mary Clay's furious and aggrieved brothers, who are behind the violence Pindar and Gleason encounter. The Clay brothers predict Hale's lynching in their repeated comment on the investigation and the trial: "We know how it's gonna end."

The trial itself—greatly condensed from the full month Frank's lasted to a few days—goes badly for Hale. Mary Clay's friends continue to claim falsely that Mary and Robert "were crazy about each other." Gleason points out the inadequacy of each prosecution witness's testimony, but Griffin consistently nullifies Gleason's efforts by responding with appeals to emotion: by waving Mary Clay's dress in front of a witness, for example, he provokes an emotional outburst from Mrs. Clay to keep the jury focused on her loss. Griffin had arranged for the reluctant Mrs. Clay to attend the trial for precisely such a coup de théâtre after witnessing an outburst from Hale's mother the previous day. (Mrs. Hale's action was itself inspired by Leo Frank's mother's verbal attack on Dorsey as "a gentile dog" late in the trial.) Griffin injects sectionalism into the proceedings in a way that Gleason can counter only with futile protests. When Buxton, on the stand, editorializes that he thought it would do Hale good to see the Confederate Memorial Day festivities, a spectator in the courtroom shouts out, to general approval, "Ain't nothing would've done that trash any good!" Another reversal hurts Hale's case: The barber admits on the stand that he shaved Hale on the afternoon in question, then, after a long, pregnant pause, claims he did not cut Hale; the blood must have come from elsewhere.

As in the actual trial with Jim Conley, Tump Redwine's appearance on the stand is a climactic courtroom scene, making the racial tensions informing the case the high point of the courtroom sequences. Redwine has been coached offscreen by Buxton's lawyer, Colonel Foster (played by Raymond Brown; William Smith was Conley's attorney). Under Griffin's direct questioning, Redwine testifies that he heard a loud noise early in the afternoon of Clay's murder and shortly thereafter saw Hale at the top of the stairs. Looking nervous, Hale had asked Redwine if he heard the noise. In cross-examination, Gleason gets Redwine to admit that he has changed his original story out of fear. Gleason also catches Redwine in an obvious contradiction—he was asleep that afternoon but claims he saw Hale at the top of the stairs. Redwine withdraws his claim when he realizes that his testimony will send Hale to his death.

Redwine's reversals can be seen to echo Conley's many affidavits to the Atlanta police about Phagan and Frank, each elaborating in more detail Conley's claims that Frank attempted to rape Phagan, killed her to conceal that fact, and then had Conley help him dispose of the body. Unlike Redwine, however, Conley never contradicted himself on the stand; his steadiness as he was cross-examined by the celebrated Luther Rosser only reinforced the impression that he was telling the truth. Redwine ultimately concedes that his fear of his own possible conviction or lynching led to his false statements—the same rationale Jim Conley offered to explain his dramatically different affidavits against Frank before the trial. (Redwine's recanting of his testimony actually arose, as we shall see below, from the demands of the Production Code Administration rather than from the case itself.) Fear is in fact the keynote of Redwine's character and Rosemond's performance; he more closely resembles the terrified night watchman, Newt Lee, than Conley, but his roles as a crucial witness and possible accessory allow him to function in the courtroom as Conley did in the actual case. By combining Lee and Conley into one character, the filmmakers emphasized the social subordination and fear of a southern black in a perilous position.

In the film, neither Redwine's recantation nor Hale's final plea of innocence has any effect. Hale's statement to the jury that the case should have nothing to do with enmity between the North and the South offends the jurors even more. Gleason's eloquent closing argument about the true witnesses in the case being "hatred, fear, and prejudice" is ignored; a portion of it is shot largely in long shot to convey its ineffectiveness, with Griffin and his assistant, Drake, sitting comfortably in the foreground listening. Griffin's own closing statement features soaring rhetoric about the grandeur and fairness of the South and calls for a judgment of "guilty, guilty, guilty." Dorsey's summation in Leo Frank's trial also ended with these words, and a church bell chimed after each "guilty"—a sound effect that had an enormous impact on the courtroom audience.[11] In the film, as the jury deliberates, one member receives a note threatening him with death if he votes to acquit Hale. The other jury members assure him that voting "guilty" will not compromise his reputation as a "tough guy."

Hale is convicted, and his sentence is read to a full courthouse (Frank's jury delivered their verdict to a mostly empty courtroom; not even Frank was present). As the crowd cheers, Sybil denounces them and collapses in tears. Thereafter, the film briefly alludes to Hale's failed appeals, including that to the Supreme Court. In a brief scene, Governor Mountford (Paul Everton), like Georgia's John M. Slaton, informs his wife (Ann Shoemaker) that his examination of the evidence along with the letters and petitions for and against Hale's execution has persuaded him to commute Robert's death sentence. The angry mob that gathered outside the governor's mansion even before he made his decision will not deter him. At the start of the film, during the Confederate Memorial Day parade, Mrs. Mountford had spoken aggressively of her husband's likely defeat of Andy Griffin in the upcoming Senate election. Here—toward the end of the film and her husband's political life—she simply tells him, reading her husband's mind: "I'm a little tired of public life anyway, aren't you?" Like Sallie Slaton, she supports her husband's decision. While the militia are called in to suppress the enraged mob, the Clay brothers and their friends tear themselves away from the anticipated "fun" of the riot to pursue their own plan.

The final section of *They Won't Forget* dramatizes Hale's unhappy fate. Frank was taken from Atlanta at night to the state prison at Milledgeville, where he stayed several months before he was abducted, driven to Marietta, and lynched. Hale does not make it that far. After the commutation of his sentence, he is put aboard a train to the state prison along with two unsympathetic police officers. Conspirators on the train bring it to a halt and scuffle with the policemen in the darkness of the baggage car where Hale sits. Hale attempts to escape but finds the lynch mob, led by Clay's brothers and Mary's boyfriend, Joe Turner, awaiting him when he slides open the door. They carry him off to his lynching.

In the film's coda, Griffin and Brock are gloating over Griffin's surefire election to the U.S. Senate. Governor Mountford took himself out of the running when he pardoned Hale, and Griffin has the backing of Brock's paper. Robert's widow, Sybil, comes in to return a personal check that Griffin had sent her on learning that she planned to leave town—presumably to go north. (Lucille Frank, by contrast, remained in Atlanta for the rest of her life.) Sybil refuses to ease Griffin's conscience by accepting the money. Moreover, she directly accuses Griffin and Brock of everything the audience has witnessed: their responsibility for stirring up the sentiment that created the mob violence and, in turn, resulted in the lynching. She goes so far as to tell the two men they are worse than the lynch mob because they had nothing personal at stake in Robert's conviction and execution beyond their own ambition.

After Sybil walks out, the two men seem troubled and reflective about their conduct for the first time in the film. As they watch her leave the building, Brock comments, "Andy, now that it's all over, I wonder if he really did it." Griffin replies, "I wonder." The town square bell tolls and the shot fades. The film concludes without ever explicitly identifying Mary Clay's killer.

As with Micheaux's films, no one remotely familiar with the Phagan-Frank case would have failed to recognize its outline in *They Won't Forget*. Some details from the case do not appear in the film (for example, the curious murder notes), which, like *Murder in Harlem*, refuses to name names and explicitly state its status as a docudrama. Many other crucial specifics of the case do appear in *They Won't Forget*, though: the murder of a teenage girl, her body discovered in a basement, an ambitious prosecutor, a black janitor who is a pivotal yet questionable witness for the prosecution, the unjust trial, opportunistic reporters, the governor's commutation of the convicted man's death sentence, rampant sectionalism, and the subsequent lynching of a white northerner. The final version of the story told in the film reflected an elaborate process of adaptation and revision.

Ward Greene's *Death in the Deep South*

Micheaux's film deviated from the Phagan-Frank case because Micheaux adhered to certain storytelling conventions and was perennially preoccupied with black middle-class aspirations and race relations. By contrast, the Warner Bros. film's alterations of the case derived in large part from southern-born journalist Ward Greene's 1936 novel *Death in the Deep South*.

Atlanta native Ward Greene is best known as the author of the short story "Dan, the Happy Dog"—on which Walt Disney based the successful and charming *Lady and the Tramp* (1955)—but he was also a syndicated news editor (at King Features) and a trustee of William Randolph Hearst's estate. At age twenty-one Greene became the assistant sports editor for the *Atlanta Journal*; he wrote the paper's ecstatic review of *Birth of a Nation* when that film premiered in Atlanta in December 1915.[12] He moved to the Northeast in 1921, where, while working at King Features, he published a series of novels about flawed southerners of various types—socialites, alcoholic reporters (like Brock), and KKK members—including *Cora Potts: A Pilgrim's Progress* (1929), *Ride the Nightmare* (1930), *Weep No More* (1932), and, after *Death in the Deep South*, *King Cobra* (1940). His few later novels were set in the North.

Just before *They Won't Forget* premiered, Greene recounted how he came to write *Death in the South*:

> I was a reporter on the *Atlanta Journal* at the time of the murder, the Frank trial and the lynching and I covered many phases of the case. The material for my book, therefore, came largely from my own personal observations. While I was writing the book I had access to the court record of the Frank trial, which was furnished to me by Frank's prosecutor, Judge Hugh M. Dorsey of Atlanta. I also consulted contemporary news accounts to refresh my recollection and such general books of criminology and law as the court record of the Sacco-Vanzetti case, the decisions of the late Justice Holmes and "Our Lawless Police" by Earnest Jerome Hopkins.[13]

The Phagan-Frank case clearly had a major impact on Greene. Even in 1948, twelve years after he had published *Death in the Deep South*, he chose "A Man Is Hanged"—Rogers Winters's August 1915 account of Frank's lynching in the *Atlanta Journal*—for his anthology *Star Reporters and Thirty-four of Their Stories*. Greene's introduction to Winters's piece notes that "no reporter working in Atlanta in those days will forget the jangle of his telephone toward dawn, the message to hurry to the office or the vigil we kept. We knew only that the mob, estimated by some at twenty and by others at seventy-five, had cut all wires in or out of Milledgeville, entered the prison at gunpoint, handcuffed the guards, seized Frank 'who uttered only a groan,' and vanished northward in eight automobiles."[14] Out of such vivid memories and considerable research Greene crafted *Death in the Deep South*.

Greene's novel earned extensive praise both in the Northeast and nationally. The *Books* magazine critic predicted that its "picture of prejudice, violence, stupidity and blood-lust will remain long in . . . memory. . . . [It] is a fascinating story, but it is also an indictment." Leigh White of the *New Republic* called it "a study of mob hysteria far more terrible than the most assiduous of murder mysteries." E. C. Beckwith of the *New York Times Book Review* ("starkly realistic throughout") and William Rose Benet in the *Saturday Review of Literature* ("a significant narrative concerning American justice") agreed.[15]

The novel received positive reviews even in Atlanta, although they were understandably less direct in their praise. The keynote of the *Constitution*'s review, written by Greene's former competitor Ralph T. Jones, was caution. Jones described Greene's novel as "an enthralling murder story. The kind of book you can't possibly put down unfinished after you have read the first few pages." Most of the review balanced such enthusiasm with caveats of various kinds. For example, Jones advised potential readers who might be put off by the novel's deviations from the case to keep in mind that it is a work of fiction. Furthermore, Jones warned readers that "it is not complimentary in many places to the character atmosphere of the South, but then it is a story largely about a mob and no mob ever ranked high in mentality." Entertainment critic Frank Daniel of the *Atlanta Journal* concurred with Jones, calling Greene "a shrewd student of southern character and of human nature in general." He also praised Greene's decision to update the story to the 1930s (to show, for example, the impact of radio news broadcasts) and agreed with Greene's decision to eliminate "some of the complicating factors, making his narrative one of justice confused by sectional prejudices and misunderstandings, without involving racial feelings" (that is, anti-

Semitism).[16] *Death in the Deep South* was thus a critical success even in publicity-sensitive Atlanta.

Greene's novel and *They Won't Forget* differ from the actual Phagan-Frank case in several important respects. To take the most important divergence, neither the novel nor the film overtly dramatizes the anti-Semitism that existed in the Phagan-Frank case. Neither even specifies the Hales' religious affiliation.[17] Casting played a part in the film's disregard of the issue as well. Leo Frank was a short man with unusually large eyes and full lips. Edward Norris, who portrayed him, was a cross between the elegant Robert Montgomery and the all-American James Stewart (like both, Norris was at that time under contract to MGM); and his low-key performance, though it has moments of hauteur, is hardly neurotic or alienating. Another crucial difference: *They Won't Forget*, following *Death in the Deep South*, offers no demagogue Tom Watson character to stir up antagonism against Hale on the basis of sectionalism or anti-Semitism. The closest the film comes to designating a Watson character is Brock, whose motive is career ambition, not political power.[18]

We can only speculate about why Oscar Micheaux did not make Brisbane Jewish in *Murder in Harlem*. In the case of Greene, the answer is clear. Writing in 1948, Greene argued that anti-Semitism was not a crucial factor in the case's earliest stages.

> Leo Frank was a Jew. It was a fact not emphasized when he was arrested nor soon afterward; there were five Jewish citizens on the grand jury that indicted him. It seems extremely doubtful that the South would have become inflamed against Frank, the balance of evidence being as equal as it was, had the issue remained simply that of white man versus black man. But it did not so remain.
>
> Frank was educated, cultured, of high moral and civic standing. . . . Conley was a "cornfield nigger" gone citybad; he had a jail history. The contrast raised banners for Frank. But eventually banners went up for Conley, too; every "underdog" gets his rooters.
>
> Leading Atlanta Jews, as things began to look dark for Frank, formed a Frank defense committee. They prepared a ringing statement which they took to an Atlanta newspaper. Its managing editor, himself a Jew, prophetically advised against publication. His advice was not taken. That was the wind. Two years later the whirlwind roared full force.

Greene argued that sectionalism and state pride created Georgia's anti-Frank sentiment:

The people of Georgia loved justice more than Tom Watson. But they did not love "outsiders" telling them how to run their state. They fumed between two fires. And so by May 10, 1915, the date on which Frank was sentenced for the fourth time to hang, the "case" had become a storm of racial, sectional and political crosswinds in which little Mary Phagan, dead in her holiday dress, mattered no more than an archduke's riddled tunic in the middle of World War One.[19]

While few would agree with Greene today, clearly he saw enough dramatic material in the Faulknerian setting of the Frank case without adding anti-Semitism to the mix. He likely wished to avoid the hornet's nest of controversy that might arise had he incorporated it. When Griffin in the film speaks of his admiration for the North, his speech transposes Dorsey's statements of admiration for Jews in his actual summation.

Film historians have attributed the absence of anti-Semitism in *They Won't Forget* to the squeamishness of Hollywood's studio heads (the Warner brothers, LeRoy, Kandel, and Rossen were all Jewish). And it is true that prior to World War II Hollywood studios and their Jewish executives were reluctant to depict Jews on-screen. There were a few exceptions, such as Warner Bros.'s own *Life of Emile Zola* (released in 1937 just prior to *They Won't Forget*), about the Alfred Dreyfus affair in France and widely understood to be a commentary on Nazi anti-Semitism. Film historian Ruth Vasey notes, however, that "the PCA [in the 1930s] had a policy of not approving stories that dealt with ethnic bigotry, on the basis that such treatments were 'provocative and inflammatory.'"[20] In the case of *They Won't Forget*, LeRoy and Kandel, who wrote the screenplay's first draft, simply followed Greene's lead in leaving out the anti-Semitic aspects of the Phagan-Frank case.

Aben Kandel's First Draft Script

The decision to make a film of Greene's novel was influenced less by its excellent reviews than by Greene's subject and cinematic writing style. Moreover, the novel appeared at a point when Hollywood seemed to be searching for new stories of the current South rather than moonlight and magnolia romances, which had culminated in 1939 with David O. Selznick's *Gone with the Wind* (a project Mervyn LeRoy later recalled that he refused to option).[21] *They Won't Forget* instead would show how much the southern past lived on in the southern present.

Warner Bros. studio executive Jack L. Warner optioned the book shortly after it was published and in early December purchased the film rights expressly for LeRoy for five thousand dollars. Indeed, the similarities between LeRoy's earlier triumph *Fugitive* and Greene's novel are striking. Both films feature a northern man who is the victim of circumstance and southern prejudice; likewise, the authorities are corrupt, other institutions are easily hijacked, and the individual loner suffers for it. True to many social problem films, neither story ends happily. LeRoy later claimed that he made *They Won't Forget* "because it was a good story. Any sociopolitical message it may have had was purely a by-product of its story." Yet in one publicity piece in 1937, LeRoy hoped *They Won't Forget* would "aid in curbing two of our greatest sociological problems—race hatred and lynch law."[22]

LeRoy had his own production unit at Warner Bros. at this time, giving him greater creative authority and autonomy than he had enjoyed as a contract director.[23] LeRoy exercised that creative muscle in hiring Aben Kandel to write the script. Kandel was not an obvious choice, given that he had not worked on message movies before. A Romanian-born World War I veteran, New York University law school graduate, published novelist, and protégé of singer-actor Al Jolson, Kandel by the early 1930s was a fledgling New York playwright. His hit comedy *Hot Money*—about a swindler soliciting investments in a fake company—was adapted into several films. (In 1940 Kandel would adapt his own 1936 boxing novel, *City for Conquest*, at Warner Bros.) In fact, LeRoy probably found Kandel suitable for adapting Greene's novel because of his facility with ruthless, amoral characters—such as Griffin and Brock.

By the time he began work on *They Won't Forget*, LeRoy was a highly successful veteran film director with ten years of experience. In addition to *Fugitive* he had directed *Little Caesar* (1931), a major early-sound-era gangster film whose success helped to jump-start the genre and cemented Edward G. Robinson's perennial identification with it. Another LeRoy film, *Five Star Final* (1931), also starring Robinson, dramatized an unscrupulous newspaper publisher and his star editor, who needlessly destroy a woman's family purely for the sake of increased circulation—a preview of Bill Brock's activities in *They Won't Forget*. Although LeRoy had also directed successful comedies (*Tugboat Annie*, 1933), musicals (*Golddiggers of 1933*), and prestigious adaptations (*Anthony Adverse*,

Director-producer
Mervyn LeRoy, a boy
wonder in the 1930s.
(Courtesy of the
Academy of Motion
Picture Arts and
Sciences.)

1936), *They Won't Forget* was understood to be a return to the message movie genre he had crystallized under Darryl F. Zanuck's supervision in 1932. The later film certainly featured the hallmarks of his earlier work in the genre: fast pacing, imaginative staging, and an evocative re-creation of Depression despair.

Kandel's first temporary script, completed in late January 1937, showed that he aimed (with LeRoy's input) to preserve Greene's stark presentation of the Phagan-Frank case's many unsavory aspects. Yet, in terms of narrative incident and characterization, the film could hardly be as explicit as the novel. For example, the draft did not use the word *nigger*, constantly uttered by nearly all the characters in the novel. Andy Griffin's line in the novel, "Bosh! Any fool can ride to glory on helpless niggers and crooked cops. I don't play ball that way" became "Bosh! Any fool can ride to glory on a helpless Negro janitor. I'm out for bigger game."[24] Kandel nevertheless retained enough of Greene's indictment of the southern setting, and especially Hugh Dorsey and the Atlanta police force, to extend well beyond what Joseph Breen at the PCA considered the boundaries of acceptable Hollywood entertainment.

Writing to reassure studio lawyers that none of the people portrayed in the film was likely to sue Warner Bros. for libel (*I Am a Fugitive from a Chain Gang* and *Black Legion* [1936] had generated several lawsuits), Greene provided a concise assessment of his view of the case:

> I personally covered the Frank case, [*sic*] while I was writing the book I read every word of testimony in a transcript . . . and I checked newspaper accounts of the case to refresh my memory. This was not only to give me a pick of actual facts for the book but to guide me in guarding against libel.
>
> Now, of the characters concerned in the Frank case, Judge Roan is dead, Mary Phagan is dead, Hugh Dorsey read the book and was not at all offended by it. . . . There is nothing in the picture libelous of Mary Phagan, who is revealed in the actual evidence as a worse little girl than Mary Clay. Her family is not going to sue on that account. She had, so far as I know, NO brothers, so you're safe on the score that her brothers are portrayed as actual lynchers. (The actual lynchers of Leo Frank, according to public knowledge in Georgia, were citizens of Marietta, led by the son of a U.S. "statesman"). I can't for the life of me see anything libelous of Hugh Dorsey in the picture. Griffin isn't crooked, he's a politician and God knows Hugh Dorsey DID ride to glory on the Frank case and WAS elected Governor. Jack Slaton, accused of taking Jewish gold, should have no quarrel with conscientious Governor Mountford. As for the cops and detectives, there was never a bigger crook than the detectives in the Frank trial and all the evidence of planted bloody shirts on Newt Lee, the framed testimony that Frank was a pervert, etc. etc. proves it. And so it goes.

Greene was misinformed on one point: Mary Phagan had three brothers, one of whom was serving in the U.S. Navy at the time of her death, and a sister. None of them was known to have been part of the lynching party.[25] But Greene was right: no lawsuit followed the film's premiere. And as Greene commented in this same letter, "Warners shouldn't have made it in the first place if they didn't expect to be daring."

Greene would have loved Kandel's first script draft because it retained the novelist's uncompromising interpretation of the case—it delineated a small southern city in which little happens and lynching is routine. An early scene has the restless reporter Brock walking through town on the night of Confederate Memorial Day, passing a sidewalk group of bored, drunken men with time on their hands. Kandel's stage directions specified giving viewers "the impression which the town radiates—the feeling that there is nothing to do here—that all these people are yearning for something that will excite and appease them."[26] One of them comments, "It's a lovely night for a necktie party," and is answered by "roars" of laughter. Kandel retained other details, such as numerous scenes of the police, the reporters, and Redwine drinking alcohol.

In fact, Kandel's depiction of the police followed directly from Greene's descriptions of their conduct. The "n" word was removed, but the detectives' brutality was not. In the novel, the police handcuff Redwine, who is naked, bloody, and sweaty; he is kicked in the groin and loses consciousness. Greene was inspired by the Atlanta police's reputation for brutality in general and their treatment of Newt Lee in particular. Leonard Dinnerstein reports that "they allegedly tortured him mercilessly. For three days they kept the night watchman manacled to a chair and put him 'through a searching, grilling third degree' that left him weeping and nerveless." Jim Conley likewise was abused while the detectives sought to extract a usable affidavit from him. Accordingly, in Kandel's script, the police work Tump over with a rubber hose, pails of water, and the like for four hours. Griffin callously instructs them to "bring him to and keep him alive. I may need him." The officers behave no better away from the jail. One detective, Laneart (named after Detective Lanford of the Atlanta police), punches his wife in the mouth and steps on her hand when she berates him for his clumsy perjury in support of Griffin's case during the trial. Here again, Kandel drew directly on scenes from Greene's novel.[27]

Moreover, Kandel's first draft script has Griffin in charge of all phases of the police actions to frame Robert Hale. At Griffin's direction, they plant evidence (a bloody shirt) against Redwine that will compel him to commit perjury—something the Atlanta police tried unsuccessfully with Newt Lee. Griffin even chooses the lawyer to coach Redwine as he rehearses his perjury. At another of Griffin's suggestions—"there are occasions when a little persuasion helps a man make up his own mind"—the police in Kandel's script (as in Greene's novel) intimidate the barber who could provide a crucial alibi for Hale into leaving town.[28]

Kandel departed most dramatically from *Death in the Deep South*'s final pages by choosing to depict Frank's lynching. Greene's novel describes in just over one page how the train taking Hale to the state prison is stopped, his police escorts are surprised by armed masked men, and Hale is told to "get up." Greene then shifts the point of view to Brock for the rest of the novel, and Hale is already dead and hanging from the tree when Brock arrives on the scene. Brock watches while a local judge and his two black assistants cut down Hale's body to return it to Atlanta "for a decent burial" and a member of the crowd tries to degrade the corpse further. As the body is being driven back to Flodden in a wagon, Brock jumps on and wonders if Hale really did murder Mary Clay—the final dialogue line in the novel.[29] Kandel by contrast elected to show the mechanics of Hale's abduction from the train and placed Sybil in the scene to fight off Hale's killers. The masked men brutally hit her twice, and Robert is kicked in the groin when he tries to resist. Kandel's version also visualized the entire "lynching sequence" as it appears in the final film. This constitutes the most powerful addition Kandel created in the course of adapting Greene's novel—and the most potent element of the film's antilynching protest.

Rather than end with Brock accompanying Hale's corpse, however, the first draft script's epilogue poured on the ironies and the outrage over Hale's lynching: it described Sybil crusading ("like Joan of Arc") to ensure that the judicial system works properly in future cases. Superimposed over these shots were to be vignettes of Griffin being elected senator, defeating the governor who pardoned Hale; Detective Laneart being promoted to chief of police; and a newspaper publisher planning to raise advertising rates because the case has increased his circulation by thirty thousand readers. (Hearst's *Atlanta Georgian* and Watson's *Jeffersonian* tripled their circulation in August 1913 and in 1915, respectively.)[30] Such details were entirely consistent with Greene's sense of the affair ("Dorsey DID ride to glory on the Frank case") and were also in accord with the historical facts of the case as they were known at the time. The bad guys won.

Joseph Breen and Script Revisions

Ward Greene's novel set the template for the narrative of *They Won't Forget*, but Joseph Breen and the PCA dramatically altered it.[31] Critics of the Breen office often accused the PCA of keeping reality out of American movies. Breen's response to Kandel's first script draft may be the starkest illustration of this policy in Hollywood history. Breen's assessment was unambiguous: the film could not be made at all because the script violated so many provisions of the Code. Breen's January 30, 1937, letter to production head Jack L. Warner described both the large-scale issues and the detailed problems he saw with Kandel's script:

Production Code Administration head Joseph Breen reviews a document with his associate and successor, Geoffrey Shurlock. (Courtesy of the Academy of Motion Picture Arts and Sciences.)

The story, as we read it, is basically the story of stark perversion of justice. It is the story of the condemnation, under the law, of an innocent man, charged with murder, the conviction being brought about by a corrupt and dishonest prosecuting attorney, in collusion with a corrupt and dishonest police department and a corrupt and dishonest lawyer (Foster [the attorney whom Griffin, in this draft as in Greene's novel, unofficially assigns to coach Tump into his perjury]). In addition, the script is marked by numerous scenes of unnecessary drinking and, at least, one scene of drunkenness, perjured witnesses, a corrupt and dishonest jury, brutalizing by the police, excessive brutality, and a suggestion of mob violence, which leads to lynching.

Such wrongdoing might have been acceptable to Breen if the guilty parties were punished. But "against all this," he wrote, "there is nothing in the picture to suggest anything like compensating moral values. While it may be argued that this sinister and inhuman activity is shown to be wrong, it is, nevertheless, true that no one is punished. On the contrary: the dishonest district attorney succeeds in having himself elected to the United States Senate, while the honest and conscientious governor is the defeated candidate; the dishonest police detective is elevated to a captaincy; and the perjuring witnesses and dishonest jurymen are permitted to go off scot free."[32] In order for the script to receive approval, it would "be necessary to show that the dishonest district attorney, the dishonest policeman, the crooked lawyer for Trump [sic], the dishonest jurymen, and the perjured witnesses are all punished by the *processes of law*. The excessive and unnecessary drinking and drunkenness must be *entirely deleted* . . . and the brutalizing by the police must be deleted." Breen proceeded to itemize several pages of scenes and dialogue lines that would have to be cut.

Though the tone of Breen's letter was discouraging, Hollywood pros like LeRoy knew that Breen would work with them to address such objections. LeRoy had already brought a new writer into the project for a fresh perspective. Robert Rossen is now best known for the films he wrote and directed in the 1940s and later, such as *All the King's Men* (which earned Best Picture and Best Director awards in 1949) and *The Hustler* (1961). He had come to Warner Bros. under contract to LeRoy in 1936 from the New York theater scene, where among his many activities he had directed *The Tree*, a play about lynching. *Death in the Deep South* was only his second script project for the studio (earlier that year he had worked on the hard-hitting Bette Davis vehicle *Marked Woman*). He was a writer of decidedly leftist sympathies who joined the Communist Party in the spring of 1937, during or shortly after his work on *They Won't Forget*. The American Communist Party at the time was part of the American Popular Front, a broad-based alliance of liberals and leftists who were antifascist, pro–New Deal, and active in civil rights matters such as the defense of the Scottsboro Nine. This affiliation informed Rossen's creative work: Griffin's use of the phrase "my aristocratic friends" in his scene with the town leaders was Rossen's addition, as were Shattuck Clay's heartfelt statement of family sadness at Mary Clay's murder and the identification of the Clay brothers as the leaders of the lynch mob. Rossen's revisions were so extensive, in fact, that his name was listed first on the screenplay. The LeRoy film was apparently his favorite among all the scripts he wrote for Warner Bros.[33]

Rossen joined LeRoy in a meeting with Breen just a few days after Breen had rejected Kandel's draft script. The three men agreed that LeRoy

Robert Rossen (right) posing with actor Mel Ferrer in a publicity still for Rossen's *The Brave Bulls* (1951). Rossen's revisions to the script for *They Won't Forget* earned him first name credit for the screenplay. (Courtesy of the Academy of Motion Picture Arts and Sciences.)

and his team would address the detailed list of problems Breen had given them and hit on a new strategy that Breen described as a "basic" change in the story. "Instead of indicating that there has been a serious perversion of justice, by way of collusion of the district attorney, Foster [Tump's lawyer], and the jurymen, which results in the conviction for murder of an innocent man," Breen decided, "the new version will remove this entirely. A new story is to be written, the basic point of which will be that the man will be convicted, honestly, on circumstantial evidence. This is important."[34]

In response to Breen's directives, LeRoy, Kandel (who continued working on drafts through February), and Rossen made several significant changes that ultimately made the project acceptable to Breen. Five of the changes stand out particularly in the finished film. The filmmakers (1) changed their portrayal of police corruption and brutality so that it is evoked but not directly depicted; (2) modified Griffin's conduct of the case so that he is not directing the police to tamper with evidence or controlling Redwine's testimony; (3) changed the film's rendering of possible suspects; (4) altered the "suggestion of mob violence" when Hale is taken from the police; and (5) devised "punishment" for the villains that Sybil Hale delivers in the film's final scene, evoking the power of memory in the process. Each of these changes illustrates Hollywood's ability to revamp horrifying episodes in history into acceptable entertainment.

The Flodden Police and Andy Griffin

Script revisions cleaned up considerably the depiction of the police. The scene of Detective Laneart physically beating his wife was gone, as were the bloody shirts planted to frame Redwine. More significant, Redwine's police interrogation scene underwent a major change. Rather than beating him, the detectives in the film simply bark at Tump ("Come clean, Tump!" "You did it." "You'll burn for it"). But the script retained Kandel's instructions for a quickly cut series of shots from the discovery of Mary Clay's body in the elevator shaft to Tump's interrogation in the jail, linked by Tump's repeated declarations, "Ah didn't do it." The last two of these shots are particularly powerful: a head-on shot in which Tump is surrounded by the police "like figures in Rembrandt's 'The Anatomy Lesson,'" and a vertiginous high-angle shot of Tump surrounded by the police in a cell, echoing the earlier, extremely dark shot in which Redwine and the police looked down on Mary Clay's body at the bottom of the elevator shaft.[35] Detective Laneart tells Griffin they will have a confession from Tump within an hour. Griffin replies, "There'll be no rough stuff." Laneart slowly responds, "You do things your way . . . we'll do 'em ours."[36] We may not see violence in the cell with Redwine, but the shots of Tump's grilling and that exchange establish the routine nature of police brutality in the town. Rosemond's performance as Redwine—his trembling line delivery, nearly paralyzed mouth, and shaking hands—embodies absolute terror. Like Arthur Vance and Lem Hawkins in the presence of Myrtle Stanfield's dead body, Redwine understands his desperate situation. The word *lynch* never appears in the script, but it need not be uttered.

The police's treatment of Timberlake—the barber who can provide Hale with a crucial alibi about the blood on his jacket—was likewise changed. The police do not frighten the barber into leaving town before the trial

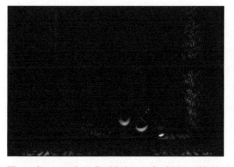

The police use their flashlights to find Mary Clay's body in the elevator shaft.

A reverse-angle shot reveals Tump Redwine kneeling beside the police and intoning, "Ah didn't do it."

There is a quick cut to Redwine continuing to protest his innocence as the police interrogate him, arranged around him, in Kandel's stage directions, "like figures in Rembrandt's 'The Anatomy Lesson.'"

As the sequence continues, the film quickly cuts to a high-angle shot of Redwine surrounded by the police that echoes the previous shot of Mary Clay's body in the elevator shaft. This shot was eliminated for screenings in Maryland.

as they did in the first script draft; instead, the barber simply refuses to cooperate with the northern detective, Pindar.[37] We are left to surmise that the barber, like the rest of Flodden, resents a Northern "snoop" trying to help Hale.

Griffin in the film is less a corrupt individual who abuses his power to orchestrate the campaign against Hale than an opportunist with political ambitions. When Laneart tells Griffin ominously, "You do things your way . . . we'll do 'em ours," Griffin responds, "Oh, no you won't. Not this time. This isn't a petty larceny case that nobody cares about. It's important. A girl's been murdered. A young girl. There's a lot of people in this town that have daughters that age. They want a conviction. I'm going to give them one and when I do it's going to be the guilty party, not someone you can get a confession out of because they're scared out of their wits and you're too lazy to go out and dig up every possible fact in the case."[38] Griffin here clearly lays out the situation in which Dorsey and the Atlanta police force found themselves when Mary Phagan was murdered.

Griffin also signals his awareness of the stakes of the case for his career and his determination to convict the guilty party. He tells his assistant, Drake, while looking out his office window at the crowds outside the business school, "They will think a lot of the man who gets that conviction." He claims to be interested only in justice when he tells Brock, "Politics or no politics, I'll prosecute no one in this case until I'm positively sure!" The cynical Brock retorts: "Sure of what—his guilt or a conviction?" We later see the answer when Griffin decides to arraign Hale after he hears the talk of the town in the local watering hole. Thus the revisions Rossen and Kandel effected in the script create another kind of complexity that is rare in Hollywood social problem films—*They Won't Forget* pits what Griffin says against what he does. His courtroom theatrics and his injection of sectionalism at every turn help him secure Hale's conviction through underhanded means. Yet having Griffin say the right thing was apparently enough to satisfy Joseph Breen and the PCA that Hale was "convicted, honestly, upon circumstantial evidence."

One other revision the filmmakers made to the script is crucial: the scene in which Brock and Griffin make a "deal" whereby Brock will give Griffin his tip that "Mr. X" (the suspect) is Hale only if Griffin will give Brock exclusive information ("first crack") about the progress of the case. Their partnership alludes to the *Atlanta Constitution*'s cozy relationship with Atlanta police. The *Constitution* received many exclusive scoops on the progress of the investigation and in exchange often endorsed the police and Hugh Dorsey's case against Frank, printing damaging rumors and unsubstantiated discoveries of evidence that were either too subtly retracted to be effective or not corrected at all. Brock is the first reporter on the murder site only because he fell asleep in the backseat of a squad car—just as Britt Craig, the opportunistic reporter for the *Atlanta Constitution*, had done. Brock's opportunism also echoes Craig's. Steve Oney describes Craig as a writer of "marred prose" with "spotty" accuracy but plenty of "luck and pluck. . . . Whether it was the gee-whiz grin he flashed from beneath his snap-brim cap or his willingness, as a police matron put

Brock falls asleep in the back of the police car and is fortuitously taken to the murder scene—just as it happened for *Atlanta Constitution* reporter Britt Craig. Brock's chief rival, Price, is laughing in the background.

At Brock's insistence, Griffin shakes on their deal: Brock will give him a tip on a suspect; if it is correct, Griffin will give Brock exclusive information on the progress of the investigation.

it, to be 'a bad boy to get news he has no business to have,' Craig often came up with stories his rivals couldn't crack." In *They Won't Forget*, Brock's deal with Griffin shows us why he did. By contrast, Greene's novel mentions only that Griffin and Brock drive off alone to talk—we are never told what they talk about.[39]

These February revisions not only build up the circumstantial evidence against Hale but also strongly imply that the local populace actively embraced Griffin's aims. The barber Timberlake refuses to be honest with Pindar, and when Timberlake takes the stand and Griffin asks him the crucial question of whether or not he cut Hale during a shave, Timberlake hesitates before answering that he did not. The film's audience sees a series of cuts to close-ups of Robert and Sybil; then Timberlake looks to the jury box, where a juror moves a hand first to his ear and then to the side as the film cuts to a shot of Mary Clay's brothers waiting for his answer. The significance of the juror's motion is unclear because the shot is taken from behind him. He is trying to hear Timberlake, but in this setting he could also be trying to signal to the barber that he had better give the "right" answer. The intimidating stares of the Clay brothers are not so ambiguous. The jury's subsequent coercion of the one holdout makes it clear that they are aligned with the police, the press, Griffin, and Mary Clay's brothers and friends to ensure Hale's conviction and eventual execution. The script changes were designed to make the finished film more acceptable as a depiction of justice gone wrong

Right after Griffin asks the barber Timberlake the crucial question of whether he cut Hale while shaving him, a juror in the foreground lifts his hand to his ear—to hear better, to intimidate Timberlake, or perhaps both.

Timberlake looks offscreen right as he hesitates to give his answer.

The next shot shows what Timberlake sees: the Clay brothers listening intently as they wait for him to give the "correct" answer.

by coincidence, but in fact they broaden the web of collusion, creating a picture far more disturbing than if one person, Griffin, had coordinated them all.

Revising the Other Suspects—Redwine, Buxton, Hale

Griffin and the police were not the only characters significantly modified as Rossen and Kandel undertook script revisions in accordance with Breen's directives: Redwine became a more pathetic figure, frightened of a potential lynching and repeatedly pleading (with Clinton Rosemond's considerable sincerity), "'Fore God, I swear I didn't do it." In Greene's novel, Redwine is a comic "coon" figure more like Lem Hawkins in *Murder in*

Harlem, shuffling to strains of "Dixie" on Confederate Memorial Day and refusing to respond immediately to the elevator buzzer because he is too involved in his pornographic magazine. All these details—plus Redwine's long list of previous arrests—suggest that he is Mary Clay's killer.[40] In the film, although he is first seen hiding his *Parisian Nights* magazine—presumably a publication like the one George Epps ogled in *Murder in Harlem*—Redwine has no other obvious negative qualities.

Tump's testimony also changed. In the actual case, Conley was coached by Atlanta police, by Dorsey and his associates, and by his personal attorney, William Smith, as he spun elaborately specific accounts of his whereabouts on the day of Mary Phagan's murder. During script revisions for *They Won't Forget*, Redwine's perjury got shorter with each draft and his character became more earnest, more closely resembling the pathetic if slightly suspicious character Clinton Rosemond portrays. In the finished film, Professor Buxton and Colonel Foster visit Tump on the occasion of Detective Pindar's arrival in town. It is Buxton, not Griffin, who has hired Colonel Foster to represent Redwine—to protect the name of the business college, he claims, although Buxton's dislike of Hale is apparent from their first encounter early in the film.

Redwine's fear makes him susceptible to perjury. He initially asserts his basic honesty when Buxton and Colonel Foster visit him in jail: "I'll tell [Pindar] the same thing I say to Mr. Griffin." But Foster and Buxton play on sectionalism across the color line to gain Redwine's cooperation, telling him that the "fellers from up North" are "tricky" and you "got to be careful what you say"—Tump might be tricked into incriminating himself and getting the electric chair. Foster then hints at what else might befall him—lynching. "Maybe if Hale goes free . . . that crowd won't wait for no trial . . . they'll come and get you . . . no matter how far you run or where you hide . . . and then it'll be worse." When Redwine admits he is afraid, Foster reassures him, "Now you don't have to be scared, Tump . . . not if you listen to me, you don't." The scene ends as Foster continues to advise him.[41]

But to satisfy Joseph Breen's demand that perjurers be punished, the filmmakers chose to have Redwine recant his perjury entirely. In response to Gleason's cross-examination questions, which imply that Tump is guilty of Clay's murder and make it clear that Tump's testimony could result in Hale's death, Tump recoils. "No—No—Ah cain't—Ah won't—Ah don' care what they do to me—Ah won't—what Ah said befo'—Ah wuz all mixed up—that don' count—Ah ain't gonna send no man to die 'count of

Professor Buxton brings Colonel Foster to represent Redwine both to protect Redwine and to ensure Hale's conviction. The two white men terrify Redwine into agreeing to perjury so that he will not be convicted or lynched for Mary Clay's murder.

A terrified Redwine can barely give his testimony; Griffin has to complete it for him.

me. Ah don't know what went on in that buildin'—Ah was asleep—Ah didn't see nobody—Ah didn't hear nothin' [sobbing now]. All Ah know is that Ah didn't do it—Ah didn't do it—Ah didn't do it!"[42]

In recanting his perjury, Redwine gains greater moral stature in the film because he knows the consequences of refusing to ensure Hale's conviction. Yet his recantation allows *They Won't Forget* to have it both ways: there is no perjury to be punished, per Joseph Breen, and yet—as Brock later comments—no one in the courtroom or on the jury believes Tump's disavowal of what he claimed moments before.

These changes to Tump's character were also part of the filmmakers' strategy to make the identity of Mary Clay's killer a mystery. Kandel's first draft script exonerated all the suspects by showing a "Mr. X" leaving the school building before the discovery of Mary Clay's body; he is never seen again.[43] The revised script and finished film dispense with the Mr. X scene, hinting instead that any of the three main suspects might be guilty. The film thereby presents a compelling test of American (and not just southern) justice: On the one hand, the crime must be punished; on the other, reasonable doubt as to who is actually guilty prevails.

For example, when Mary comes up the college stairs for her compact because she feels "naked" without her lipstick, Buxton was supposed to look after her as she went through the door, then turn to the camera with a look of "unmistakable lust on his face and cunning in his eyes."[44] LeRoy

Professor Buxton, one of the initial suspects, greets Mary Clay as she enters the college.

Per the script's stage directions, Professor Buxton's gestures and expressions suggest he lusts after Mary Clay.

Buxton's exit from the shot shows that he cannot be guilty.

backed off slightly from these stage directions when he shot the scene: Buxton does bend leftward to watch Mary go through the door and then turns toward the camera; his eyes are darting about and he is rubbing his hands. More important, though, he exits the frame once she goes inside rather than remaining on the steps or following her. He cannot be guilty so far as we know.

Likewise, in the next scene, Redwine clearly gets back into the elevator to return to the basement when he hears footsteps (presumably Mary's) on the stairs. Later, when Mary's boyfriend, Joe Turner, arrives at the school's front steps, Redwine quickly comes out of the building, followed by Hale. After Redwine and Hale dissuade Joe from entering the school and Hale leaves for the day, Redwine looks after Joe with a long, almost fierce look. This lingering glance suggests that Redwine may be hiding something or that he—understandably—does not like the persistent and rude Joe.[45] Redwine then goes back inside the building.

Redwine informs Joe Turner that no girls are inside the school building as Hale emerges from the college's front door.

Redwine has given Hale a friendly goodbye but scowls in Turner's direction. Is it because he does not like Turner or because he has something to hide?

If the filmmakers planted hints that Buxton and Redwine could be guilty, they also gave Hale some subtly suspicious behavior as well. The film's Hale is altogether more likable than Greene's. Questions arise, however, when Hale abruptly responds to Sybil's questions about how he spent the afternoon of Confederate Memorial Day, how he got the bloodstain on his jacket, and why he smells of perfume (he claims both are from the barber). In a scene after the murder, he abruptly cuts off Sybil's questions about Mary Clay. To add to our doubts, when Brock tries to interview Hale outside the business college and mentions Mary Clay, the normally slow-moving Hale quickly excuses himself as if he has something to hide; in Kandel's initial script, he had a legitimate excuse—a class to teach in two minutes.[46]

These touches fleetingly suggest that Hale might be Mary's killer and why he could become a suspect, but the greater part of the film strongly implies his innocence. Although the forces arrayed against him—sectionalism and newspaper sensationalism—are broad and impersonal, they are activated by character types: the ambitious politician (Griffin) and the heartless reporter (Brock). Perhaps the film's weakest moment, because it is so contrived, ties Hale's fate to bad luck. Robert kisses Sybil as he leaves to send the telegram accepting a teaching job in Chicago; she observes that the last time he kissed her on the forehead that way he lost his job. Their luck runs true. Robert is immediately accosted in the hallway by two police officers. As they ponder his motives in leaving town so soon (after illegally grabbing the telegram draft out of his hand), the delivery boy arrives in the hallway with a cleaned suit and takes the trouble to

Heartless reporters photograph Sybil rather than catching her when she faints at the news of her husband's arrest.

While Sybil recovers in her living room, Brock and his rival Price rummage through the Hales' bedroom.

Dolly Holly encourages Sybil Hale to confide in her about her marriage while the male reporters look on; Sybil unsuspectingly reveals that her husband feels uncomfortable in the South.

Holly's front-page account of her interview with Sybil Hale turns local sentiment decisively against Hale.

inform Robert that the cleaner could not remove the blood stain on it. Greene's novel has neither the "incriminating" telegram nor the presence of the police when Hale receives the bloodstained jacket; they are Kandel's cinematic shorthand for showing the mounting circumstantial evidence against Hale. Present-day audiences might find such a coincidence laughable, but 1930s audiences would have recognized the contrivance as a representational convention often deployed in social problem films. In any case, *They Won't Forget* builds its story forcefully and plausibly from this point onward.

True to the conventions of the genre, *They Won't Forget* depicts Robert and Sybil as loners in Flodden. While Greene's novel gives them some acquaintances in town and money to seek northern support for Robert's defense, in the revised script and the film they have no friends and no money. All this adds to the Hales' victimization by Griffin, by the townspeople, and particularly by the newspapers.

Indeed, *They Won't Forget* powerfully portrays the newspapers' role in ruining the Hales' lives. Brock may have the upper hand thanks to his deal with Griffin, but his rivals are equally despicable. Their invasion of Sybil's apartment shows unscrupulous reporters at their worst, betraying the naïve and vulnerable Sybil's trust.[47] Significantly, this aspect of the novel and Kandel's first draft script remained intact after Breen's review—a testament to the frequent appearance of jaded reporters in 1930s films, especially after Ben Hecht's and Charlie McArthur's hit play and film *The Front Page* (1931) and LeRoy's *Five Star Final*, to how little the industry feared offending journalists, or both.

The "Suggestion of Mob Violence"

LeRoy and the screenwriters were determined to tell Hale's story to its bitter conclusion, but lynching could not be shown explicitly in Hollywood movies of the 1930s under the Production Code's General Principles and its section on "Crimes against the Law," which forbade the explicit portrayal of "brutal killings" and "revenge in modern times." Another section, entitled "Repellent Subjects," specified that these subjects were to be "treated within the careful limits of good taste." The first three actions the Code characterized as "repellent" were "actual hangings or electrocutions as legal punishments for crime," third-degree interrogations, and "brutality and possible gruesomeness."[48] It was partly on these grounds that Breen had objected to, for example, the police brutality in Kandel's first script draft.

Breen's concern about the climactic scripted scenes of mob violence in *They Won't Forget* likely owed much to the public outcry over Fritz Lang's film *Fury* the previous year. Inspired by the actual lynching of two white men outside San Jose, California, earlier in the 1930s, *Fury* depicts the plight of Joe Wilson (Spencer Tracy), an innocent man en route to marry his fiancée, Katherine (Sylvia Sidney), when he is arrested on highly circumstantial evidence for a kidnapping in a small town west of Chicago.[49] The kidnapped victim is a young girl, and the townspeople want quick justice. Despite the sheriff's best efforts, the men in town, shown drinking and arguing in a bar, ultimately decide to "have some fun." Kandel had envisioned just this sort of "bored, restless" townspeople who want a "necktie party" for Flodden. In *Fury*, they are motivated not by sectionalism or prejudice, or even personal dislike of Joe Wilson, but by base human nature willing to act against a helpless stranger.

In Lang's film, the governor refuses to intervene to save Joe, and the mob ultimately sets the jail on fire so that he will burn alive, another form of lynching. The film details the glee of the lynch mob with chilling directness, creating, to use Tom Gunning's word, a "carnival" atmosphere as the mob approaches the jail, taunts the authorities, and sets the jail on fire when they cannot get to Wilson's cell. The carnival spirit—something documented in real lynchings—informs both segments of the mob violence sequence in *Fury*. The first half shows the mob happily forming and committing its violence, and a second, quiet half (marked by the belated arrival of Joe's fiancée on the scene) has them sitting back and enjoying the results of their efforts (in a way that Gunning identifies as "post-orgasmic"; one ringleader is smoking a cigarette and beaming in satisfaction). Individual, low-angle medium shots, and close-ups show townspeople smiling at the blaze, a woman holding up her toddler to watch (as Amy Wood notes, an image inspired by a newspaper photo from the San Jose lynching), a boy eating a hot dog as he watches the blaze with rapt attention—and a newsreel cameraman gleefully recording it all.[50]

Fury shows in explicit detail the dynamics of a lynch mob in action. Even though Joe Wilson is white—the PCA would not permit the filmmakers to show black lynching victims—the film features several minor black characters to remind the audience of this reality. The lynchers refuse to name names when the town is brought to trial—but newsreel cameras have captured their faces. More important, Wilson survived their attempt to kill him. While some, including Lang, criticized the film-ending kiss that signifies Joe's eschewal of vengeance against his would-be murderers, film critics praised it for the powerful treatment of its subject.[51]

Six months after *Fury*'s release, Breen was alarmed when he read the scene in Kandel's first draft script in which Hale is abducted and lynched. Although it would have lasted only a fraction of the length of Lang's extended sequence in *Fury*, Breen had plenty to say about what Kandel and LeRoy had in mind: "The business of the masked men, with guns, holding up the detective and taking Hale off, presumably to hang him, will have to

A scene from *Fury* (1936) in which the lynchers, unable to reach Wilson, burn down the jail to kill him.

A "postcoital" moment in *Fury* as one of the mob's ringleaders smokes a cigarette while enjoying the sight of the burning jail.

be entirely eliminated. So, too, will all business of brutality, such as the action of one of the men (page 168) striking Sybil in the mouth and kicking Hale in the groin. Please note that no censor board, anywhere, will allow any such scene as that set forth, beginning on page 167, showing masked men taking a prisoner from an officer of the law."[52] Breen received considerable support on this point: in early April 1937, as LeRoy neared the end of principal photography on *They Won't Forget*, New York's chief censor, Irwin Esmond, complained to Warner Bros. regarding the studio's recent film *Mountain Justice*, in which a backwoods girl is almost lynched after the accidental death of her father. The film features an extended sequence in which hooded town residents forcibly remove the heroine from the jail and march her through the town's streets to her lynching before friends rescue her. Esmond warned of taking "drastic action" if the current trend in films continued "to get closer and closer to the borderline of inhumanity and disregard for law."[53]

Accordingly, Kandel's and Rossen's script revisions for *They Won't Forget* reenvisioned the scene of Robert's abduction. In the final version, his killers are no longer masked, and Sybil is not on the train. Darkness covers the scuffle between the lynch mob and the guards on the train. On the other hand, the filmmakers added more subtle suggestions of widespread collusion in Hale's murder. Unlike the friendlier guards in Kandel's early script, who are genuinely surprised when the train suddenly halts, the detectives accompanying Hale in the film are quietly shown to be completely unsympathetic—if they are not already in on the plan to abduct him. We

A smiling townswoman holds up her baby to get a better view of the burning jail in *Fury*, an image inspired by a photo from an actual lynching.

In *They Won't Forget*, after the governor's pardon, Hale is escorted to the state prison by unsympathetic guards.

cannot be sure which is the case because it is dark in the train car when they "lose" custody of Hale.

Most striking of all, the scene was scripted during revisions and staged so that Hale is confronted with his killers when he slides open the train car door to escape. The opening of the train door, shot from behind, is like a curtain opening on a proscenium. It reveals Shattuck Clay (Trevor Bardette) standing at the front of the mob with his brothers and Joe Turner. "Come on, Hale," an enraged Shattuck tells him through gritted teeth. "We've been waiting for you for a long time." An unidentified hand from inside the train car pushes Hale out into the crowd—but in the previous shot, we saw one of the escort guards standing directly behind Hale. He must have been the one to push Hale into the mob. Hale is carried away, hysterically pleading for mercy and restating his innocence. This mob, it should be noted, is *not* the "cold-blooded" group Greene described in his recollection of the event in *Star Reporters and Thirty-four of Their Stories.*[54]

Kandel's indirect portrayal of the act of lynching itself, perhaps inspired by the widely distributed British documentary *Night Mail* (1936), is ingenious. Within the setting of an abandoned train station and in "almost black night," Kandel's script specifies:

> We can see two receding objects. To one side of the CAMERA we see Hale disappearing—dragged by a mob of about fifty men. To the other, the train is proceeding on the tracks out of view. CAMERA PULLS BACK TO INCLUDE A

Hale tries to escape his attackers by opening the train door, only to find his lynchers awaiting him, with Mary Clay's brothers and boyfriend at their head.

Hale is carried away as another train approaches the camera.

Aben Kandel's ingenious staging of Hale's lynching substitutes a mailbag for Hale's body.

The oncoming train snatches up the bag representing Hale's body.

RAILROAD ARM, which juts out from track NEAREST CAMERA. From it hangs a mail bag, which gives us the impression of a man's body being suspended by the neck. The sack sways gently in the breeze. Suddenly from the direction opposite to the one our train departed, the LIMITED CROSSES CAMERA in front of deserted station, and as the mail car of the LIMITED reaches CENTER, the mail bag is snatched from the railroad arm. The Limited continues on ACROSS SCENE without slowing down until it disappears.

Lynchings did occur near railroad lines, and lynchers had been known to charter trains for participants and spectators at such atrocities. But this indirect, symbolic image of the hanging—an example of what critic Stephen Prince has called "metonymic displacement" of screen violence—is

Another example of Kandel's visual ingenuity: the camera tracks into the empty oval for Mr. X, the unidentified suspect for the murder of Mary Clay, and then dissolves.

The next scene is a graphic match of the previous one, with Robert Hale fixing his tie in an oval mirror just before he is arrested. The necktie foreshadows his ultimate fate.

Hale is arrested when his bloodstained suit arrives just after the police have found Hale's draft telegram accepting a job in Chicago.

both imaginative and shrewd; more important, it was well within the Code's bounds of good taste.[55] Although it deprives the viewer of the spectacle, it refers unmistakably to what it does not show. The inert, dangling mail sack resembles Hale's body, and the post on which it hangs resembles a gallows. The shot is visually stunning in and of itself, but it also directs viewers to compare the momentum of the angry mob to the implacable force of an onrushing train literally railroading Hale to his death. Yet because it obeyed the Code by displacing the actual violence, Kandel's design provoked no objections from Joseph Breen. The scene, which depicts the undepictable, is Kandel's most memorable visual flourish. Rossen and LeRoy retained it for the final script and the finished film.

It is worth noting that many critics, including the circumspect Frank Nugent in 1937 and William Johnson in 1996, have credited this staging to LeRoy—and for good reason: LeRoy films often featured scenes with such visual flair. Yet Kandel provided several of the striking visual and aural touches that give *They Won't Forget* its relentless momentum. Redwine's pleas of innocence over successive shots of the college elevator shaft and the jail interrogation cell are Kandel's designs, anticipating the kind of dialogue-driven dramatic cutting that Orson Welles would use to such powerful effect in *Citizen Kane* (1941). Another example occurs when Griffin decides to bring in Hale for questioning after Brock's tip-off: from the empty oval for "Mr. X" in Griffin's diagram of suspects the scene dissolves in a graphic match to an oval mirror where Hale adjusts his tie just before he is arrested—another image that foreshadows his ultimate demise.[56] Yet, without a doubt, the lynching scene was Kandel's most powerful visual flourish of all, one that brings home its full horror.

Justice of a Sort

Kandel's portrayal of various villains profiting from Hale's conviction and demise was the final major problem Breen directed the filmmakers to revise. But LeRoy and Rossen were reluctant to rewrite the scenes of Hale's abduction and his antagonists' lack of punishment per Breen's specifications. Their intransigence was one reason Breen had passed censor Irwin Esmond's comments on to LeRoy. Further, LeRoy was already well along in principal photography on the film, having started production on March 3 with the Buxton classroom scenes. He was a quick worker on the set: he typically did no more than five takes of any given shot and often printed the first take. LeRoy was capable of covering between ten and twenty-seven setups—or two to eight script pages—a day. He had scheduled only one day for retakes.[57] The principal photography thus might well conclude with the abduction scene intact and the villains unpunished. Hence, at the end of March, Breen reiterated to the studio his concerns about the issue of punishing the lynchers:

> It is our belief that most censor boards would not permit the showing of successful and unpunished mob violence at the present time, in view of conditions generally. We believe therefore that, if this element is to be retained at all in your picture, it will be necessary to indicate definitely later on that this mob

was punished for their crime. This indication could be quite brief, either in newspaper inserts, or perhaps better still, covered by some line in Sybil's speech in Scene 411. However it is done, we believe it will be important that this point be made quite clear.[58]

"Conditions generally" referred to several current developments, perhaps most prominently the rising tide of antilynching sentiment that, late that very spring, would see Representative Joseph A. Gabagan of New York introduce a bill in Congress.[59] Moreover, southern injustice was also constantly in the headlines. Besides the ongoing Scottsboro trials, never out of the papers for long since 1931, there was Angelo Herndon—a black labor organizer and Communist Party member who had been freed on bail in August 1934 after being wrongly sentenced to life imprisonment for his labor-organizing activities. The Supreme Court overturned Herndon's conviction on April 26, 1937, the traditional date of Confederate Memorial Day (and, as it happened, the twenty-fourth anniversary of Mary Phagan's murder).

In their last round of revisions, Rossen and LeRoy took Breen's own suggestion for the simplest option to punish the perpetrators and beefed up Sybil's climactic speech to Griffin and Brock in the film's final scene. Kandel had already made Sybil the voice of the film's conscience, changing her personality from the meek, overwhelmed, somewhat passive, but good-hearted woman of the novel into a more active, aggressive character who became a crusader in Kandel's final sequence.[60] As they revised the script overall, Kandel and Rossen rethought Sybil's personality, turning her into a woman who is overwhelmed by events but strikes back in modest ways (confronting Griffin about Robert's innocence, speaking angrily to Pindar of the press's treatment of her, and scolding the courtroom spectators who cheer the jury's guilty verdict before she collapses in tears). As performed by newcomer Gloria Dickson, Sybil is a demure but perceptive, spirited, and supportive wife before Robert's arrest, conviction, and lynching. She temperately embraces the South, works hard to cheer up Robert, and suggests tactfully to him that perhaps he erected the barrier between himself and their neighbors.

The PCA's insistence that the villains be punished encouraged the writers to reshape Sybil's appearance in the film's final scene. She thus took her place alongside the barber Timberlake's wife (who slaps him for not cooperating with Pindar and looks disgusted when he lies on the stand) and Mrs. Mountford as the three women of integrity in the film. In the revised script, and as shot, Sybil interrupts Griffin and Brock as they speculate

They Won't Forget's final scene as revised begins with Griffin not yet elected senator but pronounced a sure thing by Brock.

Griffin and Brock's discussion of Griffin's election is interrupted by Sybil Hale's appearance in the office.

on Griffin's likely election to the U.S. Senate. After Sybil rejects Griffin's effort to "buy [her] peace of mind," Griffin and Brock express their regret about Robert's lynching, claiming that they were only doing their respective jobs of prosecuting and reporting the case. Griffin, in fact, promises "to prosecute every one of the men" responsible for Robert's death. This statement could be construed as providing at least some of the compensating moral values Breen had sought. (Griffin never makes such a promise in the novel.) Griffin's pledge is dubious, though. Prosecuting Joe Turner and Mary Clay's brothers—who had clearly expressed their intent to lynch Hale—would certainly damage his bid for the U.S. Senate. In 1915, Hugh M. Dorsey was not in a position to investigate Frank's lynching, and Governor John Slaton's successor, Nat E. Harris, only went through the motions of doing so.[61]

Sybil clearly does not believe Griffin, who can barely look her in the eye as he makes his pledge. Her reply, shot in a long take, medium close-up that becomes a close-up when she leans in over Griffin's desk, forcefully provides the "voice of morality" Breen wanted in the script:

Responsible? You're the one who is responsible! They at least had a reason for what they did—they, too, had someone they loved, killed—and they wanted to kill in return—just like I want to right now! But I'd rather have you live . . . to remember. . . . You're the ones who stirred up all the hatred and the prejudice down here . . . for no reason than that it suited your ambitions—that it made a good story—and for those reasons you took the life of an innocent man! But it's not over with his death. This kind of thing you've done is never over. It will stay

Sybil leans into close-up for emphasis as she forcefully informs Griffin and Brock that she, and they, will never forget what they have done to her husband.

After Sybil has left Griffin's office, he and Brock are reflective for once.

In the final shot of the film, Griffin and Brock watch Sybil leave the building and wonder whether the man they convicted was actually guilty. The window bars suggest their own imprisonment by guilty consciences.

with you as long as you live . . . because deep down in your hearts and souls, you know it's the truth!

Sybil's speech is of a type that was a consistent feature of message movies in the 1930s, a way for filmmakers to show that at least one of the characters recognizes the malfeasance of the villains and says so face-to-face. LeRoy had shot a comparable scene, in fact, at the conclusion of *Five Star Final*: here the fiancé of the ingenue—whose parents commit suicide after the paper's exploitative reporting—delivers the film's judgment: "You'll go on hunting down little, unimportant people who can't fight back. You'll go on with your filthy newspaper, pulling the clothing off women and selling their naked souls for two cents. You've grown rich on filth, and no one has ever dared rise up and crush you out." After the couple departs, the editor quits his job at the paper.

Sybil's accusations in *They Won't Forget* do not have quite this salutary effect. Griffin and Brock do not explicitly concede that Sybil is right, but they are shamed into silence and offer no further defense of their actions. They go to the window and watch her leave the building. Brock starts to express his sense of guilt to Griffin but decides—completely in character—to say only, "I wonder if he really did it." The two men, in questioning Hale's guilt, in fact affirm their responsibility for his murder. The bars on the window of Griffin's office suggest that the two men will in fact be troubled for the rest of their lives.

Justice and Memory

Sybil's solitary promise to remember this southern injustice serves the function Breen prescribed for it. But Sybil's speech also picks up a major thread of the film from its opening moments and even its title: remembrance and forgetting. LeRoy struggled to find a title for this film; when he submitted the first script draft to the PCA office, he used "In the Deep South," removing "Death" because, as he joked, "there is no use killing the picture before it goes out." Another possibility was "It Did Happen" (which would have made the link to the Phagan-Frank case unmistakable). LeRoy settled on the final title in early June.[62]

They Won't Forget was appropriate not only because of Sybil's climactic speech but also because of the film's opening minutes,[63] when the credits appear as hardened earth in relief on the ground while a medley of Civil War–era and southern tunes ("Dixie," "Swanee River," and "My Old Kentucky Home") plays. A shot of the Lincoln Memorial, accompanied by "The Battle Hymn of the Republic," dissolves into a quotation from the Gettysburg Address (the "proposition that all men are created equal"). The film then fades in on the famous 1866 statement of Robert E. Lee engraved on the pedestal of his statue in the small southern town of Flodden: "All that the South has ever desired was that the Union, as established by our forefathers, should be preserved and that the government as originally organized, should be administered in purity and truth." The film immediately creates a carefully balanced sectional dialogue and battle of memories.

The opening credits for the film appear as if bursting from the ground, anticipating the Civil War veterans' speech about rising out of their graves to remind southerners of their sacrifice.

The Confederate veterans rest and reminisce at the start of the film by the statue of Robert E. Lee; the pedestal includes his statement about the South's desire for a preserved union.

Beside this statue on Confederate Memorial Day, as the town clock chimes noon (it will chime again at the very end of the film), veterans in full dress uniform waiting to march in the parade reflect on their dwindling numbers. If southerners forget these veterans' sacrifice after the old soldiers have all passed on, one remarks, invoking the film's title, "We'll get up out of our graves and remind them" (this line is delivered by Harry Davenport, who went on to play Dr. Meade in *Gone with the Wind*). Audience members realize in retrospect that this is what the raised soil of the opening credit letters illustrated. The title of Steve Oney's book on the case, *And the Dead Shall Rise*, conveys the same sentiment. Greene's novel lacks this dialogue and these allusions.

The film's opening scene (the last actually shot, on April 9) of the Confederate veterans displays southern pride at its source. Yet the scene also portrays—literally—the fertile soil from which the suspicions, accusations, and venom against Hale will grow. One of the infirm old veterans gloats that more Confederates than Yankees remain alive in the town. The idea that southern pride outlasts death suggests a ferocity of feeling that belies these infirm old men's statements. Hale's ordeal will show that southerners have not forgotten, but this opening scene and the film's very title pose the question of how that remembrance is best preserved and observed.[64]

A less humane aspect of remembrance is immediately apparent in the next scene—one described but not dramatized in Greene's novel. Profes-

Robert Hale stops to correct the class work of a very pleased Mary Clay, portrayed by Lana Turner in her first major role.

Professor Buxton appears abruptly and instructs Hale to dismiss the class in observation of Confederate Memorial Day.

sor Buxton is drawn in the screenplay and is performed in the film (by E. Alyn Warren) as a stereotypical "southern colonel" type: stage directions for his first appearance in the revised script read, "He has a great deal of what is known as 'Southern dignity.' Apparently he is very indignant." [65] Buxton abruptly enters Hale's shorthand class and orders him to "dismiss the class" because it is Confederate Memorial Day.

Though surprised, Hale good-naturedly observes, "In my part of the country, we call it Decoration Day—and it comes a month later." His hands on the front of his jacket, Buxton retorts, "In your part of the country, sir, you can call it whatever you and all the other Yankees please—but down here it's Memorial Day and at Buxton Business College, sir, it's a half-holiday!" He then turns to the students (in long shot) and announces: "It is quite evident that Mr. Hale is badly in need of some instruction himself." Thus the film portrays Buxton's devotion to the Lost Cause (or his dislike of Hale, or both) as so great that he is willing to humiliate one of his own employees in front of the students, who laugh. The camera tracks into a medium shot of Hale to register his embarrassment. It also tracks in on Mary Clay, who is not amused. Later that day, when Joe Turner angrily comes looking for Mary Clay, Hale sarcastically comments to Turner on the front steps of the school, "Don't you know it's Memorial Day?" When Turner angrily responds, "I know that without you telling me," Hale replies, "I'm only trying to help." Turner takes an immediate dislike to Hale and indeed will be among the leaders of the lynch mob. These events set the stage for Hale's decision to return to the North and take the job he has been offered in Chicago.

The gentle, compassionate Governor Mountford
trades barbs with the ambitious Andy Griffin after
Mountford's speech at the city cemetery.

Governor Mountford provides a more humane alternative to the kind of
vengeful southern remembering Buxton and Turner display. In his annual
speech at the cemetery honoring the Confederate dead, Mountford prays
"once more that the prejudices and hatreds lie buried under this hallowed
ground, never again to be resurrected in the cause of death and destruc-
tion." When Griffin churlishly insults the governor (saying Mountford
spoke as if he had seen the Civil War himself), the governor replies, "The
more I see of my contemporaries, the more preferable the past becomes to
the present." Mountford briefly expresses a feeling of nostalgia for days
gone by that Mary Phagan and her family, themselves confronted with the
confusions of industrialization and modernization, probably shared. The
compassionate Mountford's gentle but proud acts of commemoration are
overridden by events that enable the film to position the Frank case as (in
the words of Brock) the start of the Civil War "all over again."

Thus *They Won't Forget* foregrounds the issues of memory, sectionalism, and racism that informed the Phagan-Frank case. Yet, following the
blueprint of Greene's novel, the film also shows how class resentment
multiplied these sentiments. Mary is murdered in a business college rather
than a factory—a setting that shifts the class locale from blue-collar to
white-collar labor yet retains overtones of industrialization. As a teacher,
Hale enjoys authority and inspires animosity among his students, albeit
not as deep as that the National Pencil Company factory's employees felt
for their supervisor Leo Frank. Hale is not the ultimate authority at the
school, and he makes pitifully little money as a teacher. (Dolly Holly characterizes the Hales' premarital dating as a "white-collar courtship": they

worked in the same New York office.) The issue of class also comes up when Griffin confronts the town's leading businessmen in his office: the upper-class Flodden residents also want Hale's blood.[66]

The lower-class aspect of this alliance against Hale is even more clearly established. Mary Clay's very name is redolent of her family's impoverished rural background as well as Georgia's famous red soil. Mary's brothers are clearly working class (their home is "across the tracks" and by "the mill"). Here again, script revisions went even further than Greene's novel to give the audience a sense of the brothers' motivation for the vigilante justice they ultimately enact. Rossen added a powerful speech for Shattuck Clay to deliver about the impact Mary's murder has had on their family. When Griffin asks the brothers to tell everything they know about Mary, Shattuck responds: "Everything!! There's just this much to tell, mister . . . us Clays never had much . . . 'ceptin' her . . . like a flower she was to all of us . . . ever since she was that high . . . and it was nice to come home at night from the mills . . . and hear the laugh of her . . . and see her smilin'. . . and now we don't . . . anymore . . . she's dead . . . and there's nothin' to come home to but the cussin' of the old man and the heart-breakin' wailin' of my mother . . . that's everything."[67] Though Trevor Bardette's delivery is stylized in its immobility (to suggest the character's awkwardness in formal clothes and his intimidation at speaking to a public official), his evocation of inconsolable grief in this speech is stirring. Even the cynical, ruthless Griffin is moved to respond, "I'm sorry." Shattuck's speech evokes his family's emotional trauma and their desire for some kind of closure—specifically, finding, convicting, and executing Mary's killer. The Clay brothers are manifestly unsatisfied with Griffin's condolences: "Sorry don't get us nowhere," one brother replies.

The opening scene with the Confederate veterans and these scenes with the Clay brothers constitute *They Won't Forget*'s attempt to explain to a national audience why Robert Hale—and by implication Leo Frank—was lynched. Southerners believed in the myth of the Lost Cause and were convinced that they had been ill-treated since the Civil War; further, certain Georgians felt compelled to right Governor Slaton's perceived wrong in commuting Frank's death sentence. Significantly, Greene's novel does not identify the men who pulled Robert Hale off the train, even though Greene knew who they were. In Rossen's revisions and the film, we clearly see Mary's brothers and her boyfriend, Joe, leading the mob outside the train.

Sybil's speech in the final scene about remembering what Brock and Griffin have done replies to the veterans' promise in the film's first scene.

Her accusations transform the remembrance of the Confederate dead and the South's sacrifice into a memory of the recent injustices that have taken Robert's—and by extension Leo Frank's—life. Here, memory holds a crucial place in the cinematic telling of the Mary Phagan–Leo Frank story, just as it did in *Murder in Harlem*'s many flashbacks.

Thus, multiple factors shaped *They Won't Forget* into a dramatization of the Phagan-Frank case in its entirety—from the initial murder to the final lynching—that includes a powerful rendering of some of the case's most unpleasant aspects. In fact, the film unfolds as if it were a barely embellished treatment of Leonard Dinnerstein's nonfiction book about the case. At the same time, the adaptation of Ward Greene's novel was heavily inflected by the PCA, whose directives required the filmmakers to omit, downplay, or only allude to certain subjects.

A straight interpretation of *They Won't Forget* would argue that Breen succeeded in making the film less inflammatory than the filmmakers had planned. The finished film does have elements of circumstantial evidence and compensating moral values. And in fact, *They Won't Forget* played without censors' cuts across most of the North.[68] Perhaps Joseph Breen and the Production Code Administration had done their job after all, although Amy Wood reports that there is no evidence that the film played in certain sensitive southern markets where Warner Bros. had previewed it, such as Dallas, Texas, and Charlotte, North Carolina, where censorship might have been a factor. Film historian Gregory Black makes precisely this case for the PCA's effectiveness: "While it is impossible to watch *They Won't Forget* and not come away convinced that Hale was the innocent victim of an ambitious and unscrupulous prosecutor, there is no direct dialogue stating in clear and explicit terms that a deal had been struck, money had passed hands, or future elections had been rigged. In fact, the entire film points to a system of justice trying to be fair but overcome by Southern customs that demanded 'an eye for an eye.' This was enough for Breen."[69]

Following a similar line of thought, Black argues that Griffin's promise to do the right thing and all the other efforts to give Hale due process were sincere:

Voices throughout the film told the audience that the system was trying to be fair: Griffin pledges not to move until he finds the guilty man, and refuses to allow the police to beat a confession out of the black janitor; a real investigation is conducted; the city fathers express concern over the hysteria the trial is generating; Griffin tells the jury Hale is innocent until proven guilty; and the governor states forcefully that he believes Hale was convicted on slender evidence. However, the system cannot overcome individual prejudice and hate. It is hatred and public opinion that lynch Hale, not the state. The very title of the movie reinforced that message: *They Won't Forget*.[70]

Certainly, hatred and a desire for vengeance outweigh Griffin's promise to ensure that justice is done. But I would argue that Griffin's promise and virtually every one of the incidents listed in the quotation above are equivocal as staged, shot, and placed in the narrative. The film piles on the ironies of Hale's ordeal. Breen was successful here, as elsewhere, in guiding filmmakers to create a kind of ambiguity that might permit multiple readings—naïve and sophisticated, or here literal and ironic—of what actually transpires in these scenes.[71]

Thus the PCA's efforts to shape *They Won't Forget* were more than merely prohibitive; they were also creative. In encouraging the filmmakers to focus on circumstantial aspects of the case against Hale, the PCA did not prevent the film from being a powerful indictment of social ills and the worst aspects of human nature. *They Won't Forget* is yet another instance in which the industry's effort to make films less overtly offensive resulted in an equally if not more powerful treatment of what was deemed provocative.

Breen's exhortations to remove specific scenes of police malfeasance and collusion with Griffin enabled LeRoy and the screenwriters to make the causes for Robert Hale's sad fate more ambiguous than they were in the novel and the actual trial, thereby rendering the fictionalized treatment of the Phagan-Frank phenomenon in some ways just as frightening as the actual case. Instead of depicting the perversion of justice as the result of particular characters who abuse their power, the finished film indicts an entire town—from the business school's president to the school's janitor, from barbers to pool-hall hooligans, from interested townspeople gathering outside the factory and the courthouse to newspaper readers and the guards taking Hale to prison. All of them worked together toward Robert's conviction, and their collusion creates a disturbing rendition of the power of sectionalism and vigilante justice.[72] *They Won't Forget* refuses the typical social problem film's standard conclusion: that malfeasance in America is the result of just a few bad apples in positions of power.

Mervyn LeRoy went on to direct higher-profile films with much bigger budgets and major stars. He left Warner Bros. for MGM in 1938 as a producer-director (with *The Wizard of Oz* among his produced properties) and settled into that studio's house style. He was awarded a Best Director Oscar for the Greer Garson vehicle *Random Harvest* (1942) and a special Oscar for producing and directing the 1945 pro-tolerance short *The House I Live In*, starring Frank Sinatra. He became a freelance director-producer in the 1950s and 1960s, perhaps most famously succeeding John Ford on the set of *Mister Roberts* (1955), and received the Irving Thalberg Memorial Award for career achievement in 1975. When LeRoy died in 1987, he received a special tribute from Nancy and Ronald Reagan, whom he had introduced.[73] His many later achievements aside, however, *They Won't Forget* remains one of LeRoy's most outstanding efforts.

Promotion and Reception

As LeRoy and Warner Bros. prepared to send *They Won't Forget* out to theaters in early summer 1937, they hoped audiences would greet the film enthusiastically as a stunning, stark indictment of prejudice and legal injustice. The good news was that there was not a huge negative cost to recover ($346,000).[74] The bad news was that selling the film at all represented a challenge. For starters, it had no star power. Edward Norris (Robert Hale) was so minor an actor that his weekly salary of $175 was dwarfed by the $2,000 a week drawn by Otto Kruger (the northern lawyer Gleason) in a much smaller role. These circumstances left the Warner Bros. sales department with the "authorial option"; that is, they could sell *They Won't Forget* as based on Ward Greene's book or as the creation of producer-director LeRoy. Unfortunately, Greene's name did not mean enough for the studio to keep the novel's title, and the name LeRoy was likely even less familiar to audiences than the film's unknown cast.

Still, Warner Bros.'s marketing department chose to build up LeRoy by stressing his achievements as director of the previous year's *Anthony Adverse* and *I Am a Fugitive from a Chain Gang*. Doing so allowed the marketing staff to draw genre connections between the classic message film *Fugitive* and their new release. One publicity piece, still using one of the interim titles for the film, typified this strategy while emphasizing the story treatment Breen and LeRoy had agreed on: "Not since Mervyn LeRoy made *I Am a Fugitive from a Chain Gang* has Hollywood offered such a powerfully daring drama as LeRoy's second independent production, *The Deep South.* . . . *The Deep South* is a dramatic, uncompromising indictment of the legal and social system which can railroad an innocent man to his death solely on the strength of circumstantial evidence."[75] Some film critics simply used or paraphrased this copy in their published reviews.

LeRoy encouraged Warner Bros. to stress the film's realism and in fact to use a newsreel format for the trailer. Director of Advertising and Publicity Charles Einfeld was informed: "Mervyn advised against using any courtroom scenes—which would make it look like a courtroom picture— or any inference to the prejudice angle. Both these angles would be obviously wrong. Therefore, the trailer will present the characters of the story with a suggestion of the plot. If we can make all these characters look as interesting as they are in the picture, then we ought to have a great trailer. The newsreel type [titles in the trailer] is to get over the inference that the story is an actual news event without saying so."[76] The courtroom angle was old hat; the prejudice angle (sectionalism as well as racism) might drive viewers away. Lynching was, of course, not to be mentioned—ever. Instead, the "newsreel-type" trailer stressed the story's suspense angle as well as its realism. A *March of Time*–styled voiceover narrator introduced the key characters in the story against brief scenes of Tump being grilled, Joe Turner being questioned, Robert at home with Sybil, and Griffin's standoff against the town's business leaders—all scenes geared to provoke viewer curiosity ("What will happen?").[77]

That emphasis on suspense also informed Micheaux's marketing of *The Gunsaulus Mystery* ("Was Leo M. Frank guilty?"), but unlike Micheaux, Warner Bros. had no desire to link *They Won't Forget* to the case it dramatized. Shortly after the film's preview, the studio inserted a prefatory disclaimer about the story's resemblance to actual people and events in response to initial reviews that emphasized the connection to the Phagan-Frank case. If the studio did not include the disclaimer, a studio attorney explained to LeRoy, the film's connection to the Frank case would be implicitly endorsed and lawsuits might well ensue.[78] Ads thus downplayed the film's basis on a real case and instead stressed its many generic appeals and hard-hitting qualities (mother's love, wife's love, "the kind of vital drama that makes the screen fairly pulse with life," "a picture that shocks audiences out of their smug self-complacency").[79]

Likewise, advertising made the best of a bad situation with LeRoy's casting choices—mostly unknowns in the major roles—rendering them as a deliberate aesthetic strategy to enhance the film's realism. The press book "quoted" LeRoy as claiming: "'*They Won't Forget*' is such a powerful human story and so true to actual life, that I want people seeing it to believe they are watching life move before their eyes. If they see actors who look to them just like people on the street, rather than actors they have seen in a number of different pictures, they will believe the story, feel it more convincingly." Claude Rains as Andrew Griffin was the only actor with possible name recognition; in 1933 he had starred in *The Invisible Man* (an ironic leading role, given that he was, in fact, invisible for much of the film) and had a prominent role as a villain in *Anthony Adverse*. *They Won't Forget* appeared one year before Rains's spirited performance as the evil usurper Prince John in Michael Curtiz's *Adventures of Robin Hood* (1938) opposite Errol Flynn, two years before he appeared as James Stewart's corrupt father figure in Frank Capra's *Mr. Smith Goes to Washington*, and five years before his iconic performance as Captain Renault in *Casablanca* (1942). Rains confided to a *New York Times* reporter just before the film's premiere that he had been "frightened to death" at playing Griffin because of the southern accent but had worked with a dialect coach in Louisiana. It must be conceded, however, that Rains's southern accent does at times have a cockney lilt.

Otto Kruger is perhaps best remembered as Charles Tobin, the suave saboteur in Hitchcock's 1942 film *Saboteur*, but in 1937 he might have been known for playing the older man in the Joan Crawford–Clark Gable romantic triangle *Chained* (1934). Allyn Joslyn (Bill Brock) had worked only on the stage prior to *They Won't Forget*, most notably as one of the leading-role screenwriters in *Boy Meets Girl*; he went on to enjoy steady work in major Hollywood films and television, most notably as one of Cary Grant's fliers in *Only Angels Have Wings* (1938).

Clinton Rosemond had regular work in the 1930s playing servants in contemporary and period films (including Warner Bros.'s *The Green Pastures* [1936]). Except for his dignified but dialogue-free star turn in an MGM short—*The Story of Doctor Carver* (1938), directed by future A-list director Fred Zinnemann—he would have no greater role than Tump Redwine. Elisha Cook Jr. went on to become a staple in films noir, beginning with the gunsel Humphrey Bogart repeatedly humiliates in *The Maltese Falcon* (1941). Character actor E. Alyn Warren was probably best known in 1937 for playing Stephen Douglas opposite Walter Huston in D. W. Griffith's *Abraham Lincoln* (1930).

As for Sybil and Robert Hale, *They Won't Forget* was Gloria Dickson's Hollywood debut; a Warner Bros. contractee, she is better known for

Mervyn LeRoy (center) with his cast of unknowns (left to right): Allyn Joslyn as the reporter Brock, Edward Norris as Robert Hale, Lana Turner as Mary Clay, Gloria Dickson as Sybil Hale, and Claude Rains as Andy Griffin. (Courtesy of the Academy of Motion Picture Arts and Sciences.)

playing John Garfield's love interest in *They Made Me a Criminal* (1939). Her career was cut short when she died in a house fire in 1945. Edward Norris had played only bit parts under contract at MGM, such as a customer with a reluctant girlfriend at the freak show in the opening scene of *Mad Love* (1935); he would be better known after appearing with Spencer Tracy and Mickey Rooney in *Boys Town* (1938).

Lana Turner was also at this time an unknown, but LeRoy put her under personal contract and filmed all her scenes to emphasize the qualities he wanted for the role—"young and desirable, yet [with] a childlike innocence, an untouched quality." Her soda shop scene early in the film became part of the legend of her discovery by Hollywood. LeRoy refashioned Turner's costume to emphasize her physical assets (from a modest polka-dot country dress with a lace collar to a tight V-neck sweater belted snugly around her waist).[80] In doing so, LeRoy emphasized the not-so-unconscious lust Mary Clay could inspire in older men such as Professor

Buxton, Robert Hale, Tump Redwine, and her killer. In his memoir, Le-
Roy makes much of Turner's "superb figure" and describes directing the
film score's composer to create music in a rhythm that matched the motion of her breasts as she walks to the Buxton Business School. Kenneth
Anger wrote of Turner's walk to the college in *Hollywood Babylon*, "The
rest of the film was an anti-climax."[81]

After an early June preview at Warner Bros.'s Hollywood theater, trade
paper critics thought otherwise; they raved about *They Won't Forget* as
a landmark film of social consciousness with an outstanding cast. *Daily
Variety* praised its "essential fidelity" to Greene's novel and saw the film
as a test case for topical movies that passed through the PCA's hands.
LeRoy's film had

> a shocking kind of courage and honesty, as compared to the ordinary cinematic
> pussyfootings that pretend to deal with mob passions and sociological affairs. It
> has the controversial heat which is not separable from this kind of narrative, no
> matter how many seals of approval may seek to negate its implied indictments
> and possible local resentments. . . . The passions which entertain are not all soft
> and civilized. The same emotions which excite to violence also have the power
> to attract and hold show audiences, and it is in superb statement of these harsh
> entertainment elements that Mervyn LeRoy makes his picture memorable.

The paper praised the "new faces" in the cast, singling out Clinton Rosemond, "who gives his scenes indelible impress in wailing terror and final
courageous honesty so that his coached testimony may not convict an
innocent man." The *Hollywood Reporter* and even the typically more
cautious *Motion Picture Herald* agreed.[82]

With marketing and labeling poised to position the film somewhere
between fact and fiction, and strong praise from the trade press, Warner
Bros. initially opened *They Won't Forget* just in New York's Strand Theater in July, where it did a respectable initial business in a slow summer.
The studio's distribution plan for the film entailed what is today called a
platform release—a distribution pattern in which a film opens in a major
city or two before it is sent to theaters nationwide—to showcase and build
up critical praise for it.[83]

New York critics—as a group usually more blasé than the trade critics—mostly raved about *They Won't Forget*, much as book reviewers had
praised Greene's novel. *Life* magazine made the film its "Movie of the
Week" in mid-July and gave it a major multipage spread following a two-
page spread featuring photos of the remaining Scottsboro defendants. The

review extolled Warner Bros. for again evading standard studio escapism by going "strongly sociological" with a film from which preview audiences "emerge literally limp with spent emotions." The reviewer added it "to the meager handful of U.S. cinema classics." Frank Nugent of the *New York Times* praised the film as well. *They Won't Forget*, he gushed, "reopens the Leo M. Frank case, holds it up for review and, with courage, objectivity and simple eloquence, creates a brilliant sociological drama and a trenchant film editorial against intolerance and hatred." In a subsequent profile of LeRoy, he further praised *They Won't Forget* as "a grim and savage drama of the Southland, courageous in its conception, relentless in its execution, uncompromising in its conclusion."[84] Nor was this enthusiasm for the film's social critique confined to liberal newspapers. The *Wall Street Journal* likewise praised the film to the skies:

> Not in a long time has there come to the screen a production which illustrates so forcefully the possibilities of the moving picture as a relentless searchlight to be turned on bigotry and prejudice underlying our public life as does the current Strand offering. . . . [N]o attempt has been made to adorn it with a moral, nor to offer a solution. Rather, as if armed with a razor edged scalpel, the producers have laid bare the passions and hatred and unshackled ambitions lying beneath the outer covering of human lives. . . . The word powerful, often applied to moving pictures by over-exuberant press agents, is not misplaced in this instance.

The *Christian Science Monitor*'s thumbnail review reported that the film's objective presentation of the facts made it a "memorable social drama" that "attacks the underlying problem of fear, prejudice and hatred rather than the individuals whom it involves." Otis Ferguson of the *New Republic* compared it favorably with Lang's *Fury*. Nugent wrote on this point: "Not so spectacular, or melodramatic, or strident perhaps, yet it is stronger, more vibrant . . . through the quiet intensity of its narrative, the simplicity of Mervyn LeRoy's direction, its integrity of purpose, the even perfection of its cast, whose performances deserve commendation." Graham Greene, writing in London, was amazed that the film had even been made: "Occasionally a film of truth and tragic value gets somehow out of Hollywood on to the screen. Nobody can explain it."[85]

Thus *They Won't Forget* clearly fell outside Warner Bros.'s self-proclaimed purview of "harmless entertainment." Film reviewers viewed social criticism as the key criterion for critical plaudits, and many saw the relevance of LeRoy's film for current history. The antilynching movement was at its peak, and the Scottsboro case, which had begun in 1931, was still in the headlines; trials, retrials, and appeals continued throughout the 1930s. All nine men were tried twice and convicted twice, but all were eventually freed, some of them shortly before and during the film's premiere. In late August, as the film continued to be screened in limited locations, several of the freed Scottsboro Nine reenacted their trial in a Harlem theater. Frank Nugent wrote in the *New York Times* that *They Won't Forget* could not "be dismissed as a Hollywood exaggeration of a state of affairs which once might have existed but exists no longer. Between the Frank trial at Atlanta and the more recent one at Scottsboro is a bond closer than chronology indicates." Similarly, the *Brooklyn Daily Eagle*'s critic invoked the Scottsboro case and stated that the film "should be seen by every citizen of the United States . . . it teaches a lesson that can be taken to heart by people in every section of the country." A reviewer for the American Communist Party's *New Masses* and documentary filmmaker Pare Lorentz in *McCall's* followed suit.[86]

They Won't Forget instantly achieved the status of an outstanding film. Nugent ranked it "unquestionably" the month's best picture and put it on his ten-best list for the *New York Times*. The National Board of Review likewise ranked the film as one of the year's ten best. Bosley Crowther, in 1940, would hold up the courtroom scenes in *They Won't Forget* and *Fury* as among the finest yet produced in Hollywood.[87] Writing in 1976, nearly forty years after the film premiered, James Baldwin singled out *They Won't Forget* in his book-length essay *The Devil Finds Work* as one of the key films of the 1930s that dramatized the anguish of being African American. Baldwin wrote of the haunting quality of Rosemond's performance and the film's "icy brutality," apparent in the final revelation that Griffin and Brock did not believe in Hale's guilt. Film historians and critics continue to hold *They Won't Forget* in high regard.[88]

The film's box office performance was not so clear-cut, however. *They Won't Forget* never really had a shot at a positive box office performance in the South. *Variety* noted that the film "appears certain to run up against difficulty there." Archer Winsten went so far as to suggest that southerners who saw the film might "want to lynch the Warner Brothers and Producer Mervyn LeRoy. On the other hand, maybe they will want to elect Claude Rains county prosecutor and set up a small shrine in the form of tree and rope to the Clay boys." Such comments affirm that the film was indeed seen as indicting the South, regardless of its suggestions (primarily through Gleason's showboating) that the North was equally to blame for Hale's and Leo Frank's fate. *Daily Variety*'s critic, on the other hand, argued that the film was "no more a polemic against citizens below the Mason and Dixon line than those above it. East, West, North and South, the shoe fits."[89]

Ward Greene accurately predicted that *They Won't Forget* would not be popular in Atlanta, "but Atlanta doesn't like any publicity that isn't indorsed [*sic*] by the chamber of commerce," he added. *Motion Picture Daily* further predicted that "exhibitors operating in territories assumed to be the locale of the story may expect that powerful influences will be brought to bear to prohibit its showing." One such powerful influence was Atlanta's film censor in 1937, Mrs. Alonzo Richardson, who went right to work to keep *They Won't Forget* out of the city. At the end of August, she wrote to Joseph Breen: "You will be interested to know that we have succeeded in keeping THEY WON'T FORGET out of the state entirely. Written by an Atlanta man, recalling one of the darkest pages of the state history, capable of reviving conditions which would be ghastly in the tragedy of results; exhibitors, newspapers, populace have joined us in asking that this thing will not be done to our state. The common consent has been obtained, and we will not have the picture in the state. Nobody wants it!—not even the most morbidly curious!"[90] Warner Bros. tactfully refrained from advertising the film as "banned in Atlanta."

There was indeed a "common consent" to keep *They Won't Forget* out of Atlanta, and one influential constituency in agreement was the city's Jewish leaders—still fearful that a movie about the Phagan-Frank case would reignite anti-Semitism in the city. The August 27, 1937, issue of Atlanta's *Southern Israelite* carried a news item indicating that interdenominational leaders had requested that the film not be shown in the city in response to "an open controversy which has raged since the picture was released nationally." An editorial commented that "cinema fans may be disappointed, but it is safe to wager that the majority of Atlantans are grateful to Warner Brothers for withholding, at considerable financial loss to the film producers, the showing in Atlanta. . . . At the same time, that debt [to Warner Bros.] is increased by the knowledge that the film's great message of social justice is being heard by thousands throughout the country." *They Won't Forget* has never been shown in a commercial film theater in Atlanta—although the *Atlanta Daily World* did publicize Clinton Rosemond's central role in the film.[91]

While a few future Hollywood films would depict lynchings and near lynchings—most powerfully in *The Ox-Bow Incident* (1943)—none attempted to depict the Phagan-Frank case again. But the story was not forgotten. Television took up the case using a new approach; this time the spotlight would shine on Governor John M. Slaton. Had Atlanta's censor allowed *They Won't Forget* to play in her city, Slaton would have had the pleasure of seeing himself depicted as the "conscientious" Governor Mountford in his hometown, where mobs had massed against him just over two decades earlier. Had he lived until 1964 (he died in 1955), he might have had the pleasure of seeing himself apotheosized on national broadcast television.

Interlude

From Film to Television

GIVEN THE Phagan-Frank story's obvious appeal and the many omissions of the two 1930s films, its thirty-year absence from screens—of any size—is a mystery. Why did the case fade from public memory for so long?

One answer resides with the filmmakers. Oscar Micheaux was unique among race film writer-director-producers in finding the case so compelling—perhaps because, as he alleged, he actually was in Atlanta as Frank's trial unfolded. Mervyn LeRoy saw a worthy sequel to *I Am a Fugitive from a Chain Gang* in Ward Greene's novel *Death in the Deep South*. Both films were quintessential 1930s Hollywood social problem films. But *They Won't Forget* barely broke even. Against its $346,000 negative cost, it grossed about $300,000 in the United States and $204,000 in foreign markets. This was no runaway hit waiting to be remade (as was *Fugitive*) by Warner Bros. or any other studio.[1]

America's involvement in World War II certainly overshadowed the relevance of the Phagan-Frank story, given that fascistic demagoguery and mob violence were more obviously rampant in Germany and Italy than in the United States. With American armed forces fighting to defeat totalitarianism, this was not the time for Hollywood films to question American society or institutions of justice. As Bosley Crowther of the *New York Times* would note in 1942, *They Won't Forget* and the few comparable serious films that he admired (*Black Legion*, *Fury*, *Dead End*, *The Grapes of Wrath*, and *Citizen Kane*) were not suitable fare to send abroad to present an "accurate picture" of "the America that most of us know"; and they certainly did not represent "the America that counts." (For the record, Crowther instead recommended *Sergeant York*, *Mr. Deeds Goes to Town*, *Mr. Smith Goes to Washington*, *Our Town*, and *Four Daughters* for export.)[2] Even *The Ox-Bow Incident*—the exception that proves the rule—had other elements to encourage its production. That film's straightforward depiction of a lynching and its aftermath was based on Walter Van Tilburg Clark's popular novel and was safely set in the past, on the western frontier.

The postwar period in America did see more bold dramatizations of anti-Semitism in America, in the form of Elia Kazan's Oscar-winning *Gentleman's Agreement* (1947) and *Crossfire*, made that same year by Edward Dymytryk for RKO. Robert Rossen would write and direct his own indictment of southern politics, *All the King's Men* (1949), adapted from Robert Penn Warren's novel. But by 1952 Rossen and other Hollywood "lefties" were blacklisted; Hollywood's self-censorship—via personnel rather than film content—discouraged the production of films explicitly critical of America's failure to live up to its ideals.

Many of Hollywood's most topical postwar message movies *did* focus on flaws in American society, but most concerned civil rights for African Americans—*Pinky*, *Lost Boundaries*, *Home of the Brave*, and *Intruder in the Dust* appeared in 1949, all from different studios—and packaged their social criticism in melodramatic plots that offered carefully calibrated, reasonable pleas for tolerance and understanding. Indeed, the adaptation of William Faulkner's *Intruder in the Dust* features a black farmer accused of murder who remains calm, stoic, and unbowed as he faces whites gathering in the Oxford, Mississippi, town square in hope of lynching him before he is brought to trial. Actor Juano Hernandez's dignified characterization represents a sea change in the portrayal of black suspects in southern towns. The year 1950 witnessed Sidney Poitier's film debut as a hospital doctor in Twentieth Century–Fox's *No Way Out*, a drama centered on an urban race riot. Poitier was Hollywood's leading player in films about race relations for the rest of the decade and into the early 1970s, and other actors would follow Hernandez in portraying falsely accused southern blacks of considerable integrity, as did Brock Peters, for example, in his remarkable performance as Tom Robinson in *To Kill a Mockingbird* (1963). Hollywood's coming to terms with depicting African Americans as self-respecting, multidimensional, and fully human individuals would in turn have consequences for the portrayal of Jim Conley in future screen treatments of the Phagan-Frank case.

If Hollywood filmmakers could build films on more progressive attitudes (acceptable in at least parts of the country) toward race relations, they also could take advantage of the more tolerant version of the Production Code in effect by the end of the 1950s. Directors and screenwriters were emboldened by the Supreme Court's landmark 1952 *Miracle* decision and subsequent rulings that finally granted the movies First Amendment protection and undermined the legal basis for state and city censorship boards. Films about seducing virgins (*The Moon Is Blue* [1953], released without a PCA seal of approval), drug abuse (*The Man with the Golden Arm* [1955]), and homosexuality (*Tea and Sympathy* [1956]) created major milestones through the early 1960s, showing formerly taboo topics with surprising frankness. Films in several genres—from Anthony Mann's western *The Man from Laramie* (1955) to Orson Welles's film noir *Touch of Evil* (1958) to Alfred Hitchcock's *Psycho* (1960)—depicted violence in unprecedented, gruesome detail. Moreover, other notorious murder trials received theatrical docudrama treatment: *Compulsion* in 1959 dramatized the murder trial of Nathan Leopold and Richard Loeb, while *Inherit the Wind* (1960) dramatized the Scopes "Monkey Trial" of 1925. *Judgment at Nuremberg* (1961) dramatized the prosecution of Nazi war criminals (including the testimony of a sterilized concentration camp inmate, played by Montgomery Clift).

This more permissive atmosphere meant that a screenwriter and director could dramatize the unpleasant details of Mary Phagan's murder, the trial, the unseemly and shocking accusations against Frank of sexual perversion, the sensational testimony Jim Conley gave at the trial, and other important evidence that weighed in Governor Slaton's decision on Frank's appeal. Although some filmmakers may have tried to realize such a film—indeed, Stanley Kramer optioned the 1965 Harry Golden book *A Little Girl Is Dead*—none did.

In part, the movies' new subject matter was intended to contrast with television's more restrained dramatizations. Television—already popular in 1948 and then allowed by the Federal Communications Commission to expand its channel licensees in 1952—had to be far more careful about broaching controversial subjects than 1950s theatrical films because it was broadcast directly into American homes. Like Hollywood movies before World War II, most television programs were intended for entire family viewing. All the same, television did occasionally take more risks in choice of subject matter—such as the Holocaust—than did theatrical films.[3] In any case, by late 1964, television had succeeded the movies as America's most popular and influential consensus medium.

One might speculate that by the time the *Profiles in Courage* series episode on Governor John M. Slaton was broadcast on December 20, 1964, the themes of justice and the moral high ground were so idealistically enshrined in mass media storytelling that visual storytellers could turn to Slaton's commutation of Frank's death sentence and finally revisit this horrible history and portray the role of anti-Semitism in the case. Indeed, the notion that a mob could kidnap a white prisoner from state authority and lynch him might have seemed as historically remote as the Salem witch trials. The publication in 1956 of Charles and Louise Samuels's book on the case, *Night Fell on Georgia*, provided evidence of renewed interest in the Phagan-Frank story. Nine years later, Harry Golden published his account.[4]

Of course, the lynching of blacks in the South was not remote enough. Less than a decade had passed since the murder of Emmet Till in 1955, perhaps the single most notorious instance of vigilante justice since Leo Frank's lynching. The suppression of civil rights in the South—addressed implicitly in race relation films of that decade such as *The Defiant Ones* (1958)—was a source of national shame by the early 1960s. Medgar Evers was assassinated in June 1963; the following spring the Ku Klux Klan burned more than sixty crosses around Mississippi, and shortly afterward, in June, Congress of Racial Equality members James Chaney, Andrew Goodman, and Michael Schwerner were murdered in that state. These atrocities only reinforced the relevance any program about vigilante violence and the denial of civil liberties might have. The Phagan-Frank case, accordingly, appeared on the smaller screen.

John M. Slaton as a Profile in Courage

This case was marked by doubt. —JOHN M. SLATON

IN MIGRATING FROM motion pictures to television, the Phagan-Frank case received a pronounced shift in emphasis from the pessimistic protest of *They Won't Forget* to the inspiring selflessness of Governor John M. Slaton's decision to commute Frank's sentence. In the early 1960s—at the height of the civil rights struggle and in the immediate aftermath of President John F. Kennedy's "New Frontier" presidency—a new generation of visual storytellers reinterpreted the Phagan-Frank case. Like their Hollywood predecessors, with whom they shared liberal political sensibilities, the *Profiles in Courage* team faced tough decisions about whether or how to depict some of the perturbing aspects of the case—anti-Semitism, racism, lynching, and the charge that Slaton saved Frank's life for selfish reasons. Five decades distant from the case, they addressed these challenges with much greater frankness than their predecessors had done.

Profiles in Courage: From Book to Television Series

Based on John F. Kennedy's 1956 best-selling, Pulitzer Prize–winning book of that title, *Profiles in Courage* had the further distinction of being the only television series based on an American president's book that was not a memoir. By design, the show aired for just one season (November 1964–May 1965). The twenty-six episodes, shot on 35 mm film at Desilu

The series credits for *Profiles in Courage*, designed by Saul Bass.

Studios, were framed in an anthology format: a different cast and story each week, and no continuing host. Like Kennedy's book chapters, each program focused on individuals—politicians and private citizens—who in a public arena displayed moral courage and extraordinary integrity.

The series's producer was Robert Saudek, by the early 1960s one of the most respected television producers in America. His television work to date was unanimously acclaimed as setting the highest standards in prime-time public affairs and documentary television. Saudek, one *Los Angeles Times* television columnist noted, had granted "television its first measure of artistic stature" with *Omnibus*, a series that aired on CBS from 1953 to 1956, on ABC from 1956 to 1957, and on NBC from 1958 to 1961. The producer, the columnist continued, had "consistently given [viewers] islands of quality in television's murky seas." Among these "islands" were broadcasts of Leonard Bernstein conducting the New York Philharmonic, Agnes de Mille, Leopold Stokowski, Pablo Casals, Marian Anderson, Dr. Seuss, and Orson Welles (the latter in a ninety-minute version of *King Lear*). Saudek accomplished all this, as well as the *Profiles in Courage* series itself, before the creation of the Public Broadcasting System and the Corporation for Public Broadcasting. By the end of his career Saudek had been awarded eleven Emmy Awards and seven Peabody Awards, in addition to serving as the founding president of the Museum of Broadcasting (now the Paley Center for Media) and as the head of

Robert Saudek discusses his ideas for the *Profiles in Courage* series with President Kennedy in 1961. (Courtesy of Steven Saudek and the Saudek family.)

the Library of Congress's Division of Motion Picture, Broadcasting and Recorded Sound.[1]

President Kennedy shared the general high regard for Saudek, whom he had met during the production of two *Omnibus* episodes in the 1950s, one of which ("Call It Courage") the then-senator narrated. Not surprisingly, many producers were eager to adapt *Profiles in Courage* to television—indeed, a one-time show adapted from the Andrew Johnson chapter of the book aired in spring 1956—but Saudek got the nod in February 1961 after he proposed the series to President Kennedy through Special Counsel to the President Theodore C. Sorensen. Their confidential negotiations continued through spring 1963. Meanwhile, the Kennedy administration selected Saudek to produce a closed-circuit television special that kicked off the fundraising for what came to be named the Kennedy Center in Washington, D.C.[2]

The contract for *Profiles in Courage* gave the president (and Sorensen, acting on his behalf) the right to approve the sponsors, publicity, and advertising for the series, as well as to approve any additional subjects not in Kennedy's book. The negotiations required payments to Kennedy in the form of a $5,000 signing payment, $13,500 on the broadcast of each episode, and 10 percent of the income from subsequent broadcasts. Per Kennedy's specifications, this income was to be paid to the Roman Catholic archbishop of Boston. After President Kennedy was assassinated, Cardinal Cushing directed that the funds go to the creation of Kennedy's presidential library in Boston.[3]

According to Saudek, it was television-savvy President Kennedy who insisted that the series consist of the then-standard twenty-six episodes. But the book's profiles did not provide enough material for a full season. Thus, one of the first challenges Saudek and his team faced was to find additional subjects beyond the five senators (such as Sam Houston and Robert A. Taft) covered in the book's main chapters and other figures briefly mentioned in Kennedy's penultimate chapter ("Other Men of Political Courage") such as Presidents John Adams, Andrew Johnson, and Woodrow Wilson. Moreover, Saudek told the press in March 1964, "President Kennedy did not think the series should be limited to political figures, as his book was. He felt that the show should demonstrate that courage is possible in any kind of job, at any time and regardless of social origin. He was insistent that by courage he meant non-physical courage— moral courage." Other individuals Saudek, Kennedy, and Sorensen considered portraying included Roger Williams, Tom Paine, Clara Barton, Harriet Tubman, Susan B. Anthony, Elizabeth Cady Stanton, Clarence Darrow, and Fiorello LaGuardia.[4]

Saudek's informal memoirs record that these names came from a list he and his associates "had moved swiftly" to prepare, "researching the biographies of politicians of [two and a half] centuries for acts of courage, preparing briefing papers on 50 American figures." When Saudek met with Kennedy to present them, he was hurried into the Oval Office, where Kennedy went over the list of suggested profiles while "a small knot of Cabinet officers waited in the outer office, their arms loaded with papers."[5]

The final lineup of profiles in the series was most notable for going beyond the book's focus on great white American men. Television historian Daniel Marcus's superb analysis of the series points out that women's rights and civil rights were not quite as central to Kennedy's political concerns when he published *Profiles in Courage* as they would become when he entered the White House. One television episode focused on the ex-slave abolitionist Frederick Douglass, the only African American in the series. Three shows built on Kennedy's and Sorensen's January 1958 *McCall's* article, "Three Women of Courage," published in response to the criticism that *Profiles in Courage* had neglected such figures. The three were Anne Hutchinson, the Puritan-era proponent of religious tolerance who was expelled from the Massachusetts Bay Colony; the ostracized New England teacher Prudence Crandall, who for eighteen months in the 1830s ran a school for African American girls; and pacifist Brooklyn Latin teacher Mary McDowell, who refused to sign a loyalty oath after America entered World War I.[6]

John M. Slaton was not on the first list of subjects Saudek brought to JFK in the White House, but he was on the schedule by summer 1963.[7] His profile was not a stretch to include. Kennedy's book briefly mentions one figure who closely resembled Slaton: Governor John Peter Altgeld of Illinois, who had in the late 1880s saved an anarchist from execution for participating in the Chicago Haymarket Riot of 1886 by reversing a guilty murder conviction on the grounds that the defendant had not received a fair trial. Like Slaton, Atgeld did so at the price of his own political career; *Profiles in Courage* devoted an episode to Altgeld as well.

Thus, Slaton's story fit perfectly with the ideas in Kennedy's book. In fact, when Sorensen read Don Mankiewicz's draft script for the Slaton episode in late January 1964, he wrote to Saudek that it was "excellent—the best thus far submitted. Assuming it is historically accurate in all respects, it will be an asset to your series—and I regret that President Kennedy and I did not have this material nine years ago for I am certain that he would have wished to include it in his book." In March 1964, eight months before the series began, Saudek singled out Slaton as an example of the way that the series had been able to expand the book's subjects and keep faith with its ideas.[8]

Two men advised Saudek on philosophical consistency and historical quality control for the series: Sorensen, who was officially credited as Kennedy's research associate for *Profiles in Courage* (at least one newspaper columnist suggested that Sorensen had ghostwritten it),[9] and Allan Nevins, DeWitt Clinton Professor of American History emeritus at Columbia University and a two-time Pulitzer Prize winner for biographies of Grover Cleveland and Hamilton Fish. Nevins, who had been the historical consultant for *Profiles in Courage* and for *Omnibus*, attended to the broad sweep of history as portrayed in the scripts, to nuances of interpretation, and to historical accuracy (the de Forest Research firm on the West Coast double-checked the details). In fact, Nevins contributed significantly to the Slaton episode's depiction of anti-Semitism.[10]

Bernard Weinraub, who later covered world news and the Hollywood beat for the *New York Times*, did most of the research. Weinraub's thorough work along with Sorensen's and Nevins's participation allowed Saudek to promise the press that the series would not depart from the facts. "When there are unrecorded conversations, we will allow the writers some latitude," he noted, "but we will not violate the spirit of the story." Indeed, historical accuracy was a keynote of the series's publicity, which highlighted cases whose dialogue was taken verbatim from the historical record.[11]

Yet, historical authenticity comprised just one-half of the series's appeal. The episodes were also advertised as "modern chronicle play[s]" such as those Shakespeare and his contemporaries wrote: "Each profile—in its fidelity to fact—is a *chronicle* of human courage, as manifested in a single personal act; but in its structure—scenes, acts, climax and denouement—each profile is a *play* capable of utilizing all the creative strength of the dramatic form." When he viewed a rough cut of the first episode—on Alabama senator Oscar Underwood—Saudek enthused that it had "a quality of great theatre about it such as I have never before seen in a television show . . . watching this show is like seeing a play. It is intricate, suspenseful, and filled with real characterization."[12]

This combination of historical verisimilitude and theatricality helped to make *Profiles in Courage* both compelling and informative. The entire idea of the book and the series embodied a broadly defined Kennedy-era liberal framework endorsing political progress built on the assumption that an informed public would be a wise, politically engaged citizenship. While the series was inspired by Kennedy's book, Marcus notes, it also functioned as an answer to FCC chairman Newton Minow's famous complaint that broadcast television in the early 1960s was a "vast wasteland." The series was seen as providing an antidote to the dumbing down of television, a civics lesson from American history.[13] It also had the singular advantage of being based on a book by the president who appointed Minow to his post.

Many television critics in the nation's newspapers and news weeklies shared Minow's viewpoint and had high hopes for *Profiles in Courage*. Paul Gardner of the *New York Times*, for example, wrote that the series "was not planned for the simple-minded viewers who sit beside their babble box day in, day out, watching comic strips performed by actors instead of reading bubbles above pen-and-ink characters." Its creators had hopes of "luring back to television the reasonably intelligent people, who, some sociologists believe, turned off the set five years ago," as well as attracting "the vague blob that has apparently lost all free will."[14] These high expectations, again, arose from Saudek's track record.

That record was built in part on the hard work of Saudek's New York–based team, including associate producer Walter Kerr, who later became the drama critic for the *New York Herald Tribune* and *New York Times*. Saudek later recalled that Kerr joined his production company to adapt Greek plays for *Omnibus*, and his contributions "gave authority to our dramatic productions." Another member of the Saudek team, Mary V. Ahern, had worked in the U.S. Army's World War II Chemical Warfare Service and ABC's Public Affairs Department. She had worked with Saudek on all his previous series and special broadcasts (particularly *Omnibus*, the Leonard Bernstein–New York Philharmonic broadcasts, the *Constitution* series, and *Life of Samuel Johnson*). For *Profiles in Courage*, she served again as script editor, an indispensable member of the team who provided keen criticism of screenplay drafts as the writers sent them in.

Yet, *Profiles in Courage* was a major departure from Saudek's earlier documentary and news programs. In fact, NBC insisted that Saudek hire a seasoned television producer to oversee production and suggested Saudek's ultimate choice: Gordon Oliver. A Hollywood veteran film and television actor since the 1930s, Oliver had turned producer in the 1950s and created shows such as *Peter Gunn* (for NBC) and, before that, the *Four Star Playhouse*. He would go on to produce the Robert Wagner hit series *It Takes a Thief*. Oliver later explained that Saudek had hired him to give the shows "dramatic flair. He didn't want to be merely recounting incidents or giving viewers a straight history lesson as in some television projects." "Dramatic flair" meant Hollywood film production values and energy. Oliver's success is apparent in *Life*'s review of the series, which recognized that *Profiles in Courage* "might easily have emerged as pretentious,

Actor-producer Gordon Oliver was in charge of producing *Profiles in Courage* at Desilu Studios. (Courtesy of the Academy of Motion Picture Arts and Sciences.)

sermonizing, silhouettes" but instead caught "the magic of the book."[15] Oliver was involved in planning and executing every phase of production in Hollywood, while Saudek remained primarily in his Rockefeller Center office in New York. Oliver also provided the brief prologue and penultimate voiceover narrations for each episode.

Chief among Oliver's assistants was Harvard graduate Michael Ritchie, a documentary crew veteran and future film director who is now probably best remembered as the director of the Robert Redford films *Downhill Racer* (1969) and *The Candidate* (1972), as well as other films with a semi-documentary style, in addition to popular comedies such as *The Bad News Bears* (1976, starring Walter Matthau, the star of the Slaton episode) and the Chevy Chase comedy vehicle *Fletch* (1985). Saudek saw in Ritchie a fresh, creative young man who was "enthusiastic, practical, witty, mature." Working in Hollywood alongside Oliver, Ritchie served officially as associate producer on *Profiles in Courage*—he provided input on script and production development; he was instrumental in helping Saudek hire Oliver and set up the Hollywood operation at Desilu Studios; and he helped Oliver secure the series credit sequence. This last featured an eagle and a ringing bell designed by famed title designer Saul Bass and

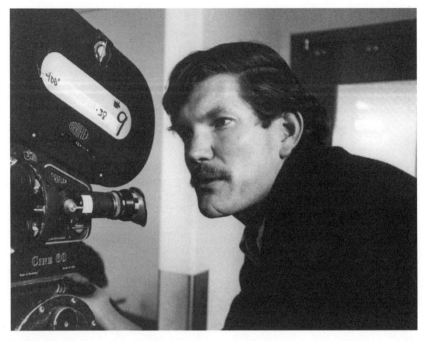

Michael Ritchie, Saudek's and Oliver's assistant, went on to become a director in his own right. (Courtesy of the Academy of Motion Picture Arts and Sciences.)

used "The Boys of Wexford," an Irish air that Patricia Kennedy Lawford identified as President Kennedy's favorite tune.[16]

Saudek and Oliver set about hiring the best talent available to script, perform, and direct the episodes. Their first choices were stage playwrights, including Lorraine Hansberry (of *A Raisin in the Sun* fame) to write an episode on Harriet Tubman (never produced) and Robert Bolt (who had written the play—and would write the script for the film of—*A Man for All Seasons*) to script the show on Anne Hutchinson. Saudek also approached southern playwrights Horton Foote (for the episode on Andrew Johnson) and Lillian Hellman to draft the Slaton episode.[17] None proved available given Saudek's limited budget.

The writers Saudek actually hired were highly skilled film and television industry professionals. Perhaps the best known today is Hollywood screenwriter and blacklistee Walter Bernstein, who in the early 1960s was just beginning to rebuild his career and who later wrote the screenplay for the blacklist black comedy *The Front* (1976), starring Woody Allen.

NBC initially balked at Saudek's decision to hire Bernstein to write the episode on Richard T. Ely, a pro-labor, pro-union University of Wisconsin professor who nearly lost his job for his beliefs, but the Saudek team, particularly Mary V. Ahern, stood firm. Indeed, during the early preparations for the series, Michael Ritchie created a list including several liberal/left, previously blacklisted writers, including Nedrick Young (who had coauthored the script for the interracial drama *The Defiant Ones* [1958]); Carl Foreman (who had, under a pseudonym, cowritten the Oscar-winning screenplay for *The Bridge on the River Kwai* [1957]); and, most striking of all, Robert Rossen (coauthor of the script for *They Won't Forget*).[18] Saudek Associates' willingness to consider—and, in one instance, hire—a writer such as Rossen provides the most tangible link between *Profiles in Courage* and Warner Bros.'s social consciousness movies such as *They Won't Forget*.

For directors the Saudek team hired a variety of talents, ranging from Ritchie and another future feature film director, Daniel Petrie (who would complete the direction of *The Murder of Mary Phagan* [1988]), to theater veteran José Quintero and actor-director Cyril Ritchard. Most of the episode directors were television series regulars such as Sherman Marks, Michael O'Herlihy, and Lamont Johnson, who received the Television and Film Directors' Award for Best Television Director of 1964.

The actors chosen for the episodes included prominent stage, screen, and anthology actors such as Rosemary Harris as pacifist Mary S. McDowell (flown in for the week's shooting from a stage engagement opposite Sir Laurence Olivier in London), David McCallum as John Adams, Robert Hooks as Frederick Douglass (along with Claudia McNeil and Frederick O'Neal in secondary roles), Tom Bosley as George Norris, and Wendy Hiller as Anne Hutchinson.[19] Kennedy in-law and Hollywood "Rat Pack" member Peter Lawford starred in the episode on Brigadier General Alexander William Doniphan, who refused a superior's command to execute Mormon leader Joseph Smith. Walter Matthau portrayed both John M. Slaton and Andrew Johnson.

By November 1963 the Saudek team had everything in place: NBC had approved the budget; Saudek Associates had assigned half the episodes to writers; Desilu Studios had been engaged for ten months beginning in January 1964; and the first episode, on Senator Oscar Underwood of Alabama, was set to begin filming on January 27, 1964.[20] Kennedy's assassination on November 22, 1963, brought production preparations to a standstill for several weeks. Saudek tactfully waited until the first week of December to write Sorensen regarding the necessity to move forward in a timely fashion: "I cannot express to you how hesitant I am about intruding on your thoughts and responsibilities at this time. It is because I am determined to make *Profiles in Courage* one of the finest living memorials to President Kennedy that I do write to you now." Kennedy's death had also produced some strains in Saudek's relationship with NBC. As the Saudek team prepared for the series's principal photography start date in late January 1964, NBC held up payment for the Slaton episode on the grounds that Kennedy's death made his approval of the topic impossible to obtain; the network also attempted to cut the series back to eighteen episodes. Saudek later attributed the network's immediate attempt "to cancel the series" to the fact that Lyndon B. Johnson, "no admirer of Kennedy's," was now president. Only Sorensen's assurance that Kennedy had delegated authority to approve new subjects (he had actually approved Slaton before his assassination), as well as Saudek's airtight contract, persuaded NBC to go forward.[21]

President Kennedy and NBC had agreed that the series would not air until late fall 1964. This decision was ostensibly to avoid the appearance of partisanship in an election year, although the subjects profiled were not exclusively Democrats. Associate producer Michael Ritchie admitted to a *Washington Post* reporter that Saudek also delayed the premiere to avoid the potential embarrassment to Kennedy before the 1964 election of not having a sponsor lined up for the series. ABC had already had to postpone a series based on Harry Truman's memoirs because of lack of support. When *Profiles in Courage* premiered in October 1964, only the Canadian company Aluminum, Ltd.—which had also backed the *Omnibus* series—was willing to sponsor the series. Apparently, NBC never was able to persuade another company, including any American company, to sign on, in spite of the general adulation of Kennedy after his death.[22]

Regardless of its lack of sponsors, critics judged *Profiles in Courage* a major success in the realm of public affairs and educational programming, a rare item in the schedules of the three major broadcast networks—ABC, NBC, and CBS. Reviews of the first two episodes, which aired in November (Oscar Underwood and Mary McDowell), were virtually unanimous in their praise. The *Los Angeles Times* called *Profiles in Courage* "unquestionably . . . commercial television's most distinguished weekly show—perhaps the only real program of stature this year." A February 1965 piece in the same paper called the series television's "best bet" "for high quality every week, for stories that have importance and intellectual content and for drama that is always staffed by excellent performers." Jack Gould of the *New York Times* hailed the first episode as "the season's most substantial and distinguished hour of theater." The *San Francisco Chronicle*'s television critic felt that the Underwood episode "provided, in its best moments, more political convention excitement than all three networks were able to muster for the nomination in 1964." The critics writing for national news magazines were likewise impressed. *Newsweek* noted that criticisms that the series was all talk and little action "ignore the brilliant exploration of history that makes its characters engrossingly human"; the magazine dubbed the series as a whole "superb." *Time* and the *Saturday Review* agreed.[23]

In short, *Profiles in Courage* conformed to what major television critics saw as the best possible television programming. Not surprisingly, the series ultimately won a prestigious George Foster Peabody Award, a Silver Gavel Award from the American Bar Association, and several other awards and citations. Newton Minow himself wrote the Peabody citation: "A Pulitzer prize–winning book written by a President of the United States is a formidable challenge to the television producer. To Robert Saudek and his associates, and the National Broadcasting Corporation, we present a Peabody Award for their faithful, artistic, and sensitive portrayal of some of the most moving episodes in American history. By adapting this book to the television screen, Mr. Saudek and NBC have added the vital dimensions of sight and sound to enrich the nation's understanding of its past and to deepen the nation's perceptions of its heritage." Minow had already written to Saudek in February 1964 that he thought the series "the best thing on television in years. I think it's outstanding in every respect, and only wish it could be repeated over and over again so that every American could see it." He informed Saudek that his entire family found a recent program on Daniel Webster "exceptionally fine," and joked, "Can you get us into the Nielsen sample?"[24]

If the approval of the man who termed television a "vast wasteland" was not enough, Saudek could also take great satisfaction in the fact that Kennedy family members and Theodore Sorensen reacted positively to the series episodes they watched. He could also capitalize on the series's educational potential, as NBC wisely sent junior and senior high school instructors more than 100,000 "teachers' guides" sparking interest in possibly renting 16 mm copies of the episodes when the series's network broadcast ended. Adults learned history from the series as well. Robert Kennedy, still serving as attorney general in the Johnson administration, was apparently surprised to learn from the Oscar Underwood episode that half of the 1924 Democratic delegation from Michigan were KKK members.[25]

Great reviews could not ensure high ratings, of course. Aired from 6:30 to 7:30 on Sunday nights and leading into *Walt Disney's Wonderful World of Color*, *Profiles in Courage* was, as *Variety* noted, "slotted at a good time for family viewing but, significantly, still outside the primetime precincts." Its market share was low in overall terms—at most, 19 percent of American homes watching television at the time of its broadcast. This was a high score for an informational show, however—certainly higher than any of the *Omnibus* episodes ever achieved. *Profiles in Courage*'s straight ratings (a percentage of all American homes, whether they watched television or not) was typically 12 percent. (Not surprisingly, the Washington, D.C., ratings doubled those in the rest of the country.) The series's biggest audience, estimated at 15.5 million viewers, was for the "Frederick W. Douglass" episode aired on January 31, 1965, suggesting considerable public interest in seeing African American history dramatized on prime-time television. The series's overall success was such that Saudek Associates contracted with Bantam Books to publish eight episode scripts as a book, *Eight Great Americans*, which had sold ninety thousand copies by June 1966.[26]

Without question, the *Profiles in Courage* series was appreciated on its merits; yet viewers and critics alike were also enthusiastic about the show as a very public delineation of John F. Kennedy's legacy to a nation still in mourning. The premiere of *Profiles in Courage* roughly coincided with the first anniversary of Kennedy's assassination and the flourishing of the Camelot image of Kennedy's family and White House. At least one television critic suggested that the series could have even more relevance to contemporary America: "Why not have [an episode on] JFK himself? Surely, his standing up to Khrushchev on Cuba, his battle for civil rights, his determination to wipe out poverty and his efforts to advance this country's goals more than qualify him." NBC actually considered this idea but decided not to pursue it.[27]

Even without a Kennedy episode, every profile in the series enshrined a high-minded individual whom Americans could admire for embodying the greatest values of American democracy. In the Saudek team's interpretation of history, Governor John M. Slaton fit right in.

The John M. Slaton Episode: Preproduction

Bernard Weinraub undertook painstaking research in preparation for the Slaton episode. He obtained copies of the major publications on the case dating back to the 1910s, including the 1915 *Forum* article that publicized the view that anti-Semitism was responsible for Frank's death. Weinraub also consulted C. Vann Woodward's biography of Thomas Watson; *Night Fell on Georgia* (1956); and Franklin M. Garrett's *Atlanta and Environs*, a multivolume history of the city.[28] Saudek's attorney obtained pages from the trial record of Conley's and others' testimony about the blood found near the lathe machine that had been mistakenly identified as Mary Phagan's. Weinraub himself read the memoirs of individuals with direct or indirect connections to the case. He secured from the Anti-defamation League Archives personal correspondence relating to the case, such as a copy of Lucille Frank's note begging Slaton to commute Frank's sentence and Slaton's own August 1915 letter to Atlanta's Bishop Warren A. Candler asking for the bishop's public support. Weinraub even arranged to interview Slaton's nephew and namesake in New York.

As he assembled information about the case, Weinraub prepared memos for the production team on particular points of history. He constructed a detailed chronology of the case—annotated as to uncertain incidents (such as Watson's offer of support for Slaton's U.S. Senate bid if Slaton would reject Frank's appeal)—and other details. Weinraub also added his own insights into key aspects of Slaton's part in the Phagan-Frank story, including the reasons Slaton lost his bid for the Senate in 1914 and the conflict-of-interest charge raised against Slaton when he commuted Frank's sentence.

Weinraub reviewed the script drafts and checked them against his research. "We have done a lot of digging in preparation for this script," he wrote to Ahern after reading the first draft, "and on the whole I should say that the digging has paid off. In all that really matters, the script is quite accurate factually." After reviewing some other points of fact, he observed that where two sources conflicted (in this case Slaton's recollections of the mob violence aimed against him versus an account in the *New York Times*), "we are justified in combining the two as drama demands." Weinraub concluded, "None of these condensations and slight alterations are really serious, and are probably justified by dramatic lisence [*sic*]. No one really knows what happened, for no mature historical investigation has ever been made. But we should be aware of . . . changes from known fact (these are very few) or extrapolation from sketchy knowledge (these are necessarily frequent)."[29] Weinraub affirmed Saudek's principle of allowing "the writers some latitude" and his determination not to "violate the spirit of the story."

To write the Slaton episode the Saudek team had hired Don M. Mankiewicz, the son of legendary Hollywood screenwriter Herman Mankiewicz (most famously, coauthor of *Citizen Kane* [1941]). Mankiewicz had attended law school, had been a reporter for armed forces publications during World War II, and had been a press agent for Alfred Hitchcock's 1949 Ingrid Bergman vehicle *Under Capricorn* before writing novels and scripts for such 1950s anthology dramas as the *Kraft Television Theater* and *Playhouse 90*. He was also active in New York Democratic circles and even ran for public office in the 1960s.

Two of Don Mankiewicz's earlier projects seemed particularly pertinent to the Slaton story. His second novel, the Harper Prize–winning *Trial*, concerned a sensational rape-murder case involving a Mexican defendant and white victim, mob violence (and a near lynching), and a defense attorney who tries to rig the case to benefit the Communist Party. Mankiewicz adapted *Trial* into a 1955 feature film starring Glenn Ford, Arthur Kennedy, and Dorothy McGuire. Mankiewicz's Academy Award–nominated screenplay for *I Want to Live!* (1958; directed by Robert Wise), about Barbara Graham—a b-girl, petty thief, and gambler executed in California in the 1930s for the murder of an elderly woman—was also relevant to the Slaton story. Susan Hayward received an Oscar for Best Actress for her portrayal of Graham, who was convicted on the basis of circumstantial evidence in part because of tabloid-style press coverage of her trial. Both *Trial* and *I Want to Live!* criticized the press distortions and political motivations that often accompanied the prosecution of sensationalized murder cases. Both Barbara Graham and Leo Frank underwent comparable ordeals that resulted in their deaths, although Graham was executed by the state rather than by vigilantes.[30]

Casting was also crucial to the episode's success. Walter Matthau at this time had enjoyed fourteen years of steady work in supporting roles on television and in films. He had played a villain in *The Kentuckian* (1955), a sympathetic school coach in *Bigger than Life* (1956), and a hawkish political scientist in *Fail Safe* (1964). His breakthrough came two years after his appearance in *Profiles in Courage*, however, when Matthau received an Oscar for his supporting role in Billy Wilder's *The Fortune Cookie* (1966) as the shyster lawyer brother-in-law opposite Jack Lemmon's injured, lovelorn television cameraman. Matthau is surely best remembered for reteaming with Lemmon for the film version of Neil Simon's play *The Odd Couple* in 1968.[31]

The only other prominent cast member in the Slaton episode was Michael Constantine, cast as Tom Watson, the politically powerful anti-Frank crusader. Constantine had regular work as a guest star on many popular series and later starred as a high school principal in the 1969 comedy series *Room 222*; more recently, he appeared as the proud Greek father in the 2002 sleeper hit *My Big Fat Greek Wedding*. Thus, casting for the Slaton episode settled on a Ukrainian American Jewish star (Matthau was born Matuschanskayaski) and a Greek American actor for the leading roles of two aristocratic sons of the South.

Robert Gist, a veteran of major television series in the 1950s and 1960s such as *Peter Gunn*, *The Naked City*, *Route 66*, and *The Twilight Zone*, directed the Slaton episode (and later the "Daniel Webster" episode as well). Gist supervised principal photography on the Slaton episode from March 18 through March 25, 1964, using Desilu's "40 Acre Ranch" for exteriors (of the courthouse and the statehouse where Slaton's successor, Nat Harris, is sworn in as governor) and Desilu sound stages for every other scene, including the set of the pencil factory. The completed fifty-minute episode aired nine months later, on December 20, 1964.

"Governor John M. Slaton"

The "Governor John M. Slaton" episode dramatizes the later phases of the Phagan-Frank case. In the opening scene, a mob has gathered outside the Fulton County Courthouse to await the verdict in Leo Frank's trial. The singer Fiddlin' John Carson (Jon Locke), here blind although the historical John Carson was not, strums his guitar and sings his infamous "Ballad of Mary Phagan" while a rabble-rouser (David Bond) stirs the crowd into cries for vengeance against Leo Frank for the death of Mary Phagan. Inside the courtroom, Judge Leonard Roan (Donald Foster) confides to his colleague Judge Powell (Whit Bissell), "To me, the man's [Frank's] innocence has been demonstrated to a mathematical certainty."

After the series credits, an expository breakfast scene sets up the situation two years later. Talking with his wife, Sallie (Betsy Jones-Moreland); his confidante and brother-in-law, John Grant (Frank Marth); and his secretary, Martin Burley (Anthony Costello), Slaton expresses his desire to remain in politics after he steps down as governor in a few weeks. He also reveals his lack of opinion on the Frank case and his uncertainty regarding what he would do were Leo Frank to appeal to him for clemency.

The scene shifts to Slaton's office, where Tom Watson arrives immediately after the Georgia Prison Commission has rejected Frank's appeal for commutation of his sentence. Watson urges Slaton to likewise reject Frank's appeal for mercy, suggesting that Roan's belief in Frank's innocence was shaped by outside influences. Watson also threatens Slaton with the powerful opposition of his followers should he grant Frank's appeal and offers his support for the governor's U.S. Senate candidacy should Slaton reject it. When Slaton refuses to do Watson's bidding, Watson threatens to publicize Slaton's law partnership with Luther Z. Rosser, Frank's initial chief defense attorney, as a conflict of interest—even though Watson acknowledges that Slaton is not truly so compromised. Slaton throws him out.

After briefly conferring with Judge Powell, who affirms Judge Roan's rectitude, Slaton decides to call a hearing of interested parties on the Frank case: two speakers for Frank and two against him. Slaton subsequently decides to review the case personally and works late into the night with Burley, setting forth the issues of the case and pondering Judge Roan's belief in Frank's innocence. Slaton infers that Conley might have confessed his guilt to his attorney, Wheeler, who in turn could have confided in Roan. Slaton, Burley, and Grant briefly interview Wheeler about Conley's possible confession of guilt, but the attorney refuses to answer these questions, respecting attorney-client privilege.

Slaton, Grant, and Burley next visit the pencil factory, where they read Conley's testimony about Frank's murder of Phagan, inspect the lathe machine where Mary Phagan allegedly hit her head, and test the elevator on which Conley alleged that he and Frank had carried her body to the basement. The men are surprised and shaken by their discovery that the elevator stops only when it actually hits the basement floor. Given this fact, and the fact that Conley claimed Phagan was bleeding profusely when he and Frank took her down in the elevator but no blood was found there, Slaton infers that Conley committed perjury on the stand. Slaton decides to commute Frank's death sentence even as John Grant predicts that Frank will be lynched if he does. Slaton asks Sallie for her approval, noting that his actions could cost him his political career, his livelihood, and perhaps even his life. Her answer is affirmative.

Slaton delivers his decision to the press, and public reaction is as he anticipated. He is booed at the inauguration of Governor Nat Harris, and he and Sallie are assaulted by a mob as they get into his car after the proceedings. That evening, he entertains friends at his home, refusing to be cowed by the mob assembling outside. A newspaper headline reports that troops had to be called in to quell the riot; a swish pan to another story features an actual photo of Leo Frank lynched under a headline announcing that news. In the series epilogue, Slaton affirms at a San Francisco press conference the rightness of his decision to commute Frank's death sentence. The narrator informs us that Slaton practiced law for the rest of his life and never again held public office.

Mankiewicz's script for the John Slaton episode followed the television show's general formula and the book's approach to history: most episodes focused on a charismatic protagonist. Saudek recognized the appeal of a hero who "dominate[s] the events and deliberately shapes them." Television historian Daniel Marcus notes that Saudek's "decision led to a focus on personal commitment and charismatic display, rather than on the workings of organized groups within a context of institutionalized power."[32] Accordingly, the Slaton episode downplays the larger forces at work—industrialization, modernization, class warfare, the yellow press, sectionalism, and anti-Semitism—to stress Slaton's heroic stand.

Slaton, like his counterparts in other episodes, remains true to his principles and ideals regardless of outside pressure. Also like the others, Slaton embodies Kennedy's notions of moderation and pragmatism in politics and the late president's desire to establish some kind of consensus to end the nation's turmoil. Marcus argues that "the series frames the struggles of the individual heroes within a narrative of national progress that has led ultimately to a contemporary sense of civic-minded nationalism."[33] That sense of progress was essential to the series's success. The unmistakable conclusion of the "Governor John M. Slaton" episode is that Slaton's unpopular decision in the Frank case placed him ahead of his time.

The Historical Record

Weinraub's careful research is apparent throughout the "Governor John M. Slaton" episode. For example, Sallie Slaton's agreement with Slaton's decision on the Frank case appears in Judge Arthur Powell's memoir, which Weinraub read and which includes the detail of Sallie kissing Slaton, as she does in the show, after she tells him: "I'd rather be the widow of a brave man than the wife of a coward." Weinraub also shared with writer

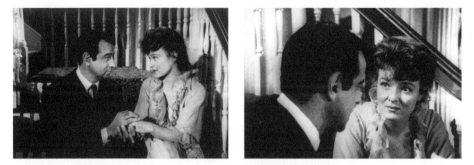

Slaton asks for Sallie's permission to commute Leo Frank's sentence. She replies, "I'd rather be the widow of a brave man than the wife of a coward."

Don Mankiewicz a copy of Slaton's 1953 correspondence with Samuel Boorstin affirming that Sallie formulated her assent in the precise words uttered in the episode.[34] Like Oscar Micheaux, Mankiewicz found suitable dialogue in the historical record.

Mankiewicz found more usable verbiage in Slaton's twenty-nine-page statement to the press announcing his decision to commute Frank's sentence to life imprisonment. In the episode, Slaton's statement borrows lines from the end of Slaton's actual summation. Slaton reads:

> Responsibility rests where the power is reposed. Judge Roan calls to me from another world to do that which he should have done. I can endure misconstruction, abuse, and condemnation. But I cannot stand the constant companionship of an accusing conscience.
>
> This case has been marked by doubt. The trial judge doubted. Two judges of the supreme court of the state of Georgia doubted. Two judges of the Supreme Court of the United States doubted. One of the three prison commissioners doubted. Acting in accordance with what I believe to be my duty under the circumstances, it is ordered that the sentence of Leo Frank is commuted from the death penalty to imprisonment for life.

Slaton's actual summation reads, in part:

> The performance of my duty under the Constitution is a matter of my conscience. The responsibility rests where the power is reposed. Judge Roan, with that awful sense of responsibility, which probably came over him as he thought of that Judge before Whom he would shortly appear, calls to me from another world to request that I do that which he should have done. I can endure mis-

construction, abuse and condemnation, but I cannot stand the constant companionship of an accusing conscience, which would remind me in every thought that I, as governor of Georgia, failed to do what I thought to be right. There is a territory "BEYOND A REASONABLE DOUBT and absolute certainty," for which the law provides in allowing life imprisonment instead of execution. This case has been marked by doubt. The trial judge doubted. Two judges of the supreme court of the state of Georgia doubted. Two judges of the Supreme Court of the United States doubted. One of the three prison commissioners doubted.

In my judgment, by granting a commutation in this case, I am sustaining the jury, the judge and the appellate tribunals and at the same time am discharging that duty which is placed on me by the constitution of the state.[35]

Slaton's repetition of the verb "doubt" ties the episode together—from Judge Roan's early comment on Frank's innocence through Slaton's own questions about why Roan would feel certain Frank was innocent. Slaton's statement to the press in the episode also is notable for what it omits. Beyond the eloquent phrase about "an accusing conscience"— which would serve as a keynote for the writers of *The Murder of Mary Phagan* in 1988—Slaton asserts that he is upholding the judgment of certain of his predecessors.

A similar reliance on the historical record informs Slaton's dialogue in the episode's epilogue, in which he affirms his belief that he did the right thing even though Frank died as a result. This epilogue underwent dramatic changes in its various drafts. Mankiewicz originally envisioned using documentary footage of Slaton's 1956 Atlanta funeral, with the narrator commenting that Georgia flew its state flags at half-mast. The Saudek team sent Nevins the first draft script after Ahern, Kerr, Oliver, Ritchie, and Saudek had gone over it. (Sorensen received a copy at this time as well.) Allan Nevins discouraged the use of this ending, noting that such a tribute was routine at the death of a former governor. Although Nevins did not specify an alternative ending, the very issue of a conclusion inspired him to reflect on Georgia as it was in 1915 and Georgia in 1963:

Georgia has seen an approach to a social revolution since Tom Watson's death. The county unit system is heavily damaged—is going if not gone. In Atlanta all minorities are now justly respected. The principal hotels and motels have been opened to Negroes. I know this because the Civil War Centennial Commission holds a meeting there next May, and we refused to thing [sic] of going to the city unless it assured equal accommodations to blacks and whites. Jews are respected and admired as in other cities. The Atlanta Constitution and Journal have been among the most liberal dailies of the nation. Everything that Slaton stood for has moved forward. Could not this be brought out in a way that would be more effective than the customary half-mast flag?[36]

Nevins's comments affirm the episode's view that Slaton was more enlightened than his fellow Georgians crying for Frank's blood. Yet, acknowledging the present progressiveness of Atlanta would take the program too far afield from its focus on courageous individuals from the past.

Mankiewicz instead created an ending to the program based on Slaton's actual words and actions. Several days after Harris's inauguration, the Slatons left town on a previously scheduled vacation and heeded advice that they not return to Georgia anytime soon. The episode's epilogue rejoins Slaton in San Francisco in August 1915, where he and Sallie actually vacationed. Inside a hotel room, Slaton puffs on a cigar, waves around a rolled-up newspaper, and speaks to local reporters about Frank's lynching. He makes several pronouncements, all of which they jot down eagerly: "Any man proved to be engaged in the lynching should be treated as a murderer. Any man who *approves* the lynching is no true Georgian and should be driven from the state. As should any newspaper which condones this *utter disgrace* to civilization." These comments are a barely paraphrased version of Slaton's comments to the California Civic League: "The act was a consummate outrage and every man engaged in the lynching should be hanged for he is an assassin. . . . Any man who approves of this action of this mob of murderers is unworthy to be a Georgian. Any man or newspaper who condones this offense ought to be driven out of the state."[37]

A San Francisco reporter had paraphrased John Grant's earlier comment to Slaton—that pardoning Frank would only change the locale of his execution from a prison to a tree—which constituted the most powerful criticism about Slaton's course of action. Adding flames to that fire, the San Francisco reporter now notes that commuting Frank's sentence made him "just as dead" and "his death even more horrible" than a state execution. Slaton disagrees: "I am *ashamed*. Every true Georgian must be deeply ashamed that this lynching did take place. But his execution by the state would have been something far more shameful. . . . [Music begins.] Brutal as these words may sound, for Frank to have been hanged by the state of Georgia would have been worse than he was [*sic*] lynched by a mob. Lynching strikes at the *body* of civilization; execution without proper cause strikes at the soul." Slaton's final comments in the episode are again taken almost verbatim from Slaton's actual talk in San Francisco: "I would prefer Frank to be lynched by a mob rather than that he be hanged by judicial mistake. One attacks the soul of civilization; the other merely reaches the body."[38]

After these pronouncements from Slaton, the series narrator wraps up the episode: "To permit the death of an innocent man was unthinkable to Governor Slaton. An outright pardon would have required the disclosure of privileged information. So the course he chose was a just one." This final narration forcefully lays out the ways in which Slaton could be said to occupy the "vital center" that Arthur Schlesinger delineated in his 1949 book of that name: Tom Watson, John Grant, and Martin Burley implored the governor not to touch Frank's appeal, and if he considered it, not to pardon him. Wheeler's refusal to divulge information about his client Jim Conley denied Slaton the grounds for an outright pardon. This positioned him as taking a principled stand between two extreme courses of action—consigning Frank to his execution, on the one hand, and freeing him, on the other. This final narration asserting Slaton's wisdom has less impact than it might have had because we have never seen or heard Slaton considering the possibility of an outright pardon.

Even the concluding narration, which, typical of the entire series, provides information on the courageous individual's career and other reflections on his or her actions, recites the historical record accurately. The camera tracks in from a long shot of Slaton talking with the reporters, cigar in hand, to a medium close-up: "John Marshall Slaton returned to Georgia as he had planned. But his unpopular decision of June 21, 1915, left him entirely without support. Tom Watson was elected to the Senate. John Slaton spent the last half of his life in political obscurity." Indeed, after the Slatons' extended trip in summer and fall of 1915, and until his death in 1955, Slaton continued to practice law in Atlanta. Slaton also held several prominent positions in Georgia's legal community. He was president of the Georgia Bar Association from 1928 to 1929, chair of the Board of Law Examiners for twenty-nine years—a post he attributed to the legal community's respect for his judgment in the Frank case—and a member of the General Council of the American Bar Association. He was also a member of the Fulton County Public Library Board in the 1930s that oversaw the work of the city's film censor. On his death, Slaton received several respectful obituaries, including one on the editorial page of the *Atlanta Constitution*, which had never taken Frank's side in the case.[39]

"Double Caution"—Depicting Leo Frank's Lynching

Excerpts from the historical record helped to make the case that Slaton was indeed a profile in courage, but the episode's creators faced many other challenges in telling his story. How to depict Leo Frank's lynching was perhaps the most straightforward one.

Using a device common to low-budget productions (such as Oscar Micheaux's *Murder in Harlem*), the filmmakers inserted a newspaper headline—instead of a costly crowd action scene—to depict the police's response to the mob outside Slaton's home. From a headline reading "State Police Disperse Mob" the camera immediately whip-pans to another one reading "Brutal Lynching." The accompanying image in the paper is an actual photo of Frank's limp body hanging from a tree. Although the image appears on-screen for only a second before the camera quickly zooms back to take in the entire front page for another second or two, its impact is palpable. It is shocking. By quickly cutting from headline to headline, the filmmakers showed the cause and effect of mob unrest and vigilante violence. Unlike *They Won't Forget*, the episode makes no visual substitutions for the brutal act itself.

The decision to use that lynching photo was, of course, controversial for Saudek Associates and NBC. Mankiewicz's first draft script called for a fully staged scene, but one that delayed the revelation of the lynching victim's identity:

III—56: FULL SHOT OAK TREE

The very end of the Frank lynching. We cannot see who has been lynched. Now, as we move in, the body is cut down, drops to the ground. A struggle. A man comes forward and deliberately drives his heel into the dead man's face. As the body is turned over, carried away, we see the face. This is not Slaton. Over this scene, we will superimpose the single word "lynch." Then as the scene itself fades, we will pull back to see another *New York Times* front page, this one describing the lynching of Leo Frank.[40]

The possibility that the lynched man might be Slaton is fleeting, but for an instant the two men are equated. A Marietta man, Robert E. Lee Howell Jr., did drive the heel of his shoe into Frank's face.[41]

At the command of NBC's Standards and Practices Department (then called the Broadcast Standards Department), the filmmakers opted to use only the newspaper headline and photo. As the financier of the series and

Newspaper headlines were used to reveal the handling of the case and lynching.

A whip pan leads to this image of a fake newspaper with an actual photo of Frank's lynching. The show's creators had to carefully calibrate how long to leave this disturbing image onscreen.

its distributor, NBC was entitled to have input on the shows, although the network's creative involvement was typically minor. Some of their suggestions the Saudek team ignored; others, they could not.[42] On reading Mankiewicz's first version of Frank's lynching, one NBC employee advised the series creators: "Please caution against use of visual or aural effects which would shock or alarm the viewer. Double caution must be used in the handling of this scene, don't show Frank's body swinging from the end of a rope, don't show the body drop to the ground, and if we must see the face, please caution that the mouth and eyes are closed. Acceptability of this scene will be established at rough-cut viewing." After receiving this advice, Oliver and Ritchie substituted the version of the lynching used in the episode.[43] The program fades out after the image of the newspaper front page, but the photo's powerful impact remains: it is, after all, the actual corpse of Leo Frank hanging from the tree. John Grant's prediction in an earlier scene—that Slaton's commutation would only change the location of Frank's execution from a gallows to a tree— has come true.

Slaton's Momentous Decision

Yet another element of the case that required some creative thinking from Saudek's team involved the actual evidence Slaton would discover as a basis for deciding that Conley must have committed perjury. Noting that Conley told two versions of how Mary Phagan came to be killed—one before the trial and one at the trial—Slaton decides to visit the factory with Grant and Burley to determine which version is false. They go at night (to avoid a "howling mob," Slaton explains, but the scene was actually staged to create a more visually striking, low-lit image on a set that would require minimal dressing for principal photography). Slaton actually did visit the factory (twice, in daylight) during his deliberations. On the second day of his hearings, accompanied by Police Chief Beavers; Hugh Dorsey; and Frank's new attorney, William Schley Howard, Slaton examined Frank's desk and office, the lathe machine in the metal room where Phagan allegedly hit her head after she and Frank struggled, the elevator, and the basement where Mary's body had been found. Slaton returned to the factory during the period when he was reviewing the documents pertaining to Frank's situation. Logically, Mankiewicz combined the two visits into one for the episode.

As the elevator in the pencil factory descends, a series of close-ups and hand-held shots show Slaton trying frantically to stop it by flicking switches. The elevator does not stop, however, until it hits the ground with a violence that sends the men reeling into each other. After the elevator rises back up to the first floor, Slaton recalls that Mary Phagan had a deep wound on her head that must have bled profusely. He points out that the factory elevator was never cleaned (a detail Mankiewicz likely gleaned from *Night Fell on Georgia*), and that Conley had wrapped Phagan's body in a thin cloth (none of Mankiewicz's sources mentioned the thickness of the cloth). Mankiewicz here included some of Conley's trial testimony, which Slaton reads verbatim in the scene, that Mary Phagan's "hands . . . went down easily"—that is, rigor mortis had not set in when her body was conveyed to the basement.[44]

The detail on which Slaton focuses in the episode—the absence of blood on the factory elevator—was never an issue in the Frank team's actual appeal to Slaton. Don Mankiewicz here wove together several strands of key evidence that Slaton had double-checked when he visited the factory in June 1915. At the actual commutation hearings, Slaton had heard the argument of Howard that no blood appeared on Mary Phagan's dress above the waist. This evidence suggested that her deep head wound could not have been caused, as Conley alleged, by hitting the lathe machine when she and Frank struggled.[45] More likely it resulted from a blow to her head committed somewhere else, and by her murderer.

Slaton's June 1915 statement accompanying his decision to commute Frank's sentence outlined all the evidence suggesting that Frank might not be guilty (after listing the evidence for his guilt). Specifically, he was impressed that the hair at the lathe machine could not be identified as Mary Phagan's—so there may have been no struggle at all between Phagan and Frank—and he doubted that Frank could have committed the murder and then done a perfect job of bookkeeping for the next several hours. The biggest reason to commute Frank's conviction to life imprisonment, however, involved Jim Conley's very likely perjured testimony. To begin, there were Conley's differing affidavits. To this could be added the similarities in vocabulary and phrasing that Conley's attorney, William Smith, and Smith's schoolteacher wife detected in the murder notes found beside Mary Phagan's body and in Conley's obscene, utterly explicit love letters to Annie Maude Carter written while he was in prison serving his sentence as an accomplice to Leo Frank. (Slaton invited Smith to his Buckhead home during his deliberations to discuss these matters further.) Slaton also took due note of the possibility that the pad on which the murder notes were written could have been from the factory basement—and hence need not have been written at Frank's dictation in his office, as Conley contended. Slaton dismissed out of hand Conley's allegations that Frank was a sexual pervert and the factory girls' testimony that he was overly flirtatious and physical with them.

And then there was the matter of "the shit in the shaft." The police had mashed Conley's excrement in the elevator shaft on Sunday morning when they took the elevator down to the basement to retrieve Phagan's body. Since Conley had admitted relieving himself Saturday morning before Mary Phagan's murder, the previously undisturbed excrement indicated that Conley and Frank could not have used the elevator to transport her body on Saturday afternoon. In Slaton's view, Conley must have been lying; and if Conley lied about this fact, his entire testimony was questionable.[46]

But of course Conley's feces in the elevator shaft was not a detail that could be showcased in a network broadcast television show in the early 1960s—Mankiewicz never even tried to depict that part of the story. Instead, he used the elevator's clumsy (and highly visual) stopping mechanism together with the absence of blood in the elevator as evidence that would persuade John Slaton that Conley had lied on the stand. Mankiewicz did not come up with these details right away. His first script outline noted of the factory inspection: "We will see only that what they find does not disprove the possibility of Conley's guilt."[47] More precisely, the scene would raise the possibility of Frank's innocence. Mankiewicz's substitution was not elegant, but it did the job.

Yet, Mankiewicz and the Saudek team faced another challenge that went far beyond finding a suitable and relatively isolated detail of evidence on which Slaton could base his suspicion of Conley's likely perjury: What motivated Slaton to even consider Frank's appeal, and on what basis did he actually commute Frank's sentence? The episode needed to show that in spite of the somewhat ambiguous historical record, Slaton acted out of the best motives and then stood his ground even when confronted with powerful pressures to relent—that Slaton was unmistakably a profile in courage.

Slaton's starting point for commuting Frank's sentence resides with Judge Roan's belief in the "mathematical certainty" of Frank's innocence, which Roan states in the opening scene. Here, Judge Powell looks at Roan in surprise, and Roan at this point holds his head in his hands in pain as the jury enters to render their verdict. Judge Roan's pronouncement is a keynote of the episode, yet many historical accounts of the Phagan-Frank case do not include it. Roan's doubts about the case are well known; his "mathematical certainty" is less certain. Weinraub's source for this detail was Judge Powell's 1943 memoir, *I Can Go Home Again*, which Mankiewicz read. The Phagan-Frank case shows up late in Powell's volume, when he recounts that while he avoided the trial ("the spectacle there was utterly disgusting to me"), he did confer with Roan from time to time, at Roan's request, on points of law. "When he was preparing his charge to the jury, I sat on the bench at his side and he said to me, 'This man's innocence is proved to mathematical certainty.'" The *Profiles in Courage* creative team decided to dramatize Roan's alleged statement to Powell and make it the primary basis on which Slaton decides to hear Frank's appeal for mercy. (In this regard, it is interesting to note that Don Mankiewicz's first draft outline for the episode began with Roan on his deathbed at the Mayo Clinic, not on the bench declaring Frank's innocence.)[48]

The team was encouraged in this decision because other sources corroborated Judge Roan's dissatisfaction with the course of Frank's trial, including Atlanta judge and attorney Allen Henson's 1959 volume *Confessions of a Criminal Lawyer*. On this score, Henson's book is something of a sequel to Powell's. Henson's account alleges that Conley's attorney, William Smith, informed Judge Roan that Conley had confessed to him. Conley claimed that, having drained a bottle of "corn whiskey,"

Judge Leonard Roan informs his colleague Judge Powell that he believes in Frank's innocence absolutely, then grabs his head in pain (from the cancer that was to kill him).

he had entered Frank's empty office following Mary Phagan, who began screaming. Conley could remember no more than that, he told Smith, but when he came to his senses, she was dead. Roan knew that this information could not be introduced at trial because of attorney-client privilege. He instead consciously relied on the likelihood that a higher court would overturn Frank's conviction or that Slaton would commute Frank's sentence after Roan denied a motion for a new trial.

Henson's memoir explicitly explains that he was revealing all these details about Conley's "confession" to Smith because Powell had refused to divulge in his own memoir how Slaton could have had such doubts about Frank's guilt. By 1959 both Slaton and Powell were dead, and Henson felt liberated, in effect, to reveal what neither man had been free to say. (Conley never actually confessed to Smith; Smith inferred Conley's likely guilt.) Yet another confirmation of Roan's awareness that Conley had lied on the stand that impressed the Saudek team came from Atlanta mayor William B. Hartsfield, who repeated this point in a letter to the de Forest Research firm, which Saudek had hired to check facts after the Slaton episode was shot.[49]

In his statement accompanying his decision to commute Frank's sentence, Slaton began his conclusion by referring to Judge Roan's doubts about Frank's guilt. Hence, using Roan's "mathematical certainty" as the prime motivation for Slaton's consideration of the case made perfect sense for the *Profiles in Courage* team. Yet, Slaton was hardly alone among Georgians closely connected to the case who doubted Conley's honesty. After Frank's trial ended, William Smith was forthright in expressing his view that Conley was guilty.[50] Smith's statements provoked heated debate in legal circles as to their propriety because they violated attorney-client

Jim Conley's actual attorney, William Smith, as a young man. (Courtesy of the Cuba Archives of the Breman Museum.)

privilege, an axiom that compels the defense to make its strongest case for a defendant and do nothing to impair that legal representation. That Smith actually turned against his former client was yet another troubling aspect of the Frank case's saga. In fact, Smith acted from the best of intentions and motives. He was devoted to the uplift of African Americans, as proved by his many community volunteer activities as well as his decision to represent Conley, but he abhorred the thought that he had aided in the conviction and possible execution of an innocent man. Smith was still proclaiming his firm belief in Frank's innocence on his deathbed decades later.[51]

In the episode, Wheeler remains mute in the face of Slaton's questions, a major departure from the historical record. Mankiewicz's script, drawing on his own legal training, presents the lawyer with precisely the dilemma Smith faced. Wheeler's silence can be read in two ways. If Wheeler gives even an inkling of his suspicions of Conley's guilt to Slaton, he has undercut his obligation to Conley. Wheeler's silence can also be read, however, as tacit encouragement that the governor is on the right track. Most of

Slaton asks Conley's attorney, Wheeler, about his client's possible confession of murder as John Grant and Burley look on.

Wheeler remains impassive, his silence an ambiguous answer.

all, reducing Smith's role in Slaton's deliberations to that of a virtual by-stander allowed the *Profiles in Courage* team to keep the focus clearly on Slaton's heroism without offering a distracting parallel act of courage (Smith received death threats in response to his public statement of belief in Conley's guilt). Besides, Slaton alone held the power to save Frank's life.

Slaton's fundamental integrity—the basis for his actions—is established in the episode's first scene after the courthouse prologue. John Grant and Burley beg Slaton not to consider Frank's appeal for commutation if it comes before him. The dialogue reveals that Slaton will be in office for just two more weeks, while Frank is entitled to a month to prepare his appeal. In fact, Slaton did have to consider Frank's appeal in hectic circumstances. The Supreme Court rejected Frank's final appeal to have his case heard in mid-April 1915. The Georgia Prison Commission, after eight days of deliberation, declined his appeal for clemency on June 9 and recommended to the governor that Frank's death sentence be carried out. Georgia governors usually followed the commission's recommendations. Frank's execution was set for June 22. Slaton's term ended June 26.

In the episode, when Grant asks him what he will do if the appeal comes before him, Slaton replies, "I am probably the only man in Georgia who can read who doesn't have a firm opinion one way or the other about what should be done with Leo Frank. The only man who doesn't know what he'd do if he were governor *is* the governor." Slaton's open-mindedness about the case was one reason Frank's legal team preferred to make their

The first post-prologue shot of the episode places the emphasis clearly and squarely on John M. Slaton as a charismatic hero.

Watson makes himself at home in Slaton's office by putting his shoes up on an open desk drawer.

appeal to Slaton rather than his successor, Nat Harris. In November 1914, more than five months before Frank's lawyers had to make this decision, Slaton had told reporters, "I shall be guided solely by the merits of the case and my own conscience. . . . If Leo M. Frank is guilty, he ought to be hanged. If he is not guilty, then he ought to be saved." Nat Harris, by contrast, promised that his judgment in the matter would be guided only by Georgians and by what was good for the state, pointedly excluding national opinion on the matter. Arthur Brisbane, Hearst reporter, editor, and intimate associate of Hearst himself, informed Frank supporter Louis Marshall that Slaton was Frank's better hope; Brisbane was in a position to know, given that Hearst and Slaton were on very friendly terms.[52]

In scene 4 of the episode, Slaton faces a great deal of pressure over the Frank case before he even begins to consider Frank's appeal—and all of it is embodied in one character, Tom Watson. Their depiction of the conflict between the two men is where Don Mankiewicz and the Saudek team took the greatest dramatic license. Historically, Slaton's and Watson's relationship was a tenuous one. Although Watson did support Slaton's gubernatorial campaign in 1912, it is doubtful that they ever met outside the confines of a political gathering. C. Vann Woodward's biography of Watson reports that Watson and Slaton both indicated that the few communications they did have—on the two topics of Slaton's possible run for the U.S. Senate in 1914 and on Frank's appeal to Slaton in 1915—took place through third parties.

The Saudek team could corroborate this fact. Weinraub had the transcript of Samuel Boorstin's interview with Slaton in 1953, in which Slaton described how Tom Watson, "who agitated this case with his magazines and newspaper, wrote me [Slaton] a letter that if I would let Frank hang, he would make me a U.S. Senator." After researching the issue, Weinraub admitted, "We do not know the exact date of Watson's offer of support to Slaton for the Senatorship, if Slaton would promise to let the Frank execution take place." He thought it most likely that the offer was made "some time between February and September, 1914 . . . after the primary election, when it was apparent that Slaton could not control enough delegates to win the nomination on the first ballot."[53] The episode's depiction of a face-to-face showdown was for dramatic effect.

In the scene, Watson's arrival interrupts Slaton's work on other state business (taxes). Informed that Watson wishes to see him, Slaton harshly condemns the man's rank hypocrisy for viewers' benefit: "Tom Watson. He claims to be the poor man's friend. Why is it he never came to see me about farmer-market roads? Where was he when I was trying to get the State to help the rural schools? He's done more harm to the state of Georgia than any man since William Tecumseh Sherman." Over the objections of his assistant, Burley, Slaton admits Watson to his office, noting that as governor he must make time even for his enemies.

Actor Michael Constantine's Watson is a sleazy, rather sweaty southern caricature with a thick accent. He is dressed in a seersucker suit typical of the time and place, thumbs resting in his belt loops, and he does not rush to remove his hat. Waving around a rolled-up copy of his newspaper, the *Jeffersonian*, as if he were getting ready to swat flies, he prowls around Slaton at his desk like a tiger stalking its prey. Praising Slaton as a "good" if unobtrusive governor, Watson sits down, opens one of Slaton's desk drawers, and casually parks his shoes on it and loosens his laces as Slaton looks on distastefully.

As this brazen gesture of informality indicates, Watson is certainly a man of the people, but he is also a flamboyant, irreverent, presumptuous villain. Constantine's performance and appearance have an almost comic aspect that amuses at the risk of undercutting the severity of Watson's threats. Watson proceeds to offer Slaton his support for the Senate; Slaton refuses to accept it. The flavor of their confrontation can be seen in this dialogue exchange, which is accompanied by shot–reverse shot cutting:

Slaton [reaction shot]: Are you offering me some kind of a deal?
Watson [reaction shot, medium close-up]: No. I can't make no deals. Anybody who accepts my support becomes unclean. You know what the *Atlanta*

Watson leans up close to threaten Slaton: "But Governor, . . . *I can oppose*."

Constitution said about my support? "Lie down with dogs, get up with fleas." [Music swells in the background.]

Slaton [medium close-up]: Yes, I rather liked that editorial.

Watson [medium close-up]: I thought you would. [He leans into the camera and into close-up.] But Governor, even if I can't support anybody [threatening horn music begins softly], *I can oppose*. And when I oppose, my people oppose. Thousands of them farmers with empty bellies got more votes than shoes. When they read in my paper that man is a scalawag, a limber back, a tool of the interests that ought to be run out of public life, they run him out. They vote him out. [The horn music, like a warning sound, peaks here, underlining the seriousness of Watson's threats.]

Slaton [medium close-up; rolls his eyes]: I'm not going to debate the extent of your power over the mob.

When Slaton refuses to bow to his intimidation, Watson tries to undermine Judge Roan's comments about Frank's innocence. During Frank's appeals, Tom Watson had written in the *Jeffersonian* that Judge Roan's misgivings about Leo Frank's death sentence were the result of Roan's clouded mind as he suffered with terminal cancer. Watson implied that Frank's allies had guided, if not dictated, the prose in one of Roan's letters declaring his belief in Frank's innocence: "He [Roan] certainly could not have prepared such a letter as Frank's lawyers presented *without assistance*."[54] In the episode, Watson proceeds to dismiss Judge Roan's doubts on precisely these grounds. He suggests that "they" had gotten to Roan in his final days and influenced his weakened mind.

When Slaton remains unconvinced by this allegation, Watson plays the ace up his sleeve: political blackmail. Slaton, should he decide even to *consider* Frank's appeal, could be vulnerable to accusations of conflict of interest. As it happened, just before Mary Phagan's murder in spring 1913 Slaton's law firm had agreed to merge with that of Luther Z. Rosser in July of that year. Slaton did not practice law while he was governor, but his name remained affiliated with the firm. Indeed, that merger was another reason the Frank legal team decided to appeal to Slaton, who had strong ties to Atlanta's Jewish community, rather than wait to appeal to Nat Harris, whose ties were to Tom Watson.[55] Watson hammered away at the conflict-of-interest issue in his publications.

In the episode, the soundtrack trumpets blare again as Watson promises to publicize the merger of the firms. When Slaton argues that Watson knows that he is not a practicing member of the firm, Watson responds: "That's true. [I know it,] . . . but hundreds of thousands don't. They will believe in the event that you permit yourself to consider this application that . . . Frank bought himself a lawyer to appear in court and . . . get the services of the senior partner." Watson's unscrupulousness—his willingness to use any means, no matter how reprehensible, to get his way—is now clear. Slaton later concedes to Burley that Watson is correct: there will be a *perception* of conflict of interest if he commutes Frank's sentence. But Slaton minimizes the issue, as does the episode.

Why did the episode downplay this awkward issue, given that Slaton's and Rosser's films had in fact merged before Frank's trial? Its creators knew that denying this fact would be as inaccurate as not raising it at all. They found this middle ground through Weinraub's research.

Weinraub summarized his understanding of the merger as follows: "Slaton's partner, one Phillips, was an office lawyer, while Slaton was a courtroom man. With Slaton now governor, Phillips could not perform both functions adequately enough to maintain the Slaton-Phillips practice. Therefore, the firm of Slaton and Phillips (with only Phillips practicing) merged with Rosser and Brandon. . . . Slaton would not actually join the firm until his governorship expired." As to the merger's impact on Slaton's conduct, Weinraub had copies of correspondence in Slaton's handwriting denying the conflict-of-interest charges. Perhaps the most powerful piece was Slaton's explanation of his decision to commute Frank's sentence to Atlanta Bishop Warren A. Candler in August 1915. Writing the bishop to ask for his public support, Slaton stated:

There was no other course open to me, unless through personal cowardice or unscrupulous ambition, I was willing to let a man die against my convictions. I would rather lie in a cemetery than do this.

Watson endeavors to intimate that a law partnership influenced me. I had no earthly connection with this firm except I lent my name to preserve the business of my partner, and this arrangement was made and quarters engaged before the murder was committed. In addition, Rosser dropped out of the case a year ago and the only meaning of Watson's insinuation is that I was bought. This is so contemptible that I can hardly think it can find credence anywhere. I have spent [illegible—likely "money"] which came only from my family in political contest, and why I should sacrifice a political future except from a compelling sense of duty for a man whom I never saw, ought to appeal to everyone.

As Slaton noted in his letter to Bishop Candler, Rosser had indeed relinquished leadership of Frank's appeal efforts more than a year earlier. Weinraub and the *Profiles* group's perception that Slaton acted honorably was corroborated in yet other sources Weinraub consulted.[56] Where it was not corroborated, Slaton's potential conflict of interest was downplayed: *Night Fell on Georgia* refers to the issue only as a false rumor. Arthur Powell and Allen Henson did not even discuss it in their memoirs.

There was, in short, plenty of support for Weinraub's reading of Slaton's situation. Slaton was a noble public servant of conscience and compassion. When Watson's great-grandson complained about the show's handling of the issue, Robert Saudek told an NBC executive, "I will not address myself to Mr. Brown's charge about Slaton's ethics as they related to his law firm connection. The program itself stated the facts with complete precision and I stand on those facts."[57]

Moral and Physical Courage

President Kennedy had told Robert Saudek that he wanted the series to stress moral rather than physical courage. Yet the Slaton episode includes two scenes that emphasize Slaton's physical courage in making his decision and standing by it—even when threatened with violence to his person.

Slaton did display considerable physical courage during his post-decision ordeal. Thousands of Georgians—not to mention Hugh Dorsey and the friends and family of Mary Phagan—were outraged by the governor's decision, which they viewed as overturning the jury's verdict, meddling with the judicial system that had convicted Frank, and thumbing a nose at the appeals process that had functioned properly in denying Frank's appeal. Mobs surrounded and invaded Atlanta's downtown government offices after Slaton's announcement, and a crowd of some two thousand people marched the six miles north from downtown Atlanta to Wingfield, Slaton's home in suburban Buckhead. City police proved insufficient to protect Slaton, and the governor was compelled to declare martial law. Smaller groups twice again attempted to attack Slaton's home. He was hanged in effigy in Marietta's central square; pinned to the dummy was a sign reading, "John M. Slaton, King of the Jews and Traitor Governor of Georgia."[58]

His vilification notwithstanding, Slaton appeared at the public ceremony to pass the state seal to his successor in Georgia's statehouse on Saturday, June 26, and performed his duties to hisses when his name was spoken. Disgruntled Georgians awaited him both outside the hall and outside the building, and Slaton was barely saved from a potentially lethal attack by a citizen carrying a five-foot metal pipe.[59] After pretending to leave Atlanta for New York (his car stopped at Terminal Station) immediately after the ceremony, Slaton attended Harris's inauguration luncheon at the Ansley Hotel.

The television episode shows much of this and more to dramatize Slaton's fearlessness. At Harris's swearing-in, newsboys hawk the *Jeffersonian* and the crowd mutters about Slaton's "million dollar prize" (alleged payment from Frank's supporters) for commuting Frank's sentence. Many of the people wave signs reading "Hang Slaton" and "Death to All Traitors." Harris is cheered, Slaton is booed—as he actually was—and the police have a difficult time restraining the crowd from attacking Slaton as he, Sallie, Burley, and Grant make their way to his car. Even though the episode does not portray the attempt on Slaton's life, it does show one citizen getting on the hood of Slaton's car; others join him and rock Slaton's car back and forth before it can pull away.[60] This is a visually exciting sequence because once again the filmmakers used hand-held cameras to place the viewer within the mob.

A rock breaks the rear window of the car, prompting a cut to a similarly broken windowpane in Slaton's dining room, where Sallie is serving coffee several hours later to Slaton, Grant, Burley, and other guests after dinner. Slaton's dinner guests are aghast that Slaton attended the party in honor of Governor Harris. All of them, including one judge, have come to the Slaton mansion armed. Mankiewicz took this detail from Arthur Powell's memoir, which describes a number of Slaton's friends carrying guns into Slaton's home: "When we got inside the house we found a dozen or so of the city's best and most prominent citizens there similarly armed. Jack

An agitated crowd appears at the inauguration of Slaton's successor.

Shooting again from within the crowd, this shot shows a mob rocking Slaton's car, with one man getting on top of it.

Slaton and his wife were the calmest of all the party."[61] In the episode, his guests plead with Slaton to leave town ahead of his scheduled departure date, which is several days away. Slaton is unmovable: "To the extent I change the course of my actions to suit the mob, I become part of it." When his colleagues, family, and friends beg him to change his mind, Slaton responds angrily that the decision is his: "The people of Georgia gave me certain powers and they paid me for my judgment in using it. Some of them may regret what they did. That is their privilege. And their right. That does not entitle them to make my plans for me. I will leave exactly when I had arranged to leave."

As Slaton makes this speech to his friends and allies, the sounds of the crowd offscreen grow louder, and Slaton must be restrained from going out to talk with them. ("Some of them must have voted for me!" he insists as he gets up to go outside.) Sallie, in a reaction shot, beams at him with pride—her "brave man" in action. This depiction of Slaton's bravery likely stemmed from sources such as Powell's and Henson's memoirs; the latter, for example, wrote, "Jack Slaton was not a man to run from a mob." The scene also reveals that Slaton's friends have arranged for the Georgia National Guard to protect his home, since Slaton is no longer officially the governor. In fact, in 1915, Slaton had to impose martial law on the state and order state troopers to reinforce the local police surrounding Wingfield.[62] John M. Slaton Jr. confirmed this fact to Bernard Weinraub. (In actual fact, the mob marched on Wingfield before Slaton stepped down as governor. The episode rearranged this chronology to further dramatize Slaton's bravery.)

Slaton apparently never expressed a wish to speak to the mob that night. Moreover, he was reportedly amazed to see twenty-six Georgians arrested on the grounds of Wingfield early in the morning of his last day in office. According to guards who were present, Slaton "stood still for a moment" and then turned away "as if his heart was breaking."[63] The ferocity of their anger had not quite registered with Slaton until this encounter. The *Profiles in Courage* episode does not include this dramatic incident, nor, per Powell, Slaton's refusal to swear out warrants for the captured men's arrest. "Let these deluded men, who thought they were acting in a good cause, go home to their families who need them. Tell them that I did what I knew was right, and I forgive them for any wrong they intended against me," Powell quotes him as saying.[64] In the episode, Slaton—with an almost suicidal fervor—retains his firm belief in his connection with his constituents.

The episode's epilogue in San Francisco affirms Slaton's certainty that he acted correctly in the Frank case. After the image of Slaton talking to the San Francisco reporters diminishes, and after Oliver's brief narration about Slaton's subsequent life and career, we hear Kennedy's voice reading a paraphrased version of the final lines of *Profiles in Courage*: "These stories of past courage can teach, can offer hope, and they can provide inspiration, but they cannot supply courage itself. For this each man must look into his own soul."[65] Kennedy's exhortation to civic action guided by conscience, implicit in the episode, is now explicitly stated.

Anti-Semitism Rears Its Head

The *Profiles in Courage* team's interpretation of the historical record is most apparent in their dramatization of Slaton's motivations for tackling the Frank appeal, his resistance to Watson's threats, his status as a law partner with Luther Z. Rosser, and his fearlessness in the face of the mob. If Slaton's potential conflict of interest was the most sensitive of these to dramatize, the role of anti-Semitism in the Phagan-Frank case was perhaps the most explosive.

The episode's prologue raises the issue in a sharp if brief manner. It is shot with an immediacy that places viewers in among the agitated mob. The camera fades in on an extreme close-up of Fiddlin' John Carson isolated in a beam of light as he sings the first verse from "The Ballad of Mary Phagan" ("Little Mary Phagan / Left her home one day

/ She went to the pencil factory, to get her weekly pay"), tilts down to his guitar, and then tracks to the right through a crowd. Titles reveal the place and time as the Fulton County Courthouse in Atlanta, Georgia, on the night of August 25, 1913, the date Leo Frank was convicted. The camera continues panning and tracking right through a crowd whose members are also eagerly looking right, in front of others holding torches high overhead. The shot ends on a guard with a gun as trumpets in the soundtrack blare an almost atonal alarm. We cut to a long shot of the torch-carrying mob in front of the courthouse; one torch is center frame in the foreground.

A cut to a low-angle, medium-long shot, as if from the point of view of the crowd, reveals a lone rabble-rouser (David Bond) on a balcony, quoting Scripture: "Vengeance is mine, saith the Lord." He asks the crowd, "And what is vengeance? Is there one law for the rich and another for the common people?" Now in close-up, he looks into the camera: "Are we to submit to the murder of a Georgia girl? Is justice to be sold for Jew money?" In high-angle, point-of-view reaction shots, the crowd shouts back, "No!" after each question. The crowd cries, "Hang him!" And when they are asked "Who?" they shout, "Leo Frank" again and again. As they do so, the camera makes an ironic point in tilting down from the speaker's balcony to a plaque engraved with the Georgia state motto, "Wisdom, justice, moderation."

The fact that the scene is staged and shot at night rather than in the afternoon, when the jury actually announced its guilty verdict to the acclaim of a huge crowd gathered outside the building, provides visual punch to this crucial moment, building on the visual tradition of the torch-bearing lynch mob in Hollywood films. It was also a cost-saving device requiring less set dressing and conveying the sense of a larger crowd than was present on the set.

Later, when focus has shifted to Slaton's office and Watson refers to "they" who got to Roan on his deathbed and convinced him to proclaim that Frank was innocent, Slaton asks Watson point-blank, "Who is 'they'?" Watson merely replies, "You can read all about it in my paper." This is the second mention of Georgians' resentment of northern opinion and Jewish efforts to mold the nation's views of the case. Watson here trades on the "polite" language of anti-Semites who believed that Jews controlled the country in every respect. The shocking cry of "Jew money" in the prologue links up here with Watson's deeper accusations of Jewish influence on and bribery of Roan and Slaton. Governor Slaton,

The opening shot of the "Governor John M. Slaton" episode is an extreme close-up on singer Fiddlin' John Carson, who is singing "The Ballad of Mary Phagan" outside the Fulton County Courthouse.

A shot of the mob gathered outside the courthouse to hear the jury's verdict places the viewer within the crowd.

A rabble-rouser appears on top of the courthouse to stir up the crowd, yelling about "Jew money" and calling for Leo Frank to be hanged.

like any viewer familiar with the Phagan-Frank case, knew perfectly well who "they" were.

Bigotry was a prominent theme in other episodes of *Profiles in Courage* (for example, those portraying Frederick W. Douglass, Prudence Crandall, and Oscar Underwood), and anti-Semitism more specifically was the centerpiece of the episode on Woodrow Wilson and his nomination of Jewish attorney Louis Brandeis to the Supreme Court. Don Mankiewicz and the Saudek team had to weigh how much emphasis to give anti-Semitism in this script. In mid-October 1963, while working on his first draft, Mankiewicz commented, "Thing that bothers me the most now, not only did Frank not do it, but that Connally [*sic*] did it. Connally [*sic*] confessed to his attorney. As a policy do we want to go so far as to saying this [is] corruption of justice, Frank was a northern Jew, and convicted on that?" The episode's creators pondered that question and whether or not to portray Conley. They ultimately decided to leave Conley and Frank out of the episode entirely. Neither one ever appears on-screen. That Conley was black is never even stated. To imply that a black man committed perjury about the murder of a white girl was too risky in the early 1960s, crucial years in the civil rights struggle.[66]

While the production team made the decision to depict Slaton's alleged conflict of interest as a false issue on their own, on the broader topic of anti-Semitism and its role in the case they took guidance from Allan Nevins. After reading Mankiewicz's first complete draft in fall 1963, Nevins forthrightly argued against stressing the anti-Semitic angle in the case. This early draft had the rabble-rouser on top of the Fulton County Courthouse calling out, "What shall become of the Jew?" and the mob below chanting, "Hang the Jew!" several times in response to his retort, "I can't hear you."[67] In a subsequent scene, Slaton was himself to raise the issue of Frank's religion and then to dismiss it out of hand.

Nevins praised the first script for showing Slaton's heroism and Watson's villainy, but, citing V. O. Key's *Southern Politics* as a source, urged Mankiewicz to render anti-Semitism as but one factor in anti-Frank sentiment. Nevins's comments not only offer details about Mankiewicz's first draft script, they also summarize the political situation in Georgia at the time of Frank's conviction:

A slight change in the emphasis or slant of the early scenes would seem to me serviceable to historical truth and dramatic appeal alike. For more than one reason, it seems to me a mistake to emphasize Anti-Semitism in a heavyhanded [sic] way, as in the speech "an unbeliever has defiled the flesh of a Christian girl." AntiSemitism [sic] was a reality, of course, but not the deepest reality, not the ultimate source of the maladies ruining Georgia.

The deepest reality, I think (and I may be in error) was the poison which Tom Watson and other demagogues had spread in the veins of the State by their shrewdly calculated appeals to a whole gamut of phobias. They appealed to sectional prejudice, South as against North; race prejudice, whites as against Negro; economic prejudice, poor as against rich; and of course the prejudice of the rural voters as against the slickers of the cities. The main appeal was to poor white farmers and tenants as hostile to the prosperous people of the towns, for under Georgia's county unit system governmental power rested with the small rural counties.

Watson has published his "lies" about Slaton's conflict of interest in the case. In tight close-up, a Marietta farmer who reads Watson's newspaper challenges Slaton to prove there is no conflict of interest by denying Frank's appeal.

That is, prejudice was excited by Watson against Frank as a Jew. But it was excited against him still more as an Atlantan, and hence an enemy of the rural folk; as a prosperous manufacturer, and hence an enemy of the poor; as a member of a minority group, and hence somehow vaguely identified with the Negro minority. I think it will be better history to treat the ignorant, blatant, boorish prejudice in these large terms. And in doing so we shall have better drama, in that we get a larger theme, and we avoid touching on sensitivities pro and con that are better avoided; touching on them, at any rate, in a semi-sensational manner.[68]

Watson's reference to "my people," the subsequent threatening statement of a Marietta farmer about what he reads "in the papers" at Slaton's hearing, and the anonymous crowds outside the courthouse and, later, the statehouse all represent Georgia's poor whites and their "ignorant, blatant, boorish prejudice." A small detail in the later scene of Nat Harris's inauguration features a protest sign among the crowd that reads "Were [*sic*] is justice?"

Thus, Nevins, in the name of taste and the actual historical forces that shaped the Phagan-Frank case, guided the episode's creators to downplay anti-Semitism as a factor in Frank's fate and Slaton's dilemma. Nevertheless, the "Governor John M. Slaton" episode has the distinction of being the first moving-image dramatization of the case to represent anti-Semitism as a factor at all.

Assessing *Profiles in Courage*: "Governor John M. Slaton"

The *Profiles in Courage* episodes are of a piece with other dramas of clearly delineated right and wrong within the political arena. In that regard the series is reminiscent of Fred Zinnemann's Oscar-winning film of Robert Bolt's play *A Man for All Seasons*—the drama of Thomas More (Paul Scofield), who, at the price of his life, refused to sanction Henry VIII's divorce of Catherine and his proposed marriage to Anne Boleyn. No wonder that Saudek had tried to recruit Bolt to write the Anne Hutchinson script.

The "Governor John M. Slaton" episode more specifically resembles *A Man for All Seasons* in the epigrammatic dialogue and rhetorical flourishes in Mankiewicz's script. After their visit to the factory, for example, John Grant objects to Slaton's decision to commute Frank's sentence: "It seems to me that all you'd be doing is changing the place of his hanging from a gallows to a tree." Slaton replies, "The state cannot always control the mob, but God help us if the mob controls the State." That Slaton himself was capable of such utterances only enhanced the episode's historical accuracy. As with his closing comment that "lynching strikes at the *body* of civilization; execution without proper cause strikes at the *soul*," Slaton's rhetorical flourishes resembled what commentators have called "the reversible raincoat." The term refers to the turns of phrase that Theodore Sorensen drafted for Kennedy's speeches, most famously, "Ask not what your country can do for you; ask what you can do for your country." In fact, when he read Mankiewicz's revised script in January 1964, Sorensen singled out such lines, commenting that they "have a certain Sorensenian ring to them which I enjoy."[69]

The Slaton episode is equally striking for its extremely narrow focus on Slaton. Only the prologue unfolds without him. This is appropriate given both the episode's "profile" orientation toward an individual and its detective story framework. (Which of Conley's two versions is true? What will visiting the factory reveal?) In fact, the focus is so narrow that an uninformed viewer would have no idea what the Frank case was. The prologue shows a mob enraged about Leo Frank's guilt, mentions the murder of a little girl, and references "Jew money," but the precise issues surrounding the case remain unexplored at this point. Surprisingly, they remain unspecified for another ten minutes of the fifty-minute program.

Mankiewicz's strategy is designed to create suspense and arouse viewers' curiosity—in a sense, it also keeps viewers as free of information on which to make a judgment as Slaton claims to be—while keeping their attention squarely on the figure profiled. The same strategy informed the exposition of other episodes: for example, the program on George M. Norris begins with him alone in an auditorium awaiting utter character assassination in 1917 for reasons we must wait twenty minutes to learn (he was one of only six senators to vote against America's entry into World War I). Mankiewicz took this strategy to such an extreme degree, however, that some of Saudek's team questioned it. Walter Kerr, reading the script's first draft, commented that the breakfast scene in Slaton's home was a "dangerously static way of learning all this [that is, about Slaton's political options and the Frank case]; All talk: when there's colorful material at hand (murder)." He complained that viewers never even see Frank, and that the handling of the case was "all terribly abstract . . . can only go so long sans knowing details."[70] Yet Mankiewicz's final script adhered to this strategy.

The opening scene also fulfills the predominant principles Oliver articulated for the series' visual style. In their discussions months before shooting started, Oliver noted that "this is a program of ideas and characters. I want the secondary aspects of it—i.e., sets, costumes, etc. to be greatly subordinated to the ideas and the characters." He wanted "unimaginative designing—suggestive in feeling rather than literal." Oliver and Ritchie intended to use the actors' words and expressions to convey the story: "Television is a close-up medium," Oliver wrote in a memo to Ritchie. "We are telling stories of insight into character. We will never be able to match the old MGM historical epics or the Bronston sea of Spanish extras. And we don't want to. . . . Up to now, we have been agreeing in general terms about the use of close-ups and indicated backings."[71] Saudek's Hollywood staff understood that close-ups were crucial not only for the smaller, more intimate television screen but also for a series emphasizing courageous individuals. In the Slaton episode, the most threatening characters—Fiddlin' John Carson, Watson, the Marietta farmer—are shown in extreme close-ups to express the imminent danger they pose to Slaton and to law and order.

Beyond its more intimate visual style, the narrowness of the episode's focus on Slaton was also consistent with the series' individualist philosophy. Mankiewicz had toyed with the idea of having Slaton broach the larger forces at work in the Frank case in a discussion with Burley: "It is not that Leo Frank is a Jew, and that the murdered girl was native-born, and fourteen years old, and attractive. I am not concerned with the fact that he was an employer of child labor; he was, himself, an employee of the factory, and not an owner, but it would not matter if he had personally fixed the wage scale. Much of the activity in his behalf was ill-advised; and if I act favorably on his petition, many people will put an ugly interpretation on it, but that doesn't matter."[72] The creators of "Governor John M. Slaton" made a conscious decision to remove such direct references to all the sources of resentment against Frank.

Perhaps this is not so surprising. One could argue that the brief but piercing references to anti-Semitism in *Profiles in Courage* marked some progress in the medium's level of comfort with naming this form of preju- dice, at least in the context of southern barbarity. The same might be true of the show's potential to demonstrate the rift between blacks and Jews over the Frank case at a time when Jewish liberal activists had joined with black activists in the civil rights struggle. Moreover, in the episode as we have it, even sectionalism is minimized. Frank is barely identified as being from the North, for example, and when Slaton reviews the case with Burley, the governor mentions that Mary Phagan was murdered on a "holiday" but does not specify that it was Confederate Memorial Day. In class terms, the lower class (the Marietta farmer, the mob, and their leader, Watson) is arrayed against the forces of upper-class reason and jus- tice. Constantine's performance as Watson may be a comic stereotype, but Matthau is an elegant incarnation of Slaton—though it may be difficult for present-day viewers to take Matthau seriously because of his subse- quent performances in comic roles. Matthau portrays Slaton as a con- trary, independent-minded, sardonic, yet idealistic and self-assured chief executive. He is far more refined than Watson. No wonder that John M. Slaton Jr. wrote Saudek's team of his utter satisfaction with the episode: "My wife and I enjoyed the program very much. We feel that an excellent job was done in portraying Gov. Slaton and wish to congratulate Robert Saudek Associates and the actors. Every Sunday night we look forward to *Profiles in Courage*. You are rendering the country a great service."[73]

Nor is it surprising that the least-satisfied viewer of the episode was Tom Watson Brown, Tom Watson's great-grandson. A practicing attorney in Atlanta, Brown—in 1964 and until his death in early 2007—believed in Leo Frank's guilt, in the honor of his great-grandfather's actions against Frank, and in the charges against Slaton of bribery and conflict of interest. Both Brown and his father wrote NBC in early 1965 to demand a retrac- tion from the network and show's producers along with a withdrawal of the program from rebroadcasting and syndication.[74] Brown expressed his dissatisfaction to NBC about the "libelous" depiction of Tom Watson in no uncertain terms: "The portrayal of Mr. Watson was base and false, and so far removed from reality as to bespeak a recklessness tantamount to malice on the part of NBC. The program portrayed a fat, slovenly, cowardly, uncouth, hypocritical, semi-literate, dishonest and self-serving yellow journalist and black-mailer. Watson was none of these. I found particularly loathsome your implication that he was dishonest and hypocritical in championing the cause of the common people."[75]

In truth, Brown's description of Constantine's portrayal was not inaccurate. Bernard Weinraub had anticipated Brown's complaints in his comments on Mankiewicz's first script draft in November 1963:

> In the first part of the dialogue between [Watson] and Slaton, Watson talks in cracker fashion. The fact is that he was an extremely intelligent man, the author of biographies of Jefferson and Jackson, and a history of France. Later his words become more refined, possibly deliberately on Don's part, but the first section is misleading. Watson is a fascinating man, and a complex one. Slaton and Watson represent two sides of the new South, the one allied with respectability, the other slightly demagoguic [sic]. I had hoped that their confrontation would reveal the similarities between them as well as their differences. This is, of course, not a matter of fact but a difference in interpretation. Watson was no cracker; in fact, he was worth at least a million dollars by this time.[76]

Indeed, one would not think Constantine's Watson capable of any such achievements except wealth. The actor's performance clearly diverges from Weinraub's "interpretation" of the man, which Brown might have found less repellent. Brown further assured NBC that while Watson and Slaton never met as depicted in the episode, if they had, "There can be little doubt as to Watson's dominating any meeting between the two. Intellectually, in terms of political power and in terms of courage." He continued: "Elevating Slaton's stature beyond perspective does not bother me. His act in commuting Frank's sentence was indeed courageous, albeit personally advantageous in some particulars and a duty which was not properly his. Ethically it was questionable for him to act on a case in which his law firm had a direct financial interest. But your desire to praise him does not justify the vicious distortion and portrayal of Watson."[77]

Tom Watson Brown's complaints about this episode are worth dwelling on because they illustrate the existence, even in 1963, of diverse views of the Phagan-Frank case. As he is portrayed in this episode, Tom Watson conforms to the series's general approach to its heroes' antagonists—as described by the *Saturday Review*'s critic—as "ignorant and bigoted."[78] Still, Watson *was* a demagogue. Saudek wrote a point-by-point refutation of Brown's missive to NBC executive Robert Kasmire, quoting from already published characterizations and quotations in Woodward's biography of Watson. Had he wanted to, Saudek could also have drawn on unpublished characterizations of Watson such as those of Allan Nevins and Atlanta mayor William B. Hartsfield. The latter, in a letter to the de Forest Research firm, wrote: "The man who whipped up the hatred and anti-Jewish sentiment in Georgia was Thomas Watson, through his paper the Jeffersonian. He traded on this politically, for years and finally became U.S. Senator and dictated the election of several Governors. Watson was an opportunist, who stirred also a lot of racial prejudice. But when seeking political support in his early years, he courted the negroes, having them in his home."[79]

Hartsfield's comments implied, and many critics pointed out, the series's relevance to contemporary politics. The mob mentality, though directed against a Jew, had obvious implications for southern racism and anti-segregation sentiments in the early 1960s—as the murders of Andrew Goodman, Michael Schwerner, and James Chaney in Mississippi in 1964 demonstrated. In fact, viewer Harold C. Bailey of Seattle, Washington, had suggested that the series should be dramatizing the student protests and civil rights struggles occurring right then: "You have dredged up out of the comfortable archives quite a series of remote and now fashionably innocuous Galahads for whom to beat your breasts." Bailey continued: "I suggest you lay down your telescope and look about you. There is no dearth of examples crowding around us today, timely, pertinent, and embarrassingly offensive to our delicate sensitivities." Citing Medgar Evers, Mississippi's Student Non-violent Coordinating Committee members, HUAC victims, and others, he continued, "It's easy to admire and support courage in 1893 on the college campus of Wherever, No-Land. It's more impressive to tender a cup of water to one whose blood still flows, and whose features have not yet become ennobled by the passage of time and passion. I fear you are more adept at saluting courage than . . . in demonstrating it."[80]

Even without overt tributes to contemporary American heroes, the *Profiles in Courage* episodes that highlighted Slaton's stand against the "madness abroad in Georgia" and Oscar Underwood's insistence on condemning the KKK at the 1924 Democratic Party convention were seen as very timely in the 1964–65 television season. The series as a whole reinforced the rightness of Kennedy's and Lyndon B. Johnson's endorsement of the civil rights struggle. The *Profiles in Courage* production team often placed the series within that framework, even while their public statements cast the series as nonpartisan.

In October 1964, for example, as *Profiles in Courage* approached its initial broadcast, Saudek stressed that "the series is not just a history lesson. The stories must have contemporary application and the characters should be an inspiration to us." He made this connection explicit in private correspondence on at least one occasion. In defending a script for a planned episode on President Woodrow Wilson that Sorensen found faulty, Saudek wrote that in supporting the nomination of Louis Brandeis to the Supreme Court, "Wilson did take a substantial career risk in the politically most fateful year of his Presidency. . . . These examples of courage must inspire Americans, as those in the book surely do." Saudek continued:

> Perhaps the extraordinary Goldwater syndrome blighting this west coast, leads me to argue at such length for Wilson and Brandeis. Their stories, like the others, would be seen here alongside all the Goldwater bumper-cards, television shows, and billboards which Californians are being exposed to. These two men (Wilson and Brandeis) may not be Sir Launfals [a member of King Arthur's round table], but their hearts are purer and their stories far more inspiring than what is readily available and going virtually unchallenged, in Southern California this year.[81]

Saudek could not have been more explicit about the role he saw the series playing in contemporary American politics, especially in response to Goldwater's reactionary conservatism.

Certain television critics connected the dots as well. Jack Gould of the *New York Times* felt the series fulfilled its aim of relevance. The program, he wrote after seeing the episode on Oscar Underwood, "succeeds entirely in its dual mission: to stand on its own as excellent entertainment, and to capture in dramatic form history's exciting pertinency to current events." Gould saw unavoidable connections to recent American history in Underwood's story. "For those who remembered references to the Klan during the heated floor colloquy over the John Birch Society at last summer's Republican convention, the parallels between 1924 and 1964 were nothing short of fascinating." John Marshall Cuno of the *Christian Science Monitor* had a similar reaction to the episode on New York governor and associate Supreme Court justice Charles Evans Hughes, who disagreed with those anti-communist forces in the 1919 state legislature that sought to deprive elected representatives suspected of being Communists of their standing in state legislatures. Cuno saw the episode as dramatizing "the kind of anxiety, witch-hunting and political expediency antedating the McCarthy era of our own time."[82]

Besides Tom Watson Brown's, there are no letters from other Georgians in the Saudek papers that indicate their reactions to this dramatization of Georgia history. Television critic Dick Gray of the *Atlanta Journal-Constitution* wrote that "some of Georgia's most unpleasant history will be brought to life on the nation's television screens tonight—and it might be a good lesson if everybody watched the show." Gray devoted roughly half of his column to the memories of one Atlanta woman alive at the time of Frank's trial and appeals. This woman recalled the gathering of "angry" Georgians when Frank's sentence was commuted, the call for militia protection of Slaton's estate, and the rush to see Frank's body when it lay in repose in the funeral parlor. Gray's piece implied that the Mary Phagan–Leo Frank case, with all its attendant passions, was very much in the past; Allan Nevins would have agreed.[83]

The "Full" Treatment

The Murder of Mary Phagan

I'm talking about humanity. . . . The little man is hurtin'.—TOM WATSON
I cannot abide the companionship of an accusing conscience.—JOHN M. SLATON

ON SUNDAY, MARCH 7, 1982, the *Nashville Tennessean* published a "Special News Section" devoted to the Phagan-Frank case. Page 1 focused on Alonzo Mann's claim (verified by lie-detector tests at the paper's request) that, as the front-page banner headline had it, "An Innocent Man Was Lynched."[1] Mann, "now 83 and ailing with a heart condition," recounted that when he was fourteen and working as Leo Frank's office boy, he saw Jim Conley just after noon on Confederate Memorial Day carrying Mary Phagan's limp body in the lobby of the National Pencil Company's factory. Conley used a trap door (the "scuttle hole") that led via a ladder to the basement where her body was later found. Mann was unsure whether Phagan was unconscious or dead, but he definitely recalled what Conley had said to him at that moment: "If you ever mention this, I'll kill you." The *Tennessean* helpfully enhanced the front-page story with photos of the principals and an artist's rendering of Mann's traumatic encounter with Conley.

On the advice of his mother, and fearing Conley, the teenaged Mann did not reveal what he had seen when he was called to testify at Leo Frank's trial. Both Mann and his parents believed that Frank would be exonerated. Once he was convicted, Mann's parents advised their son that he and they could do nothing to change the verdict; had he tried, the mob waiting outside the courthouse would probably have attacked him. "You

Mary Phagan   Jim Conley   Alonzo Mann   The Lynching   Leo Frank

SUNDAY, March 7, 1982

THE TENNESSEAN

A GANNETT NEWSPAPER

Special News Section

An Innocent Man Was Lynched

By FRANK RITTER
JERRY THOMPSON
and ROBERT SHERBORNE
Copyright 1982, The Tennessean

LEO Frank, convicted in 1913 and lynched in 1915 in one of the most notorious murder cases in American history, was innocent, according to a sworn statement given by a witness in the case.

The testimony used to convict Frank was perjured, and the real killer of 14-year-old Mary Phagan was the man who gave that false testimony, the witness has disclosed to The Tennessean.

ALONZO MANN of Bristol, Va., is the witness. Now 83 and ailing with a heart condition, he was Frank's office boy in 1913 at the National Pencil Co. factory in Atlanta. It was there on Confederate Memorial Day in April that little Mary Phagan was slain when she went to collect the $1.20 she was owed for 10 hours of work the previous Monday.

"Leo Frank did not kill Mary Phagan," Mann said. "She was murdered instead by Jim Conley."

Mann's memory is not perfect when he is recalling people, places and events of nearly 70 years ago. But he remembers vividly the confrontation with Jim Conley, who had the limp form of Mary Phagan in his arms.

Mary's battered body was found face down on a pile of sawdust shavings in the factory basement. A cord was knotted around her neck and there was massive bleeding from a deep wound to her head. Cinders were found under her fingernails, showing she had clawed the ground in her struggles. Her underclothing was ripped but there was no evidence indicating she had been raped.

Alonzo Mann, 1982

THE SLAYING shocked Atlanta and, after an investigation, police arrested Frank, the Jewish superintendent of the factory. The prosecution's star witness was Jim Conley, who worked at the factory as a sweeper. He said Frank committed the murder.

But Mann has told The Tennessean that he saw Conley on the day of the murder with the limp body of Mary Phagan in his arms. He believes he saw this only moments after Mary had been knocked unconscious, but apparently before she was murdered. And he believes that if he had yelled out, he might have saved Mary's life.

But Mann says he did not yell out, and that Conley told him:

"IF YOU EVER MENTION this, I'll kill you."

He was frightened and ran out, Mann says. After riding a trolley home, he told his mother what had happened. She directed him to disobey his conscience and not get involved. He obeyed her.

Mann's statement puts him in direct conflict with the testimony to which Conley swore during the trial. Conley testified he was ordered by Frank to dispose of Mary Phagan's body by burning it in the basement's furnace. He said he and Frank were together the whole time they took the body from the second floor of the factory directly to the basement, using the elevator. He said he was not on the first floor with the body.

MANN, HOWEVER, says he saw Conley alone with Mary Phagan on the first floor of the building, standing near the trapdoor that led to the basement. It later became apparent — after the trial — that the elevator did not go to the basement that day. This fact was cited as crucial by Georgia Gov. John Slaton when he commuted Frank's sentence in 1915 to life imprisonment.

There is no way that what Mann says today can be reconciled with the version of events which Conley related in court in 1913. Either Conley lied then, or Mann is lying now.

Because of the historical significance of what Mann is saying, The Tennessean asked him to submit to both a lie detector test and a psychological stress evaluation examination — procedures designed to determine if someone is lying. The tests were given by the Ball Investigative Agency here, and investigator Jeffery S. Ball provided the newspaper with a formal statement saying Mann responded truthfully to every question he was asked.

THE TENNESSEAN, after an extensive investigation which included the examination of files and records in several states and interviews with people knowledgeable about the case, concluded that Mann's story needed to be made public.

This is the first time that Mann has spoken publicly about what he knows of the brutal murder which led to the most blatant display of anti-Semitism in the nation's history and to a revival of the Ku Klux Klan — an irony because Conley, the chief witness, was a black man.

Mann says he told relatives and friends about what he knew. Once, while in the Army, he got into a fight with another soldier who disputed his statement that it was Conley and not Frank who killed Mary Phagan. And he tried once to tell his story to an Atlanta reporter.

FOR NEARLY 70 years his story has been a secret, and it has preyed on his mind. Now that he perhaps does not have long to live, it is vitally important that the truth come out, he told The Tennessean.

"I want the world to know the truth," Mann explained in a series of interviews with the newspaper. "The testimony which Conley gave at the trial to convict Frank was a lie from beginning to end."

That trial, surrounded by mob hysteria and violent anti-Jewish sentiment, was the most sensational in Atlanta's history. No other trial even comes close, except perhaps that of Wayne Williams, convicted a week ago in the deaths of two young Atlanta blacks and suspected of being the mass murderer who terrorized Atlanta for months.

ALTHOUGH MARY PHAGAN was not raped, Frank was denounced as a sexual pervert, however, Conley was the only witness to suggest that.

The star prosecution witness made four separate statements to police in connection with the case, the first one saying nothing to implicate Frank. However, each of the three statements that followed increasingly involved Frank.

During the trial, it was the fourth and last statement that formed the basis for Conley's court testimony. On cross-examination he repeatedly acknowledged that he had made numerous mistakes in his earlier statements to police, but efforts by the defense to break down his tale were largely unsuccessful.

FRANK WAS FOUND guilty and sentenced to hang, but appeals delayed the execution. Two years later his sentence was commuted to life in prison after the case had created a furor across the nation.

At that point — August 1915 — a group of vigilantes stormed the prison where Frank was being held, abducted him at gunpoint and lynched him. Four blacks had been lynched in Georgia the month before.

Although he possessed information in 1913 which he believes would have cleared Frank, Alonzo Mann did not tell authorities what he knew. He says he did not speak out because Conley threatened to kill him if he did and because his mother and father convinced him he should keep silent.

NOW, FINALLY, HE has come forward with his story.

"I wish I had done it differently," he says. "I wish I had told what I knew. But I never thought Mr. Frank would be convicted. And once he was convicted, I was sure he would eventually get out of it. I knew he was not guilty.

"I never fully realized until I was older that if I had told what I knew Leo Frank would have been acquitted and gone free. Instead he was imprisoned. After he was convicted, my mother told me there was nothing we could do to change the jury's verdict. My father agreed with her. I continued to

(Turn to Page 2, Column 1)

—Drawing by Pat Mitchell

An artist's interpretation of the confrontation between Alonzo Mann, then 14, and Jim Conley, holding the limp form of Mary Phagan on the first floor of National Pencil Co.

JUSTICE BETRAYED
a sin of silence

● Page 2
The historical significance of the Mary Phagan-Leo Frank murder case.

● Page 3
The lie detector tests given Alonzo Mann. A moment of terror — the confrontation between Lonnie Mann and Jim Conley.

● Page 4
Alonzo Mann's visit to Mary Phagan's grave. The Ballad of Mary Phagan.

● Page 5
The eight key personalities in the Leo Frank story.

● Page 6
An analysis of the evidence that convicted Leo Frank.

● Page 7
An analysis of the evidence implicating Jim Conley.

● Page 8
A chronology of the Phagan-Frank case. Lonnie Mann's incomplete testimony at Leo Frank's trial.

The impact of a book by Harry Golden on the Phagan-Frank case.

● Page 9
Alonzo Mann's sworn affidavit.

● Page 10
Georgia Gov. John Slaton — a "profile in courage."

Nashville Mayor Hilary H. Howse's urging leniency for Frank.

The Phagan-Frank case — a boon to newspaper circulation.

The front page of the March 7, 1982, *Nashville Tennessean* reports on Alonzo Mann's new revelations. (© 1982 The Tennessean. Reprinted with permission.)

know," he told Steve Oney in 1984, "you think entirely different when you're fourteen. And out in front of the courthouse, there were hundreds of people. Some of 'em had sticks, and one of 'em had an ax." Mann stepped forward with this story in 1982 because he was terminally ill and burdened by a guilty conscience; he told the paper: "I know, of course, that because I kept silent Leo Frank lost his life."[2]

Mann was too hard on himself. Oney points out that Mann's statements—though both startling and utterly believable—were nevertheless inconclusive evidence of Conley's guilt: his recollections proved only that Conley did not take the elevator and therefore gave perjured testimony on the stand. Mann's comments did not definitively exonerate Frank and convict Conley of Phagan's murder. It is possible—though highly implausible—that Conley was acting as Frank's accomplice when Mann saw him carrying Phagan's body.[3] But why would Conley lie about this if not to hide the fact that he killed Mary Phagan?

In 1983, inspired by Mann's revelations, the Anti-defamation League (ADL) petitioned Georgia's Board of Pardons to pardon Frank. The board refused because a complete pardon required absolute proof of the accused's innocence. In response to the ADL's second appeal in 1986, the board overruled Frank's conviction—not because he was irrefutably innocent but because, in Leonard Dinnerstein's words, "his lynching prevented his continued appeal of his conviction and . . . the state had failed to bring his killers to justice." Mann's revelation and the ADL's pardon requests inspired two new books on the case—one asserting Frank's innocence, the other his guilt.[4] Oney began writing his massive study of the case at this time as well.

When Mann made his confession, producer George Stevens Jr. had already begun preparing a two-part television miniseries on the case that would air under the title *The Murder of Mary Phagan*. First broadcast on NBC in late January 1988, the miniseries still constitutes the most thorough and painstakingly produced dramatization of the Phagan-Frank case. Its producers gave it the "full treatment"—realistic visuals created by shooting on location and a talented cast. Like the *Profiles in Courage* series, the miniseries earned many enthusiastic reviews and a Peabody Award, and also a Christopher Award for affirming "the highest values of the human spirit."[5] The miniseries also received five Emmy nominations in several categories and won in three, including Best Miniseries of the Year.

The Murder of Mary Phagan appeared at a time when the rise of cable and satellite television had already diminished the dominance of network broadcasting in the American television marketplace. The miniseries remained a powerful form of special programming, however—a more elaborate variation of the networks' made-for-TV movies and "Movie of the Week" original programming of the late 1960s and early 1970s. Made-for-TV movies often treated controversial subject matter; indeed, media historian Douglas Gomery has characterized the genre as a direct descendant of the 1930s social consciousness movies of the sort that Warner Bros.'s *They Won't Forget* typifies. While critics initially dismissed such special programming as low-budget cinema wannabes, by the late 1970s it was clear that miniseries could become major cultural events—as, for example, with *Roots* (1977), *The Holocaust* (1978), *The Day After* (1984), and *Shogun* (1988).

Given five hours of broadcast time (221 minutes without commercials), *The Murder of Mary Phagan* in effect combined all the previously depicted aspects of the case into one dramatization. It begins just before Phagan's murder and ends with Alonzo Mann's revelation in 1982. The expanded running time and the distance of seven decades allowed the filmmakers to depict nearly all the major figures in the case by name rather than via fictionalized personae. The miniseries also portrayed many other significant "characters" in the case who had not appeared in previous dramatizations, such as Alonzo Mann and Annie Maude Carter, the object of Jim Conley's unrequited prison "crush." Equally significant, the miniseries depicts the broader impersonal forces that affected Leo Frank's fate, and thereby provides insight into Georgians' outrage at what befell Mary Phagan.

Whereas previous dramatizations of the case could only hint at its unseemly aspects, *The Murder of Mary Phagan* deals explicitly with the coroner's discussion of Phagan's enlarged vagina and the suspicion that she had been raped before she was murdered, the accusations that Frank was a lecher and a pervert, the anti-Semitism of the jury and the lynchers, and the racism informing white Georgians' and the Frank legal team's view of Conley. Though NBC's Standards and Practices Department had to ensure that the miniseries was not too gritty, the network was far more tolerant of unsavory drama than it had been at the time of the *Profiles in Courage* series, in part because of the comparative freedom afforded competitive premium pay channels such as HBO.

Like the *Profiles* episode before it, *The Murder of Mary Phagan* emphasizes the heroism of John M. Slaton by omitting the troubling issue of the governor's conflict of interest in the case and by focusing most of part 2 on his reinvestigation of the trial evidence and his eventual decision to commute Frank's death sentence to life imprisonment. Some of the greatest fictional embellishments of the historical record—and grounds for criticism of the miniseries—reside here. By dramatizing Slaton's reflections on the case as a series of hearings that approximate a second trial and by portraying Slaton, Hugh Dorsey, and Tom Watson as political allies, the series deviates significantly from the known history of the case, complicating its status as a signal achievement in screen dramatizations of the Phagan-Frank case. The creative team took this approach to create a more powerful drama and to avoid a simple black-and-white account of the principals involved. But in doing so they also reignited the more general debate over the historical docudrama's accuracy.

Production Background

Although its timing seems to indicate that *The Murder of Mary Phagan* was made to capitalize on Alonzo Mann's sensational revelations in the early 1980s, producer-writer George Stevens Jr. and veteran television director Billy Hale had conceived the project well before Mann reappeared on the scene. Stevens and Hale had served together in the U.S. Air Force as motion picture officers in 1954 and were reunited when Hale worked as a second-unit director on *The Greatest Story Ever Told* (George Stevens Sr.'s 1965 epic about the life of Christ). Hale had been a documentary filmmaker in the intervening years and had become an A-list director of network television series episodes in the 1960s and 1970s. Many of the episodes he directed involved law and order; for example, *Judd for the Defense*, *The Streets of San Francisco*, *Cannon*, *Barnaby Jones*, *Kojak*, and *The Paper Chase*. Hale grew up just fifty miles from where Frank was lynched and had always thought the Phagan-Frank story would make a great television drama.[6]

Stevens attributed his general interest in the Frank case to the influence of his celebrated father, whose most successful films dealt sympathetically with loner figures longing to be part of mainstream society: George Eastman (Montgomery Clift) in *A Place in the Sun* (1951), the title character (Alan Ladd) in *Shane* (1952), and Jett Rink (James Dean) in *Giant* (1955). In publicity for *The Murder of Mary Phagan*, Stevens Jr. noted that such films focus on "an outsider who gets entangled with the machinery of justice and meets an unhappy end. But they explore the human spirit and

A young George Stevens Jr. poses with his father, a major Hollywood veteran director. (Courtesy of the Academy of Motion Picture Arts and Sciences.)

the human heart."[7] Leo Frank's position as the resented, college-educated, upper-middle-class Jewish northerner in Atlanta certainly fit that description. It was Stevens's unique insight that Slaton was Frank's mirror image in this respect: a consummate insider when he considered Frank's appeal, and a scapegoat and outsider after he commuted Frank's sentence.

Stevens Jr. also had a strong connection to the same liberal Democratic political and cultural world that revolved around President Kennedy and resulted in the *Profiles* series. He had worked with Edward R. Murrow in the early 1960s as head of the Motion Picture Division of the U.S. Information Agency. Given his background, it was not a huge leap to move from documentaries to docudramas. After initiating the Kennedy Center Honors in 1978 and serving as founding director of the American Film Institute, Stevens was ready in the early 1980s to produce his own projects—and it was then that he and Hale turned to the Phagan-Frank project.[8]

Both Hale and Stevens were further inspired to develop this project by a 1965 book entitled *A Little Girl Is Dead*, written by Jewish columnist, editor, humorist, and civil rights activist Harry Golden, whom Stevens had met while working on *The Greatest Story Ever Told*. Golden's book is a novelistically detailed account of Phagan's murder, the trial, and the Frank lynching; and it clearly relies on newspaper accounts and personal recollections. Though positively reviewed on its release, the book was generally overshadowed by the publication of another true-crime bestseller that appeared that same fall: Truman Capote's *In Cold Blood*.[9]

Stevens and Hale wanted to buy the rights to Golden's book, but producer Stanley Kramer—famous for his own message movie courtroom dramas such as *Inherit the Wind* (1960) and *Judgement at Nuremberg* (1961)—had already done so in the late 1960s.[10] Undeterred, Stevens and Hale decided to research the Phagan-Frank case on their own, consulting "stacks and stacks of the original newspapers and court documents," as well as other published accounts of the case: "We were starting from scratch as it were. . . . But if we had chosen to acquire one of the other books, we would have done that work anyway, because you just want to tell your story, not somebody else's story." For legal reasons the script's coauthor, Jeffrey Lane, had to corroborate every story point from newspaper accounts, trial transcripts, or both. Consulting historical materials had the added benefit of furnishing details for story action and character personalities—what Stevens called "texture." Lucille Frank's love of opera was one such detail; detective William J. Burns's love of peanuts was another.[11]

After enlisting NBC's support, Stevens persuaded his Washington, D.C., neighbor, Texas novelist Larry McMurtry, to write the script for a two-hour movie-of-the-week dramatization. McMurtry, who was already famous for his novels and their successful film adaptations (including *Hud* [1963], *The Last Picture Show* [1972], and *Terms of Endearment* [1983]), agreed.[12] After McMurtry had completed his script, an NBC network executive balked at proceeding with the project, but the network subsequently signed Orion Television to produce a two-part miniseries on the Phagan-Frank case, and network head Grant Tinker invited Stevens to join the Orion team. By that time, however, McMurtry had moved back to Texas and was immersed in other projects. So Stevens turned to Jeffrey Lane, his writer for several televised American Film Institute tributes and an experienced prime-time television writer. Lane had also authored scripts for *Lou Grant* (in 1977), *Ryan's Hope* (1978–83, for which he won two Emmys and three Writers' Guild Awards), and *Cagney and Lacey*, and would go on to write for and produce the hit series *Mad About You*.[13]

Stevens and Lane brought unique talents to the project: Stevens's political experience gave him a feel for "what worked in the political sense," he noted, and Lane provided "more detail and more characters. He was especially good at creating details of Frank's relationships, particularly Frank's with his wife." McMurtry ultimately received "Story by" credit for the miniseries, and Stevens and Lane received screenplay credit. Lane's extensive story conferences with Stevens and Hale enabled him to expand the script into its four-hour form within a brisk seven months.

Of their decision to give Governor Slaton extensive screen time in part 2, Stevens recalled:

> Billy Hale and I both had a feeling from the outset, that we didn't want to make that kind of "it couldn't happen here" story, in which the primary audience involvement was, "Isn't this an outrage?" You need more than that. You know it's a terrible thing that happened, but if that's all that you have going for you in telling the story, it's not enough for the audience, or it's not enough for us as filmmakers. And the character of the governor gave you an opportunity for there to be a character in whom you could yourself invest, who did not have the entirely tragic aspect of Leo Frank.
>
> And also, the governor's story is a very good story of investigation and political commitment and, eventually, political sacrifice.

NBC's interest in a two-part miniseries allowed the filmmakers to combine the social protest of *They Won't Forget* ("it can't happen here") with the inspirational focus on John M. Slaton of the *Profiles* episode.

Publicity reports on the miniseries variously pegged the budget between seven and nine million dollars.[14] Though small by miniseries standards of the period, that amount allowed Stevens to hire a first-rate group of actors and an accomplished production team. Jack Lemmon, for instance, one of Hollywood's premiere dramatic and comic actors, took on the role of Governor John Slaton after Stevens's first choice, Jimmy Stewart, turned it down. (According to Stevens, "It seemed he [Stewart] thought the script was a liberal tract, with its civil rights angle. This was during the Reagan years, and he just wasn't comfortable with it.") Stevens secured Lemmon by telling him about the project during a golf outing. Lemmon had already received Academy Awards for Best Actor (for *Save the Tiger*, 1973) and Best Supporting Actor (for *Mr. Roberts*, 1955). His credits included Billy Wilder's *Some Like It Hot* (1959), *The Apartment* (1960), and the Neil Simon 1968 smash hit *The Odd Couple*. Just prior to *The Murder of Mary Phagan* Lemmon had starred in Jonathan Miller's revival of Eugene

O'Neill's *Long Day's Journey into Night*. In 1988, the year the miniseries was broadcast, Lemmon received the American Film Institute's Life Achievement Award.

The cast also featured a number of other talented and seasoned professionals. Playing the role of private detective William J. Burns was Paul Dooley, an established television series actor and cocreator of PBS's *The Electric Company* but now probably more familiar for his roles in Christopher Guest's "mockumentaries" *Waiting for Guffman* (1993) and *A Mighty Wind* (2003). Richard Jordan was cast as Hugh M. Dorsey. Jordan is today best known for his performance as National Security Adviser Dr. Jeffrey Pelt in *The Hunt for Red October* (1990) and Brigadier General Lewis A. Armistead in *Gettysburg* (1993), but in 1987 he was a two-decade veteran of theater, television series, and films. Stevens cast Washington, D.C., Arena Stage and film veteran Robert Prosky to play Tom Watson. Prosky's movie credits to that time included *Thief* (1981), *The Natural* (1984), and *Broadcast News* (1987). By 1988 he was much acclaimed for playing Sergeant Jablonski on *Hill Street Blues*. Kathryn Walker (Sallie Slaton) and Kenneth Welsh (lead defense attorney Luther Rosser) had appeared in several major Broadway productions and a number of feature films.

Equally striking about the miniseries cast is the number of actors then new to movies (not unlike Gloria Dickson, Allyn Joslyn, and Lana Turner in *They Won't Forget*) who are now film and television stars. Jeffrey Lane even drafted some of the roles with these actors in mind. Kevin Spacey portrayed the alcoholic reporter Wesley Brent—a composite of Britt Craig and other reporters on the case—five years before his breakthrough role as a desperate real estate agent in *Glengarry Glen Ross* (1992). In 1987, however, Spacey would have been recognizable for appearing as Jamie Tyrone opposite Lemmon onstage in *Long Day's Journey into Night* and his role on television's *Wiseguy*. Similarly, Peter Gallagher, as Leo Frank, had won praise and a Tony nomination for his performance opposite Spacey and Lemmon as Edmund Tyrone. The miniseries appeared one year before Gallagher's central role in Steven Soderbergh's independent film phenomenon, *sex, lies and videotape* (1989). For the pivotal role of Jim Conley, Stevens cast Charles Dutton, who had already starred in the Broadway premiere of August Wilson's *Ma Rainey's Black Bottom*. William H. Macy, now famous as the sleazy car salesman Jerry Lundegaard in *Fargo* (1996), was cast as Mary Phagan's neighbor Randy. Dylan Baker (Dr. Curt Connors in *Spiderman*

Some of the miniseries's all-star cast: (standing) Jack Lemmon as Governor Slaton, Robert Jordan as Hugh M. Dorsey, and Robert Prosky as Tom Watson; (seated) Rebecca Miller as Lucille Frank and Peter Gallagher as Leo Frank. (Courtesy of the Cinema-Television Library, University of Southern California.)

2 [2004] and *Spiderman 3* [2007]) was cast as Ravenal, Slaton's executive secretary.

The smaller women's roles went to equally promising performers. Loretta Devine, who had starred in the Broadway production of *Dreamgirls* and had a regular part on the 1987–88 season of the *The Cosby Show* spinoff *A Different World*, played Annie Maude Carter, the woman to whom Conley writes lascivious love letters in jail. Cynthia Nixon, now best known as Miranda Hobbes in the *Sex and the City* series, portrayed Mary Phagan's friend and coworker Doreen Camp, who gives crucial testimony at Leo Frank's trial. Sculptor and visual artist Rebecca Miller, daughter of playwright Arthur Miller and photographer Inge Morath, made her professional acting debut as Lucille Frank—a part for which Stevens also had considered Sarah Jessica Parker and Joan Allen. All in all, the miniseries featured an outstanding cast.

By the time production designer Veronica Hadfield joined the crew (after a three-year stint as international art director on the mammoth 1988 miniseries *War and Remembrance*), Stevens, Hale, and their scouts had settled on downtown Richmond, Virginia, as the appropriate location for Atlanta exteriors and interiors. (As George Cukor had discovered fifty years earlier while visiting Atlanta in preparation for David O. Selznick's *Gone with the Wind* [1939], William Tecumseh Sherman and enthusiastic redevelopment had left few vintage buildings suitable for shooting a period project in Atlanta.) Richmond's Greek-style state capitol, designed by Thomas Jefferson, was well suited to stand in for the governor's mansion. The forbidding old city hall, with its tower, served reasonably well as the Fulton County Jail. The grand interior of the Jefferson-Sheraton Hotel in Richmond provided the setting for the Democratic Party soiree interrupted by Lucille Frank and Frank supporters from around the country.[15] Hadfield secured authentic antiques, including Lucille Frank's wind-up gramophone and automobiles from the early twentieth century, and with set decorator Deborah Schutt dressed interiors and exteriors for a period feel. For the costumes Stevens and Hale hired Merrily Murray-Walsh and, most notably, veteran Judy Moorcroft, then admired for her work on David Lean's *A Passage to India* and *The Killing Fields* (both 1984).

Equally important to the production design was the availability of abandoned factories in downtown Richmond that were about to be converted into condominiums. The one chosen to represent the National Pencil Company's factory, with its high ceilings and wooden beams, proved perfect for the alternately oppressive and mysterious mood of the factory

The old city hall in Richmond, Virginia, was the Fulton County Jail in the miniseries.

The Fulton County Jail with its tower. The press dubbed Frank "the silent man in the tower" because he refused to give interviews. (Courtesy of the Kenan Research Center at the Atlanta History Center.)

scenes. It included an office on the second floor (used as Leo Frank's) and an old-fashioned industrial elevator with vertically sliding wooden doors. The Musgrave Pencil Company in Shelbyville, Tennessee, loaned the production circa-1900 machinery used for hand-laid lead pencil manufacturing and its employees showed the cast how to use it.[16] Like all the locations used, the factory's prominence in the opening sequence added to the series's period realism.

The choice of Nic Knowland for series cinematographer was, like the hiring of Veronica Hadfield, part of the producers' strategy to shoot *The Murder of Mary Phagan* like a film rather than a television program. Knowland, a British cinematographer, made little distinction between shooting for film and for television. George Stevens corroborated this assessment: "I had called a director who had done a large historical miniseries because both Billy and I didn't want the television look. The networks at that time felt that everything should be brightly lit, everything in close-ups, that television was a close-up medium. And we wanted to give it a cinematic look." Knowland's use of camera cranes—when Mary Phagan's body is loaded into a hearse, when Leo Frank speaks in his own defense at the trial and at Slaton's hearing, and when Slaton hands over the state seal to his successor—adds an epic quality to the miniseries.

Knowland had shot a number of John Lennon's and Yoko Ono's short films, as well as The Who's performance at the Isle of Wight rock concert. His credits also included such high-profile television films as the controversial *Death of a Princess* (1980) and an adaptation of Thomas Mann's *Death in Venice* (1981). A television director told Stevens that Knowland's work was comparable with that of master cinematographer Vittorio Storaro, famed for his lush and painterly use of lighting and color in such Oscar-winning work as *Apocalypse Now* (1979), *Reds* (1980), and *The Last Emperor* (1987).

Knowland's previous work on documentaries gave him the confidence to shoot off the cuff and without a lot of preplanning, which was invaluable given how late he arrived on the production. Knowland later recalled spending perhaps three days looking at the chosen locations and conferring with Hadfield about the look and tonality of the sets and the shots; they chose darker sets and lighting schemes to counter the tendency of network technicians in the late 1980s to brighten the film image. Given that principal photography lasted just eight weeks—from May through early July 1987—Knowland's ability to work quickly was essential, as was the ability of the very professional cast to shoot scenes without prolonged rehearsals.[17] Moreover, Knowland was known to be skilled at shooting darker-skinned characters after his experience in *Playing Away* (1987), a film about Indian cricketers in London. Considering the prominence of Jim Conley and Annie Maude Carter in the script, that talent, Stevens said, "was the frosting on the cake."

A final, major production coup for the miniseries was hiring the prolific veteran composer Maurice Jarre, who had scored such epics as *The Longest Day* (1962), *Lawrence of Arabia* (1962), *Dr. Zhivago* (1965), *Ryan's Daughter* (1970), and *A Passage to India* (1984); he received Oscars for the latter three. Jarre also had written music for more personal dramas, the best of which included *Witness* (1985) and *The Mosquito Coast* (1986). Stevens decided on Jarre after seeing *Fatal Attraction* (1987), whose score has the same minimalist effect Stevens was seeking. Although Jarre was "too big for this project," Stevens recalled, he agreed to do it. The two watched *The Murder of Mary Phagan* and together decided where music would enhance the film. "Often," Stevens noted, "composers are lobbying to have more music in the film. But Maurice would say, 'Tell me why you need music here.' Maurice is a filmmaker and . . . very rigorous, and I so valued his collaboration in deciding where music should be and his restraint about where not to overlard it." Indeed, Jarre's score plays for thirty minutes at most during the entire duration of the miniseries.

Jarre's music features both an ominous melody and a more wistful main theme, which are heard in succession in the opening shots. The ominous theme plays at inauspicious moments—such as when Mary Phagan enters the factory alone, when Leo Frank realizes that the police consider him a suspect, when Dorsey has Conley reenact his "lookout" role for Frank at the factory, and when Lucille fears that Leo has been unfaithful to her. It crescendos when John Slaton asks Alonzo Mann what he knows about Mary Phagan's murder. The more hopeful major theme is associated with Mary Phagan and working-class Georgians—for example, we hear it as Phagan performs in *Sleeping Beauty*, when her body is loaded into the hearse, and when Dorsey and Watson confer in the countryside; it is also the melody at the wedding dance in part 2. Jarre's participation furthered Stevens's and Hale's aim to make the miniseries more cinematic than televisual.

Thus, by late spring 1987 Stevens and Hale had in place the scripting, casting, production design, and cinematography to mount their dramatization of the Mary Phagan–Leo Frank case.

The Larger Forces at Work

Befitting the extensive research on which the script is based, the sweeping impersonal forces that shaped the fates of Mary Phagan and Leo Frank are apparent from the very first moments of *The Murder of Mary Phagan*. An examination of those moments shows how carefully the series's creators established them.

The Phagan family's dislocation in leaving tenant farming in rural Georgia to seek work in the city is immediately evident. With the fade-in at the start of the miniseries, the camera tilts up from spare, unpicked cotton plants to reveal a field full of languishing cotton and then pans right to a long shot of a dilapidated farmhouse (presumably in Marietta).[18] As music plays in the background, the Phagans say farewell to family (or

The first image of the miniseries emphasizes tenant farmers' difficulties by focusing on sparse cotton plants.

The shot then tilts up and pans right to the Phagan family preparing to leave their home for Atlanta.

perhaps neighbors) and begin their trek on foot to Atlanta. As the family continues walking, the narrator (George Stevens Jr.) provides a very general description of the story's time and place: "It was early in the twentieth century. In the South, cotton had fallen to five cents a pound. Families were losing their farms. Their hope lay in the cities, where new industry promised opportunity and jobs. It was a time of change, and with change would come conflict." The scene eventually shifts to Mary standing on an Atlanta street, shot from a low angle behind her as she looks at the posted flyer advertising jobs at the pencil factory and then turns and approaches the factory.

As the credits continue, a cut takes us to the factory's interior, where we see girls at work. The overwhelming noise and poor lighting provide jarring contrast with the countryside and lyrical music of the preceding scenes. The pencil-making machinery is prominent in a few shots, and Hadfield's production design and Knowland's low-key lighting re-create the dark, sepia-toned, barely lit, suffocating quality of the factory in spite of its expansive spaces. A vague haze (courtesy of a "smoker" pumping compressed air through a fifty-gallon barrel of liquid paraffin) hangs over these scenes and also evokes stifling heat.[19] The soundtrack mix emphasizes the machines' deafening noise; we can barely hear any dialogue—not that the workers are allowed to talk to each other. It is clear how alien the factory must have been to the many young women who worked there—dark, unnatural, and unhealthy. These opening scenes—countryside and factory—build on a principle that Veronica Hadfield credited to Dan Curtis, the director of *War and Remembrance*, which was also broadcast

The series title credit features Mary Phagan walking toward the pencil factory after reading a help-wanted sign.

The National Pencil Company factory around the time of Mary Phagan's murder. Terminal Station is visible in the background at right. (Courtesy of the Kenan Research Center at the Atlanta History Center.)

in 1988: "Seduce the audience from the get-go. . . . If you spend money on the first five, ten minutes, they are with you for the rest of the program."

If Mary Phagan belongs to the countryside, the factory interior scenes are clearly Leo Frank's domain. Although Frank has been visible in the establishing shots of the factory interior, we first see him clearly in medium shot as he exits the elevator during the credit sequence—a nice touch because the elevator will prove crucial to the commutation of his sentence. Frank walks around the facilities, checking on the work of "his" girls. These shots indicate the source of unspoken conflict between labor and

The first shot inside the pencil factory shows Leo Frank looking over the girls' work.

The Musgrave Pencil Company's antique machinery is featured in the opening scene at the factory.

management that will motivate much of the girls' testimony against him at the trial. Frank pauses to tell one girl (Doreen Camp, as it happens) that her stamping on the pencils is uneven, and she responds with an uneasy smile, "Okay, Mr. Frank." This exchange shows both that Frank does not bother to learn his employees' names and that he directly and freely criticizes them. Here, Lane and Stevens may have drawn on Alonzo Mann's 1982 recollections of Frank: "When he wanted something done, he wanted it done right away, and if it wasn't done correctly, he would tell you about it."[20]

As a case in point, Frank abruptly enters the girls' changing room and catches them flirting with the boy sweepers outside the window. When Frank scolds the girls, saying that they should flirt on their own time, one replies, "We're undressing here, blame it," adding, "We're just getting some fresh air." Oney recounts this episode in *And the Dead Shall Rise* and its later use in Frank's trial. In the late stages of the prosecution's case, a witness testified that Frank had barged into the girls' changing room un-announced and "just stood there and laughed. Miss Jackson said, 'Well, we are dressing, blame it,' and then he shut the door." Dorsey portrayed this incident as evidence of Frank's lechery. The defense claimed it was simply Frank's conscientious approach to his job—one girl even admitted on the stand that they did flirt with boys outside the window.[21]

The ambiguity of Frank's motivations for these actions generates a fur-ther irony. Although he may want the girls to work more assiduously, he is also acting in loco parentis to protect them from the kind of free encounters with members of the opposite sex that their parents feared. Historian Nancy MacLean notes that a significant portion of the outrage

Leo Frank catches his employees flirting with boys at their locker-room window.

against Frank expressed by the parents of pencil factory employees was motivated by these very perceptions: "Some spoke as parents who had entrusted their children to employers' custody in exchange for the wages that their labor could bring. They now felt furious at Frank's alleged betrayal of that trust."[22] Frank's supervisory actions might have been part of the solution to their fears, but his alleged lechery was ultimately perceived to be the problem.

The second half of this brief scene reinforces our sense that Frank is protective of his employees. After the flirtatious girls leave, Frank finds another employee prostrate with pain (from "cramps," she informs him) on a locker room bench. While not a specific incident in the case, this detail alludes to the Frank defense's alternative explanation of the blood found on the lathe room floor: it was not Mary Phagan's blood from a rape or attempted rape in which she hit her head, but menstrual blood from one of the factory girls. A medium shot reveals that while Frank is disappointed that the stricken girl cannot work and extremely uncomfortable to hear this very personal information, he is somewhat sympathetic to her plight and suggests she rest until the pain passes. While Frank may take his work seriously—he may even be a tense, neurotic workaholic—he is not a slave driver. Nevertheless, his quiet nervousness is part of what unnerved his employees and coworkers.

Indeed, Peter Gallagher's performance—here and throughout the series—is delivered complete with a New York Jewish accent and a flutter of eyelids to convey how uncomfortable Frank feels in his own body and around others, even when that "other" is his wife. Gallagher's casting is notable because, while the rest of the cast differs dramatically in physical appearance from their historical personages, Gallagher closely resembles Leo Frank—appropriately so, since Frank's appearance was part of what encouraged Atlantans to demonize him—although Gallagher's larger build and photogenic qualities mitigate what some described as Frank's physically unappealing appearance. Jeffrey Lane recalled that casting Gallagher as Leo Frank was a key strategy to show Leo Frank in a less-than-innocent light:

> A lot of people had started to sanitize Leo Frank. And make it like he was this poor victim. He was *weird*—there was something very odd about him. In fact, when we went to cast Leo Frank, and we brought up Peter Gallagher, NBC's view was that he was too handsome. . . . They wanted . . . a nebbishy little Jewish guy. And it could have become this "Oh, this poor victim and these horrible southerners." And that wasn't the case. Number one, we didn't want to do that dramatically. But more to the point, it wasn't the truth. There was something odd about this guy. I do believe he might have looked at the girls, so who knows? I don't believe he was guilty of the murder. I do believe he might have made these girls uncomfortable or . . . they might have interpreted it that way. But we had to show why they interpreted it that way—whether it was actually lecherous or not.

Lane's sentiment about Frank's interest in women is explicitly expressed by Luther Rosser in part 1; during a recess in the trial, Rosser tells his associate, Reuben Arnold, "Flirting doesn't make you a murderer."

The filmmakers planted another hint about Frank's character soon after the scene in the changing room. At the end of the workday, Frank watches the girls intently from behind his glass office door as they file out. He displays an unusual interest in Mary, following her with a hard stare. She returns his gaze briefly and then giggles something to the girl in front of her as they walk away. (He has already briefly smiled at her while making the rounds early in the factory sequence.) The accusation that Frank lusted after Mary Phagan could have been built on just such a fleeting exchange of looks. When he subsequently tells Mary Phagan on Confederate Memorial Day, "Miss—you look very pretty today," and then says, "I hope my observation doesn't offend you," he adds to our uncertainty about his connection to her. He may have claimed that he did not know the girls in his employ by name, but these verbal and visual exchanges demonstrate that he knew Mary by sight at least. At the same time, is not his apology to Mary evidence of his fundamental decency? Could this man really be a lecher, even a murderer?

Leo Frank and Mary Phagan give each other a sustained look.

Exiting the factory that day, Mary sees Leo Frank through his office window.

Leo Frank gives Mary Phagan a hard stare in return. He is frequently shot behind doors, windows, and bars.

The shot of Frank looking at the girls from behind the glass window inaugurates a visual motif that will develop throughout the film—the visual framing of Frank. His face viewed through the glass panes and bars of the window visualizes ambivalence in Frank's position in the factory—the manager who oversees the girls from a place of power is also isolated from his employees, an outsider. For example, immediately after Jim Conley's first appearance—in which Conley demands a dime from Alonzo—we see Frank through the window bars of his office as he prepares to work on the books. Later, of course, we will see him through bars and window frames when he enters "the Tower" of the Fulton County Jail.

Although the bulk of the miniseries focuses on other major figures in the case, *The Murder of Mary Phagan* takes more time than any previous dramatization to convey a sense of Mary Phagan's home life and community. After the factory sequence, a subsequent scene shows Phagan portraying Sleeping Beauty in a church play attended by appreciative friends (includ-

Mary Phagan (in the background) leaves home after her father (actually her stepfather) has asked her to get her pay.

ing Alonzo Mann, who told the *Nashville Tennessean* of attending that performance two weeks before Phagan's murder).[23] After Frank's trial, in part 2, Mary's neighbors Lund and Randy, who also attended the performance, assault detective William J. Burns when he crashes a neighborhood wedding to ask question about the Frank case. These scenes evoke the sense of neighborhood that binds working-class Atlantans, something the Franks never enjoy.

On Confederate Memorial Day, Phagan prepares to go downtown for the parade: she puts on a straw hat and, at her mother's insistence, takes an umbrella. As Phagan leaves, her father mentions that they are "running kinda short this week" and asks her to pick up her pay; when she is gone, he comments to Randy, "I never thought a daughter of mine would have to work in the factory." Her father briefly verbalizes the humiliation, his and his family's, of being uprooted from their farm and forced to move into the city, then having to send his daughter to work. His comment also hints at the economic forces that predisposed poor Georgians against Frank when he was accused. Randy's teasing comment when he declines to accompany Mary into town—that she is going to meet "a fella"—picks up on parents' fears of adolescent girls' sexual vulnerability in the big city. Frank symbolized everything working-class Georgians resented about their lives.

As in *They Won't Forget*, the Confederate Memorial Day celebration introduces us to the major political figures in the case. Slaton, Sallie, and Tom Watson ride together to the park (not to Atlanta's Oakland Cemetery, where the ceremonial speeches were actually made), where Slaton shows his skill as a politician. He pauses for a photo with children in Confederate uniform and pinches a child's cheek, all without missing a beat as he heads

Governor Slaton takes advantage of a photo opportunity with young Atlanta children waving Confederate flags on Confederate Memorial Day.

Mary Phagan walks against the holiday crowd en route to the pencil factory, her umbrella held high.

Mary Clay en route to the Buxton Business College on Confederate Memorial Day in *They Won't Forget*.

for the grandstand. He and Watson join Hugh Dorsey, who is seen escorting the widow of General Stonewall Jackson (a false detail in Golden's account) to the podium.[24] En route to the stand, Slaton jokes with Dorsey about the latter's ambitiousness: he would marry frail old Mrs. Jackson if he "thought it was worth fifty votes." On the platform, Slaton gives an impassioned, well-received speech about bringing new industry to Georgia and the state's unlimited promise.

Before Slaton's speech, however, there is a cutaway to two different locales. First, we see Phagan en route to the factory, walking against the crowd rushing to see the festivities. This shot follows the logic of the shot of Mary Clay in *They Won't Forget* as she returns to the Buxton Business School for her makeup. At one point, all we can see is Phagan's yellow umbrella sticking up above the crowd—foreshadowing its importance to the case.

This point-of-view shot as Mary Phagan enters Leo Frank's office visualizes how the safe door could obscure Frank's presence.

Jim Conley is seen for the first time in the foreground as the camera pans left with Alonzo Mann, who is making his way to the factory.

Inside the factory, Knowland for the first time used a handheld, first-person shot to create a sense of mystery and danger as Mary approaches Frank's apparently empty office. Frank rolls into view on his office chair from behind the huge safe door when she calls his name. The fact that the safe door could obscure Frank's presence in his office was a point the defense made at his trial. Monteen Stover (Doreen Camp in the series) claimed Frank's office was empty when she came for her pay after Phagan had come for hers. The implication was that Frank was elsewhere in the factory attacking Phagan.

The other crucial cutaway from Slaton's speech is to young Alonzo Mann, who is approaching the festivities. As the camera pans left with Alonzo in the background, it reveals Jim Conley lying beneath a tree in medium shot. Conley is imposing in the frame as he calls out commandingly to Alonzo, "Stop. Give me a dime, white boy." When in shot–reverse shot Alonzo claims that he does not have a dime, Conley cries out, "Just one dime, Alonzo, I want a beer." This short scene illustrates Mann's recollections in the *Nashville Tennessean*: "Although it was early in the morning, Conley had obviously already consumed considerable beer. He drank a lot, even in the mornings. He spoke to me. He asked me for a dime to buy beer. A dime could buy a good-sized bottle of beer in those days. . . . I told Jim Conley I didn't have a dime. That was not the truth. I had some money in my pocket, but I had let Conley have a nickel or a dime for beer before. He never paid me back."[25]

This exchange efficiently establishes Conley's perpetual drunkenness, his slothfulness, and the kind of power he wields over Mann. Significantly, here Conley calls him "white boy" and by his first name, whereas he will call all the white adults "boss." We can easily imagine this Conley threatening Mann to keep silent about what he saw in the factory lobby. The miniseries does not depict or even describe in any detail that particular encounter aside from a brief shot of Mann fleeing the factory to ominous music. Conley's desire for a dime here also sets up his likely motivation for killing Phagan: he tried to steal her pay envelope and then killed her so she could not accuse him of the crime. This line of thought is what Alonzo Mann recounted to Steve Oney in December 1984, shortly before he died: "I know what I know. I know why he had the little girl, too. He wanted her money. He'd wanted to borrow money from me earlier in the day."[26]

By this point, the exposition of *The Murder of Mary Phagan* is complete; we have met nearly all the major characters. The series proceeds to provide details on the key personalities involved in the case. Each character illustrates a social and cultural force that was crucial in ensuring Frank's conviction and lynching.

Case Details: Newt Lee, Wes Brent, and the Atlanta Police

The Murder of Mary Phagan takes advantage of its extended running time to depict an extraordinary number of incidents from the case. There is Frank atypically asking Newt Lee to come back to work later on that Saturday; Frank's confrontation with fired employee John Lund (standing in for bookkeeper James Milton Gantt), who appears at the factory on Confederate Memorial Day to retrieve his shoes from his locker; Frank's atypical call to Lee that night to make sure everything is all right; the scene in which reporter Wes Brent is drunk and asleep in the back of the police car when they drive to the factory after Lee reports finding Mary's body; Brent discovering the murder notes, reading them aloud, and then jotting down notes for an article ("Child murdered in factory identifies her killer"—a detail recounted in Golden's book); Frank trying to delay getting into the police car early the following morning when he is asked to identify Mary's body; Frank trying to get Newt Lee to tell him what he knows and informing the terrified, handcuffed Lee that they "are both going straight to hell"; Frank removing his jacket to show his police interrogators that there are no scratches on his body, indicating he could not have struggled with Mary Phagan or killed her.[27]

Fired employee John Lund asks Leo Frank and Newt Lee if he can retrieve his shoes.

Wes Brent sleeps off a binge in the back of a police car, as did Britt Craig of the *Atlanta Constitution* and the reporter Brock in *They Won't Forget*.

Wes Brent discovers and reads the murder notes as Newt Lee prays in the background (left) and Mary Phagan's body rests in the foreground (right).

The series also emphasizes the role of the crowd and the press in pre-venting a fair trial for Frank. Wes Brent recognizes the importance of the crowds that form outside the pencil factory, the funeral parlor, and police headquarters. "This isn't some colored woman getting cut up," he tells his skeptical editor. "It's not even another lynching. It's a little girl, a little white girl, poor, working in that factory for northerners at twelve cents an hour. It's on the people's faces outside: they wrote it." Like Brock, his predecessor in *They Won't Forget*, Brent knows a good story when he sees it. Also like Brock, Brent's reporting turns the crowd against Frank almost immediately: at the start of the following scene, the camera cranes up from the red headlines blaring out Brent's story to reveal the crowd reading it outside the funeral home where the Phagan family is receiving visitors. As the Franks and Uncle Sig Montag arrive, we hear the disgusted comments

Wes Brent listens as a brothel madam tells him and a police detective that Leo Frank was a regular customer with perverted tastes, and that he wanted to hide Mary Phagan's dead body in the brothel.

Wes Brent writes the madam's story, although he knows it is untrue.

from the crowd: "Look at that car, would you?" "Rich Yankees. They got that little girl working twelve cents an hour and let this happen." Brent's exchange with Doreen Camp in this scene—getting her name and having the photographer take her photo—is virtually identical with Brock's questioning of Mary Clay's gossipy friend Imogene in *They Won't Forget*. Inside the funeral home, Uncle Sig correctly observes to Frank, "The papers are blowing this all out of proportion." Part 1 is punctuated with newspaper headlines that drive the story forward; as they did in 1913, the newspapers here name Frank "the silent man in the tower" because he refuses to give interviews.

The Murder of Mary Phagan thus portrays the press as reflecting the priorities, sentiments, and suspicions of ordinary Georgians. By the time Brent writes a front-page article entitled "Leo a Pervert," based on the dubious claims of a brothel madam that Frank sought to hide Phagan's body in her house, Brent's contribution to Frank's fate is unmistakable. Further, Brent writes the story even though he shares Hugh Dorsey's skepticism that this tale is "a vaudeville act" that the police arranged.[28]

The visit to the brothel is one of the few scenes in the miniseries that dwell on the police's hand in turning public opinion against Frank and securing his conviction. The Atlanta police were held in low regard (for corruption and for their failure to solve crimes) at the time of Phagan's murder, and were under great pressure to find the culprit quickly. Frank's attorney Luther Rosser suggests that the police chief's job "may be in trouble, for all I know." In part 1, the Atlanta police brutally interrogate Newt Lee to get his confession (we can hear his cries of pain offscreen). In part 2, at Hugh Dorsey's direction, they force detective William J. Burns out of town to prevent him from uncovering evidence that might support Frank's appeal to Slaton. Yet they are not as corrupt, venal, and abusive as the miniseries might have depicted them. In any case, Lucille Frank late in the trial clearly blames Brent, not the police, for her husband's dire situation. Her pleading with Brent to report on her husband's humanity shames him into abandoning his attempted interview of her in front of her home and plants the seed of his character's change of heart in part 2.

Wes Brent is not the only character who understands the significance of Phagan's murder for ordinary Georgians: so do Hugh Dorsey, John Slaton, and—most of all—Tom Watson. Their fictionalized affiliation forms the dramatic backbone of the miniseries.

The Watson-Dorsey-Slaton Alliance

Like the *Profiles in Courage* episode on John Slaton, *The Murder of Mary Phagan* treats the political aspects of the Phagan-Frank case in highly personal terms to amplify and intensify the consequences of Slaton's decision to commute Frank's sentence. "When you're doing something like this [miniseries]," George Stevens said, "you try and relate the characters to one another. It's hard to say where fact guided us and invention begins . . . . I have my own guideline. It has to do with something I would regard as the essential truth as opposed to the unvarnished fact. And I believe that as long as one is true to the essential truth of the story, then I consider it a valid way of proceeding." This dramatic thread constitutes the miniseries's most fantastic fictionalization of the case.

Stevens and Lane may have been encouraged to create the Watson-Dorsey-Slaton alliance by Golden's book, which emphasizes the connections among the three men more than any other account of the case. In any case, the miniseries, particularly Robert Prosky's performance, portrays Watson as the grand old man of the Democratic Party, a dignified if alcoholic and opportunistic kingmaker, part father and part ruthless politician—a troubling combination.

Watson became fiercely interested in the Frank case not during the original trial but during the appeals process. As individuals and organizations across the nation began agitating on Frank's behalf, and as pro-Frank articles such as the *Forum*'s 1915 piece began to appear, Watson began to rail: against Frank personally, against outside influence on Georgia justice, and against anyone who challenged the jury's verdict. C. Vann Woodward's biography of Watson describes Watson's broadsides as consisting of "rumors, half-truths, special pleadings, merciless slander, every device known to the skilled criminal lawyer. . . . He pulled all the stops: Southern chivalry, sectional animus, race prejudice, class consciousness, agrarian resentment, state pride. Aside from these resources there were the sociological constants of human cupidity, ignorance, and gullibility. He was convinced, he said, that Frank had had as fair a trial as a man could possibly have had."[29]

Indeed, Watson's fulminations against Frank, a man he never met, as excerpted in Woodward's biography are jaw-dropping: "Here we have the typical young libertine Jew who is dreaded and detested by the city authorities of the North for the very reason that Jews of this type have an utter contempt for law, and a ravenous appetite for the forbidden fruit—a lustful eagerness enhanced by the racial novelty of the girl of the uncircumcised." Watson could tell that Frank was a "lascivious pervert" just by looking at his photo, which he reprinted frequently along with exhortations to examine it closely: "bulging, satyr eyes, protruding fearfully sensual lips; and also the animal jaw."[30] Watson's politics in 1913 may have been a far cry from the interracial populism he had espoused in the 1890s, but it was lucrative and enhanced his influence: his editorial stance on the Frank case tripled the *Jeffersonian*'s circulation.

Though Watson has moments of rudeness, and though he bullies Slaton in a dramatic confrontation in part 2, nothing in the miniseries even approximates the hatefulness of his writings against Frank. That relative mildness was a conscious decision by the scriptwriters. Stevens commented that in delineating Watson's character, he and Lane sought to make him more sympathetic than he would have been at the time: "That comes more to my view of drama than of history. I've always found it interesting to have adversaries or, if you will 'villains,' that are credible and believable. If it's too easy for the audience to dismiss them, then the strength of the drama is diluted. So, I think we were probably trying to create a credible— for our times—adversary in that situation." Jeffrey Lane agreed: "Tom Watson was much more of a nightmare than we portrayed him. And we wanted to show some humanity. And again, not make [the miniseries dramatize] 'this poor little Jew who was being hunted down by the rednecks,' because everybody had their reasons." In making Watson a paternal figure of mild prejudice, extreme opportunism, and cordial friendship, Lane and Stevens made it difficult for Slaton to reject his exhortations—certainly more difficult than it was for Slaton to ignore the "threats, promises and lies" of the buffoonish Watson in the *Profiles* episode.

Watson's storied past as a prominent populist is evoked quickly through a camera pan across an array of photographs at his home, Hickory Hill, but the series accurately shows that Watson's power and influence on the case derive in large part from his keen understanding of—and pandering to—ordinary Georgians' anger and sorrow at Mary Phagan's murder. In virtually all his scenes after Confederate Memorial Day, Watson reminds anyone listening—John Slaton, Hugh Dorsey, the out-of-town reporters, and always the audience—of the larger forces at work: the failed cotton crop, the shame of the tenant farmers' poverty, and their feeling of powerlessness in the cities. When Slaton resists—in the name of the Phagan family's private grief and his reluctance to take political advantage of it—Watson's suggestion (inspired by Dorsey) that they all attend Mary Phagan's funeral, Watson pointedly instructs Slaton in the politics of the common man:

> I'm talking about Humanity. Don't ever make the mistake of thinking the man who votes for you loves you. Voting in our democratic society is touted as a positive act. It's not. It's negative. Cause most people go out to vote *against* somebody. . . .
>
> Now people are gonna be there at that funeral tomorrow to wave the train off that's carrying that child home to Jesus, and I'm talking to you about people and their feelings, not about politics. . . . Hard times, John. Hard times. The little man is hurtin'. Crops down to five cents, a man can't get work so he sends his young ones to factories for wages that would embarrass his slave. He's poor, he's worried and now he's bitter. 'Cause underneath it all, he's decent.

Such dialogue dramatizes Watson's hard-edged feel for poor Georgians for whom the pre–Civil War South is still a vivid memory and a legacy.[31] Watson repeats these comments twice in the course of the series: to Lucille Frank and Uncle Sig when they ask him to defend Leo (Watson did claim that Frank's supporters—and perhaps Frank's attorneys, if not his wife specifically—had asked him to lead Frank's defense counsel), and to northern reporters in part 2.[32]

If the relationship among Slaton, Watson, and Dorsey was far more distant and tenuous than the series depicts it, so too was Watson's anomalous position in Georgia politics in the 1910s. Watson led a "nondescript army" after 1910, notes Woodward. It was not a "party" at all but rather an "amorphous, mercurial, and unstable . . . following" with no platform but prejudices and a master rather than elected candidates.[33] Watson was much more clear about what he stood against (Catholicism, capitalism, and eventually Jews) than what he stood for, in line with his comment to Slaton that a vote for one candidate is in actuality a vote against someone else.

Historically, Watson *was* a kingmaker in Georgia politics in spite of his former allegiance to the Populist Party. Woodward writes:

> Democrats of both factions kept a beaten path to Hickory Hill, and news of Watson's favor or disfavor made or unmade many a candidate. As a boss his power was not absolute: the power of no boss is absolute. His influence waxed and waned. Yet there was no governor of the state between 1906 and the time of Watson's death, a period of sixteen years, who did not owe at least one of his terms, in a greater or less degree, to Tom Watson's support. Some of the men whom he elected he as surely defeated; in fact, that was the rule rather than the exception, for rarely did he support the same man twice.[34]

In the *Profiles in Courage* episode, Slaton and Sallie discuss how Watson supported Slaton and then turned against him. In the miniseries, the men's relationship is more durable, but Watson eventually turns against Slaton in favor of the politically ambitious Hugh Dorsey.

Hugh Dorsey and the Trial

As Slaton's teasing of Dorsey at the Memorial Day festivities demonstrates, Dorsey and Slaton are friends at the start of the miniseries; their relationship could not be more different from the cool disregard Andy Griffin and Governor Mountford display for each other in *They Won't Forget*.[35] Slaton's alienation from Dorsey grows in stages. It begins at Phagan's funeral, where Dorsey offers Mrs. Phagan his condolences; assures her, "We knew [Mary's] soul," when she questions the politicians' presence at this sad event; and announces that "this tragedy has not gone unnoticed" and that he will personally take charge of the case. "Neither I nor the people of this state will rest until justice has been done. The man who did this to little Mary will hang."

Neighborhood men nod in approval in the background as Dorsey says this, but quick reaction shots catch the surprise on the faces of Slaton and

Tom Watson, Wes Brent, and John Slaton look on as Hugh Dorsey announces at Mary Phagan's funeral that he is taking charge of the case. Watson gives him a look of shrewd appraisal.

Watson and Dorsey celebrate Dorsey's court victory.

reporter Brent. Dorsey's speech is a power grab in public (unlike Griffin's move behind closed doors in *They Won't Forget*).[36] Slaton is critical of this move, but Watson approves. He encourages Dorsey to prosecute Frank ("you will have the gratitude of every decent person in this state"); attends Dorsey's trial summation (he confidently tells Slaton's assistant, Ravenal, that Dorsey is "gonna slip the noose around Frank's neck"); and rides with Dorsey in an open car as Atlantans cheer the solicitor general for convicting Frank.

Slipping that noose around Frank's neck was in fact a desperate goal for Dorsey, who had just lost several relatively clear-cut cases. Convicting Phagan's murderer was generally regarded as Dorsey's last chance to prove himself a capable prosecutor.[37] In *The Murder of Mary Phagan*, dialogue provides quick allusions to these past failures. Dorsey eagerly boasts to Slaton that he will win the case: "Oh, I may have lost a few cases lately but those days are over. I told those people [i.e., the Phagan family] I'm gonna set it right, and I mean to." Subsequently, Dorsey will angrily inform Slaton that he no longer needs Slaton's help to succeed.

Dorsey carries his common touch and opportunism into the courtroom. He outmaneuvers Luther Rosser—portrayed as smart but ineffective—at every turn, in keeping with historical accounts that Frank's attorneys badly mishandled the case. One commentator went so far as to characterize the defense's case as "one of the most ill-conducted in the history of Georgia jurisprudence."[38] When the defense is finally able to present favorable witnesses who can testify to Frank's honorable character, Dorsey

Another black employee at the factory speaks against Jim Conley: "He ain't one of mine."

quickly tears them down. Alonzo Mann testifies that he never saw women in Frank's office on a Saturday.[39] Dorsey, however, quickly gets Mann to concede that just because Alonzo did not see girls in Frank's office does not mean Frank did not host them there.

Dorsey is even more impressive when he cross-examines the northerners—the dean of the engineering school at Cornell, Frank's alma mater, and an insurance company executive—effectively nullifying their steady assertions of Frank's rectitude by stirring the pot of sectionalism and class resentment into a very powerful courtroom mix. When Dorsey has a series of factory girls testify to Frank's evil ways, Rosser refuses to cross-examine them, explaining to a dubious Lucille that each of them is an image of Mary Phagan: "If Luther even suggests that one of those Mary Phagan's [sic] might be lying, it will alienate the jury, in a way that will do nothing but harm your husband." The actual defense team did challenge one group of employees but declined to interrogate another group of the factory girl witnesses, recognizing that doing so would give Dorsey more opportunities to elicit destructive details from them in his redirect examination.[40] In the miniseries as in the trial, Dorsey takes advantage of Rosser's and Arnold's decision to introduce the issue of Frank's character as a last-ditch defense strategy after they failed to break Jim Conley on the stand. The character defense was a risky one, Oney notes; when Dorsey's turn came to present character witnesses *against* Frank, "The bill for placing Frank's character in evidence had come due, and Dorsey intended to see that it was paid in full."[41]

Dorsey allows the testimony of just three defense witnesses to stand. An accountant testifies that Frank could not have strangled a girl and then done four hours of painstaking accounting "as neat as a pin" in the same afternoon. A young employee testifies that she believes Frank is "as innocent as the angels in heaven" (she stands in for Julia Fuss, a seventeen-year-old factory employee who used this exact phrase in her testimony).[42] This same girl, like several witnesses at the actual trial, comments about Jim Conley that the Bible on which he had sworn "would not mean much to him." A third witness, tellingly, is a black employee at the factory (Carl Gordon) who claims he never saw women in Frank's office or witnessed Jim Conley stand watch for Frank: "Most of the time he'd be asleep, drunk, out back." When Rosser asks him why he would speak "against one of your own like this," he replies, "Excuse me, sir. But he ain't one of mine." Lane and Stevens extrapolated this scene from a brief paragraph in Golden's book that references the defense's use of black witnesses against Conley's character, people who likely shared the *Atlanta Independent*'s harsh view of him.[43]

Jim Conley

The key to Dorsey's case against Frank in the miniseries, as in the actual trial, is, of course, Jim Conley's affidavits and testimony. Prior to the trial we have seen Conley only briefly—accosting Alonzo Mann for a dime, awaiting his turn to give evidence at police headquarters, and demonstrating his testimony at the factory for Dorsey—all of which Conley actually did in 1913 (although the last took place without Frank being present).[44]

Later, well dressed in a new suit courtesy of the public prosecutor, Conley holds a pretrial press conference in his cell. Stevens and Lane drew on the sentiments, if not the precise wording, of Conley's 1913 pretrial statements of relief about "coming clean" in his testimony. The newspapers reported that Conley had been worried about what he alleged he was holding back: "I couldn't sleep and it worried me mightily. I just decided it was time for me to come out with it and I did. I . . . told the truth, and I feel like a clean nigger."[45] In the series, Conley tells the press (most prominently Wes Brent): "I was gonna help Mr. Frank like we agreed. Then people started accusing me of killing that little girl. It got to working in my head so much . . . I couldn't keep it in no longer. I just decided it was time to come out with it. And Mr. Dorsey has been mighty fair to me. And I feel a whole lot better now telling the truth."

After the judge clears the courtroom of women except for Lucille, Conley provides an elaborate description—paraphrasing Conley's actual

At Dorsey's request, Conley acts out his "watching" routine for Leo Frank as Frank looks on.

Conley holds a press conference before the trial at which he speaks of his relief at finally being able to tell "the truth" about what happened to Mary Phagan.

trial testimony—of Frank's sexual peculiarities when he had "chats" with the girls in his office: "I *seen* one of the young ladies lying back on his desk. He doin' stuff I don't know *how* to talk about." Luther Rosser's objections are overruled when Dorsey comments, "This crime against nature is most relevant." Conley goes on to allege that Frank said to him, "Damn it, why should I hang? I have wealthy people in Brooklyn behind me!" Conley reiterates that he initially avoided the police for fear they "would try to put it on me." Rosser later tells Frank, "I've never seen a colored handle himself quite like that," and his efforts to trip Conley up—by getting Conley to confirm new details that might contradict others—are futile. In the series as in the trial, the defense team's dwelling on the details of Conley's account only made it seem more truthful.

Conley even confronts the issue of his possible perjury head-on in the series. Denying that Dorsey coached his testimony, Conley, as he did in 1913, admits to lying in his various affidavits—about whether he was in the vicinity of the factory on the day of Phagan's murder and about whether or not he could write. Rosser tells him, "You are a liar. Every word you've spoken in this courtroom has been a lie, hasn't it?" Conley's response, shot in profile from a slightly low angle, is surprisingly blunt: "See, like they say, a nigger will lie and lie until he finally decides to tell the truth. I just finally [cut to a reaction shot of the jury box] got my fill of telling lies that weren't even my own. I figure, Mr. Frank, if he want to, can go on telling them for both of us. And that's the truth, before Jesus." Rosser nervously looks at the jury, the judge, and then back at Conley, as-

Luther Rosser fails to shake Conley's story.

As Frank completes his statement, the camera cranes up to the ceiling of the courtroom.

tounded both that Conley is so explicitly acknowledging whites' prejudice against blacks and that he is carrying this off so well on the stand.[46] His "before Jesus" places Conley in commonality with the white members of the jury and the courtroom and in opposition to Frank. Conley may be black, but he is a Christian son of the South.

Just as it did in 1913, Conley's testimony places Frank in serious trouble; the subsequent witnesses—John Lund and the factory girls (far more numerous than the schoolgirls in *They Won't Forget*)—ensure his conviction. Frank's pleas on his own behalf are futile. In a statement that, by Georgia law, is immune to cross-examination, Frank begins by awkwardly standing as the camera slowly tracks in on him. As he concludes, the camera begins to track right around him and cranes upward: "Some newspaper men have called me the silent man in the tower. And I have kept my silence advisedly, believing under the American system of justice there would be a time and a place to speak. This is the time, this is the place." By now the camera is up to the full height of the courtroom, and the ceiling fan is visible in the shot. Frank concludes in this high-angle long shot: "I've told you the truth, the whole truth, so help me God." The courtroom is silent as Frank sits down, and the scene fades out. Frank's four-hour address to the jury in the actual trial is dramatically condensed here, but his words about the silent man in the tower and his innocence are taken verbatim from the trial record. They are given their due force and power here by virtue of the sweeping camera movement.

When the series fades in again, Dorsey begins his summation. He speaks directly to the jury and waves Mary's clothes in their faces. As in 1913 and in the Warner Bros. film, he ends with climactic cries of "guilty, guilty, guilty." A church bell rang in 1913 as Dorsey said these words, and it chimes again in the miniseries. *The Murder of Mary Phagan* does not even show the futile Rosser-Arnold summation in defense of Frank; Dorsey has the case sewn up.

Anti-Semitism in *The Murder of Mary Phagan*

The specter of anti-Jewish sentiment in Leo Frank's trial is indicated in the miniseries by small details, direct and indirect, whose impact gradually accumulates. The police chief in part 1 and Tom Watson in part 2 refer to Frank as "the Jew," and a police detective on the stand describes Frank as nervously "rubbing his hands the way 'they' do" (an allusion to the stereotype of greedy Jews). When Conley testifies that Frank did things with women that he could not describe—something no previous dramatization of the case could state—the series alludes to Conley's actual assertion that Frank performed cunnilingus on women in his office because, Frank had told him, "he [Frank] wasn't built like other men." During Slaton's actual hearing on Frank's appeal for commutation of his death sentence, a new Atlanta defense attorney, William Schley Howard, argued that Conley's comment about Frank's genitalia was based on Conley's vague knowledge of the Jewish practice of circumcision.[47] The rest—the sexual practices Conley alluded to—were Conley's extrapolation of what sex for a childless Jewish man would entail, although neither the historical Conley nor the miniseries Conley ever explicitly referenced Leo Frank's Jewish identity.

Anti-Semitism appears more forcefully late in the miniseries trial. When the insurance company's representative mentions Frank's leadership of B'nai Brith, the courtroom bursts into laughter. When Uncle Sig Montag testifies, open courthouse windows reveal a mass of people on nearby rooftops who now can hear and see the proceedings. A series of fictional details follow: neighbor Randy derisively yells, "He's lying," after Uncle Sig gives his name; another yells out, "Jew," after Montag identifies himself as owner of the pencil factory. The outdoor crowd sings "A Mighty Fortress Is Our God" as Uncle Sig tries to continue his testimony. Though utterly fictional, these expressions from the crowd dramatize how much

The open windows allow the crowd outside, including Mary Phagan's neighbor Randy, to yell into the courtroom.

Hugh Dorsey finds Governor Slaton hosting a group of national Jewish leaders, as well as Sig Montag (second from right), who express their concern about anti-Semitism in Frank's trial to Dorsey.

the people gathered outside the courtroom influenced the proceedings within. At this point, Rosser demands a mistrial: "Leo Frank isn't being tried in this courtroom. He's being tried in the streets of Atlanta." As happened at the trial, Judge Roan insists on completing the nearly finished trial. Though Dorsey subsequently—and accurately—denies to a group of Jewish leaders that he explicitly fomented the anti-Semitism on display outside the courtroom, it is clear that the spectators' and the jury's anti-Semitism was activated by a chain of associations that Dorsey exploited. This is ironic, given the Franks' identification with Atlanta's highly assimilated German Jewish community. We see Leo and Lucille observing Jewish ritual only once in the miniseries, when they celebrate the Jewish Sabbath in a brief one-shot jail cell scene in part 2; their ordeal has inspired them to take solace in this observance.

Dorsey's interview with Slaton and the Jewish leaders pushes the prosecutor and the governor further apart. They have a testy exchange in private:

> *Dorsey:* I'm just doing my job, and I resent your taking sides.
> *Slaton:* Nobody is taking sides. This trial is your baby, Hugh, but it is *my* state. [Close-up.] And I do not want a mess in my state.
> *Dorsey [close-up]:* You think I'm still your boy. Going around losing cases and then the big man has to come along and smooth it over. [Reaction shot of Slaton.] Well, rest easy old friend. [Close-up of Dorsey.] That's not something

Dorsey tells Slaton that he resents Slaton's role in confronting him with the Jewish leaders and informs him that he no longer needs Slaton's help.

In a pattern of staging and framing, the man who gets the last word leaves his rival within the shot.

you're gonna have to worry about any more. [Close-up of Slaton as Dorsey walks out in the background.]

Here as in many of their other curt exchanges, the man with the last word leaves the other behind in the frame of the shot. Dorsey proceeds to address the anti-Semitism issue in his summary, instructing the jury to "put out of your minds the fact that Leo M. Frank is a Jew." He pays tribute to Jews in history: "I honor the race that produced such men as Disraeli and Judah P. Benjamin" (the latter served as both secretary of war and secretary of state in Jefferson Davis's Confederate administration) but argues that "human character is a shifty thing."

The miniseries thus follows the interpretation that Leo Frank's Jewishness became an overwhelming factor as the trial progressed (Watson is seen in part 2 telling out-of-town reporters that there was no anti-Jewish feeling in Georgia "until now"). Dorsey is technically correct in claiming that anti-Semitism has nothing to do with his case against Frank, but it quite obviously does. As with Griffin's statements and behavior in *They Won't Forget*, Dorsey's actions and the way the trial unfolds belie his claim.

Lucille Frank and a Ray of Hope

Part 1 of *The Murder of Mary Phagan* ends with Lucille visiting Leo in prison and playing her favorite duet from *La Bohème* to cheer him up, remind him of home, and express her love for him. The miniseries format allowed the filmmakers to make Lucille an even fuller character than Sybil Hale was in *They Won't Forget*. Lucille's love of opera is another way of distinguishing the Franks' upper-class existence from that of the factory workers; the duet she plays for her husband contrasts implicitly with the "people's music," such as "The Ballad of Mary Phagan," which Governor Slaton overhears schoolgirls singing near the end of part 1.[48]

This Lucille Frank is a confirmed romantic. Her first scene with Leo, at their home on Memorial Day night, begins as we hear the love duet "O Soave fanciulla" ("Oh lovely girl") from *La Bohème*, sung when Mimì and Rodolfo discover their love for each other at the end of act 1. Lucille lip-synchs the libretto (as Mimì boasts of her garret, "And when the spring comes, the first rays of sunshine are mine"), and the music soars on the hand-cranked phonograph player but then comically slows down before Mimì can finish her shift to higher notes—the effect undercutting the grand emotions of the song. Lucille, a native Georgian, associates New York with the opera and "mysterious people" such as Leo. When Leo points out, "Brooklyn isn't exactly Paris," she replies, "Well, it is compared to here. You people up there, you have all those other lives, all those different ways. That's what I thought of the night I met you. I thought, this isn't just a man I'm meeting; this is a world." In her admiration, Lucille subtly expresses the kind of fascination with Leo Frank's "foreignness" that the Atlanta mob will share.

Slender and frail as portrayed by Rebecca Miller, Lucille is a dreamer. In Lane's conception, Leo Frank initially saw Lucille as a "silly little southern girl who was forced to grow up through these events" rather than the stoic, statuesque figure Lucille Frank always appeared to be in public. She weakens temporarily after the factory girls' courtroom testimony of lechery against Frank. "Wasn't I enough for you?" she asks Leo at one point—a feeling of doubt Lucille Frank was never known to have expressed but which Lane reasonably ascribed to her. When Leo reassures her, "You are all that I have ever needed," she once again becomes his most ardent champion, exhorting Luther Rosser to present a stronger case. In part 2, to protest Frank's conviction, she leads a group of national leaders to a political gathering hosted by Watson.

Following Leo's conviction, Lucille plays the *La Bohème* duet for him in his cell, now emphasizing Rodolfo's lines. When Leo asks, presumably for the first time, for a translation of the song, Lucille recites through the bars, "Heart to heart, soul to soul, love binds us." In a reverse-angle shot, Leo approaches her and states his belief in his ultimate vindication. Their

Lucille has brought a gramophone and opera recording into the jail to cheer Leo up after his conviction at the end of part 1.

The final shot of part 1 has the governor's mansion in the foreground and the jail in the background, showing Frank's current plight and his eventual "court" of last resort.

parallel with Mimì and Rodolfo is complete—the opera couple and the Franks both discover their passion for each other but cannot be together for long. Rays of light come through the cell window to visualize this sense of hope as the music continues playing. If Lucille's playing of one of opera's most passionate duets was ironic before, here it becomes sincere.

Part 1 ends with a cut to an exterior zoom-out shot that encompasses the jail tower and the governor's mansion. The setting was crucial for establishing continuity in the miniseries. The proximity of Richmond's old statehouse (used in the miniseries as Slaton's mansion) to the jail building, Stevens told a reporter, "allowed us to juxtapose the machinery of the law and the jail with the governor's office [and] . . . gave the film an unusual thrust that we couldn't have achieved otherwise."[49] That thrust visually foreshadows Frank's final recourse to Governor Slaton in part 2.

Detective William J. Burns

Part 2 begins after Leo Frank's various legal appeals have failed, indicated as the camera pans a wall of newspaper clippings in his jail cell. Then Frank's self-proclaimed "last best hope" appears: the celebrated detective William J. Burns.

Detective William J. Burns convinces Wes Brent
to be his ally in investigating the Frank case. They
are well-matched allies—cynical and smart.

Actually, Burns was hired (his fees were paid by Jewish Chicago advertising innovator Albert Lasker) to work on Frank's behalf well before the Supreme Court appeal. Burns, a boastful publicity hound, came to Atlanta amid great fanfare, making brash and baseless pronouncements to the press that he would soon solve the case. His work for Frank backfired: he was accused of paying witnesses to get testimony favorable to Frank, and in the end he proved to be of little help.[50]

Burns fares slightly better in the miniseries. He is given a mysterious buildup when he is introduced, remaining faceless as he packs and drives to Atlanta—almost as if he, and not Governor Slaton, will be the hero of part 2. As Burns, Paul Dooley is quirky (with a penchant for shelled peanuts) and disinterested in Frank's guilt or innocence. ("Are you innocent? Good. That tends to make things easier sometimes.") He is unimpressed when Frank quotes the memorable line from Justice Oliver Wendell Holmes's dissent from the Supreme Court's rejection of Frank's appeal—"Mob law does not become due process of law by securing the assent of a terrorized jury"—because he knows it will not save Frank's life. Most of all, Burns is overconfident: he introduces himself as the world's greatest living detective and presents Wes Brent with a photo of himself for the article he imagines that Brent will write; he even dictates the headline, "World's Greatest Detective Saves Frank from the Jaws of Death."

In the miniseries, Burns's self-aggrandizement provides some welcome comic relief. His love of publicity, however, gets him into serious trouble.

The Wm. J. Burns International

Detective Agency, Inc.

REPRESENTING AMERICAN BANKERS' ASSOCIATION

Healey Building, Atlanta, Georgia

WILLIAM J. BURNS, Principal
New York

RAYMOND J. BURNS,
Secretary and Treasurer
Chicago

F. BOURGEOIS, General Manager
Chicago

Civil and Criminal Work
Done Anywhere
In the United States
Or in Any Country
of the
Civilized Globe

The depiction of Burns as a self-promoting publicity hound in the miniseries is based on fact; this is an ad Burns placed in an Atlanta newspaper around the time of his investigation of the Frank case. (Courtesy of the Breman Museum.)

The actual Burns was physically attacked in Marietta while he was investigating the case,[51] and Pindar in *They Won't Forget* is beaten (offscreen) simply for showing up. The miniseries has Burns roughed up after he obnoxiously crashes a wedding celebration, flatters and dances with Doreen Camp until she is dizzy, and asks the other neighborhood teenagers intrusive questions about Frank. He gets no helpful answers. Instead, a group of neighborhood men (including Lund and Randy) recognize Burns from his picture in Brent's newspaper. The threatened violence is a form of poetic justice for Burns's hubris. He is saved only by the intervention of Mary Phagan's mother, who persuades the men not to harm him, then spits in his face when he thanks her. In actual fact, Burns fled for his life, protected by Judge Newt Morris, who later planned Frank's lynching.

Burns and Brent develop a rapport—they even sit together at Slaton's hearings—that seems appropriate because they are the two most overtly cynical observers of Frank's fate. An offscreen tip from Brent leads Burns to a helper; he recruits a clearly starstruck young Fulton County jail guard

Burns gets some crucial information
from a factory employee and pig farmer.

to keep an eye on Conley for evidence useful to Frank (in the actual case, Burns had several such operatives working at the jail).

In the course of his work, Burns pursues a line of investigation that provides a crucial perspective on Jim Conley—and on southern blacks in the 1910s. He visits the black factory worker–farmer who testified against Conley at the original trial. The farmer says of Conley: "He's a good talker. He puts it over on you folks." His comment signals a view of the case from the black side, namely that Conley was performing a role—appearing simple and obsequious, just as Lem Hawkins did toward Brisbane in *Murder in Harlem*—to fulfill white Atlantans' stereotypes of southern blacks. The farmer admits, however, that he is not sure if Conley is lying about Frank: "Everything I know about him [Conley], I'm still not sure. Guess that's how good he really is."

The farmer is a significant alternative to the terrified Newt Lee, on the one hand, and the deceptive, murderous Conley, on the other. The farmer's appearance, dialogue, and behavior are a testament to the shifting representation of African Americans in Hollywood and on television two decades after the height of the civil rights era. In terms of television history, viewers had already enjoyed *The Jeffersons* (CBS, 1975–85), *Good Times* (CBS, 1974–79), and the heyday of *The Cosby Show* (NBC, 1984–92). To find a cinematic antecedent for this dignified farmer in a screen treatment of the Leo Frank case one must go back to attorney and author Henry Glory in Micheaux's *Murder in Harlem*.

In the miniseries, Slaton's own investigation into the case ultimately corroborates the farmer's claims. In fact, Burns's ineffectiveness contrasts with Slaton's success. Slaton's investigation—held in a crowded hearing room that excludes the rabble—retraces the steps of the original trial and outdoes Dorsey's own brilliant work at Frank's trial.

The Slaton of *The Murder of Mary Phagan* is marginally younger than his cinematic predecessor, Governor Mountford in *They Won't Forget*, but older than his *Profiles in Courage* incarnation in Walter Matthau. Jack Lemmon was sixty-two when the miniseries was shot; Matthau was forty-three when he acted in the episode; Slaton himself was forty-nine when he commuted Frank's sentence. Slaton undergoes a "conversion narrative" similar to that of Rick Blaine (Humphrey Bogart) in *Casablanca* (1942) or—even more appropriate, given the case's general similarity to France's Dreyfus affair—the title character played by Paul Muni in *The Life of Emile Zola* (1937). Like Matthau's Slaton, Lemmon's Slaton begins the program uninterested in the Frank case and focused on his own political fortunes and likely future as a U.S. senator—he is an aging "good old boy" wealthy by virtue of his marriage to Sallie Slaton. Although he decides to reopen the case almost on a whim, doing so eventually reminds him of his highest ideals of political leadership. It is as if the viewer is waiting for the decent Jack Lemmon—a star image established through countless film roles—to appear.

This well-intentioned but highly political John Slaton barely appears at all in part 1. He does not attend Frank's original trial, but gets an update in a barbershop from Ravenal, who describes Conley's amazing testimony. When Slaton asks if he believes Conley, Ravenal evasively notes, "No white man has ever been convicted in this county on the testimony of a black." Slaton quickly and shrewdly replies, "Yes, but the white man is a Yankee, and the black man is southern—try that on for size." Yet Slaton forgets all about the fascinating trial when Watson enters the barbershop to tell him the "boys in the back room" want to put him up for senator next fall. "This is one old horse that's raring to go," he tells Watson.

Governor Mountford in *They Won't Forget* may have preferred older, calmer times, but this Slaton is forward thinking, well connected, and pro-development. Such a characterization fits with John Slaton's historical profile—a corporate attorney who worked to bring modern business to Georgia only half a century after the Civil War's conclusion. Slaton's Memorial Day speech in the miniseries clearly states his position:

> Folks, do you know that there are *still* those *today* who think that Georgia *only* means cotton. And when you speak to them of industry and factories, when you speak to them of iron and steel and textile manufacturing, they're like that

Slaton listens as his assistant, Ravenal, describes Conley's extraordinary testimony.

Slaton's interest in the Frank trial is instantly forgotten when Watson tells him he will be the party's nominee for the U.S. Senate in the fall.

old farmer who said, "Oh, you can't get there from here." [The crowd laughs; Slaton has his thumbs in his vest.] Well they are wrong. They are as wrong as that old farmer. We can and we will. We live in a time of *prosperity*. A great era of challenge. And the people of Georgia, they, they are hearty, industrious people. [The audience applauds in a reaction shot.] And they can meet that challenge. They can bring new prosperity to this great state. [Head-on medium close-up of Slaton.] Industry means employment, and that employment means a fair wage for every man that wants to work. And, and, I mean to see that we *do* get there from here. [Reaction shot of crowd applauding.]

Slaton actually spent that Confederate Memorial Day in Manhattan at the home of William Randolph Hearst, and as governor-elect rather than governor. In the miniseries, however, it is of obvious dramatic value to place Slaton at the celebration. His speech on this day renders him a prophet of industrialization and Georgia's unlimited future—not unlike Atlanta's celebrated journalist, editor, and New South prophet Henry Grady.

Slaton wants to bring northern industry to Georgia, perhaps as a means to solve the problem of statewide poverty. By contrast, in persecuting Frank, Watson undertakes a more vivid, superficial, and crowd-pleasing approach to mitigating their despair (this is another, unspoken reason why he refuses to defend Frank). Both men understand the fundamental decency of ordinary Georgians, but they are on a collision course in terms of the way they see Georgia's problems and in their approach to politics. Slaton sees industrialization as Georgia's long-term salva-

Slaton speaks of Georgia's readiness for industrialization in his Confederate Memorial Day speech.

tion; Watson regards it as the state's short-term humiliation. Watson also understands his ability to shape the common people's views, telling Sallie Slaton that political "popularity is clay to be molded." In general, Slaton appeals to Georgia citizens' hope and better nature when he tells the cheering Memorial Day crowd his vision of coming prosperity. By contrast, Watson—and Dorsey after him—appeals to their resentments, frustrations, and darker side.

As governor, Slaton did try to convince northern businesses that Georgia's economy had diversified away from agriculture—hence his reference in the speech to the unimaginative Georgia farmer. Industrialization, of course, led to the exploitation of child labor, but the series depicts Slaton as aware of and concerned about that issue as well, referring at Phagan's funeral to "our bill to protect little girls like Mary." In actual fact, Slaton did little or nothing to combat child labor, and the influence of farmers and businesses was so powerful that no efforts to abolish or even regulate child labor in Georgia succeeded.[52] As the series would have it, Slaton and Frank each tried in his own way to look after the most vulnerable workers in Georgia; it is all the more ironic, then, that so many Georgians demonized them both by 1915.

The series further embellishes Slaton's turnaround by suggesting he wants no part of Frank's appeal for mercy when Dorsey forces him to confront the issue. Frank's legal team urged the Georgia Prisons and Parole Board to make its ruling on Frank's appeal for life imprisonment as quickly as possible so that they would have time to appeal to Slaton— whom they preferred over his successor, Nat Harris—in the likely event of an unfavorable ruling.[53] In the series, Dorsey insists that Slaton take up the appeal. When Wes Brent informs Slaton at Terminal Station that the

Lucille Frank leads a delegation of representatives from around the country to ask Watson to use his influence to get Leo Frank's sentence commuted. Her protest interrupts Watson's soiree in honor of Slaton and Dorsey.

prison board has turned down Frank's appeal, Slaton is visibly upset. As they drive home, he discusses the issue with Sallie and Ravenal:

> *Slaton:* He [Dorsey] knows how to stick it to a fellow.
>
> *Sallie:* He learned from a couple of masters.
>
> *Slaton:* Now that he's riding high he wants me to shine his shoes. If I hang Frank, it's Dorsey's victory.
>
> *Ravenal:* And if you don't?
>
> *Slaton:* They'll hang me.

However distant he was from the original trial, Slaton is thoroughly familiar with how most Georgians view the case.

Slaton's annoyance with Dorsey, evident in the "shining shoes" comment (and in his pique at the publicity the New York papers gave to Dorsey after the conviction), has built since Dorsey spoke up at Mary Phagan's funeral. The two rivals trade barbs at a Democratic Party celebration presided over by Tom Watson. Slaton is clearly even more disturbed when the party is interrupted by Lucille Frank and Sig Montag, who lead an array of state representatives from across the country, North and South (including then-Virginia governor Gerald L. Baliles as that state's representative) to create a sense of the national outcry regarding the Frank case.[54] Lucille's plea to Tom Watson to arrange with "the men you run" for Frank's clemency shows that she knows exactly where the power lies. If she was a "silly little woman" in her husband's eyes at the start of part 1, she has matured dramatically since.

This national protest, among other things, persuades Slaton to avoid Leo Frank's appeal in a momentary bout of cowardice unthinkable to the *Profiles in Courage* Slaton. The next scene shows him instructing Ravenal

After angering Watson by not agreeing to dismiss Frank's appeal out of hand, Slaton soothes him in a gesture that demonstrates their close friendship.

to prepare his public statement on why he will let his successor rule on the issue: "I only have eight days left as governor. I can't possibly give that petition for clemency the time and thought that it deserves." Sallie Slaton, impressed by the huge sacks of mail arriving in his office, persists in asking her husband what he thinks about Frank's possible innocence. He finally and curtly replies, "To tell you the truth, Sallie, it's none of my concern." She is visibly offended.

Given his obvious desire to avoid the Frank appeal, Slaton's resistance to Watson's strong-arm tactics in the following scene is all the more striking. Watson has invited him to Hickory Hill to find out "what you gonna do about the Jew?" Watson is at his ugliest here as he tries to bully Slaton into rejecting Frank's appeal. Like his earlier incarnation in *Profiles in Courage*, this Watson suggests that Slaton take "the easy way." When Slaton tells Watson that he will let Nat Harris decide the matter, Watson replies that he will not "let the people of this state elect a man senator who won't carry out their will. Who can't bring himself to act on the business of his office. The last thing we need is a coward." Watson urges Slaton to deny Frank's appeal so that the party, the state, and the people can "move forward"—a line of argument that the historical Watson used in the *Jeffersonian*.

When this rhetoric has no impact on Slaton, Watson accuses the governor of ingratitude for Watson's past support, momentarily rising out of his chair to argue more fiercely before sinking back in response to a throbbing pain in his forehead. This detail alludes to Watson's mental health problems at the time of Frank's appeals, as documented by Woodward, adding to the series's repeated suggestions that Watson is a heavy drinker.[55] Slaton stands behind Watson and rubs his temples, a gesture of great intimacy (like Watson's stance behind Slaton in the barbershop) that further emphasizes how much is personally at stake in their present dispute. Slaton has angered Watson this way before, but Slaton has been able to calm him down. Their dialogue suggests a different outcome this time.

In the miniseries, pushing Slaton to act on Frank's appeal does not work as Watson had planned. Even Watson's gift of a beautiful new gilded buggy—meant to remind Slaton of his debt to Watson—fails to sway Slaton. If anything, it has the opposite effect.

Slaton's Hearings and Investigation

Oney observes that Slaton almost certainly would have preferred to spend the final days of his term celebrating his accomplishments rather than considering a controversial life-and-death case. "His decision, whichever way it went," Oney notes, "would offend thousands while overshadowing the accomplishments of a governorship that had seen Georgia's debt refinanced at an advantageous rate and taxes reduced." Slaton had received telegrams, letters, and petitions from around the country and within the state urging him to show mercy; he also had heard plenty of arguments about why Frank should be hanged. To step in and reconsider a jury decision that no appeals court had reversed would be an assertive, dramatic move. Twenty-five hundred people had gathered on the steps of the state capitol to urge the prison board to deny Frank's appeal. Another huge crowd gathered there during a weekend recess in Slaton's hearings; this is where Fiddlin' John Carson debuted "The Ballad of Mary Phagan."[56]

On June 12, 1915—two weeks before his term ended and ten days before Frank was to be executed—Slaton began his hearing on Frank's appeal in a room jammed with spectators. The defense again made the case for Frank's life. The new lead attorney, William Schley Howard, emphasized many points, including presiding Judge Roan's doubts about Frank's guilt; Conley's lascivious letters describing his own guilt to Annie Maude Carter; William Smith's study of the murder notes that ascribed their authorship to Conley; and the significance of the excrement Conley had left in the elevator shaft Saturday morning. Howard argued that Conley had carried Phagan's body to the basement through the "scuttle hole" linked by a ladder to the basement rather than using the elevator—an argument Alonzo Mann's recollections would corroborate nearly seventy years later.

On the other side of the question, a group of eminent Marietta citizens—including former governor Joseph M. Brown, who later helped to plan Frank's lynching and likely served as liaison between the lynchers and Tom Watson—warned Slaton that if he offered "mercy" instead of "justice," he would only strengthen the practice of lynch law in the state. During a weekend recess, Slaton continued to receive pleas for mercy from prominent figures across the country. Back in the hearing room, Hugh Dorsey presented all the reasons Slaton should not commute Frank's sentence: Frank's trial had been fair; the mob did not influence the jury's decision; the defense team did not challenge the factory girls' testimony and had waited far too long to ask for a mistrial. Dorsey further suggested that even without Conley's testimony the evidence against Frank was overwhelming. Dorsey filled his allotted time without interruption by any spectator in the room.[57]

The miniseries depicts Slaton's hearings as an extended and less formal event than they actually were. In spite of Watson's bullying, Slaton has chosen to hold an initial hearing to help him decide whether to consider Frank's appeal for mercy. Frank's defenders, led by Luther Rosser, inform Slaton that they seek a commutation of sentence rather than a new trial—not because there is doubt about Frank's innocence but because they think he would not live long were he acquitted. (Frank's actual defense team decided on this course because they felt a pardon would be too much of a stretch given Frank's many unsuccessful appeals.) In response to Slaton's query as to whether new evidence has become available since the trial, Burns is allowed—in a show of remarkable informality—to introduce from the back of the room the fact that Conley has a long police record and that other aspects (unnamed) of the case disturb him. In fact, Burns was not even in Atlanta in 1915.

But the keynote of this initial hearing scene is the Dorsey-Slaton rivalry. Each time Slaton poses a question to Rosser or anyone else, Dorsey interrupts the proceedings, trying to end the hearing via various legal arguments. He uses some of the assertions actually made by Dorsey when given the floor at the 1915 hearing. Dorsey's interruptions and the sparring between the two former allies intensify the antagonism between them. Most provocative of all, toward the end of the hearing, Dorsey suggests that Slaton is out of his depth investigating a criminal case because his only legal experience is in corporate law, and that he cannot make an informed decision because he has not interviewed the witnesses in the trial. Their testy exchange is punctuated by the standard shot–reverse shot

While making his case for Slaton to deny Frank's appeal peremptorily, Dorsey leans in to remind an annoyed Slaton that doing so will help both of them politically.

editing of a debate. Dorsey's challenge to Slaton's competence in criminal cases backfires, however, as Watson's strong-arm tactics did earlier: "You've made the point that my background in criminal law is incomplete," Slaton tells Dorsey. "Maybe it's time I got some experience. I'm just gonna call your Mr. Conley in here. I think I should hear this chief witness myself." Slaton gets the last word and leaves Dorsey in the frame. As Slaton gets into his car with his assistant, he comments, "I don't know, Ravenal, I guess he just got my goat. Now what the hell do I do?"

This dramatic license departs from the two previous screen dramatizations of this decision. In both *They Won't Forget* and *Profiles in Courage* Slaton accepted Frank's petition after considering it in a sober, dispassionate fashion, as was the case historically. The miniseries's shift makes Slaton a more human figure. "We did not want to make anybody a saint," Jeffrey Lane later recalled. "We wanted to show that everybody had a reason. Not always the best of reasons. Even the people who wind up lynching Leo Frank, horrible as they might have been—there was a reason it happened."[58]

The miniseries dramatizes Slaton's consideration of Frank's appeal by transforming the historical hearings into another trial, albeit one in which Slaton serves as judge and jury. In contrast to the limited hearings the historical Slaton held—two sessions over two days, during which he heard only from Dorsey, Frank's new defense team, and a few eminent Marietta citizens—Slaton here reinterviews all the key witnesses in the trial: Jim Conley, Doreen Camp, John Lund, Alonzo Mann, and Leo Frank. In effect, these scenes dramatize Slaton's thought processes as he reviewed the trial transcripts and witness testimony at his Buckhead estate.

Conley is obviously thrilled to be called before the governor at the hearing. He awkwardly holds his manacled hand out to shake Slaton's hand,

Conley, pleased to be called before the governor in a hearing, reaches out to shake his hand.

and Slaton takes it reluctantly. Slaton interviews Conley in a breezy, folksy style that flatters Conley by recognizing that he is capable of a high degree of self-awareness. The technique gets Conley to reveal far more about himself than the badgering of Frank's attorneys during the trial ever did. Slaton asks some questions about Conley's stints on the chain gang to remind him that he admitted, under oath, that he sometimes lies. Conley sheepishly concedes this point. When Slaton jokingly asks Conley how someone could tell that he is lying, Conley provides the crucial information that he shakes his head and plays with his fingers—two facts Conley did offer at the trial.[59] Given the division of the miniseries into broadcasts on nonconsecutive nights (Sunday and Tuesday, separated by President Reagan's State of the Union Address on the intervening Monday), viewers were unlikely to remember that Conley was shaking his head while describing his "watchin'" activities to Dorsey at the factory.

Slaton's interviews elicit numerous interesting details from the trial witnesses that the audience knows about but Frank's legal team overlooked. He learns that Alonzo Mann knows something but will not reveal it, that John Lund was fired for being a dollar short the week before the murder and never liked Frank, and that Doreen Camp could have missed Frank sitting behind the huge door of the safe in his office. Slaton thereby brings out some of the unspoken prejudices motivating the witnesses against Frank.

The series then reminds us of how widespread the sentiment against Frank is in Georgia. One of the most remarkable scenes shows Ravenal and Sallie Slaton reading a threatening letter from "the Knights of Mary Phagan" as a crowd (including Randy, John Lund, and Doreen Camp) marches to the governor's mansion singing "Bringing in the Sheaves" and

A minister who had called for vengeance for Mary Phagan's death leads a group in singing hymns outside the governor's mansion and pleads with Slaton not to be influenced by money in his decision.

"Abide with Me" (echoing the courtroom scene in which the mob sang hymns while Uncle Sig was trying to testify). The Slatons go outside and join them in singing. The crowd's leader, the minister of Mary Phagan's church, speaks to Slaton (and to the viewer) to stress that not all Georgians who believe Frank guilty are rabid anti-Semites: "We want you to know that there are decent people in this state on the side of Mary Phagan. We're being made out to be cruel people when all we want is fairness. We feel there should be one law for all. And all we ask is that Leo Frank get the same as one of us would get." When Slaton agrees, the minister continues with an awkward smile: "It don't look that way to some. To some, it looks like you might be listening to the rich—them that owns the newspapers, the railroads, them that's got truck on Wall Street. Don't let it be. That's all we're telling ya. Don't let it be."

More than any other, this scene dramatizes the genuine sorrow and rage behind the desire of many Georgians to see Frank executed, the emotions Tom Watson has spoken of throughout the miniseries. The tone of this crowd's complaint is surprisingly conciliatory, illustrating in yet another way Jeffrey Lane's guiding principle that "everyone had his reasons" for what they did. Yet the torches carried for this night scene suggest that the crowd could erupt into uncontrollable vigilante violence at any moment—making Slaton their target as easily as Frank. They are a threat to Slaton, both politically and physically. Slaton brilliantly parries the implicit threat—for the moment—by joining them. He uses their innate goodness—to which Watson only pays lip service—to try to diffuse their potential to become an angry mob seeking vengeance. This violent side emerges in a subsequent scene: as Slaton leaves the capitol after a hearing and walks along a roped-off crowd of onlookers to get into his car, Randy attempts to hit him with a lead pipe. In this way, the miniseries personalizes the historical attempt to kill Slaton that actually took place at Harris's inauguration. Here, Dorsey saves Slaton's life rather than the historical National Guard officer.[60]

In the miniseries, as in *Profiles in Courage*, nothing dramatic emerges from Slaton's public hearings. The real breakthrough comes with the appearance of Conley's love letters to fellow inmate Annie Maude Carter, courtesy of the "World's Greatest Detective." Burns's recruitment of a jail guard to keep an eye on Conley has borne fruit. Several scenes in the jail during part 2 show Conley's ingenuity in getting Carter's attention (even tipping over her wash pail so she has to come into his cell to mop up the water), while his pickup lines affirm his smooth personality. Late in part 2, Carter hands Conley's love letters to Burns at a church outside Atlanta. The city police (on Dorsey's directive) intercept Burns immediately after his meeting with Carter, but he is able to hide the letters and to get them to Brent after the police have escorted him out of town. Although the Conley letters were in fact secured by an entirely different detective hired by Frank's defense team, viewers see how a crucial piece of evidence reached Slaton's attention and played an important role in his deliberations.

When the three days of hearings ended in 1915, Slaton (and his assistant, Jessie Perry) had just six days to consider the evidence, which they took with them to Slaton's residence.[61] In the series, Brent delivers the letters to Slaton as he is deliberating on the case, and the two confer in a darkly lit scene. That the governor would reflect on the letters' significance with Brent, with whom he has had no special relationship up to this point, makes dramatic sense given the miniseries's story line. Brent stands in here for William Smith, Conley's attorney, who came to believe in Conley's guilt.

Smith and his wife, a schoolteacher, compared Conley's love letters with the murder notes found beside Phagan's body. Their considerations, which focused on Conley's predilection for using certain verb tenses and double adjectives (as in "long tall black Negro" in one of the murder notes), convinced Smith that Conley had authored the notes himself rather than at the dictation of Frank, as Conley alleged. Smith actually visited Slaton at Wingfield to answer the governor's questions about his assessment of the notes and his newfound belief in Conley's guilt. Whereas *Profiles in Courage* depicts Conley's lawyer as bound by attorney-client privilege to answer Slaton's pointed questions with ambiguous silence, the series omits the Smith "subplot" entirely.[62] Brent's function as delivery person

The lead pipe attack against Slaton at Nat Harris's inauguration is staged in the miniseries after one of Slaton's hearings sessions.

Jim Conley looks on with interest at fellow inmate Annie Maude Carter; he has spilled her pail of water inside his cell so she will have to come in to clean it up.

Annie Maude Carter hands Conley's "love letters" to Burns in the anteroom of a rural black church.

Wes Brent delivers the letters to Governor Slaton, and the two men contemplate their significance for the case.

and party to the contents of the letters also provides proof of Brent's change of heart about Frank's guilt, building on his embarrassment at Lucille's entreaty for accurate reporting in part 1. Brent's altered attitude toward Frank mirrors that of, for example, the *Atlanta Georgian*, which after remonstrations by Jewish Atlanta merchants and even an advertising boycott tempered its coverage of Frank and joined the *Atlanta Journal* in supporting commutation.[63]

The letter Brent and Slaton inspect is extremely revealing. Brent reads it aloud: "If you love me, I will be the happiest easy rider you will ever have. If you say you don't I'd as soon be ruled by the night witch." The phrase "easy rider" is a pale substitution for the graphic language Conley used in his actual letters to Annie Maude Carter ("And every time [I] read that my long dick got on a hard why I would like to hold it in one of your hipped this morning and let you take everything that I have got there with me because I love you so much and if I could put my sweet long dick in your hipped I think I could make mama call me papa one time").[64] Frank's appeal attorneys would argue that Conley's putting these desires (and boastful descriptions of his genitals) into writing suggested that Conley's accusation that Frank was a sexual pervert was in fact a projection of his own obsession.

Because the series was produced for network television, the script has Brent and Slaton focus on the phrase "night witch" rather than the sexually explicit language or the dramatically flat issue of Conley's literary style. "Night witch" had appeared in one of the murder notes beside Phagan's body: "He said he wood love me land down play like the night witch did it but the long tall black Negro did boy his slef [sic]." When the letters were first discovered and read in part 1, Brent and the police reasonably suspected that "night witch" was a misspelling of "night watch," as in night watchman Newt Lee. Dorsey, ironically, is shown having Frank write out the phrase "night witch" in part 1 during his investigation. Now, Brent explains (ostensibly for Slaton's benefit but actually for viewers') that a local black preacher explained to him that "night witch" referred to an "old colored legend": "When children cry in their sleep, the night witch is riding them. Parents have to wake them up or they wake up dead with a rope around their necks"—that is, strangled, as was Mary Phagan.

This explanation persuades both men that Conley must have written the murder notes because they used the same phrase. Brent spells out why: "He [Conley] had to. If you and I haven't heard of that legend, both born and raised here, how could a man from Brooklyn come up with something like this? He [Conley] lied about this, he lied about all of it, and he did it."[65] Frank's outsider status for once works in his favor.

Slaton agrees with Brent, but he needs more concrete evidence to prove Conley's perjury. While in the actual case Conley's likely authorship of the murder notes was but one aspect of the evidence that moved Slaton to commute Frank's sentence, here it is decisive. Conley's letters to Annie Maude Carter inspire Slaton to visit the factory in search of more evidence to affirm that Conley authored the murder notes. Slaton looks at the opening to the basement and at Frank's office, and Newt Lee takes him down to the basement in the elevator, whose abrupt stop makes him realize something. From there, Slaton proceeds to the morgue and retrieves Phagan's property, particularly her umbrella. This prop—so expressive of Phagan's youth, innocence, and femininity—has been visually prominent in various scenes over the course of the series: besides her walk to the factory on Confederate Memorial Day and Dorsey's wielding it in the courtroom, there is a shot in which a detective finds it in the elevator shaft along with her hat and some mice.

True to detective film conventions, we do not know what Slaton is thinking as he goes from the factory to the morgue and back to the factory and has Conley and Dorsey brought there in the middle of the night. Neither does the skeptical Ravenal, who comments to Slaton, "You've gone off the deep end over this." Once police and the other principals are assembled, Slaton has Conley again walk through his account of the murder and the disposal of Phagan's body. Neither of Slaton's actual visits involved Conley, but having the prosecution's most important witness there allows the series to revisit the scene in which Conley showed Dorsey and Frank how he claimed to have helped Frank by "watchin'" while Frank visited with girls in his office.

Unlike his earlier calm and cool appearance at the trial, Conley is distinctly unnerved—uncomfortable, sweating, and disoriented. When he reaffirms his account of what transpired, Conley shakes his head, giving away his deception. Slaton has Conley toss the umbrella, which is currently intact, down the elevator shaft. He confirms with the police that the umbrella now lies in the shaft in approximately the same position as it did when they found it. They all enter the elevator and ride down to the basement, and in a ground-level shot we see and hear the elevator smash the umbrella. The umbrella here stands in for Conley's "deposit" at the bottom of the elevator shaft, a substitution Stevens and McMurtry had developed in the first script. (Although Lane acknowledged that NBC Standards and Practices concerns may have been an issue in this substitution, he also noted that as a scriptwriter, he would "rather write about a broken parasol rather than about smashed feces.") Had Conley actually used the elevator as he said, the umbrella would have been smashed already. The fact that it was not proves that Conley was lying on the stand.

When a worried and uncharacteristically obtuse Dorsey asks, "What's all this rigamarole mean?" Slaton explains it for him and for us in a medium close-up: "Mary Phagan wasn't murdered on the second floor. Maybe she was murdered on the first floor, or maybe down here in the basement.

Slaton asks Jim Conley to walk him through his "watchin'" for Leo Frank and to explain what happened on the day of Mary Phagan's murder, repeating a similar request by Dorsey in part 1.

As the elevator descends to the factory basement, a shot shows Mary Phagan's umbrella being crushed.

Jim Conley is sweating and nervous as Slaton questions him at the factory.

A close-up reveals Conley's telltale habit of playing with his fingers when he lies; he has already shaken his head a few times, the other sign that he is lying.

And by somebody who was waiting to rob her when she came down here with her pay. You made up quite a story, Jim. Do you care to tell us what really happened?" While shaking his head, Conley replies, "How do you 'spect me to remember all that old stuff, boss? I've been sitting in jail for a while. I forgot all that stuff I told the newspapers. I ain't studied on no umbrella."

Slaton is not ready to let Conley off the hook. As the camera tracks in slowly on Slaton, he asks Conley: "What about the other day? Do you remember what you told me then? . . . About what you do when you lie?" We cut to a close-up of Conley's fidgeting fingers. Reaction shots show Ravenal and Wes Brent gazing at Slaton in admiration. We then cut to

As Jim Conley and Wes Brent look on, Slaton informs Dorsey that he is certain Conley committed perjury, then tells him, "Your witness, Mr. Dorsey."

After having the last word, Slaton leaves Dorsey behind in the frame.

a two-shot of Slaton and Dorsey in profile, with Conley visible between them in the background. Slaton hands Dorsey the smashed parasol and speaks in close-up: "You shaved him, you washed him, you dressed him up, you brought him into court, and *you let him lie through his teeth to convict an innocent man.*" After another cut, Slaton concludes: "Your witness, Mr. Dorsey." Slaton exits the frame, followed by all the observers. Dorsey is left alone in the basement, holding the shattered parasol, as the scene fades out.

Slaton, who has no experience as a criminal lawyer, has out-thought Dorsey and beaten him at his own game. Even if the questioning of Conley never took place at the factory with such decisive results, the scene dramatizes some of Slaton's thinking in making his decision to commute Frank's sentence—his doubts about Conley's testimony were the strongest consideration in his judgment that Frank had not received a fair trial. His final speech to Dorsey about dressing up Conley for the courtroom likely derived from the more racist comments Rosser made while cross-examining Conley at the trial: "They put some new clothes on you so the jury could see you like a dressed up nigger."[66]

After this dramatic scene, the focus shifts to Slaton's home in Buckhead. An earlier interlude at Wingfield during Slaton's hearings showed Sallie reminding Slaton of his idealistic self by pulling out an old love letter her husband had written her during their engagement: "Ideals are like the stars; we never reach them. But like the mariners of the sea, we chart our course by them." When Slaton admits that he stole this phrase from

Sallie tells Slaton she would rather be the widow of a brave man than the wife of a coward.

Montaigne (it is actually attributed to Union Army general and politician Carl Schurz), Sallie confesses that she knew it all the time but that the phrase described perfectly the yearnings of the younger Slaton—and the present one as well. Slaton is visibly moved by his wife's reminder that he is at heart a principled and honorable man.

Now, having decisively proven Conley's perjury and likely guilt, this Slaton does not need to ask Sallie's permission to commute Frank's sentence, as Governor Mountford does implicitly in *They Won't Forget* and Slaton does explicitly in *Profiles in Courage*. Nonetheless, as he prepares for bed that night after ordering that Frank be removed from the county jail to Milledgeville for his safety, Slaton stands before a mirror with Sallie and tells her that it will be "a tossup whether they lynch Leo Frank or me first" tomorrow. Her reply, drawn from the historical record, is the same as that used in the *Profiles in Courage* episode: "I guess I'd rather be the widow of a brave man than the wife of a coward." The camera holds on them for a few extra beats as Slaton looks at her in the mirror and then laughs with relief.

This scene caps a key innovation in the miniseries's depiction of the Slatons: their marriage parallels the Franks' marriage. Jeffrey Lane viewed the Slatons' relationship as "a very comfortable marriage that . . . grew through this case. In their early scenes, you feel a fondness but you don't feel a real passion. You feel her grow in her respect for him." Actor Kathryn Walker conveys these sentiments quietly. Frank and Slaton are once again mirror images.

The Commutation's Aftermath

Slaton's last public appearance comes at Nat Harris's inauguration as Georgia's new governor, an unhappy bookend to part 1's scenes of Slaton's public acclaim on Confederate Memorial Day. Now, as John and Sallie climb the steps of the state capitol, they must be protected from a huge, booing crowd amassed there. Silence falls as they enter the assembly hall past rows of unfriendly officials in a point-of-view shot. Dorsey and Watson, seated together, turn away. Someone calls Slaton a "traitor" as he takes the stage, and someone pounds a gavel for order.

Slaton said little at the actual ceremony. He was simply hissed when he handed over the seal to Harris, as was portrayed in *Profiles in Courage*. The miniseries Slaton says plenty, beginning in a frontal medium close-up:

> Before I have the honor to pass the seal of this state to my successor, I feel that I must make a statement regarding recent events that have *so* divided us. Honest people may disagree with my decision [cut to a reverse-angle shot of the assembled group, which mutters disapproval], but they must realize that all of us must be measured by our consciences. [Reaction shot of Ravenal; cut to medium frontal close-up of Slaton.] Two thousand years ago another governor washed his hands of a case and handed a Jew to a mob. Two thousand years later that governor's name is a curse. [Cut to an over-the-shoulder shot of the assembly, with Watson and Dorsey visible in the front row.] It's been my lifelong dream to serve the people of Georgia in the United States Senate. That is a dream I will not see unfold. [Cut to the medium frontal close-up of Slaton again.] I can do many things in my life. I can plow, I can hoe, and I can live in obscurity. But I cannot abide the companionship of an accusing conscience. [Reaction shots of Wes Brent and Sallie Slaton.]

As he takes the Georgia state seal from a box, Slaton adds, "And gentlemen, I did not dishonor this seal." We cut to a reaction shot of Watson and Dorsey looking at him. There is a cut to a very high angle from the ceiling in the chamber as Slaton hands the state seal to his successor, pats him on the shoulder, and walks out of the silent room with Sallie on his arm.

Lane and Stevens constructed Slaton's powerful retirement speech from at least three of Slaton's public statements. When he spoke to the press about his decision to commute Frank's sentence, he told them, "Feeling as I do about this case I would be a murderer if I allowed that man to hang.

Before handing the state seal to his successor, Slaton comments that he has not dishonored it.

A high-angle shot shows John and Sallie Slaton exiting the hall in silence.

I would rather be plowing in a field than to feel for the rest of my life that I had that man's blood on my hands."[67] In his twenty-nine-page rationale for commuting Frank's sentence, Slaton drew to his conclusion with the comments: "I can endure misconstruction, abuse and condemnation, but I cannot stand the constant companionship of an accusing conscience, which would remind me in every thought that I, as governor of Georgia, failed to do what I thought to be right." At a reception for Harris at the Ansley Hotel after Harris's inauguration, Slaton spoke of honest people disagreeing with him, of being measured by conscience, and invoked "another governor" who "washed his hands of a case and turned a Jew over to mob," a governor whose name was "accursed." Slaton, however, did not publicly state his desire to serve as a senator on these occasions.

Slaton's speeches after his decision were the keynote to Lane's approach to his character: "He was just a genuinely decent man, who in his speech said, 'I cannot abide the companionship of a troubled conscience.' The man who said that is the man that we tried to portray. That one phrase was the key to who that character was." In a sense, the aim of Lane's and Stevens's work in depicting Slaton entailed developing his character to the point at which he would utter those words credibly.

Regardless of Slaton's fine sentiments, the crowd waiting outside the statehouse in the miniseries taunts him again (there were cries of "Lynch him!" when Slaton and Harris emerged in 1915). When he gets into his car, though, Slaton discovers two admirers in the crowd—one is Ravenal, who had told him repeatedly him that considering Frank's appeal and granting him life imprisonment "was not a very politic thing to do"; the

Wes Brent tips his hat in deference to Slaton as the governor gets into his car.

other is the cynical Wes Brent, who tips his hat to Slaton. In these moments, the miniseries acknowledges that some Georgians did appreciate Slaton's actions.[68]

The Mob and the Lynching

The miniseries depicts the anger and revulsion against Governor Slaton in a far more vivid way than any previous Leo Frank dramatization had done. The phenomenon of mob violence looming throughout the series now bursts into action. The Atlanta crowds rush into government buildings and offices, as they historically did, but *The Murder of Mary Phagan* specifically includes shots of Jewish stores being vandalized, something no previous version showed. One shot of a store window being smashed evokes the infamous *Kristallnacht* ("Night of Broken Glass") of November 1938, Nazi Germany's night of vandalism against Jewish stores, synagogues, and homes.[69] Another brief shot shows Jewish parents placing their children on a train to send them to safety. We briefly see Slaton burned in effigy. Meanwhile, the state militia is called out to protect Wingfield, and Sallie and John Slaton watch from a window as the guards subdue the torch-bearing mob.

From here we dissolve to Phagan's tombstone, behind which Tom Watson speaks to a circle comprising the Phagan family and their friends. He assures them that Frank will not escape the consequences of his "vile" act. Watson also alludes to Slaton's alleged bribery. As the camera circles

The series depicts the reprisals against Jewish businesses in Atlanta after Slaton's decision.

Slaton was burned in effigy in Dacula, Georgia. (Courtesy of Vanishing Georgia Collection, Georgia Archives.)

The miniseries re-creates this detail of the case.

Police and state troopers face down the mob at Slaton's home.

slowly in front of him and cuts to reaction shots of the small crowd, a mournful Watson says, "The worst of it is that this shame has been visited on us by one of our own. Like a thief in the night he took the honor of Georgia and he *sold* it. He shall not be forgiven." This is as close as the series Watson comes to inciting mobs and vigilante justice, which the actual Watson did repeatedly. He wrote in the *Jeffersonian*, for example, that "lynch law" was the inevitable result of "no law at all," and "THE NEXT JEW WHO DOES WHAT FRANK DID, IS GOING TO GET THE EXACT SAME THING THAT WE GIVE TO NEGRO RAPISTS."[70]

Watson's actual attacks on Slaton were fierce rather than sorrowful. The historical Watson, after Frank's commutation, minced no words in accusing Slaton of corruption and treachery:

> Our grand old Empire State HAS BEEN RAPED! . . .
> We *have been violated,* AND WE ARE ASHAMED! . . .
> The great Seal of State has gone, LIKE A THIEF IN THE NIGHT, *to do for an unscrupulous law firm, a deed of darkness which dared not bask in the light of the sun. . . .*
> We have been betrayed! The breath of some leprous monster has passed over us, and we feel like crying out, in horror and despair,
> "*Unclean!* UNCLEAN!"[71]

Watson's final appearance in the series affirms his understanding and manipulation of working-class Georgians. Since we do not see Watson spreading his views through his own publications, the miniseries suggests that Watson is able to mold public opinion (and popularity) through sheer force of personality.

The Slatons, having left town, are sitting ill at ease in the dining car of a train as Slaton reads the Atlanta mayor's advice to stay out of Georgia for a while. If the Slatons are safe from the mob now, Frank is not. A true urbanite, Frank is shown working ineffectively in the fields at the Milledgeville state prison, advised by a black inmate on how to tell weeds from the cotton he tries to hoe—the very crop whose failure drove the Phagans into the city. Lucille visits Leo to plot legal strategy; she also offers to cook for him, maintaining her routine of bringing him lunch at the factory. As a parting gesture, she gives him a carnation. Their visit ends with an affirmation of love.

The series abruptly cuts to a night scene of Frank's lynchers, most recognizably Randy and John Lund (carrying the rope), preparing to kidnap Frank. *The Murder of Mary Phagan* thereby maintains the dramatic convention of *They Won't Forget* and other films with lynching scenes, identifying the lynchers as men personally connected to the victim, whereas in Frank's case they were outraged leading citizens of Marietta. They easily overpower the guards and take Frank from his cell.[72]

We ride with Frank and his killers. Lund tells him the logic of what they are doing: by lynching Frank, they are righting a perversion of justice committed by the governor. "We aim to do no more than carry out the sentence the law handed down," says Lund. "The jury found you guilty and the judge sentenced you to hang and that's good enough for us." Frank replies calmly and firmly, "Who is going to provide for my wife?" Lund looks away uncomfortably. A somber mood continues for the duration of the ride.[73] As the cars start to be noticed at sunrise, excited crowds come out into the roads as men yell, "They've got him!" Even the minister of Mary's church runs excitedly toward the lynching spot.

They Won't Forget alluded to Frank's lynching allegorically. *Profiles in Courage* briefly showed the shocking photo of Frank's lynched body. In the miniseries, for the first time, Frank's lynching is restaged and shown directly—but as an extremely calm and methodical process, as many historians and journalists (including Ward Greene) have said that it was. We see Frank's manacled legs as he walks under the tree. A brief shot shows a rope being thrown over a tree. In medium-long shot, Frank and Lund are standing on the truck bed as men put the noose around Frank's head. Lund asks him if he is guilty or innocent, and Frank simply says, "Innocent." He then takes off his wedding ring and asks Lund to give it to his wife. A surprised Lund accepts it. Randy gives the driver the command to drive. The truck drives off, and the camera remains framed on Frank's

The lynchers, most prominently John Lund and Mary Phagan's neighbor Randy, prepare to drive to the state penitentiary.

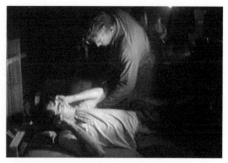

Lund awakens the sleeping Frank after the lynchers have overpowered the guards.

Leo Frank and John Lund during the ride to the lynching tree.

A group of men arrive to see Frank's lynched body, in a shot that loosely imitates several postcards and photos taken of the event.

modestly shaking shoes and then his hands as the carnation Lucille gave him falls to the ground. Although some of the details differ from accounts of Frank's actual lynching—for example, he apparently also wrote a note of farewell to Lucille—this sequence captures the subdued mood of the actual lynching quite well.[74]

We cut away to a group of men running through the field; the camera pans right and tracks left to follow them, then comes to and stops at Frank's body. This view evokes one of the Frank lynching photographs, but the "mob" here is significantly smaller than the one thousand estimated to have been present. Lund gives the command to cut down the body, and Frank is gently taken down, all in long shot. The cutaway to the men running to the scene implies an imprecise passage of time since the shot in which Frank's feet stopped shaking. The editing implies that Frank's body did not hang for hours, as it actually did, so hundreds could witness and photograph it and tear off pieces of his clothes. The miniseries likewise omits such unhappy details as the hysterical ranting and brutality of Robert E. Lee Howell, who tried to rally the crowd to burn or tear up Frank's body and stomped on Frank's face when his body was dropped as it was being carried away.[75]

In the miniseries, the aftermath of the lynching itself is melancholy. There is a dissolve to a phonograph player. Lucille listens again to Mimì's aria in *La Bohème* as an undertaker pulls up in his cart with a coffin on it, then comes up her front steps, hat in hand. Lucille instantly recognizes the significance of this visit as she goes out on her front porch to greet the man. She quickly turns away from him and toward her front door (and the camera) to compose herself—all without a single line of dialogue. Lucille expresses no outrage, as Sybil Hale did in *They Won't Forget*, partly because *The Murder of Mary Phagan* has cast the net of blame for Frank's fate far wider than the prosecutor and a newspaper reporter. Instead, Lucille is simply undone.[76]

As the closing music continues, the miniseries checks in with each of the major characters. An office boy hands Wes Brent an envelope holding Frank's wedding ring. We see Frank's coffin loaded onto the train to go to New York as Wes Brent gives Lucille the wedding ring at the train station. He then posts the letter he was typing to Slaton, informing him of the news of Frank's lynching. George Stevens's voiceover narration reappears to conclude the series, informing us of Frank's burial in Brooklyn and of the fact that Lucille lived until 1957. Over a shot of Slaton in the foreground with Brent's telegram while Sallie sits at a table in the background, we hear that Slaton learned of Frank's lynching while in California and that he practiced law "until his death in 1955. He was never again elected to public office." In a low-angle shot of Jim Conley, we learn that he was sentenced as an accomplice to Mary Phagan's murder, got out of prison less than a year later, and died in 1962. (This was for decades widely believed to be the year of Conley's death, but Steve Oney notes that no one knows precisely when Conley died.)[77] William J. Burns is seen at work with a team of detectives, and viewers learn that he became head of the U.S. Justice Department of Investigations, later renamed the Federal Bureau of Investigation, or FBI. Another shot shows Hugh Dorsey stroking Watson's temples on his front porch, as Slaton had done earlier; his assumption of Slaton's place speaks volumes. We learn

Alonzo Mann testifies nervously and quietly during the trial.

Since Alonzo Mann had passed away by the time the miniseries was shot, an actor portrayed him in the miniseries's epilogue as he visited the pencil factory.

that Watson became a U.S. senator and Dorsey became Georgia's governor. Over shots of Randy, John Lund, and even Doreen Camp, we are told that no one involved in Frank's lynching was "ever charged or brought to trial." Here, at last, is the true ending of the story that had been denied to Mervyn LeRoy and his creative team in 1937.

The final segment of the miniseries's epilogue focuses on Alonzo Mann. Mann was woven into the action all along—doing favors for the Franks, attending the *Sleeping Beauty* play and the neighborhood wedding, carrying the gramophone to just outside Frank's cell at Lucille's request, and twice testifying about Frank's character (at the trial and at Slaton's hearing). Now, a contemporary car pulls up in front of the pencil factory and an elderly man gets out to talk with reporters. (Mann had died before the series was shot.) The narrator tells us Mann's story: he told of having "seen Jim Conley *alone* disposing of Mary Phagan's body that Confederate Memorial Day. He said Conley had threatened to kill him if he ever told what he saw. Mann's testimony was validated by a lie detector test." We see Mann by Phagan's grave, an actual visit that the *Nashville Tennessean* photographed and printed as a page-wide photo.[78]

The narration concludes: "In 1986, the state of Georgia granted to Leo Frank a posthumous pardon." We see a medium close-up of Peter Gallagher as Leo Frank, slightly smiling, looking offscreen before the final fadeout—the same shot used when a bemused Leo responded to the opera Lucille played at home in their first scene together.

Assessing the Miniseries

The filmmakers involved in *The Murder of Mary Phagan* depicted the Phagan-Frank case comprehensively in both visual and narrative terms. Veronica Hadfield's production design and Nic Knowland's lighting and cinematography gave it a visual authenticity that owes little to the studio-bound stylization of previous versions. Lane's and Stevens's script gave due attention to the economic and social currents that informed the case. It also telescoped and rearranged events, and embellished or departed significantly from the available historical record when the writers deemed it dramatically appropriate. The best example of this is the Cain and Abel–like situation in which Governor Slaton and Solicitor Dorsey vie as political allies for the approval of the fatherly Tom Watson. In its totality, the miniseries demonstrates how unfair Leo Frank's trial was and how controversial and ultimately just Slaton's actions were.

Yet, even as the miniseries gives full expression to Georgians' thinking that Frank was guilty and the reasoning behind their demands that Frank be punished, even as it depicts Frank as a bit creepy and Slaton as impetuous, the miniseries elides two of the most troubling aspects of the case. As the two films and two television programs demonstrate, no dramatization can include every detail; nor would that be desirable. Some of the miniseries's omissions are not serious: for example, *The Murder of Mary Phagan*, unlike the *Profiles in Courage* episode, omits any mention of Judge Roan's post-trial misgivings about Frank's conviction. By contrast, the difficult position of William Smith—first fervently believing in Jim Conley's innocence and then announcing his conviction that Conley was guilty—would have made a fascinating subplot, although it might have distracted viewers from Slaton's own change of mind about the case. Even more significant is the omission of Watson's accusations, taken up by other outraged Georgians in 1915, that Governor Slaton had a conflict of interest in the case by virtue of his law firm's merger with Luther Rosser's firm, along with the accusation that Slaton was unduly influenced by northern, perhaps Jewish, money. The miniseries briefly mentions the latter charge twice but never the former.

Including Slaton's potential conflict of interest in the script would have made the southern mob's anger even more comprehensible to a 1988 audience and would have increased the audience's doubts about Slaton's character. Moreover, Lane and Stevens explicitly tried to give Slaton's character shades of gray. After all, they chose to depict Slaton's hearings into Frank's conviction as motivated in part by personal, somewhat petty considerations—his anger at Watson's strong-arm tactics and his rivalry with Dorsey. One might argue that in dramatizing the accusation that Slaton had "sold out," the filmmakers effectively incorporated related perceptions of Slaton as corrupt. In interviews, neither Lane nor Stevens could recall why they did not include the conflict-of-interest issue in their treatment. Lane said, "I think, if we were aware of that, . . . it would have wound up in there, because . . . we tried to make sure nobody was a saint." Stevens offered another possible rationale: "This is history and in another way it's not dissimilar to adapting a novel. . . . You have to select carefully what you include and if you drag in too many ancillary issues or details, you lose the thrust of the narrative and the drama."[79]

Perhaps the notion that Slaton finally did act from the very best motives encouraged the storytellers to neglect the conflict-of-interest issue. Immediately after Frank's initial trial, and certainly in the mid-1980s after Alonzo Mann's revelations, an overwhelming consensus held that Frank was innocent. In fact, until the publication of Steve Oney's *And the Dead Shall Rise* in 2003, no major study of the case besides Mary Phagan-Kean's took the charges against Slaton seriously. Stevens's suggestion that the conflict-of-interest issue might have been left out for reasons of narrative flow is certainly a possibility. Although the *Profiles in Courage* episode demonstrates that dramatizing the accusations against Slaton could be done in just a few dialogue exchanges, one could argue that the miniseries was committed to exploring fully all the facets of the case it did focus on; in other words, presenting the suspicion of Slaton so briefly would have clashed with the writers' approach to representing history.

Overall, however, the omission of some facets of the case and the addition of the fictional friendship among Slaton, Dorsey, and Watson cannot obscure the fundamental fact that *The Murder of Mary Phagan* is a major achievement and is likely to remain the most comprehensive dramatization of the case for decades to come.

Promotion and Publicity

George Stevens and Jack Lemmon were chief spokespeople for *The Murder of Mary Phagan*. In interviews, profiles, and previews they explained their attraction to the subject, noted its high-quality production and casting, and otherwise provided juicy quotes on the project that turned up in a number of critics' previews and reviews. Their comments focused on the multifaceted nature of the case: It was a good mystery yarn that portrayed an important trial in American history; it portrayed a conscientious politician; and Frank's guilt or innocence was ambiguous. Stevens emphasized the notion that the miniseries had been designed for an intelligent audience. Television critics, by and large, agreed with the filmmakers on all of these points.[80]

Publicity also reminded readers that Frank's ordeal was called "the American Dreyfus case" and that it was "one of the most important trials in American legal history." Slaton's tough choices and high-minded actions were another major theme in the filmmakers' publicity comments. "One of the things that attracted me most to the story," Stevens said, "was the fact that the most popular governor in Georgia history got entangled in the events, and it caused him to make a difficult choice, to test his own conscience. . . . The difficulty of a politician remaining true to himself is still a problem in our political system." Jack Lemmon seconded this view in his explanation of why he ended his twelve-year absence from television roles for this project. "Every now and again, with something like 'The China Syndrome' or 'Save the Tiger,' you can both entertain *and* enlighten. You can go a step beyond just telling a great story. You can make people *think*. And 'Mary Phagan' certainly does that.'" That Lemmon had chosen this vehicle for his return to television only reinforced the publicity's claims for the subject's importance.[81]

Lemmon's comments on the series pointed up the broadly conceived, liberal viewpoint that it shared with his major previous film projects. He specifically compared Slaton with other characters he had recently portrayed—Jack Godell in *The China Syndrome* (1979) and Ed Horman in *Missing* (1982)—men who are initially skeptical that there is a problem in society or industry or the government, but eventually recognize that they must personally intervene.[82] Moreover, Lemmon connected the miniseries to contemporary American politics in a "Special Mailer" publicity packet mailed out by NBC: "Slaton didn't do it to be a hero. He did it because he was faced with a question of ethics. And that kind of dilemma is very pertinent to what's going on in politics and business today. What is moral? Public officials behave today in ways that were unheard of a few decades ago, and yet they are not chastised; they become heroes. The bigger the crime, it seems, the more money people can make writing about it and giving lectures." Similarly, Lemmon told *Los Angeles Herald-Examiner* critic Yardenia Arar, "I've had greater parts, per se, but there's very few things that I've been in that I've felt more proud to be a part of. I felt for once, in this day and age, we can do a true story about an American politician that is not downbeat."[83]

Most broadly, Lemmon articulated Stevens's and Hale's cinematic ambitions. *The Murder of Mary Phagan*, Lemmon asserted in series publicity, "is a *film*, plain and simple. The fact that it's being shown on television is beside the point; it has the 'feel' of a finely-crafted feature." (In another publicity item, costume designer Judy Moorcroft declared the series "bloody marvelous. This is as handsome a production as anything I've ever worked on.") Lemmon told the *Washington Post*: "There are aspects of this production, if I were sitting as a member of the Academy and this were a feature, I would think of a number of Oscar nominations the film deserves: The set design—wardrobe—let alone the acting—were all top drawer." If the series represented quality, so did the audience Stevens envisioned for it: "I remember my father saying, 'Audiences don't come just to escape or to be entertained, they come to learn about themselves.' The most important lesson I learned from him was his respect for the audience. He refused to accept it when studio heads told him the public had a 12-year-old mentality. Like him, I believe the audience is very perceptive, and that's been our attitude making this film."[84]

That perceptive audience also would be invited, Stevens implied, to reach their own conclusions about the case—specifically, whether or not Frank was guilty. That question might be another selling point for the series, given all the hints that Frank was not completely innocent of the charges against him. Lemmon told Michael Hill of the *Washington Post*: "We're not trying to say he was irrefutably innocent. Slaton commuted Frank's sentence to life in prison—he didn't pardon him. But there was not in his opinion enough to even dream of saying, 'The man's guilty—hang him.'" Hill added: "Viewers will be no more certain of Frank's guilt or innocence after five hours of television than historians and others are after 75 years of controversy."[85]

In Atlanta, the series was roundly criticized in advance of the broadcast, something that likely stirred even more interest among potential viewers. Mary Phagan's great-niece, Mary Phagan-Kean, who would publish her book on the case later that year, commented to a reporter that the teleplay was "not very factual or accurate at all," and objected to the depiction of the Phagan family as so poor that they had to walk to Atlanta and relied on Mary's wages to survive. Tom Watson Brown, Tom Watson's great-grandson, agreed about the teleplay's accuracy: "So much of it is just skewed. . . . The teleplay has a factual error on every page. They've taken it from Harry Golden's book (*A Little Girl Is Dead*) right down to misspelling the same names." Brown felt compelled to write NBC again, as he had in response to *Profiles in Courage*, accusing the show of being "false and malicious, hence libelous." Steve Oney commented on the portions of the script he had read: "it is inaccurate in many, many points, both specific and in the larger spirit. . . . It takes immense liberties."[86]

Reporter Phil Kloer allowed Stevens and Lane to respond to such criticisms, which they did by addressing specific points of complaint and by invoking the docudrama's hybrid status relative to historical reality. Stevens insisted the Phagans were "portrayed as decent, hard-working people." Peter Gallagher commented: "I think one thing we tried not to do is paint the people as bloodthirsty anti-Semites, but as people still smarting from the ravages of war." More broadly, Stevens argued: "We stayed true to the case in its broad realities, and we dramatized where necessary to make it a tellable story. I believe that we have captured the general truth of the Leo Frank story." Lane commented, "We're familiar with their viewpoints, but our research was very comprehensive. . . . It's fictionalized, but I believe what we've shown is true." The miniseries otherwise received excellent publicity prior to its broadcast. The *Post* devoted three pages to it, including large photos of the cast. The greatest publicity coup may have been civil rights–era attorney and Atlanta native Morris B. Abram's account of the case for *TV Guide* the week the series aired. Abram situated the Phagan-Frank case in relation to the troubled historical relationship between American Jews and blacks.[87]

Critical Reception

For the most part, television critics lauded *The Murder of Mary Phagan*, picking up on several major themes of the network's publicity—to wit, the multilayered story's entertainment value as well as its educational value and the ambiguities of the case.[88] Like the film critics who applauded *They Won't Forget* and the television critics who acclaimed *Profiles in Courage*, late-1980s television critics praised the miniseries's sophistication, its historical re-creation of the Phagan-Frank case, and its vision of a government official intervening to right an atypical wrong in American legal history.

The strongest praise came from reviewers in weekly magazines with a national readership. John Leonard in *New York* magazine described the series as "an uncommonly scrupulous and affecting account of 'the American Dreyfus case.'" Leonard concluded his review with the observation, "I can't help thinking that *The Murder of Mary Phagan* is exactly the sort of thing network television ought to do more of: history with nuance, the sociology of culture. There's no reason, for instance, that such John Sayles movies as *Matewan* and *The Brother from Another Planet* couldn't likewise have been commissioned by NBC or ABC or CBS, instead of the forthcoming and obscenely expensive Sidney Sheldons and James Clavells." Similarly, Laurie Stone in the *Village Voice* praised the series because it "gives each factor in Leo Frank's complicated case its due, and the movie is ultimately deeply disturbing."

The *Washington Post*'s review by Tom Shales, entitled "'Murder' Most Compelling," agreed with Leonard and Stone: "Chronicles of terrible things have made strong television movies before, but 'Mary Phagan' seems extraordinarily and thoughtfully powerful. . . . Why bring it [the case] up again now? The film justifies itself every step of the way, but especially in its second half, when the script concentrates on the ordeal that faced Slaton, who threw away a political career in his attempt to prevent injustice." Shales concluded by suggesting that the miniseries "is in its way an extension of Leo Frank's pardon, a belated act of justice. Just as importantly, in recalling the sacrificial triumph of John Slaton, it's a valuable and memorable profile in courage."

Similarly, Martha Bayliss in the *Wall Street Journal* appreciated "the film" as "a beautifully crafted piece of work—muted, understated, elegiac in tone. One adjective that cannot be applied to it is sensational. Yet, paradoxically, it succeeds in telling a very sensational story." Bayliss further noted that the series "pays us the compliment of assuming that we, like Mr. Stevens, are 'interested in the subtlety of extremes, rather than in their rabid demonstration.'" Her comments are especially striking given the reputation of movies of the week and miniseries for exploitative drama.

Like Bayliss, Laurie Stone of the *Village Voice* appreciated the conceptual sophistication of the miniseries, praising it for being "clear-eyed about the particular etiology of anti-Semitism, while, from the beginning to end, illuminating the political contexts that heat this poison to a boil." She viewed the emphasis on class differences between Frank and his accusers as a virtue, providing an intriguing account of the ambivalent responses viewers might have had to different elements of the program: "The filmmakers achieve their effects by focusing less on the division between Jews and anti-Semites than on the separation between power and powerlessness. We sympathize with the poor whites and blacks until, collectively, they form a mob against Leo Frank. We dislike Leo Frank for not paying his workers better wages, but feel for his victimization." Stone's comments register the scriptwriters' effort to portray three-dimensional characters. Such evaluations placed the series on the high plane of achievement that had greeted *They Won't Forget* and the *Profiles in Courage* episode.

But what some critics found "subtle" and "elegiac" others criticized as ponderous. John J. O'Connor of the *New York Times* complained that the series "proceeds at a slow, occasionally funereal pace. An hour might have been trimmed from the production without much effort." Other critics agreed that it began too slowly. Jeff Jarvis, writing for more pedestrian *People* magazine, gave the series a C– in his "Picks and Pans" column: "Such a drama should be filled to overflowing with drama and raw emotion, but this one isn't. Everybody in the show is too restrained." The *Los Angeles Herald Examiner*'s critic likewise panned the series as not fulfilling the "terrific dramatic potential" of the actual case; it was, David Gritten wrote, "a three-hour movie masquerading as a five-hour miniseries; it's laboriously slow and the material is stretched too thin." Gritten praised the cast but speculated that the filmmakers were almost "afraid" of the subject, "as though to pump up the highly dramatic elements in it would somehow trivialize it. Lane and Stevens (and director Billy Hale, for that matter) dwell lovingly on the details of the story, but somehow they forgot to charge it with enough excitement or involvement to sustain our interest. Ultimately, 'The Murder of Mary Phagan' suffers from a surfeit of good taste."

Variety's industry-minded critic compared the series unfavorably both with the case itself and with *They Won't Forget*: "As a case, 'The Murder of Mary Phagan' still chills; as a 5-hour tele-film, there's not much conviction." *They Won't Forget*, he said, "had a dynamism and impact and purpose that eludes 'Mary Phagan.'" Tom Shales likewise reminded readers of the *Washington Post* that *They Won't Forget* "aimed to make an audience's blood boil, and it remains effective at that even now." Such reviews suggest that the filmmakers' reliance on subtlety fell flat for certain critics, and by extension for viewers. In criticizing what they saw as the program's slow pace, particularly at the start, these critics also failed to appreciate the creators' care in setting forth *all* the factors that influenced the Phagan-Frank case's unusual development. If this care and detail reflected Stevens's respect for his audience's intelligence, this segment of the audience did not appreciate it.

One point on which all the critics agreed was the quality of the cast. Many critics noted that Jack Lemmon was unusually and effectively subdued. *Variety* characterized Lemmon's work as a "controlled, well-thought performance that has impressive written all over it." The critic for the *Christian Science Monitor* hailed Lemmon's performance as "brilliant." Gritten agreed that Lemmon gave a "finely tuned performance, with subtle intimations of light and shade." Likewise, Tom Shales spoke highly of Lemmon's "tremendous" work: "This is a stirring, heartening portrait of monumentally stubborn integrity, and as Slaton painstakingly goes over details of the trial, the film is persuasively suspenseful besides." Other cast members received praise in their own right. Gritten wrote that Gallagher succeeded in a "difficult, unsympathetic part . . . [playing] Frank initially as cold, uptight and formal." Shales singled out Charles Dutton, who was "mesmerizing in scene after scene" despite a "difficult" role: "It can't have been easy for a black actor in the self-conscious 1980s to play a character like this, who groveling, addresses all white men as 'boss.' Never mentioned in the screenplay is the obvious point that if the finger of guilt had pointed at Conley in the first place, there would also have been a lynching—probably without the nicety of a trial beforehand."[89]

The series's straightforward depiction of Frank's lynching also earned praise. Shales complimented the filmmakers for not "trafficking in the kind of hysterics that surrounded the case in the first place." Instead they "toned down some of the details—even the horror of the lynching itself, which is depicted as having been an occasion of heads-bowed chagrin on the part of the lynchers." Bayliss also praised the series for avoiding the clichéd Hollywood representation of the lynch mob. She found "a certain dignity" in the scenes in which members of the crowd "chant and sing hymns in unison" outside Slaton's mansion. This softening of the lynchers was simultaneously perturbing, however. Compared with the actual mobs, Bayliss noted, "the 'Mary Phagan' mob acts like a Greek chorus, expressing relevant emotions in highly stylized form." She duly noted the miniseries's softening of Tom Watson but ultimately concluded that "by understating rather than overstating, the film makes their point of view impossible to dismiss."[90]

Part 1 earned the twelfth-highest Nielsen rating for the week, a 28 share (that is, 28 percent of the estimated eighty-eight million television sets turned on during that time slot were watching the show). It placed behind such popular shows as *The Cosby Show*, *A Different World*, *Cheers*, *Night Court*, *60 Minutes*, *Murder, She Wrote*, *L.A. Law*, *Moonlighting*, and *The Golden Girls*; and ahead of *ALF*, *Body of Evidence*, *Matlock*, *Newhart*, *Family Ties*, *Amen*, and *Designing Women*. Apparently, part 2—generally regarded as the stronger half of the series—lost audience members because it aired on Tuesday, not Monday (President Reagan's State of the Union Address was broadcast on the intervening night).

The Murder of Mary Phagan received several honors from within the television industry and outside it. It earned five Emmy nominations, and won awards for Best Miniseries and for Outstanding Editing and Outstanding Sound Editing for a Miniseries or a Special. Jack Lemmon was nominated for Best Actor in a Miniseries or Special but lost to Jason Robards (for *Inherit the Wind*), and Jeffrey Lane lost the award for Outstanding Writing for a Miniseries or a Special to William Hanley for *The Attic: The Hiding of Anne Frank*. In addition to its 1988 Christopher Award, the miniseries—like *Profiles in Courage*—won a Peabody Award for Lemmon's performance, the series's "historical detail," and its overall "exceptional quality" in allowing "a look behind the exterior of a society and its sense of justice."[91] The miniseries also had a life as a text for the study of intolerance generally. Given that Frank's conviction inspired the creation of the Anti-defamation League (ADL), it was appropriate that the miniseries had a special premiere at the Washington, D.C., American Film Institute Theater under ADL auspices. The ADL also prepared a special teaching poster for the miniseries, which provided an overview of the case, a list of crucial dates, a postscript to the case, and an explanation of Georgia's posthumous pardon. Like the *Profiles in Courage* teaching aids, the poster then suggested topics for classroom discussion. Its prose and bibliography drew analogies between the Phagan-Frank case and apartheid in South Africa, the Scottsboro trials, and the internment of Japanese Americans during World War II.[92]

The Murder of Mary Phagan received mixed assessments in Atlanta that focused on its status as a historical docudrama. Television critic Phil Kloer listed the miniseries's virtues: the "powerful feelings of class and regional antagonism run through the miniseries every bit as strongly as the strain of anti-Semitism"; Frank may seem innocent to viewers, but "the production does not whitewash Frank. This is not black-and-white, easy-answer-stuff; the many ambiguities that still dog the case suffuse the miniseries with shades of gray." He concluded that the series as a docudrama avoided huge errors of fact and created a "satisfying drama that is best watched with an active mind."

By contrast, a "weary" Mary Phagan-Kean told the Metro Marietta Kiwanis Club after viewing part 1 that she was "banking on the intelligence of the American people" to recognize that the producers had "Hollywoodized" the story and that very few incidents depicted were "factually correct"—citing in particular the portrayal of the Phagans as a poor family and the inclusion of Mary's father, John, who had died before Mary's murder. Phagan-Kean was seconded by beloved local columnist Celestine Sibley, who had authored a five-part series on the case for the *Constitution* twelve years earlier. Sibley was annoyed that the series was shot in Richmond and was particularly critical of the "ridiculous ornate, over-steepled version of our old county jail, Fulton Tower," when it could have just as easily been shot on a Hollywood back lot. She appreciated the inclusion of Fiddlin' John Carson's famous ballad, "but when the entire courtroom full of people got to their feet and started singing a hymn like the Mormon Tabernacle Choir in Salt Lake City," she "burst into laughter."

Sibley was in general "sorry [she] sat up late two nights" to watch it: "What a terrible thing to do, using the skills of fine actors and technical crews for one of those 'based on' productions! It should have been offered as either fiction or fact. . . . Using the real names of people and places and then fictionalizing their character and actions left this viewer reeling with confusion. How much was true? How much an expedient concoction by scriptwriters?" Sibley further cited disgruntled reactions from Hugh Dorsey's son and Tom Watson Brown on the depiction of their ancestors (adding, in regard to Watson's depicted attempt to persuade Slaton to reject Frank's appeal outright: "As well as I've been able to find out, there wasn't a behind-the-scenes bone in the fiery Watson's body"). She even reported that Brown believed that, in her words, "NBC was wary of doing its worst by his grandfather this time because of a set-to he had with the network in 1962 [*sic*] when an earlier version presented him as 'Boss Hawg.'" She further reported, incorrectly, that the *Profiles in Courage* episode had been "withdrawn" as a result.[93]

Sibley's comments on the series reflected the uncertain status of the historical docudrama as a form, its allegiance to historical accuracy, and the parameters of its fictional inventions. On the whole, the miniseries's omissions and divergences from the historical record can be balanced against its extraordinary achievement as a work of popular history. Among the four treatments of the case considered in this volume, *The Murder of Mary Phagan* delivers the most nuanced and fullest account of what befell Mary Phagan, Leo Frank, and John M. Slaton—and why. It incorporates the most significant elements from all the previous versions: the notion of a town colluding to convict and execute an innocent man, the perversion of justice within an American courtroom for political gain, the potential of the press to destroy lives, the power of sectionalist hatred, the role of anti-Semitic feeling and white supremacist thought in the case, and the horror of vigilante justice. Not least, the miniseries delineates the roots of class hatred of Frank and Slaton and portrays at least some southern black Americans as they really were in the 1910s: thoughtful, intelligent, and honorable.

Conclusion

BEYOND THEIR INHERENT INTEREST as dramatizations of one of the most sensational cases in twentieth-century America, *Murder in Harlem*, *They Won't Forget*, *Profiles in Courage*: "Governor John M. Slaton," and *The Murder of Mary Phagan* provide a remarkable opportunity to explore how the same historical event can be represented on-screen by different storytellers across five decades in closely related media. The differences among them—in terms of the details they emphasize, the characterizations they offer, the genre conventions they employ, and their visual style—are as fascinating as their similarities, which in turn attest to a remarkable consensus in interpreting what transpired in Atlanta between 1913 and 1915.

Only a year (or two, depending on how one counts it) separated Oscar Micheaux's and Mervyn LeRoy's films about the case. Both works fictionalize it, set it in the present, and, to remarkably different degrees, allude to the violence and legal malfeasance rampant in the South in the 1930s. The conditions under which Micheaux and LeRoy worked were worlds apart, though—in terms of filmmaking sensibilities, but also in budget, production values, and available technology. These conditions affected what could and could not be shown to public audiences. Certainly, the filmmakers' perspectives were also strikingly different.

Micheaux provided an African American interpretation of Leo Frank's corrupt character—sexual assailant, hypocritical coward, everything but a murderer—that Tom Watson and his acolytes would have applauded. Yet Micheaux concluded his story with a surprise twist that named a white boyfriend as the guilty party. This unexpected ending may reflect Micheaux's customary playfulness with his story sources, or he may have been unwilling to offend his new Jewish financiers. The true killer is punished outside the courtroom; a rough-hewn poetic justice transpires in a rough-hewn film.

The LeRoy film conveys even more forcefully than Micheaux's the utter terror a black American man felt at the unsolved murder of a white woman in that decade—a point emphasized further by the film's refusal to identify the murderer, as if the name of the guilty party is beside the point. Perhaps the most fascinating contrast between the two films concerns their conception of justice in America. Micheaux's film decries three manifestations of white dominance in American society: the effort of white criminals to frame black people; the potential injustice that black defendants routinely faced in a white-run judicial system; and implicitly, the horror that black suspects faced outside the courtroom, at the end of a lynching rope. In Micheaux's film, only the first of these three possibilities comes to pass. This is a mark of the film's optimism: *Murder in Harlem* expresses faith that the trial process—if conducted by African Americans on behalf of African Americans—will uncover the truth and at least exonerate the innocent, while fate will punish the guilty. In contrast, the Warner Bros. film shows that a (southern) legal system can be hijacked by opportunists in public office and within the press corps if they manipulate the circumstantial evidence effectively. *Murder in Harlem* takes the persistence of lynching as inevitable, even as it confines its story to the fortunes of the black characters; *They Won't Forget* unambiguously condemns lynching. In Micheaux's treatment, Jim Conley could not have committed murder. *They Won't Forget* suggests he very well might have—but also that he might be as innocent as Robert Hale, and that reasonable doubt should preclude anyone's condemnation to death.

The two television treatments of the Phagan-Frank story are notably different from their cinematic predecessors of several decades earlier. Clearly, historical distance from the actual events enabled both dramatizations to portray the case more fully—most significantly, to portray the crucial role of anti-Semitism in Leo Frank's fate while presenting their story as undisguised historical docudramas. Both seek to balance the horror and tragedy of Frank's lynching against Slaton's nobility. Both show how a trial can be unduly influenced by a mob, but how justice can be recognized even by a few and enforced, if only temporarily. Both inspire connections to their time period—the heyday of the civil rights era and the ideals of public service associated with the Kennedy administration in 1964, and the possibility of enlightened political leadership in the late 1980s. But where the studio-bound *Profiles in Courage* zeroes in on the contest of wills between Governor John M. Slaton and Tom Watson, the bigger-budgeted, location-shot, all-star *Murder of Mary Phagan* paints a much broader canvas in delineating the dynamics of the case. *Profiles in Courage* responded to the "vast wasteland" Newton Minow saw in network television by offering educational programming. *The Murder of Mary Phagan* was special-event television, a means of allowing NBC to compete with the other broadcast networks and the cable and satellite channels just beginning their encroachment on the networks' domain. Both are examples of what has come to be called "quality television."

Perhaps the greatest contrast between all these versions is visible in the depiction of the Jim Conley character. His race is never specified in the *Profiles in Courage* episode, and the show thereby ignores the troubling black and white, and black and Jewish, dimensions of the case against Frank. The miniseries's depiction of its black characters clearly benefited from the achievements of the civil rights movement and its effects on the representation of African Americans in film and television. As Micheaux's film did for Harlem, the miniseries creates a sense of diversity within the black Atlanta community rather than focusing on Jim Conley as the sole black figure in a white world. Conley was, in fact, isolated and playing to his white audience inside the courtroom and jailhouse in Atlanta in 1913. But by portraying Newt Lee, Annie Maude Carter, and the factory employee–farmer, the miniseries fleshes out a series of contrasting characters with greater dignity and integrity than Conley, much as Oscar Micheaux did with his main characters in *Murder in Harlem*. Equally significant, the miniseries also makes Conley the master of his own survival strategy rather than, as in the 1930s films, the puppet of his white lawyer or his white boss. The miniseries grants Conley an intelligence and agency that was unthinkable to 1913 Atlantans and too controversial for Warner Bros. to show in a 1930s film. If Luther Rosser in the miniseries does not know what to make of the wily Conley, the black farmer, Burns, Governor Slaton, and the miniseries's audience certainly do. He is ultimately unmasked as a perjurer. His guilt for murder is all but explicitly stated— something else that distinguishes the miniseries from its predecessors.

For all their differences, the films and television productions have striking similarities. For one thing, each complicates in several ways the claim that film and television treatments of American history simplify and distort the facts. Undeniably, all altered countless details of the case in their storylines, settings, and characterizations. Yet all four were based on extensive knowledge of the case. Ward Greene was in Atlanta at the time of the trial, read trial transcripts, and undertook additional research; Oscar Micheaux claimed to have attended the trial but knew the story intimately in any case; and the television program creators undertook considerable research that included the consultation of archival primary sources in addition to published accounts. As each storyteller discovered, the Mary Phagan–Leo Frank affair offers a dazzling array of sensational, fascinating, and often ambiguous details from which to construct a story. Yet, each interpreted the many facets of the case—the guilt or innocence of the accused, the identity of the actual killer, the reasons for Georgia's outrage, the demands for vengeance, and the motivations of John Slaton—in their own way. Each decided which elements were essential to tell their story, which elements to omit, and which alterations or embellishments were necessary to portray events with the greatest dramatic impact.

Each version was produced by a determined visual storyteller: Micheaux, LeRoy, producer Robert Saudek and his team, and George Stevens and his. Likewise, all the screen versions—even Hal Reid's 1915 films—shared a didactic purpose, however disguised it might be. Micheaux's film explores Jim Conley's informative testimony as a key witness at Leo Frank's trial and his reluctant participation in what he alleged to be Leo Frank's murder of Mary Phagan. *Murder in Harlem* reflects on Conley's centrality to the case and the ways in which black-white race relations figured into the trial's unfolding; but it also exposes and ridicules both the simpering but self-conscious Lem Hawkins and the conniving Catbird and her criminal entourage. These negative role models are implicitly contrasted with the dignified, educated, and smart utterly fictional characters Henry Glory and especially Claudia Vance, who eventually identifies the true killer of Myrtle Stanfield. Considering this configuration of characters reveals *Murder in Harlem* as another example of Oscar Micheaux's exhortations to African Americans in the 1930s to live up to their potential. Its brief references to lynching reminded the audience of that horrific possibility.

They Won't Forget powerfully denounces mob violence, lynching, and corrupt and venal politicians and newspaper reporters. The two television programs also focus on these profound problems in American life, but show that while the American justice system can be derailed and that human nature can be deeply flawed, a responsible, enlightened officeholder could at least make a stand for justice and mercy. Much as Claudia Vance and Henry Glory functioned in *Murder in Harlem*, Governor Mountford in *They Won't Forget* and John Slaton in the television programs are inspiring role models. If the emphasis in *They Won't Forget* lay in showing that "it can happen here," the two television programs about Slaton offered more hopeful history lessons to their viewers.

In presenting their vision of American life, all these visual storytellers worked within a broadly liberal philosophical framework, voiced perhaps most forcefully by Walter Lippmann's call for journalists to enlighten the citizens of democratic society about the issues of the day. Each version of the Frank case sprang from an assumption that an informed American democratic citizenry is essential to a more responsive and progressive government and nation, one capable—specifically in the arena of civil rights—of granting all its citizens equal treatment and due process.[1] All three of the mainstream media productions share the further assumption that their audience would appreciate such informative storytelling. The admiring film and television critics who praised their work suggest that they were correct.

Each visual storyteller, and many of the critics, connected the events of the past with current history. *Murder in Harlem* and *They Won't Forget* spoke to the Scottsboro trials, the ongoing lynching of African Americans in the South and around the country, and failed federal antilynching bills in the 1930s—some in the spring of 1937, months before *They Won't Forget* was released. *Profiles in Courage* embodied President Kennedy's highest political ideals and tacitly endorsed the aims of the civil rights movement unfolding as the program appeared—as when some reviewers linked the opening episode about the 1924 Democratic National Convention to the 1964 Republican National Convention. Some viewers might have seen in John Slaton's stand a ray of hope for reasonable southerners to embrace integration, even though the show did not specify that perjurer Jim Conley was black. Early 1988 marked the start of a presidential election year; the broadcast of *The Murder of Mary Phagan* was interrupted by Ronald Reagan's final State of the Union address. In this context, viewers of the miniseries might well have reflected—as did some television critics—on the persistence of hate and prejudice in contemporary America and the paucity of ethical or selfless political figures on the national scene.

It is striking in this regard to note that the creators of the three white-produced, mainstream commercial screen treatments of the case shared a more specific liberal political commitment that shaped their viewpoint on the case. In the 1930s, the Warner Bros. studio was an enthusiastic supporter of Franklin Delano Roosevelt and the New Deal, a position allied with the studio's progressive message movies (often scripted or co-scripted by leftist writers) such as *They Won't Forget*. In the early 1960s, the *Profiles in Courage* team even considered leftist blacklistees (including Robert Rossen) as writers for the series. "Governor John M. Slaton" scriptwriter Don M. Mankiewicz was active in the Democratic Party. Executive producer Robert Saudek framed the show in part as a tribute to the legacy of John F. Kennedy's presidency and as a response to Goldwater Republicanism. Jack Lemmon had lent his talents and prestige to notable liberal protest films in the 1980s before signing on to do *The Murder of Mary Phagan*. More significant, George Stevens was, like Saudek and Ritchie, a Kennedy-era liberal, having worked within the USIA for the Kennedy administration and for Edward R. Murrow, now most famous for his stance against McCarthyism in the 1950s. Remove from the series the comparatively explicit dialogue about sexual perversion and the direct depiction of Leo Frank's lynching and one can easily imagine *The Murder of Mary Phagan* appearing as scripted on the big or small screen in the 1960s. Indeed, liberal filmmaker Stanley Kramer had planned to create such a film during that decade.

The Murder of Mary Phagan demonstrates how far a screen storyteller of any political commitment can go in attempting to provide a comprehensive account of the Phagan-Frank case. The sense of decorum and propriety that informs the 1930s films—enforced by city and state censors for all filmmakers at that time—prevented Michaeux and LeRoy from dwelling on or even delving into the details of the crime, police corruption, the generalized accusations against Frank of lechery and sexual perversion, and especially the lynching itself. *Profiles in Courage* for the first time registered the role of anti-Semitism in the case, even as it downplayed the issue at the advice of its historical consultant; the writers handled the lynching phase of the story with great care, as did LeRoy in *They Won't Forget*. In contrast, the miniseries could show almost anything its creators deemed appropriate. George Stevens and his team embraced a subdued, anti-sensationalistic style that deviated so far from the usual over-the-top tone of movies of the week and broadcast miniseries that some critics found it dull.

Another factor shaping these screen versions of the Phagan-Frank story were the conventions of the many genres—the murder mystery, the wronged-man melodrama, the courtroom drama, the cynical newspaper film, the social problem film, the biopic of personal integrity—the storytellers, consciously or unconsciously, embraced. Oscar Micheaux played on the mystery story to frame an investigation into Myrtle Stanfield's death via multiple flashbacks and courtroom inquiry, concluding with the climactic revelation of the killer's identity. For good measure, he added an extended sequence including musical performances and class-based satire (directed primarily at Lem Hawkins). He threaded a romantic subplot through the film that ultimately ends in the formation of an idealized romantic couple. Most movies are generic hybrids; *Murder in Harlem* is a generic gumbo.

They Won't Forget also combines different genres, but its most creaky moment comes when the Flodden police come to take Robert Hale into custody for questioning and find him with evidence of his plans to leave town and a suit marred by a stubborn blood stain. Hale is truly a "victim of circumstance," the pivot point of the Hollywood 1930s message movie. Hale, like Arthur Vance before him and Leo Frank in the miniseries, is in the wrong place at the wrong time. *Profiles in Courage* depicts a murder mystery as an occasion for moral bravery within the framework of a biopic; the miniseries combines all of these genres as it tells the most chronologically complete story of the case.

Whatever their genre affiliations, the four screen treatments of the Phagan-Frank case share a striking consensus in their characterizations of the dramatic personae. Leo Frank, however suspiciously he behaved and however reprehensible he might have been in other ways, was innocent of Mary Phagan's murder. Robert Hale may be cool and paranoid; Leo Frank might be uptight and neurotic, and he might stare a bit too long at Mary Phagan; Anthony Brisbane may be a lecherous, power-abusing coward who does hold assignations with various women in his office. But Mary Phagan's murderer is either a third party (George Epps in *Murder in Harlem*, never identified in *They Won't Forget* and *Profiles in Courage*) or Jim Conley (*The Murder of Mary Phagan*). *They Won't Forget* and *The Murder of Mary Phagan* depict the Hales and the Franks, respectively, as socially isolated in the town. Sybil, Pindar, and Robert's mother are Hale's only visitors in *They Won't Forget*. In the miniseries, the Franks have Uncle Sig as family, but only Lucille Frank visits Leo in jail to comfort him. In actual fact, many friends, family members, a rabbi, and various celebrities visited Frank daily. Even when a screen treatment shows a national protest to save the convicted man's life, the couple effectively fight their battle alone. The magnitude of their struggle is further increased in *They Won't Forget* because they are barely getting by on Hale's salary. In both that film and in the miniseries, the marital bond of the central couple grows stronger across the jail cell bars. There is no question that isolating the Franks from one another is designed to heighten our sympathy for them, to diminish our sense of their class privilege and social power, and to further suggest Leo Frank's bad luck, if not innocence.

Andy Griffin in *They Won't Forget*, Tom Watson in *Profiles in Courage*, and Hugh Dorsey and Tom Watson in *The Murder of Mary Phagan* provide other examples of consistent characterizations across the three white-produced versions of the case. In all three, these characters are ambitious and corrupt men whose actions result in the murder of an almost certainly innocent man. Their charisma, drive, and energy make them compelling figures. The considerable disparity between what they say and do—between Griffin's stated determination to convict the guilty party and his case against Hale, between Dorsey's pretense at heartfelt sorrow at Mary Phagan's murder and his power grab, and between Tom Watson's quiet sympathy for the poor Georgian and the virulent hatred he stirs up—adds a fascinating layer of complexity. Brock and Price in *They Won't Forget* and Wes Brent in the miniseries are likewise recognizable figures of jaded, ruthless reporters—with only Brent registering substantial remorse for his role in ensuring Leo Frank's fate. Sybil's final speech in *They Won't Forget* is another convention of the newspaper or social problem movie genre often inserted at the Production Code Administration's insistence; it conforms to countless other cinematic condemnations of character malevolence in 1930s message movies.

The actions of Governor John M. Slaton are always heralded as heroic; he is a model of the political leader who acts without consideration for personal gain. Like Leo Frank, the governor enjoys a solid marriage to a supportive wife. This is in contrast to the prosecutor (Griffin, Dorsey) and Tom Watson, whose domestic solitude is subtly linked to their ruthless persecution of the accused. (Significantly, the real Dorsey and Watson were family men.) The governor has his wife's support, no matter how ambitious she has been for him, even as his assistant and other allies try to dissuade him from commuting Frank's sentence. No question is raised about the Slaton character's motives in *They Won't Forget*; his commutation of Hale's death sentence is simply one lone effort to restore justice to Hale's situation and a galvanizing event for the lynch mob. In *Profiles in Courage*: "Governor John M. Slaton," Watson churlishly threatens the governor with what are clearly stated to be false accusations of conflict of interest. The episode raises and then explains away such charges. *The*

Murder of Mary Phagan never even raises that issue, simply dramatizing the very powerful outrage in Georgia over Slaton's perceived bribery by wealthy northern Jewish interests. Most of all, the two television versions treat as definitive Slaton's determination that reasonable doubt exists about Conley's testimony and Frank's guilt.

The mobs depicted in all these treatments deserve comment because the works that give the lynchers an on-screen identity depart significantly from the historical record. *Murder in Harlem* merely alludes to the lynch mob, briefly broaching the possibility that Arthur Vance or Lem Hawkins might be in danger. The three white, mainstream treatments of the Phagan-Frank affair make vigilante justice a rumbling threat throughout, understood by the lynchers as their only recourse to correct what they perceive as the governor's perversion of justice. In *Profiles in Courage*, the mob—represented individually only by the Marietta farmer at the hearing—is stirred up not by the prosecutor or the daily newspapers, but by the opening scene's hateful rabble-rouser and by Tom Watson and the *Jeffersonian*.

They Won't Forget and *The Murder of Mary Phagan* offer another signal departure from the historical record: the mob consists of individual working-class males who have a personal connection to the murder victim. Mary Clay's brothers and boyfriend, Joe Turner, in *They Won't Forget* threaten continually to lynch Hale, and they are first in line outside when Hale opens the railroad car door to escape his abductors. In the miniseries, Mary's neighbors Randy and John Lund are the only identifiable lynchers of Leo Frank—Lund is in fact their leader. The real Mary Phagan's uncle was the only identified member of the planners or executors of Frank's lynching related or closely connected to the Phagan family. Instead, the planners were highly educated Marietta citizens, some of whom had held prominent government positions, and all of whom felt they had to avenge the outrage of Slaton's decision. Depicting the lynchers as relatives or friends of the murder victim is a way of linking diverse characters in a more dramatic way than the historical record allows, much like the miniseries's conceit that Slaton, Dorsey, and Watson were friends and political allies, and of providing some insight into the lynchers' motivations. (Certainly, the widespread sentiment that what befell Mary Phagan could have happened to any urban-dwelling, factory-employed working-class girl powerfully motivated the anti-Frank forces' desire for vengeance.) The fictional close connection of the lynchers to Mary Phagan also creates, in *They Won't Forget* and *The Murder of Mary*

Phagan, a strongly bonded community that contrasts starkly with the isolation of the Franks.

The Phagan-Frank story has been told primarily as a tale of men, with women acting as supportive partners or helpless victims. All four versions of the Phagan-Frank case portray Mary Phagan as an unfortunate, simple victim who was in the wrong place at the wrong time. If Myrtle Stanfield has little personality in *Murder in Harlem* (unlike Claudia Vance), Mary in *They Won't Forget* and *The Murder of Mary Phagan* is an attractive young woman, an embodiment of youthful innocence and unselfconscious sensuality. Her ordeal is always offscreen, in keeping with the conventions of the murder mystery and the uncertain identity of her killer. It is the trauma of her loss, an element of the story that *Murder in Harlem* and *Profiles in Courage* neglect to dramatize on-screen, that incites the mob.

Fictional generic conventions—cynical journalists; isolated, falsely accused victims; emotionally passionate mobs—do shape the depiction of historical events. They may do so, as is often asserted of docudramas, to simplify the depiction of those events by omitting certain facts or fabricating others. Yet three of the Mary Phagan–Leo Frank screen dramatizations actually depict many of the details of the case as well as its historical and moral complexities. Lem Hawkins's inconsistent character gyrations in *Murder in Harlem*—in the scene in which Anthony Brisbane dictates the murder notes to him—testify to the multiplicity of ways in which Jim Conley was perceived at the trial. They also reveal Hawkins's obsequious dissemblance in the presence of his powerful, wealthy white boss—which in turn alludes to the varied stereotypes by which American popular culture has portrayed African Americans.

They Won't Forget's refusal to specify who killed Mary Clay was rare if not unheard of for a Hollywood murder mystery/courtroom drama. The town's collusion in convicting Hale, even if this logic was inserted as a result of the PCA's requests, is a remarkably perturbing assignation of guilt. The film's explanation of the roots of southern sectionalism and the emotional anguish of Mary Clay's brothers may have been a pragmatic effort on the part of the filmmakers to minimize the insult to the South that the film's story entailed; yet it bespeaks a compassion that lesser films might exclude. Even Sybil Hale in *They Won't Forget* is moved to tell Griffin and Brock that she understands why her husband's killers sought his death— whereas the prosecutor and reporter had no reason aside from their own ambition. The film's depiction of Griffin as a prosecutor who says the right things but does the opposite attests to the contradictions inherent in human nature. The same might be said of Sybil's gentle suggestion that Hale is partly to blame for his discomfort in the South.

The Murder of Mary Phagan goes the furthest in this direction, upholding the principle that Jeffrey Lane quoted from the great film director Jean Renoir's *Rules of the Game* (1939): "Everybody has his reasons."[2] No screen version of the Phagan-Frank case suggests that such sympathies can ever justify vigilante justice; yet, combined with the oddities of Robert Hale and Leo Frank's personalities as depicted in the 1937 film and the 1988 miniseries as well as their bad luck, each treatment does provide a fuller understanding of how these men came to be so reviled. *The Murder of Mary Phagan* does this most broadly by attending to the impersonal factors that drove the Phagans to Atlanta and Mary into the pencil factory in 1913.

Mary Phagan's murder and especially Leo Frank's lynching are the two core aspects of the story and the two most difficult to portray. It is possible, but unlikely, that their stories would still have such a powerful grasp on our imaginations today had they not ended in murder. Lynching, in particular, has been a story element in several Hollywood films over the decades. But as three of the four screen treatments of the Frank case show, representing this horrible form of mob violence can be as difficult as showing the forces that resulted in it. *Profiles in Courage* opted for a flash of an actual photograph that remains shocking and searing in its directness, however brief the screen duration of the image. *The Murder of Mary Phagan* uses cutaways from the victim as it directly portrays Leo Frank's lynching in a melancholy mood, setting a tone that is not unlike the descriptions we have of the awful handiwork of Leo Frank's calm, methodical killers. *They Won't Forget* offers the most fierce, dynamic, overpowering portrayal of lynching, paradoxically by not showing it at all. The difficulty resides in the traumatic nature of such violence, its challenge to representation, and its distressing reverberations in American history and culture to this day, which challenges our sense of who we Americans are, have been, and can be.

As I hope to have made clear, each of the four screen dramatizations of the Mary Phagan–Leo Frank story rewards a close look. All keep remarkable, albeit not complete, faith with the historical record their writers' drew on for their scripts and visuals, and all tell an unwieldy tale full of fascinating and mysterious characters; brimming with uncertain facts; bookmarked by two murders; and infused with class resentment, sectionalism, racism, anti-Semitism, and seething hatred that was barely satiated by mob violence. The story also encompasses an extraordinary example of personal integrity in the face of overwhelming pressure and considerable personal loss. Most of all, the retellings on-screen of what happened to Mary Phagan and Leo Frank constitute a search for justice inside and outside the courtroom.

All of these facets have made the Phagan-Frank case compelling for both professional and amateur historians and other observers. This will always be true because of the story's many uncertainties, the fundamentally traumatic nature of the case for everyone involved, and the fact that the very elements that make the story so fascinating often elude representation. But the case's fascination endures as well because most Americans still struggle to find a solution to so many of the conflicts that animated the case: to secure some measure of social harmony in a racially, ethnically, religiously, economically, and regionally diverse country; and to ensure justice in uncertain circumstances.[3] Filmmakers and television show creators will continue to return to this tale. It will be fascinating to see what they do with it.

Appendix A

Case Chronology

1913

April 26	Confederate Memorial Day in Atlanta. Mary Phagan is murdered in the National Pencil Company factory sometime in the early afternoon.
April 27	Factory night watchman Newt Lee discovers Mary Phagan's body in the basement and calls the police.
April 29	Atlanta police arrest Leo Frank.
May 3	Hugh Dorsey takes over the investigation and prosecution.
May 23	A grand jury indicts Leo Frank for Mary Phagan's murder after deliberating for only ten minutes.
May 29	Jim Conley provides a third affidavit asserting that he helped Leo Frank carry Mary Phagan's body to the basement and that Leo Frank was the killer.
July	The law firms of Luther Z. Rosser (Frank's lead defense attorney) and Governor-Elect John M. Slaton merge.
July 28	Leo Frank's trial begins.
August 25	Leo Frank is found guilty after less than two hours of jury deliberation.

| October 31 | Judge Leonard Roan, who presided at the trial, rejects the defense's motion for a retrial. |

1914

February 17	The Georgia Supreme Court affirms the lower court's ruling. Frank's defense team subsequently announces they have hired detective William J. Burns.
March 19	Tom Watson publishes his first editorial on the Frank case in the *Jeffersonian*.
October 2	William M. Smith, Jim Conley's attorney, admits his belief that Jim Conley killed Mary Phagan.

1915

April 19	The U.S. Supreme Court denies Frank's appeal. Two justices dissent.
June 9	The Georgia Prison Commission refuses to commute Frank's sentence (one of the three members dissents). Frank is to be executed June 22.
June 12	Governor John Slaton hears Frank's petition for commutation of sentence.
June 20	Governor Slaton commutes Frank's sentence one day before Frank is to be executed. Frank is taken to the state prison in Milledgeville.
June 26	Nat Harris is sworn in as Georgia's governor.
July 17	An inmate at the state prison slashes Frank's throat and nearly kills him.
August 16–17	Leo Frank is abducted from the state prison and lynched in Marietta, Georgia.

Appendix B

Filmography

Murder in Harlem (1936) (aka *Lem Hawkins' Confession* [1935])

Production company: Micheaux Pictures Corp. Presenter: A. Burton Russell. Producer-director-writer: Oscar Micheaux. Photography: Chas. Levine. Art director: Tony Continenta. Cabaret sequences writer and director: Clarence Williams. Songs: "Harlem Rhythm Dance" and "Ants in My Pants" by Clarence Williams. Recording engineers: Harry Belock and Armond Schettin. Production manager: Chas. B. Nason. Released October 9, 1936. Length: 98 minutes.

CAST: Clarence Brooks (Henry Glory); Dorothy Van Engle (Claudia Vance); Andrew Bishop (Brisbane); Alec Lovejoy (Lem Hawkins); Laura Bowman (Mrs. Epps); Bee Freeman (the Catbird); Alice B. Russell (Mrs. Vance); Lorenzo McClane (Arthur Vance); Slick Chester (detective); Oscar Micheaux (second detective).

A DVD of the film is available as part of the Tyler, Texas, Film Collection from the G. William Jones Film & Video Collection at Southern Methodist University; see http://www.smu.edu/blackfilms/

They Won't Forget

Producer-distributor: First National Pictures and Mervyn LeRoy Productions/Warner Bros. Pictures, Inc. Executive producer: Jack L. Warner. Producer-director: Mervyn LeRoy. Screenplay: Robert Rossen and

Aben Kandel. From the novel *Death in the Deep South* by Ward Greene. Photography: Arthur Edeson. Art director: Robert Haas. Editor: Thomas Richards. Gowns: Miss MacKenzie. Music director: Leo F. Forbstein. Music and arrangement: Adolph Deutsch. Hair: Helen Turpin. Makeup: Al Bonner. Released October 9, 1937. Length: 105 minutes.

CAST: Claude Rains (Andy Griffin); Gloria Dickson (Sybil Hale); Edward Norris (Robert Hale); Otto Kruger (Michael Gleason); Allyn Joslyn (Bill Brock); Lana Turner (Mary Clay); Linda Perry (Imogene Mayfield); Elisha Cook Jr. (Joe Turner); Cy Kendall (Detective Laneart); Clinton Rosemond (Tump Redwine); E. Alyn Warren (Carlisle P. Buxton); Elizabeth Risdon (Mrs. Hale); Clifford Soubier (Timberlake); Granville Bates (Detective Pindar); Ann Shoemaker (Mrs. Mountford); Paul Everton (Governor Mountford); Donald Briggs (Harmon Drake); Sybil Harris (Mrs. Clay); Trevor Bardette (Shattuck Clay); Elliott Sullivan (Luther Clay); Wilmer Hines (Ransom Clay); Eddie Acuff (drugstore clerk); Frank Faylen (reporter Bill Price); Leonard Mudie (Judge Moore); Harry Davenport (Confederate soldier); Harry Beresford, Edward McWade (Confederate soldiers).

Not available on DVD, but sometimes shown on Turner Classic Movies.

Profiles in Courage: "Governor John M. Slaton"

Production company: Robert Saudek Associates. Executive producer: Robert Saudek. Producer: Gordon Oliver. Associate producer: Michael Ritchie. Script: Don M. Mankiewicz. Director: Robert Gist. Director of photography: William Spencer. Art director: Richard Haman. Set decorator: Frank Wade. Wardrobe: Frank Delmar. Makeup: Jack Wilson. Music: Nelson Riddle. Editor: Jason H. Bernie. Casting: Patricia Rose. Main title: Saul Bass and Associates. Production manager: Nathan R. Barranger. Historian: Allan Nevins. For the estate of President John F. Kennedy: Theodore C. Sorensen. Length: 51 minutes. First broadcast: December 20, 1964. NBC network.

CAST: Walter Matthau (Governor John M. Slaton); Michael Constantine (Thomas Watson); Betsy Jones-Morland (Sallie Slaton); Frank Marth (John Grant); Anthony Costello (Martin Burley); Donald Foster (Judge Roan); Whit Bissell (Judge Powell); Alan Baxter (Judge Fish); Tyler McVey (Wheeler); Gage Clark (clergyman); Paul Gence (prison commissioner); Robert Sorrells (farmer); Lyle Sudrow (Prosecutor Dorsey); Patrick O'Moore (Governor Harris); David Bond (rabble-rouser); Neil Rosso (news vendor); Charles Alvin Bell (court clerk); Ollie O'Toole (first reporter); Jon Locke (blind singer); Shirley O'Hara (Mrs. Addison); Lenny Geer (second juror); Elmer Modlin (jury foreman).

A DVD can be purchased from the Social Studies School Service at http://socialstudies.com.

The Murder of Mary Phagan

Production company: George Stevens Jr. and Century Towers Productions. Distributor: Orion Television. Producer: George Stevens Jr. Teleplay: Jeffrey Lane and George Stevens Jr.. Story by: Larry McMurtry. Director: Billy Hale (special thanks to Dan Petrie). Creative consultant: Toni Vellani. Associate producer: Caroline Stevens. Director of photography: Nic Knowland. Editor: John A. Martinelli. Production designer: Penny Veronica Hadfield. Art director: Vaughn Edwards. Costume designers: Judy Moorcroft and Merrily Murray-Walsh. Makeup supervisor: Gigi Coker. Casting director: Howard Feuer. Music: Maurice Jarre. Unit production manager: Bill Chase. Length: 251 minutes. First broadcast: Sunday, January 24 (part 1), and Tuesday, January 26, 1988 (part 2), NBC network.

CAST: Jack Lemmon (Governor John M. Slaton); Richard Jordan (Hugh M. Dorsey); Robert Prosky (Thomas Watson); Peter Gallagher (Leo Frank); Kathryn Walker (Sallie Slaton); Rebecca Miller (Lucille Frank); Paul Dooley (detective William T. Burns); Charles Dutton (Jim Conley); Kevin Spacey (Wes Brent); Cynthia Nixon (Doreen Camp); Kenneth Welsh (Luther Rosser); Loretta Devine (Annie Maude Carter); Wendy J. Cooke (Mary Phagan); Brent Jennings (Newt Lee); Nicholas Wyman (Lund); Dylan Baker (Ravenal); Barbara Eda-Young (Mrs. Phagan); Sam Gray (Sigmond Montag); W. H. Macy (Randy); Jordan Marder (Alonzo Mann); Ron Weyland (minister); Daniel Benzali (coroner).

Not available on DVD. VHS copies are for sale on the Web.

Notes

Introduction

1. Stewart Tolnay and E. M. Beck, *A Festival of Violence* (Carbondale: University of Illinois Press, 1995), ix, 260.

2. A list of the fictional texts based on the Mary Phagan–Leo Frank case would range from "Fiddling John" Carson's 1913 "Ballad of Mary Phagan" through David Mamet's novel *The Old Religion* (New York: Free Press, 1997) to the 1998 stage musical *Parade*, with book by Atlanta native Alfred Uhry, playwright and Oscar-winning screenwriter for the 1989 Academy Award winner for Best Picture, *Driving Miss Daisy* (1989).

3. See Nancy MacLean's superb essay "The Leo Frank Case Reconsidered: Gender and Sexual Politics in the Making of Reactionary Populism," *Journal of American History* 78, no. 3 (1991): 917–48. The classic examination of the case is Leonard Dinnerstein, *The Leo Frank Case* (New York: Columbia University Press, 1968; repr., Athens: University of Georgia Press, 1998); Steve Oney offers the most vivid and comprehensive account of the case in *And the Dead Shall Rise: The Murder of Mary Phagan and the Lynching of Leo Frank* (New York: Pantheon Books, 2003). A useful Web site on this topic is http://www.cviog.uga.edu/Projects/gainfo/leofrank.htm.

4. Eugene Levy quotes Rosser and Frank in "Is the Jew a White Man? Press Reaction to the Leo Frank Case, 1913–1915," *Phylon* 35, no. 2 (1974): 214.

5. Oney, *And the Dead Shall Rise*, 513–28.

6. Oney discusses the planners and the executioners in *And the Dead Shall Rise* (513–28) and describes the lynching itself on pp. 561–72. Among those who

planned it, for example, were Joseph M. Brown, a former governor of Georgia; Solicitor General Herbert Clay; barber Cicero H. Dobbs; and Judge Newton A. Morris, a former speaker of the Georgia House. For more general readings on the Phagan-Frank case, in addition to Oney and Dinnerstein, see MacLean, "The Leo Frank Case Reconsidered"; C. Vann Woodward, *Tom Watson, Agrarian Rebel* (New York: Oxford University Press, 1938); and Jeffrey Melnick's insightful monograph, *Black-Jewish Relations on Trial: Leo Frank and Jim Conley in the New South* (Jackson: University Press of Mississippi, 2000), which builds on MacLean's work to take a selective look at the class and race dynamics of the case.

7. Vida Goldgar, "In Leo Frank's Memory," *Jewish Times* (Atlanta), January 1, 1999, 48. Dinnerstein reports that "the police had jailed the sweeper two days after Frank's arrest because a foreman had informed them that Conley had been trying to wash blood from a shirt. Strangely enough, the authorities were inclined to attach little importance to his arrest. No one even bothered to have the city bacteriologist test the blood stains on the shirt" (*Leo Frank Case*, 21); Dinnerstein here quotes from "William Smith Tells Why His Opinion Has Changed as to Guilt of Leo Frank," *Atlanta Constitution*, October 4, 1914, 1, 6.

8. The first federal child-labor law was passed in 1916, three years after Phagan's murder, and was subject to Supreme Court rejection and revision during the next several years.

9. MacLean, "The Leo Frank Case Reconsidered," 932.

10. Dinnerstein, *Leo Frank Case*, vii; see also Eric L. Goldstein, *The Price of Whiteness: Jews, Race, and American Identity* (Princeton, N.J.: Princeton University Press, 2006), 43, 48.

11. See Allen Lumpkin Henson, *Confessions of a Criminal Lawyer* (New York: Vantage Press, 1959), 61–66; the quotation comes from page 65. I am indebted to Katherine Skinner for this formulation of the role of stereotypes in the interpretation of, and discourse surrounding, the case.

12. Dinnerstein, *Leo Frank Case*, vii. Joel Williamson, in *The Crucible of Race: Black-White Relations in the American South since Emancipation* (New York: Oxford University Press, 1984), regards Frank's fate as a forceful example of "the paranoid style in the twentieth-century South": white Georgians' sentiments against Frank followed a logic by which, after the Atlanta race riots of 1906, white southerners sublimated their fears of 'the black beast rapist' into a fear of 'hidden blackness, the blackness within seeming whiteness,' a category that encompassed 'whole congeries of aliens insidious in their midst who would destroy their happily whole moral universe." Williamson discusses southern paranoia on pp. 464–68 and the Phagan-Frank case on pp. 468–71. The quotations are from pp. 465–66 and 471.

13. The one scholarly proponent of this view is Albert S. Lindemann, who argues in *The Jew Accused: Three Anti-Semitic Affairs (Dreyfus, Beilis, Frank) 1894–1915* (New York: Cambridge, 1991), 223–72, that Jews in Atlanta were widely respected as law abiding (229–34, 245); that Frank's Jewish identity was not a factor in his initial suspected guilt (242); that neither Hugh Dorsey nor even Tom Watson were anti-Semitic prior to the Phagan-Frank case; and that, if anything, pervasive preconceptions about the Jews in Atlanta held them up as solid citizens. Lindemann's scholarship in Jewish history has been heavily criticized, however, by other historians.

14. "Mr. Louis Geffen" (obituary), *Atlanta Journal-Constitution*, January 25, 2001, B6.

15. Telephone interview with Tony and Jackie Montag, May 12, 2007, Atlanta, Georgia. Alfred Uhry's comments appear at http://www.music.umich.edu/performances_events/productions/past/01–02/uprod-parade.html, accessed June 19, 2007.

16. Oney, *And the Dead Shall Rise*, 644–49; Jane Gross, "Georgia Town Is Still Divided over the 1915 Lynching of a Jew," *New York Times*, August 26, 2000, A7. This piece also documents anti-Semitism in Marietta against a Jewish property owner. See also Bill Hendrick, "Lynching Reopens Old Scars for Some Mariettans," *Atlanta Journal-Constitution*, August 21, 2000, C2. Steven Lebow, an Atlanta rabbi, responded to Tom Watson Brown's claims in "Incendiary Comments Must Be Addressed," *Atlanta Journal-Constitution*, September 8, 2000. James Phagan, a nephew of Mary Phagan, told Carrick Mollenkamp of the *Wall Street Journal* that historian Stephen Goldfarb's posting on the Web of a list of names of Frank's lynchers is but another effort by Jews to exonerate Frank. "He's a Jew, isn't he?" Phagan asked reporter Mollenkamp about Goldfarb. "That tells you what you need to know" (A12).

17. Hugh Dorsey, quoted in Henson, *Confessions of a Criminal Lawyer*, 75.

18. *Traffic in Souls* premiered in November 1913, and *Inside of the White Slave Traffic* appeared in December, months after Mary Phagan's murder. Nonetheless, their appearance testifies to the culturally resonant fears of white slavery. On Mary Phagan's love of the movies, see Oney, *And the Dead Shall Rise*, 3–4; on Conley's account of attending them, see ibid., 135.

19. Oney, *And the Dead Shall Rise*, 534–37.

20. Ibid., 557–58.

21. Frank was born in Texas but grew up in Brooklyn.

22. "'Thou Shalt Not Kill' Preaches against Capital Punishment," *Motion Picture News*, July 31, 1915, 71. Reid's comments before the preview of his documentary film were reported in detail by *Variety*'s review "Leo M. Frank" (July 30, 1915):

Mr. Reid . . . delivered a preliminary discourse, containing a glowing tribute to Frank and his mother, with a little boom [sic] as well for the Presidential nomination of Slaton. The main reason, said Mr. Reid, why Georgia's ex-Governor should get the big seat at Washington is because he did his duty in the face of death when he commuted Frank's sentence. Reid also remarked Gov. Slaton informed him that he (the Governor) had received over 1,000 messages warning him if he did commute the sentence his death would follow. But with the confidence of his wife, who kissed him when he announced his determination, the Governor did the thing he thought should be done, added Mr. Reid, who dwells quite heavily upon this in lecture and captions. It's just as well, too, for once in a while when a fellow like Slaton looms up it might as well go on the record.

This review comments on Frank's physical appearance ("a slightly built man, of distinct Hebraic type, wearing glasses and having a studious expression") as well as the other personages, noting that Reid did not try to make a narrative out of his footage but simply shows "a series of scenes and photographs of a remarkable affair." In the lobby (of presumably the New York Theater), Reid also made available a letter from Slaton that *Variety* predicted the Circle Film Corporation would use "for press work wherever the film is shown." After noting that Reid could talk more freely of the "unpublishable phrases [sic] of the Frank murder matter that appear to bear out his assertion of Frank's persecution," reviewer Sime Silverman commented that the film itself was not sensationalistic. Rather, "so much publicity has been given the case this film should create a general interest that could be easily heightened by proper attention to the showmanship details in the smaller cities."

23. "'Thou Shalt Not Kill' Preaches"; see also the "Thou Shalt Not Kill" entry, *American Film Institute Catalogue, Feature Films, 1911–1920* (Berkeley: University of California Press, 1988), 925–26. Reid's film was not the only anti–capital punishment film to appear in summer 1915; *Motion Picture News* (August 28, 1915, 83) reviewed *Capital Punishment*, a three-reel film that again depicted a wrongly accused man, this time nearly executed after a judge's campaign fails to abolish the death sentence.

24. "Coroner to Resume Investigation Today into Frank Lynching," *Atlanta Constitution*, August 24, 1915, 1. I was able to view an incomplete surviving video copy of the Pathé newsreel at the Breman Jewish Museum in Atlanta, Georgia. My thanks to archivist Sandra Berman.

25. Kevin Brownlow, *Behind the Mask of Innocence: Sex, Violence, Prejudice, Crime: Films of Social Conscience in the Silent Era* (Berkeley: University of California Press, 1992), 379. Brownlow, drawing on a story in *Variety*, also describes Russian Jewish director George K. Rolands's film.

26. Steve Goodson, "This Mighty Influence for Good or Evil: The Movies in Atlanta, 1895 to 1920," *Atlanta History* 34, nos. 3–4 (1995): 41–44. See also Cedric Robinson, "In the Year 1915: D. W. Griffith and the Whitening of America," *Social Identities* 3, no. 2 (1997): 177–78. Robinson argues that Mary Phagan's alleged struggle to preserve her virtue at the hands of Leo Frank was "a model" for Griffith's conception and staging of Little Sister's choice, in *The Birth of a Nation*, to leap to her death rather than face "certain" rape at the hands of the black renegade Gus. Although Robinson offers no evidence for such assertions, the analogy between the two instances, I think, would have been immediately apparent to Atlanta's and Georgia's white supremacists watching Griffith's film in December 1915.

27. "Leo Frank Pictures Barred," *Indianapolis Freeman*, August 28, 1915, 4; reprinted in Henry T. Sampson, *Blacks in Black and White: A Source Book on Black Films*, 2nd ed. (Metuchen N.J.: Scarecrow Press, 1995), 156–57. See Goldstein, *The Price of Whiteness*, 69, for a discussion of Jewish sentiment in the 1910s against lynching.

28. See Robert E. Burns, *I Am a Fugitive from a Georgia Chain Gang* (1932; repr., Athens: University of Georgia Press, 1997), 133–35; Vincent Sherman, *Studio Affairs: My Life as a Film Director* (Lexington: University of Kentucky Press, 1996), xiii, 1–16; Robert Berkvist, "Vincent Sherman, Studio-Era Film Director, Dies at 99," *New York Times*, June 21, 2006, C19. On John Wood, see Oney, *And the Dead Shall Rise*, 570, 624–25.

29. As I write in January 2008, documentary director Ben Loeterman is preparing a feature-length documentary on the Phagan-Frank case tentatively titled *The People vs. Leo Frank* for eventual broadcast on PBS. A London version of Alfred Uhry's and Jason Robert Brown's Tony-winning musical *Parade* is also in preparation.

30. Dudley Andrew, "Adapting Cinema to History," in *A Companion to Literature and Film*, ed. Robert Stam and Alessandra Raengo (New York: Blackwell, 2004), 191. Andrew refers to Paul Ricoeur's *Time and Narrative*, vol. 3 (Chicago: University of Chicago Press, 1987), 154; and Hayden White's *Metahistory: The Historical Imagination in Nineteenth-Century Europe* (Baltimore: Johns Hopkins University Press, 1975). See also Thomas Leitch's chapter "Based on a True Story" in his *Adaptation and Its Discontents: From "Gone with the Wind" to "The Passion of the Christ"* (Baltimore: Johns Hopkins University Press, 2007), 280–303, which reflects on the meaning of that commonly used but ambiguous phrase as a form of adaptation; Leitch's ideas have informed my thinking on this issue, as have those of Janet Staiger and Horace Newcomb, "Docudrama," in *Encyclopedia of Television*, ed. Horace Newcomb (New York: Schirmer Books),

738–40; Steven Lipkin, *Reel Emotion Logic: Film and Television Docudrama as Persuasive Practice* (Carbondale: Southern Illinois University Press, 2002); and Derek Paget, *No Other Way to Tell It: Dramadoc/Docudrama on Television* (New York: Manchester University Press, 1988). For the debate on history in film, to which Lipkin's and Paget's volumes contribute, see Robert A. Rosenstone, *Visions of the Past: The Challenge of Film to Our Idea of History* (Cambridge: Harvard University Press, 1995); Robert A. Rosenstone, ed., *Revisioning History: Film and the Construction of a New Past* (Princeton: Princeton University Press, 1995); Marcia Landy, *Cinematic Uses of the Past* (Minneapolis: University of Minnesota Press, 1996); Robert Burgoyne, *Film Nation: Hollywood Looks at U.S. History* (Minneapolis: University of Minnesota Press, 1997); Vivian Sobchack, ed., *The Persistence of History: Cinema, Television, and the Modern Event* (New York: Routledge, 1996); Robert Brent Toplin, *Reel History: In Defense of Hollywood* (Lawrence: University of Kansas Press, 2002); Robert Brent Toplin, *History by Hollywood* (Urbana: University of Illinois Press, 1996); John E. O'Connor, ed., *Image as Artifact: The Historical Analysis of Film and Television* (Malabar, Fla.: Robert E. Krieger, 1990); and Gary Edgerton and Peter C. Rollins, eds., *Television Histories: Shaping Collective Memory in the Media Age* (Lexington: University of Kentucky Press, 2001). For a clear overview of these issues, see Janet Walker, "Introduction: Westerns through History," in Walker, ed., *Westerns: Films through History* (New York: Routledge, 2001), 1–24. For a popular version of the matter of historical representation in specific films, see Ted Mico, John Miller-Monzon, and David Rubel, eds., *Past Imperfect: History According to the Movies* (New York: Henry Holt, 1995).

31. Michael Bronski, in a provocative article on *Murder in Harlem*, generalizes about the many books and films inspired by the Phagan-Frank case to argue that the genre in which a storyteller chooses to frame the case depends on and forecloses the questioning of certain facts, such as Leo Frank's presumed innocence (in the case of a social protest film), or even the case's place in the history of relations between blacks and Jews. Genres certainly can have these effects, and clearly a majority of the people familiar with the Phagan-Frank case believe in Frank's innocence. Yet Bronski makes these generalizations apparently without having seen *They Won't Forget* or the two television shows. In fact, three of the four texts I examine go to some lengths to suggest that Frank might have been guilty or was guilty of something short of murder. *Profiles in Courage* does not question Frank's innocence, but that is in part because Frank is not even onscreen. The remaining three encourage their observers to suspect the Frank character, however briefly; only *The Murder of Mary Phagan* affirms Frank's innocence with its recounting of Alonzo Mann's 1980s disclosures—but then only in its final moments. See

Michael Bronski, "The Return of the Repressed: Leo Frank through the Eyes of Oscar Micheaux," *Shofar* 23, no. 4 (2005): 26–49.

32. Regarding the representation of violence in film at the time of *Murder in Harlem* and *They Won't Forget*, see Stephen Prince, *Classical Film Violence: Designing and Regulating Brutality in Hollywood Cinema, 1930–1968* (New Brunswick, N.J.: Rutgers University Press, 2003); and Stephen Prince, ed., *Screening Violence* (New Brunswick, N.J.: Rutgers University Press, 2000). Regarding the representation of trauma in literature and film, see Cathy Carruth's *Unclaimed Experience: Trauma, Narrative, and History* (Baltimore: Johns Hopkins University Press, 1996). Regarding Holocaust films, see Annette Insdorf, *Indelible Shadows: Film and the Holocaust*, 3d ed. (New York: Cambridge University Press, 2003); Joshua Hirsch, *Afterimage: Film, Trauma, and the Holocaust* (Philadelphia: Temple University Press, 2004); and Janet Walker, "Trauma Cinema: False Memories and True Experience," *Screen* 42, no. 2 (2001): 211–16. Regarding the representation of lynching, see Dora Apel, *Imagery of Lynching: Black Men, White Women, and the Mob* (New Brunswick, N.J.: Rutgers University Press, 2004); and Ryan Markovitz, *Legacies of Lynching: Racial Violence and Memory* (Minneapolis: University of Minnesota Press, 2004).

The book most closely allied with some of the concerns of the present volume is Amy Wood, *White Supremacy and Spectacle: Witnessing Lynching in America, 1880–1940* (Raleigh: University of North Carolina Press, 2009).

Chapter 1. Cinematic Justice across the Color Line

1. Micheaux was a writer before becoming a filmmaker, and several of his novels refer often to the Phagan-Frank case.

2. Patrick McGilligan, *Oscar Micheaux, the Great and Only: The Life of America's First Great Black Filmmaker* (New York: Regan Books, 2007), 124. Micheaux's fundraising efforts for his first film are described on pp. 120–24.

3. Micheaux did go bankrupt in the late 1920s, but he quickly recapitalized and continued filmmaking. In her biography of Micheaux, Betti Carol VanEpps-Taylor estimates that a Micheaux film grossed as much as ten thousand dollars at the Lafayette Theater in Harlem and that he earned twenty thousand dollars for one film at the height of the race film boom in 1920. See VanEpps-Taylor, *Oscar Micheaux, a Biography: Dakota Homesteader, Author, Pioneer Film Maker* (Sioux Falls, S.D.: Dakota West Books, 1999), 115.

4. The literature on race filmmaking and on Micheaux is now extensive. See Thomas Cripps, "Two Early Strides towards a Black Cinema" and "The Black

Underground," both in *Slow Fade to Black: The Negro in American Film, 1900–1942* (New York: Oxford University Press, 1978); Thomas Cripps, "Hollywood Wins: The End of 'Race Movies,'" in *Making Movies Black* (New York: Oxford University Press, 1993); Henry T. Sampson, *Blacks in Black and White: A Sourcebook on Black Films*, 2d ed. (Metuchen, N.J.: Scarecrow Press, 1995); Matthew Bernstein and Dana White, "'Scratching Around' in a 'Fit of Insanity': The Norman Film Manufacturing Company and the Race Film Business in the 1920s," *Griffithiana* 62 (spring 1998): 81–127. Regarding Oscar Micheaux specifically, see Pearl Bowser and Louise Spence, *Writing Himself into History: Oscar Micheaux, His Silent Films, and His Audiences* (New Brunswick, N.J.: Rutgers University Press, 2000); Jane Gaines, *Fire and Desire: Mixed-Race Movies in the Silent Era* (Chicago: University of Chicago Press, 2001); J. Ronald Green, *Straight Lick: The Cinema of Oscar Micheaux* (Bloomington: Indiana University Press, 2000); J. Ronald Green, *With a Crooked Stick: The Films of Oscar Micheaux* (Bloomington: Indiana University Press, 2004); and the essays in *Oscar Micheaux and His Circle: African American Filmmaking and Race Cinema of the Silent Era*, ed. Pearl Bowser, Jane Gaines, and Charles Musser (Bloomington: Indiana University Press, 2001).

5. VanEpps-Taylor draws on Joel Williamson, *A Rage for Order: Black/White Relations in the American South since Emancipation* (New York: Oxford University Press, 1986), 65–67, to argue for this assessment of Micheaux's views of blacks' place in American society: "[Booker T.] Washington's ideas of self-help, ambition, and personal achievement continued to resonate with largely silent, mobile, black families. They remained aloof from the philosophical debate raging among the factions and raised their children in Washingtonian values, similar to those of aspiring immigrants and other white families. Such was the nature of the Michaux (original spelling) family" (VanEpps-Taylor, *Oscar Micheaux*, 4).

6. McGilligan, *Oscar Micheaux, The Great and Only*, 273.

7. VanEpps-Taylor, *Oscar Micheaux*, 101–8, makes the case that post–World War I race riots inspired Micheaux in the making of *Within Our Gates*.

8. Corey K. Creekmur, "Telling White Lies: Oscar Micheaux and Charles W. Chesnutt," in Bowser et al., eds., *Oscar Micheaux and His Circle*, 148–49. Early in this essay, Creekmur suggests that traditional adaptation studies are inadequate for understanding Micheaux's creativity (148); but he concludes by suggesting that it is still "valuable" to examine the director's work of "adaptation in the conventional sense" (158), which the present chapter does. See also Sampson, *Blacks in Black and White*, 158.

9. Until this book chapter was published as "Oscar Micheaux and Leo Frank: Cinematic Justice across the Color Line" in *Film Quarterly* 57, no. 4 (2004):

8–21, little attention had been paid to the traces of the Phagan-Frank trial present in the one film of the three that is extant, *Murder in Harlem*. Micheaux scholars generally either acknowledged the case as a source and proceeded to consider other issues or did not mention it at all. To take just two examples, in *With a Crooked Stick*, Green makes no reference to the Phagan-Frank case in his fourteen-page analysis of *Murder in Harlem* (177–90); he instead references Micheaux's alleged use of the Dorothy Stanfield murder case from Atlanta (177). Creekmur reminds us in "Telling White Lies," 151, that *Lem Hawkins' Confession* and *Murder in Harlem* are allegedly based on the Stanfield case but that Micheaux did not publish his novel *The Story of Dorothy Stanfield* until ten years *after* the films appeared. (Creekmur also makes no reference to the Frank case in his essay on Micheaux's intertextuality.) Green's rich analysis demonstrates that a knowledge of Micheaux's novels and films can generate insightful readings of the film's typically Micheauxian elements (he points out, for example, Claudia's crucial role in solving the murder and securing her brother's innocence [186], as I do). Such readings of the film nevertheless miss a crucial dimension of its significance as a reenactment of a sensational case. Since "Cinematic Justice across the Color Line" appeared, one other essay has been published on the connection between *Murder in Harlem* and the Phagan-Frank case. Michael Bronski's "The Return of the Repressed: Leo Frank through the Eyes of Oscar Micheaux," *Shofar* 23, no. 4 (2005): 26–49, sees the film as a black reading of the case, as I do.

10. Sampson, in *Blacks in Black and White*, 158, discusses the actual case on which *The House behind the Cedars* is based. Micheaux is quoted in Charlene Regester, "Oscar Micheaux the Entrepreneur: Financing *The House behind the Cedars*," *Journal of Film and Video* 49, nos. 1–2: 19.

11. "Negro Films Have Good Future," *Atlanta Daily World*, May 7, 1934, 1; and "'Arrowsmith' Star Stops in Atlanta," *Atlanta Daily World*, August 5, 1934, 1. Clarence Brooks, the future star of *Lem Hawkins' Confession* and *Murder in Harlem*, accompanied Micheaux on the second visit.

12. Ad clipping in the George P. Johnson Negro Film Collection, Department of Special Collections, Charles E. Young Research Library, University of California–Los Angeles (hereafter GPJ Collection).

13. McGilligan, *Oscar Micheaux, the Great and Only*, 166.

14. Oscar Micheaux, *The Forged Note: A Romance of the Darker Races* (Lincoln, Neb.: Western Book Supply Company, 1915 and 1916), 100–107. Regarding *Circumstantial Evidence*, see the note in Charles Musser, Corey K. Creekmur, Pearl Bowser, J. Ronald Green, Charlene Regester, and Louise Spence, "An Oscar Micheaux Filmography: From the Silents through His Transition to Sound, 1919–1931," in Bowser, Gaines, and Musser, eds., *Oscar Micheaux and*

His Circle, 242. Micheaux promised he would make the film in a prospectus for *The Homesteader*. Regarding Micheaux's presence at the Leo Frank trial, Steve Oney's *And the Dead Shall Rise: The Murder of Mary Phagan and the Lynching of Leo Frank* (New York: Pantheon Books, 2003), 191, describes the courtroom as small and tightly packed; it is unclear whether any black spectators, let alone Micheaux, would have been allowed to enter and watch the proceedings. VanEpps-Taylor, *Oscar Micheaux*, quotes the "News about Town" item in the *Chicago Defender* of January 31, 1920, on p. 109. For the repetition of Newt Lee's name, see McGilligan, *Oscar Micheaux, the Great and Only*, 230.

15. McGilligan, *Oscar Micheaux, the Great and Only*, 166.

16. See the profile of the film, "Latest Race Photo Play and Vaudeville Features at Lafayette," *New York Age*, April 23, 1921, 6; reprinted in Musser et al., "An Oscar Micheaux Filmography," 241–43. See also the description of the film in Sampson, *Blacks in Black and White*, 311–12; and the entry for the film in the American Film Institute Catalog, *Within Our Gates: Ethnicity in American Feature Films, 1911–1960*, ed. Alan Gevinson (Berkeley: University of California Press, 1997), 425. Given Micheaux's fondness for muckraking journalism (as indicated in *The Conquest*), he may have chosen the name Anthony Brisbane as an allusion to the widely published *Cosmopolitan* reporter Arthur Brisbane (thanks to Dana F. White for information on this possible connection). As Oney points out, child labor was a major concern of Brisbane's employer, William Randolph Hearst, and Hearst's wife. Brisbane himself was "a fanatic on the subject" who published articles in Hearst's papers in the 1910s about those abuses (*And the Dead Shall Rise*, 14).

17. Worth noting is that many of the film's leads were played by actors from Harlem's celebrated Lafayette Players: Dick Abrams as Sidney Wyeth, Evelyn Preer as Ida May, and Lawrence Chenault as the villainous Brisbane. Preer and Chenault appeared in many of Micheaux's films; the latter played Paul Robeson's ex-convict "buddy" in *Body and Soul*.

18. See *The Gunsaulus Mystery* ad, clipping, GPJ Collection, reel 5; Musser et al., "An Oscar Micheaux Filmography," 241–42, reprints the item from the *Chicago Whip*, May 7, 1921, 6.

19. Ibid.; McGilligan, *Oscar Micheaux, the Great and Only*, quotes the *New York Age* review and Chesnutt's praise on pp. 129 and 130, respectively; the *Chicago Whip* review is reprinted in Sampson, *Blacks in Black and White*, 312–13. Information on the banning of the film in Atlanta appears in *Atlanta Journal*, February 2, 1923, 14, and February 4, 1923, 3B; see also "Gonzales [*sic*] Mystery Picture Is Barred," *Atlanta Constitution*, February 4, 1923, 5; the censor's quotation is from Ira L. Bell to W. D. McGuire Jr. (executive secretary of the National

Board of Review), February 23, 1923, "Regional Correspondence—Georgia: Atlanta, 1923" File, National Board of Review of Motion Pictures Collection, New York Public Library. I thank Emory University film studies master's student Jeremy Groskopf for bringing this letter to my attention.

20. McGilligan reports in *Oscar Micheaux, the Great and Only*, 282, that Micheaux retitled *Lem Hawkins' Confession* for distribution outside the East. On the film's production background, see pp. 274–82.

21. Steve Oney, "The Murder Atlanta Can't Forget," *Atlanta Magazine*, June 2000, 130.

22. Oney, *And the Dead Shall Rise*, 72–74.

23. Green, *With a Crooked Stick*, 187.

24. All the details of the Phagan-Frank case mentioned here and compared with *Murder in Harlem* come from Leonard Dinnerstein, *The Leo Frank Case* (New York: Columbia University Press, 1968); and Oney, *And the Dead Shall Rise*: the murder notes (Dinnerstein, 3; Oney, 20–21); Epps reporting Phagan's fears of Frank (Dinnerstein, 17; Oney, 73); Newt Lee's irregular work hours on Confederate Memorial Day (Dinnerstein, 2; Oney, 48); the false evidence that Phagan's blood and hair were found in the room across from Frank's office (Dinnerstein, 5 and 58; Oney, 46, 231, and 318); and Conley's series of affidavits accusing Frank (Dinnerstein, 21–25; Oney, 129–41).

25. Dinnerstein, *Leo Frank Case*, 41–42; Oney, *And the Dead Shall Rise*, 241.

26. "Attempt to Make Witness Accessory to Murder," *Chicago Defender*, February 28, 1914, 1; *Crisis* 9 (March 1915): 234; quoted in Eugene Levy, "Is the Jew a White Man? Press Reaction to the Leo Frank Case, 1913–1915," *Phylon* 35, no. 2 (1974): 216.

27. The quotation ("no question of his guilt") is from "Yellow Journalism," *Chicago Defender*, April 25, 1914, 8. Also see "Conly [*sic*] Must Die Because He Is Black," *Chicago Defender*, January 2, 1915, 8; and "The Condemned Murderer," *Chicago Defender*, December 12, 1914, 8. The "Every effort has been made" quotation is from "Fixing the Blame," *Chicago Defender*, May 9, 1914, 8. See also *Philadelphia Inquirer*, February 13, 1915, 4. The "We have no desire to see Frank executed" quotation is from "Dismissal of Frank's Appeal," *New York Age*, April 22, 1915, 4; see also *Cleveland Gazette*, December 26, 1914, 8. Levy, "Is the Jew a White Man?" deftly summarizes black press reaction to the Phagan-Frank case. He discusses blacks' outrage at the attention Frank's lynching received (216); whites searching for a black scapegoat (215); views of Conley's motivations for aiding Frank and Conley's innocence (217–18). The *Crisis* quote (216) is from the September 1913 issue, vol. 6, 221; the *Chicago Defender* quote (216) comes from the April 25, 1914, issue.

28. "Has Frank Had a Fair Trial?" *Atlanta Independent*, March 21, 1914, 4.

29. Dinnerstein, *Leo Frank Case*, 21; Oney, *And the Dead Shall Rise*, 132.

30. See Dinnerstein, *Leo Frank Case*, 86, for the fate of the historical George Epps. Glory's book title, *A Fool's Errand*, is a phrase that appears in Micheaux's novel *The Homesteader* referencing the title of Albion Tourgee's 1879 Reconstruction novel. In *The Homesteader*, it is the phrase closed-minded neighbors use to describe hero Jean Baptiste's struggle against a fierce storm on the prairie. It is also the title of a play by Eulalie Spence; Micheaux announced in 1923 that he would soon be adapting it, but the film never materialized. Charles Musser argues that the thrice-told tale of the Gridlestone murder in *Within Our Gates* is taken from Tourgee's novel; see "To Redream the Dream of White Playwrights: Reappropriation and Resistance in Oscar Micheaux's *Body and Soul*," in *Oscar Micheaux and His Circle: African-American Filmmaking and Race Cinema of the Silent Era*, ed. Pearl Pearl Bowser, Jane Gaines, and Musser (Bloomington: Indiana University Press, 2001), 98. On p. 307, n. 93, Musser argues that in *Body and Soul* Micheaux builds on and responds to Charles Chaplin's *The Pilgrim* (1923). J. Ronald Green invokes "Micheaux's ideas of moderation, the middle path and the middle class," which certainly applies to Henry and Claudia, in his excellent "Oscar Micheaux's Interrogation of Caricature as Entertainment, *Film Quarterly* 51, no. 3 (1998): 19.

31. See Oney, *And the Dead Shall Rise*, 395–96, for an account of Annie Maude Carter's affidavit. Jeffrey Melnick, *Black-Jewish Relations on Trial: Leo Frank and Jim Conley in the New South* (Oxford: University Press of Mississippi, 2000), 92. Melnick's characterization of Conley as a Sambo figure (93) comes by way of Eric Lott, *Love and Theft: Blackface Minstrelsy and the American Working Class* (New York: Oxford University Press, 1993).

32. Green, *With a Crooked Stick*, adds to the list of Claudia's accomplishments in the film: she knows Henry is the author of the book when he tries to remain anonymous; she gets Henry to agree that she can hire another attorney if he proves inadequate to the task of defending her brother; she anticipates the criminal behavior of her neighbors; she tracks down Henry to represent her brother when he is arrested, in spite of the awkwardness stemming from their broken-off courtship; she accompanies Henry to all hearings and the trial and to the sessions where he questions all the witnesses in and out of court (including George Epps's mother); finally, she realizes why Henry stopped seeing her three years earlier when she reads his new novel and she initiates their reunion (186).

33. Ibid., 178.

34. Clarence Brooks's biggest break came when he played a dignified, capable Haitian doctor in John Ford's 1931 film *Arrowsmith*. He was also a founder of

the Lincoln Motion Picture Company, the concern that tried to buy the film rights to Micheaux's *Homesteader* back in the late 1910s but refused to collaborate with Micheaux. Alec Lovejoy was an Atlanta native who resembled Conley in build.

35. Green, "Oscar Micheaux's Interrogation of Caricature," 23. He discusses the cutting gaze on p. 25 and Glory's interrogation of Hawkins on pp. 26–29.

36. Ibid., 28.

37. Ibid.

38. The quotation is in Melnick, *Black-Jewish Relations on Trial*, 92.

39. Ibid., 93. The defense's view of Conley would have been utterly consistent with the way in which D. W. Griffith depicted Reconstruction blacks in *The Birth of a Nation*; that is, as a degraded menace to white women who justified the creation (and renewal) of the Ku Klux Klan.

40. Ibid., 88–108. Melnick discusses each point I highlight in the text as follows: Frank's knowledge of southern black culture (98–104), Conley's unlikely drafting of the notes (90), and Conley's literacy (93–96).

41. Green, "Oscar Micheaux's Interrogation of Caricature," 28–29.

42. McGilligan, *Oscar Micheaux: The Great and Only*, 280–81.

43. Ibid.

44. Micheaux's addition of a new twist in the Phagan-Frank case broadly resembles his reworking in *Body and Soul* of Nan Bagby Stephens's play *Roseanne*, a melodramatic tale of an exploitative, cruel black minister who steals from a devoted parishioner and rapes her daughter, who ultimately dies. In the play, the mother forgives the minister, who promises to reform. In Micheaux's film, the mother forgives him, but he does not change at all; in fact, the minister kills her son before the mother wakes up to realize that the entire narrative was a nightmare. Charles Musser argues that Micheaux's reshaping of the Stephens play constitutes a critique of its white paternalistic view of black spirituality and forgiveness, and that Micheaux in effect refused to reproduce Stephens's play's sympathy for the helpless, deceived, and robbed mother and the raped daughter. See Musser's "To Redream the Dream of White Playwrights," 114–16.

45. See McGilligan, *Oscar Micheaux, the Great and Only*, 257–74, for a discussion of Micheaux's working relationship with Franklin Schiffman, who with Leo Brecher ran the four largest movie theaters in Harlem and the Apollo, and eventually sued Micheaux for breach of contract. McGilligan discusses Micheaux's relationship with Alfred Sack on pp. 280–81 and 285–86.

46. VanEpps-Taylor, *Oscar Micheaux*, 116. Green refutes this view of Micheaux as an anti-Semite persuasively in *With a Crooked Stick*, 30–32 and 33–34; as does McGilligan, *Oscar Micheaux, the Great and Only*, 280–81.

47. Green reports the comments of student Kathryn DiCiacinto on this point in *With a Crooked Stick*, 188. On the black press's response to Frank's lynching, see "Lynching of Leo M. Frank Sounds Death of Mob Law," *Chicago Defender*, August 21, 1915, 1, 2; "The Georgia Lynchers," *Philadelphia Tribune*, August 21, 1915, 4; "Lawless Georgia Mob Wreaks Its Vengeance on Leo Frank, a White Man, by Lynching Him," *Philadelphia Tribune*, August 21, 1915, 8; "We Blush," *Baltimore Afro-American*, August 21, 1915, 4; "The Frank Lynch-Murder," *Cleveland Gazette*, August 21, 1915, 2; *Washington Bee*, August 21, 1915, 4; *Richmond Planet*, August 21, 1915, 4; *Chicago Broad Ax*, August 21, 1915. For the record, the black press's response to Frank's lynching was that this murder of a white man might bring the world's and the country's attention to the lynching of thousands of black citizens violently killed "at the hands of persons unknown."

48. Bronski, in "The Return of the Repressed," 48, argues that Micheaux made George Epps the murderer to avoid depicting Brisbane's/Frank's lynching under circumstances that might make it seem justifiable (that is, Brisbane was guilty). This reasoning is unpersuasive. The factory supervisor was guilty in *The Gunsaulus Mystery*, but Micheaux did not feel compelled to stage a lynching scene in that film. In other words, he was capable of telling the Phagan-Frank story without showing the Frank character's ultimate fate. Similarly, Bronski (47–49) offers a queer reading of the film by arguing that Henry Glory's comment "I didn't know that George Epps was that sort of boy" when he learns of Epps's criminal aspirations, Epps's mother's reference to "the mark of Cain," and Neil's revelation that Epps wanted to free two men in prison all imply that Epps is gay and Jewish, like Leopold and Loeb, that is, that Epps in Micheaux's film is a shadow figure for the Jewish and allegedly sexually "perverse" Leo Frank. I find this reading intriguing, but only partially persuasive. In Bronski's reading, Frank's Jewishness appears as much in the guise of Epps as in the abusive actions of Brisbane.

49. Melnick, *Black-Jewish Relations on Trial*, 26; Creekmur, Telling White Lies," 158.

50. For another example of this kind of sensationalized docudrama of recent current events, see Matthew Bernstein, "Individuals and Institutions: *Riot in Cell Block 11* (1954)," *Velvet Light Trap* 28 (1991): 3–31.

51. "Cast of Races Greatest Stars in 81 Thriller," *Atlanta Daily World*, August 11, 1935, 7; August 12, 1935, 2; August 13, 1935, 6; August 14, 1935, 3; August 15, 1935, 3.

52. "Atlanta City Censor Report, July 1935," in author's possession.

53. McGilligan, *Oscar Micheaux, the Great and Only*, briefly discusses *Murder in Harlem's* reception: the film "ought to have revived Micheaux's stature but

most big-city scribes simply ignored the film. This was the first alarm bell that Micheaux's time had passed" (281–82).

54. The wire story, "New Micheaux Film Is 'Slow,'" appeared in the *Atlanta Daily World*, August 2, 1935, 2.

55. See Oscar Micheaux, *The Case of Mrs. Wingate* (1945; repr., New York: AMS Press, 1975), 48–52, for his treatment of this detail from the Frank case. Oney discusses Conley's uncertain knowledge of circumcision in *And the Dead Shall Rise*, 496.

Chapter 2. The Phagan-Frank Case as 1930s Hollywood Message Movie

1. William Johnson, "Deep," *Film Comment* 32, no. 2 (March–April 1996): 74.

2. See Peter Roffman and Jim Purdy, *The Hollywood Social Problem Film* (Bloomington: Indiana University Press, 1981), for a fine, historically informed account of the genre. An earlier but still valuable exploration is Russell Campbell, "The Ideology of the Social Consciousness Movie: Three Films by Darryl F. Zanuck," *Quarterly Review of Film Studies* 3, no. 1 (1978): 49–71.

3. See "'We Wanted to Be Boosters, Not Knockers': Photography, Anti-lynching Activism, and Southern Shame," in Amy Wood, *White Supremacy and Spectacle: Witnessing Lynching in America, 1880–1940* (Raleigh: University of North Carolina Press, 2009), for an account of how the meaning of lynching photos had been transformed into evidence of barbarity rather than white supremacy by the 1930s.

4. "Warner Bros.," *Fortune*, December 1937; reprinted in *Inside Warner Bros. (1935–1941)*, ed. Rudy Behlmer (New York: Viking Press, 1985), 55.

5. Ward Greene, *Death in the Deep South* (New York: Stackpole Sons, 1936).

6. Steve Oney, *And the Dead Shall Rise: The Murder of Mary Phagan and the Lynching of Leo Frank* (New York: Pantheon Books, 2003), 72–74.

7. Ibid., 9–11.

8. Oney, "The Murder Atlanta Can't Forget," *Atlanta Magazine*, June 2000, 130–33; see also *And the Dead Shall Rise*, 24–32.

9. See Oney, *And the Dead Shall Rise*, 102–3; and Leonard Dinnerstein, *The Leo Frank Case* (New York: Columbia University Press, 1968), 16, 34, 84, and 100–105, on Burns's role in the Phagan-Frank case. See Nancy MacLean, "The Leo Frank Case Reconsidered: Gender and Sexual Politics in the Making of Reactionary Populism," *Journal of American History* 78, no. 3 (1991): 926–27, for a discussion of Burns's antiunion activities.

10. MacLean, "Leo Frank Case Reconsidered," 926, quotes David L. Carlton, *Mill and Town in South Carolina, 1880–1920* (Baton Rouge: Louisiana State University Press, 1982), 246, on this point.

11. Dinnerstein, *Leo Frank Case*, 55.

12. See Steve Goodson, "'This Mighty Influence for Good or Evil': The Movies in Atlanta, 1895–1920," *Atlanta History* 39, nos. 3–4 (1995): 43, for a discussion of Greene's review of Griffith's film.

13. Ward Greene to Mr. Carl Helm (Greene's attorney) (copy), September 21, 1938, *They Won't Forget*–"Death in the Deep South" file 12685, USC Warner Bros. Archives, School of Cinema-TV, University of Southern California (hereafter WBA). Hopkins's book does not discuss the conduct of Atlanta's police department in the Phagan-Frank case but rather looks at malfeasance on a national scale. See Ernest Jerome Hopkins, *Our Lawless Police: A Study of the Unlawful Enforcement of the Law* (New York: Viking Press, 1931).

14. Ward Greene, *Star Reporters and Thirty-four of Their Stories* (New York: Random House, 1948), 131–42; the quoted passage appears on p. 133.

15. Lyle Saxon, *Books*, October 25, 1936, 6; Samuel Sillen, *Nation*, November 14, 1936, 583; Leigh Whipper, *New Republic*, December 16, 1936, 224; *New York Times Book Review*, October 18, 1836, 12; W. R. Benet, *Saturday Review of Literature*, October 17, 1936.

16. Ralph T. Jones, "Murder Story," *Atlanta Constitution*, November 15, 1936, 3K; Frank Daniel, "Death in the Deep South," *Atlanta Journal*, October 25, 1936, 12.

17. Greene's book has only a few Jewish characters: a leading town merchant who protests to Andy about the local unrest; Rabinoff, the leader of a northeastern legal defense group that comes to Robert's aid (a stand-in for any number of prominent northern Jewish figures in the case, most notably Louis Marshall); and Judah Clem, a northern publisher who is meant to suggest *New York Times* publisher Adolph S. Ochs, who took on Frank's appeal as a personal crusade. None of them appears in the Warner Bros. film.

18. The novel briefly alludes to Watson only when identifying Mary Clay's brothers as "wool hat boys." See Greene, *Death in the Deep South*, 41.

19. Greene, *Star Reporters*, 131–33; see also Greene's entry in "Topics of the Times: An Attack Gave It Importance," *New York Times*, May 28, 1915, 20. Greene's views that anti-Semitism was a factor only after the case had begun anticipates, albeit in the broadest outlines, those of historian Albert S. Lindemann in *The Jew Accused: Three Anti-Semitic Affairs (Dreyfus, Beilis, Frank) 1894–1915* (New York: Cambridge University Press, 1991), 235–37. Similarly, Judge Arthur G. Powell—a friend of the presiding judge in Leo Frank's trial, L. S. Roan—observes

in his memoir, *I Can Go Home Again* (Chapel Hill: University of North Carolina Press, 1943), that anti-Semitism was less a factor in Atlanta's sentiment against Frank than his manager-owner status at the factory. Like Nancy MacLean, Powell stresses the powerful gender considerations at play in the perception of Frank: "No girl ever leaves home to go to work in a factory but that her parents feel an inward fear that one of her bosses will take advantage of his position to mistreat her, especially if she repels his advances. This fear is readily converted into passion when a factory manager is accused of having killed a factory girl." Powell continues: "The thing that did arouse a most phenomenal racial prejudice against not only Frank but all Jews was that just about the time the trial was to occur, various writers, speakers, civil rights societies, and Jewish organizations began to protest that Frank was being persecuted because he was a Jew. This whipped into flames the passion and prejudice which had been dying down and converted them from a mere feeling of resentment against a factory boss into a spreading racial and religious hatred" (287–88). Steve Oney describes the visit of Jewish leaders to a newspaper editor (of the *Georgian*) to protest the treatment of Frank in *And the Dead Shall Rise*, 97–100. He also affirms that four Jews (not five, as Greene claimed) served on the grand jury that voted to indict Frank (although whether these four so voted is unclear); see p. 116.

20. Ruth Vasey, *The World According to Hollywood, 1918–1939* (Madison: University of Wisconsin Press, 1997), 137. For a history of Hollywood's representation of Jews, see Lester Friedman, *Hollywood's Image of the Jew* (New York: Ungar, 1982); and Lester Friedman, *The Jewish Image in American Film* (Secaucus, N.J.: Citadel Press, 1987). For general accounts of Jews in Hollywood, see Neal Gabler, *An Empire of Their Own: How the Jews Invented Hollywood* (New York: Crown, 1988); and Steven Carr, *Hollywood and Anti-Semitism: A Cultural History up to World War II* (Cambridge: Cambridge University Press, 2001).

21. "Sowing the South Forty," *New York Times*, December 13, 1936, 6.

22. R. J. Obringer, memo to Espinosa, November 17, 1936, *They Won't Forget–* "Death in the Deep South" file 12733, WBA. LeRoy's memory of the film's production is selective and faulty in some details. See Mervyn LeRoy, with Dick Kleiner, *Mervyn LeRoy: Take One* (New York: Hawthorn Books, 1974), 130–33. He forgets Aben Kandel's work on the script, for example, and claims Clinton Rosemond's role was a prototype for Sidney Poitier and black leading actors who followed. LeRoy's pro-message publicity piece is "Never Do the Same Thing Twice," *Stage* 14, no. 6 (1937): 58–59, in LeRoy's clipping files, Margaret Herrick Library, Academy of Motion Picture Arts and Sciences, Film Study Center, Los Angeles.

23. On LeRoy's production setup, see Douglas W. Churchill, "Alphabet Soup in Hollywood's Lap," *New York Times*, May 2, 1937, X3.

24. Greene, *Death in the Deep South*, 51.

25. Ward Greene to "Mitchell," July 3, 1937, in *They Won't Forget*–"Death in the Deep South" File 12685, WBA. "Mitchell" likely was Mitchel Rawson of Warner Bros.'s legal department in Manhattan. Information about Mary Phagan's siblings comes from Robert Seitz Frey and Nancy Thompson-Frey, *The Silent and the Damned: The Murder of Mary Phagan and the Lynching of Leo Frank* (New York: Madison Books, 1988), 6; the brothers' nonparticipation in the lynching is asserted on p. 105. See Steve Oney's chapters "Marietta," "Milledgeville," and "The Lynching of Leo Frank" in *And the Dead Shall Rise* for a full description of those who planned and carried out Frank's lynching. *Variety* reported in late August 1937 that the KKK was suing Warner Bros. for $113,500 for the alleged use of the organization's insignia in *Black Legion*. See "Klan Suit Helps Atlanta 'Legion' Exhib; Some Duck," *Variety,* August 25, 1937.

26. Aben Kandel, "Death in the Deep South," temporary script, dated January 8–25, 1937, Warner Bros. Collection, Mss 99AN, series 1.2, box 392, folder 4, Wisconsin Center for Film and Theater Research, Wisconsin State Historical Society, Madison (hereafter WCFTR). Kandel wrote this first draft in three stages during January.

27. On the beating of Newt Lee, see Dinnerstein, *Leo Frank Case*, 14, which quotes from the *Atlanta Journal*, April 29, 1913, 1; for Griffin's callous comment to the police, see Kandel, "Death in the Deep South," temporary first draft script, 37; for Detective Laneart's violent domestic scene, see Greene, *Death in the Deep South*, 193–96; and Kandel, ibid., 130–31.

28. See Kandel, "Death in the Deep South," temporary first draft script, 38, for the plan to plant a bloody shirt to incriminate Redwine; and pp. 76–77 on the plan to use that shirt to frighten Redwine into perjury. The police intimidate the barber in Greene, *Death in the Deep South*, 125–26; and in Kandel, ibid., 77.

29. Greene, *Death in the Deep South*, 277–83.

30. Kandel, "Death in the Deep South," 166–70. Dinnerstein, *Leo Frank Case*, 13, discusses the *Georgian*'s success in covering the Phagan-Frank case.

31. For excellent studies of the Studio Relations Committee and the Production Code Administration, see Lea Jacobs, *The Wages of Sin* (1991; repr., Berkeley: University of California Press, 1995); Vasey, *The World According to Hollywood*; Gregory Black, *Hollywood Censored: Morality, Codes, Catholics, and the Movies* (Cambridge: Cambridge University Press, 1994); Gregory Black, *The Catholic Crusade against the Movies (1940–1970)* (Cambridge: Cambridge University Press, 1997); Frank Walsh, *Sin and Censorship* (New Haven: Yale University Press, 1996); various articles by Richard Maltby, including "'Baby Face,' or How Joe Breen Made Barbara Stanwyck Pay for Causing the Wall Street Crash," *Screen*

27, no. 2 (1986): 22–45, and "'A Brief Romantic Interlude': Dick and Jane Go to 3½ Seconds of the Classical Hollywood Cinema," in *Post-theory*, ed. David Bordwell and Noël Carroll (Madison: University of Wisconsin Press, 1996), 434–59; Thomas P. Doherty, *Pre-Code Hollywood: Sex, Immorality, and Insurrection in American Cinema, 1930–1934* (New York: Columbia University Press, 1999); and Doherty's *Hollywood's Censor: Joseph I. Breen and the Production Code Administration* (New York: Columbia University Press, 2007).

Two previous studies of the making of *They Won't Forget* exist. Gregory Black, in *Hollywood Censored*, 268–74, provides a fine account of those negotiations but neglects Greene's novel. Brian Neve, in "The Screenwriter and the Social Problem Film, 1936–1938: The Case of Robert Rossen at Warner Brothers," *Film and History* 14, no. 1 (undated CD-ROM edition: 1–11), has read Greene's novel and various script drafts. He makes helpful points about the film's historical context (the Scottsboro case) and about the script revisions, but he did not have access to the PCA files.

32. Joseph I. Breen to Jack L. Warner, January 30, 1937, *They Won't Forget* File, Motion Picture Producers and Distributors Association Collection, Margaret Herrick Library, Academy of Motion Picture Arts and Sciences Film Study Center, Los Angeles (hereafter MPPDA).

33. See Neve, "Screenwriter and the Social Problem Film," for a concise overview of Rossen's pre-Hollywood career. See also Alan Casty, *The Films of Robert Rossen* (New York: Museum of Modern Art, 1969), 6, which claims that Rossen favored *They Won't Forget* among all his Warner Bros. scripts. For an excellent discussion of another screenwriter whose politics informed his scripts, see Charles Maland's "'Powered by a Ford'?: Dudley Nichols, Authorship, and Cultural Ethos in *Stagecoach*," in *John Ford's Stagecoach*, ed. Barry Keith Grant (Cambridge: Cambridge University Press, 2003), 48–81.

34. "JIB" [Joseph I. Breen], memorandum for files, February 2, 1937, *They Won't Forget* File, MPPDA.

35. John Harley Warner compares medical school dissection class photos with lynching photos in "Posing with the Cadaver: Race, Violence, and Dissection-Room Portraiture, 1880–1920" (paper presented at the Conference on Lynching and Racial Violence in America: Histories and Legacies, October 4, 2002, Emory University, Atlanta). Detective Laneart's dialogue quotation is from Aben Kandel and Robert Rossen, "In the Deep South," final script version, dated March 17–March 30, 1937, Warner Bros. Collection, Mss99AN, series 1.2, box 392, folder 6, WCFTR, 36.

36. Kandel and Rossen, "In the Deep South," revised script, March 30, 1937, 36.

37. See, for example, Kandel, "Death in the Deep South," temporary first draft script, 80–82, where Detective Laneart bullies Timberlake into leaving town because the barber remembers too accurately the time that he shaved Hale, thus providing Hale with an alibi.

38. Kandel and Rossen, "In the Deep South," final revised script, 38–39.

39. On the *Atlanta Constitution*'s police-friendly reporting, see Dinnerstein, *Leo Frank Case*, 11–16; the quotation on Britt Craig comes from Steve Oney, "The Murder Atlanta Can't Forget," *Atlanta Magazine*, June 2000, 129. The "deal" scene in Greene, *Death in the Deep South*, appears on p. 68.

40. Greene, *Death in the Deep South*, 224.

41. Whereas Greene's novel reveals some of the content of Foster's coaching, the film leaves it all offscreen; see Greene, *Death in the Deep South*, 108–9; Kandel and Rossen, "In the Deep South," final revised script, 99.

42. Kandel and Rossen, "In the Deep South," final revised script, 149a.

43. Kandel, "Death in the Deep South," temporary script, 18.

44. Kandel and Rossen, "In the Deep South," final revised script, 16–17. By contrast, in Greene's novel, Griffin dismisses Buxton as a "lecherous old goat" who is too timid to act on his desires (*Death in the Deep South*, 66).

45. In *Death in the Deep South* (74–75), Joe confesses to Andy that he has had sex with Mary. This scene built on questions during the trial as to whether Mary Phagan was in fact a virgin defending her honor against Frank's alleged advances, an allegation derived from the blood on her underwear. The coroner ultimately ruled that Phagan had not been raped. In any case, this detail of the novel presumably embodies Greene's judgmental comment in correspondence, quoted above, that "Mary Phagan . . . is revealed in the actual evidence as a worse little girl than Mary Clay at the time of her murder." In the film, Gleason's question to Joe regarding his conflicting answers about whether or not he ever kissed Mary barely hints at the question of whether or not Mary Phagan was sexually active. In any case, the PCA would not have tolerated such suggestions about Mary Clay.

46. Kandel, "Death in the Deep South," temporary first draft script, 42.

47. In *Death in the Deep South* (92) Greene creates the rivalry among the three Atlanta papers (the *Constitution*, the *Journal*, and Hearst's newly acquired *Georgian*): "A murder mystery is the best of all possible news to newspapermen. The conservative *Messenger* might play it down; the *Star* might want to; but the sensational *Advocate* would let neither forget that murder plus sex equals circulation." Dinnerstein (*Leo Frank Case*, 11) describes how Atlanta newspapers exploited the case; and Oney (*And the Dead Shall Rise*, 35–45) discusses the politics and newspaper rivalries in great detail, stressing how Hearst's *Georgian* compelled the other papers to publish yellow journalism. As in so many aspects of the

adaptation process, Greene's novel portrays the reporters as far more vulgar and hateful than the film could. While Dolly Holly interviews Sybil, two male photographers comment that they would not blame Hale for cheating on Sybil with Mary Clay; one adds, "Oh, she wouldn't be so bad . . . provided she don't cry when she does it." See Greene, *Death in the Deep South*, 104.

48. The "Don'ts and Be Carefuls of 1927" and the "Production Code" can be found in Garth Jowett, *Film: The Democratic Art* (Boston: Little, Brown, 1976), 466–67, 468–71.

49. For the most thorough account of *Fury*'s production, see Patrick McGilligan, *Fritz Lang: The Nature of the Beast* (New York: St. Martin's Press, 1997), 221–35. Kenneth L. Geist, *Pictures Will Talk: The Life and Films of Joseph L. Mankiewicz* (New York: Da Capo Press, 1978), 76–81; and Black, *Hollywood Censored*, 264–68, offer brief accounts. Tom Gunning's *The Films of Fritz Lang: Allegories of Vision and Modernity* (London: BFI, 2000) has the most thorough analysis of the film (212–34). See Amy Wood, "'Bring Home to America What Mob Violence Really Means': Hollywood's Spectacular Indictment of Lynching," in *White Supremacy and Spectacle*, for a detailed account of how *Fury*'s script drew on reports of that lynching.

50. Gunning, *Films of Fritz Lang*, 221, 222, 225, discusses how the lynching sequence, the trial's use of motion picture footage, and many other elements in *Fury* constitute allegories of cinema, one of many ways in which Lang's film dramatizes the power of vision. See also McGilligan, *Fritz Lang*, 235; and Amy Wood, "Bring Home to America What Mob Violence Really Means."

51. For example, the *New York Times* reviewer wrote, "Let it be said at once: 'Fury' is the finest original drama the screen has provided this year. A mature, sober and penetrating investigation of a national blight" (June 6, 1936, 21). On the PCA and *Fury*, see Black, *Hollywood Censored*, 265.

52. Joseph I. Breen to Jack L. Warner, January 30, 1937, *They Won't Forget* File, MPPDA.

53. Irwin Edmond to Warner Brothers, Inc. in New York, April 2, 1937, *Mountain Justice* File, MPPDA.

54. Greene, *Star Reporters*, 131.

55. Ibid., 166–67. In his *Classical Film Violence: Designing and Regulating Brutality in Hollywood Cinema, 1930–1968* (New Brunswick, N.J.: Rutgers University Press, 2003), 220–30, Stephen Prince discusses metonymic displacement as one of many different screen rhetorics for indirectly representing violence; all are forms of what he calls "spatial displacement." See pp. 205–51 for the full discussion.

56. Frank Nugent, directly in "A Boy Wonder Grows Up," *New York Times*, July 18, 1937; and William Johnson, indirectly in "Deep," 76, attribute the inven-

tion of this staging to LeRoy (Johnson characterizes it as LeRoy's one "bravura" stylistic flourish in the film). To his credit, Nugent does acknowledge that he could be wrong and that his comments might inspire a sneer from the film's screenwriters. Another example of stylization in LeRoy's *I Am a Fugitive from a Chain Gang* involves brutal violence such as whippings seen in shadow and heard from offscreen while the other prisoners' listening faces appear in close-up. See Kandel, "Death in the Deep South," temporary first draft script, 33–54 (Redwine's wailing) and 46 and 51 for the graphic match on the oval mirror.

57. Geoffrey Shurlock to Joseph I. Breen, March 17, 1937, *They Won't Forget* File, MPPDA. Information on *They Won't Forget*'s principal photography comes from "In the Deep South" File 1493B, WBA.

58. Joseph I. Breen to Jack L. Warner, March 20, 1937, *They Won't Forget* File, MPPDA.

59. Brian Neve discusses the antilynching bill introduced by New York Representative Joseph Gavagan, sponsored by the NAACP, and passed in the House of Representatives on April 15, 1937. It would be defeated in the Senate by southern senators. Neve cites Robert L. Zangrando, "The NAACP and a Federal Anti Lynching Bill, 1934–1940," in *The Negro in Depression and War: Prelude to Revolution, 1930–45*, ed. Bernard Sternsher (Chicago: Quadrangle, 1969), 181–82. See also Philip Dray, *At the Hands of Persons Unknown: The Lynching of Black America* (New York: Random House, 2002), 359–62.

60. Greene, *Death in the Deep South*, 24. Greene has fun with Sybil's preconceptions and perceptions of the South. With her husband, Sybil ventures into "the wilderness across the Hudson. . . . Her knowledge of the South was limited to popular songs, reports of lynchings and a play she had seen called *Tobacco Road*, but she voiced no fears. Still, it was rather a relief when their destination turned out to be bare of magnolias, showboats, bleeding blacks or too plainly barbarous whites. On the whole, the city reminded Sybil of Queens" (ibid., 26–27).

61. Oney, *And the Dead Shall Rise*, 582–95.

62. Mervyn Le Roy to Joe Breen, January 28, 1937, *They Won't Forget* File, MPPDA. Title changes are recorded in memos from Mervyn LeRoy to "All Departments" dated January 21, 1937, May 18, 1937, and May 28, 1937, all in file 12733; and June 3, 1937, file 2881, all in Warner Bros. Archives, USC.

63. See Kandel's temporary first draft script, 1–3.

64. The issue of the Civil War and memory has been explored most thoroughly in David W. Blight, *Race and Reunion: The Civil War in American Memory* (Boston: Belknap Press, 2001).

65. The scene first appears in the revised script dated February 15, 1937, 3–5, with pages added through April 2, in the Robert Rossen Collection, UCLA Theater

Arts Library; also see Kandel and Rossen, final revised script, "In the Deep South," 4–7.

66. Greene's novel displays a keen awareness of the social dimensions of the Phagan-Frank case, some of which is expressed in the way he has Griffin view Mary's brothers as "workworn young men, the stamp of field and foundry in their faces, the mark of privation on them from boot to brow. . . . They were the 'wool hat boys' of Georgia, the 'blue jeans' of New England; they were the serfs of their time. But they were the American male, the 'backbone of the country'" (41). Gregory Black in *Hollywood Censored*, 271, sees the business leaders' scene with Andy as another of the film's attempts to show that there is no townwide conspiracy to have Robert convicted; if so, in my view, the scene backfires.

67. Kandel and Rossen, "In the Deep South," final revised script, 41.

68. As noted on page 83, during the film's distribution, Maryland's censor eliminated the one overhead shot of Tump under interrogation. The censorship reports appear in the *They Won't Forget* File, MPPDA. Reflecting Warner Bros.'s gradual distribution strategy, they are dated July 31, 1937 (New York); August 31, 1937 (Maryland); September 30, 1937 (Kansas); October 1, 1937 (Ohio); October 6, 1937 (Japan); October 11, 1937 (Massachusetts); December 21, 1937 (Quebec); and March 15, 1938 (Dutch East Indies).

69. Amy Wood provides a thorough account of *Fury* and *They Won't Forget*'s sparse bookings in the South in "Bring Home to America What Mob Violence Really Means." Also see Black, *Hollywood Censored*, 269–70.

70. Black, *Hollywood Censored*, 273–74.

71. Indeed, a *Motion Picture Herald* article from August 1937 reported that Breen was trying to "relax" his enforcement of the code as studios turned increasingly to dramatic material and away from "nonsensical" comedies such as *My Man Godfrey* (1936). Greta Garbo's vehicle *Camille* (1936), about a courtesan, and *They Won't Forget* were specifically mentioned as examples of Breen's new approach to helping studios make more controversial films. See "Breen Office May Relax Rules a Bit," *Motion Picture Herald*, August 13, 1937. Thanks to Thomas Doherty for bringing this article to my attention. See Jacobs, *The Wages of Sin*, 111–13; and Vasey, *The World According to Hollywood*, 105–7, 111–12, on Breen's efforts to create ambiguity of meaning in certain story events concerning illicit or illegal actions.

72. Johnson, "Deep," 75.

73. For an excellent, concise assessment of LeRoy's career, see Charles Wolfe, "Mervyn LeRoy," in *American Directors*, vol. 1, ed. Jean-Pierre Coursodon with Pierre Sauvage (New York: McGraw Hill, 1983), 216–19.

74. The negative cost figure for *They Won't Forget* comes from a ledger referred to as Jack Warner's "Black Book." My thanks to archivist Sandra Joy Lee at the Warner Bros. Archives, USC Los Angeles, California, for providing me with this information.

75. Edward Selzer, Director of Publicity, n.d., *They Won't Forget* File 690, WBA.

76. George R. Bilson, memo to "Charlie" (probably Charles Einfeld), n.d., file 12685B, WBA.

77. Trailer script, "They Won't Forget," June 10, 1937, file 12685B, WBA.

78. The rationale for adding the disclaimer appears in Perkins-[Morris] Ebenstein, Coast Wire to Mervyn LeRoy, July 13, 1937, *They Won't Forget* File 12685, WBA.

79. Ad in *Variety*, August 14, 1937, for *They Won't Forget*. *They Won't Forget* Press Book, WB Campaign Plan, Academy Clippings Files.

80. Leroy, *Mervyn LeRoy*, 130, 131. Jeanine Basinger, *The Star Machine* (New York: Knopf, 2007), 180–89, discusses Turner's life through *They Won't Forget*, and on 186–87 discusses LeRoy's costume changes for Turner. Basinger has written of Turner's casting that whoever played Mary Clay "*must* leave a definite imprint in the audience's mind [and] . . . be powerful enough to keep the audience feeling the tragedy of her loss." Turner fulfilled this function very well. See Basinger's *Lana Turner* (New York: Pyramid Books, 1976), 22.

81. Kenneth Anger, *Hollywood Babylon* (New York: Dell, 1976), 269.

82. *Daily Variety*, June 9, 1937; *Hollywood Reporter*, June 9, 1937; *Motion Picture Herald*, June 19, 1937; clippings in *They Won't Forget* File, MPPDA.

83. "Inside Stuff—Pictures," *Variety*, July 14, 1937, 8; and "Tourists Aiding B'way; *Forget* Strong $30,000, *Easy Living* 2d Week with Martha Raye Sock 50G," *Variety*, July 21, 1937.

84. "Movie of the Week: *They Won't Forget*," *Life*, July 19, 1937, 32–35 (six weeks later, *Life* would do a piece on a "Tennessee Lynching"); Frank S. Nugent, "*They Won't Forget*," *New York Times*, July 15, 1937, 16; and "A Boy Wonder Grows Up," *New York Times*, July 18, 1937.

85. Leo Mishkin, "Screen Presents," *New York Morning Telegraph*, July 15, 1937; "M.F.L.," "The Theatre," *Wall Street Journal*, July 15, 1937, 8; "Monitor Movie Guide," *Christian Science Monitor*, October 9, 1937, 17; all clippings in *They Won't Forget* File, WBA. "Movie of the Week: *They Won't Forget*," *Life*; Otis Ferguson, "New Film in a Dry Month," *New Republic*, July 28, 1937, repr. in *The Film Criticism of Otis Ferguson*, ed. Robert Wilson (Philadelphia: Temple University Press, 1971), 185–87. Graham Greene, *Graham Greene on Film: Collected Film Criticism, 1935–1939*, ed. John Russell Taylor (New York:

Simon and Schuster, 1972), 178. Critics outside New York also praised the film. See "*They Won't Forget* Is a Sensational Murder Drama Loaded with Dynamite, Packed with Controversy," *Washington Post*, September 16, 1937, 14; Kenneth McCaleb, "Ward Greene's Cry against Prejudice Reverberates in a Mighty Film," *Los Angeles Daily Mirror*, July 18, 1937, magazine section, 19. One exception was the ultraconservative *Chicago Daily Tribune*'s Mae Tinee, who condemned the film in no uncertain terms: "'They Won't Forget' is a sickening picture. *An unnecessary picture*. In a world full of hates and fears, why for the love of Mike haul out a lot of old ones to rile folks up and make them miserable?" This review inspired a spirited dissenting view from a reader who found it one of the year's best films and who even took the trouble to find corroboration in other critical "best film" lists. See Mae Tinee, "Critic Aroused Because Movie Stirs Old Hate," *Chicago Daily Tribune*, January 8, 1938, 15; Helene Albrecht, letter to the editor, *Chicago Daily Tribune*, February 6, 1938, G2.

86. Neve, "Screenwriter and the Social Problem Film," 4; Amy Wood, "Bring Home to America What Mob Violence Really Means," discusses the Times Square protests. "Scottsboro Boys on % for 1st P.A. in Harlem; Re-enact Court Scene," *Variety*, August 25, 1937: 1; Gould Cassal, "The Sound Track," *Brooklyn Daily Eagle*, New York Public Library of the Performing Arts Clippings File, n.d.; *McCall's*, October 1937; and *New Masses*, July 20, 1937, are both cited in Neve, n. 28.

87. Frank Nugent, "Another Month Passes in Review; July Will Be Remembered for *They Won't Forget* and Will Be Forgotten for *Crusade against Rackets*," *New York Times*, August 1, 1937, 139; Bosley Crowther, "A Desperate Plea for Justice," *New York Times*, September 8, 1940, 129. See also Robbin Coons, "Movies Go Onward and Upward in Spite of Some Bad Company," *Washington Post*, June 23, 1940, A4; John D. Beaufort, "The Wide Horizon," *Christian Science Monitor*, September 8, 1939, 24; and Frank Daugherty, "Hollywood and 'Ideas': Should Films Say Something?" *Christian Science Monitor*, March 13, 1939. Frank Nugent placed the film fifth on his ten-best list, behind *The Life of Emile Zola*, *The Good Earth*, *Stage Door*, and *Captains Courageous*; "Ten Best, in a Pickwickian Sense," *New York Times*, January 2, 1938, 127. *They Won't Forget* was among ten films chosen to represent the United States (along with *Mr. Deeds Goes to Town*, *Showboat*, *The Informer*, and *Scarface*) in the New York Film Festival's first season in July 1938; "Sixteen Nations to Show Films in Fete Here," *New York Times*, June 3, 1938, 17. Likewise, the National Board of Review included the film behind *The Life of Emile Zola* and *Black Legion* in its ten-best list for 1937.

88. James Baldwin, *The Devil Finds Work* (New York: Dell, 1976), 23–24. V. J. Jerome's pioneering volume *The Negro in Hollywood Film* uses a publicity still

of the terrified Rosemond as its frontispiece and discusses the film (New York: Masses and Mainstream, 1950), 188. Nick Roddick views *They Won't Forget* as "Warners' most emphatic social document of the second half of the decade" and "a high-class example of a Warners contemporary social picture." See Roddick, *A New Deal in Entertainment: Warner Brothers in the 1930s* (London: British Film Institute, 1983), 153–54. See also Peter Roffman and Jim Purdy, *The Hollywood Social Problem Film* (Bloomington: Indiana University Press, 1981), 169–72. In "Deep," 74–76, William Johnson perceptively notes how *They Won't Forget* creates false hopes, not unlike those in Alfred Hitchcock's *The Wrong Man* (1956), in Sybil's somewhat clichéd words, "Somewhere, someplace, there must be someone who'll help." Detective Pindar appears, but he proves ineffective.

89. Archer Winsten, "Movie Talk: *They Won't Forget* at the Strand Theatre," *New York Post*, July 15, 1937; Gould Cassal, "How Men Die in the Deep South Is Shown in 'They Won't Forget,' a Strong Indictment of Mob Prejudice at the N.Y. Strand," *Brooklyn Eagle*, July 31, 1937. Cassal faulted the film for following Greene's "potboiler" too closely. Unsigned, "Strand Film Shows Evil of Lynching," *New York Daily Telegram*, July 15, 1937, clippings file, Billy Rose Collection, Library for the Performing Arts, Lincoln Center, New York.

90. Ward Greene to "Mitchell," July 3, 1937, file story file 12685, WBA; Mrs. Alonzo Richardson to Mr. Breen, August 31, 1937 (incomplete copy), *Artists and Models* File; and Joseph Breen, memo to Mervyn LeRoy, September 6, 1937, *They Won't Forget* File, both in MPPDA.

91. "Warners Withdraw Film from Atlanta," *Southern Israelite*, August 27, 1937, 7; "Atlanta Is Grateful," *Southern Israelite*, August 27, 1937, 6. See Wood, "Bring Home to America What Mob Violence Really Means," on the *Atlanta Daily World*'s publication of the Rosemond photo. *They Won't Forget* was shown noncommercially at the Breman Jewish Museum in Atlanta in spring 2002 as part of a film series about lynching curated by Miriam Petty, then of Emory University's Graduate Institute of the Liberal Arts, in conjunction with the exhibit at the Martin Luther King Jr. Center in 2002 of the James Allen Lynching Postcard Collection Exhibit. It was shown a second time in spring 2008 to accompany an exhibit at the Breman on the Leo Frank case.

Interlude. From Film to Television

1. This financial information comes from Jack Warner's "Black Book." My thanks to Sandra Joy Lee, archivist, Warner Bros. Archives, USC, Los Angeles, California, for providing me with these figures. Frank Nugent, in "What's Wrong

with the Movies? Producers and Exhibitors Have Had Their Say but the Public Seems to Have Its Own Ideas," *New York Times*, November 20, 1938, briefly mentions that *They Won't Forget* "lost money."

2. Bosley Crowther, "America in Films: How Truthfully Do Our Motion Pictures Reflect Our National Life?" *New York Times*, July 12, 1942, 3.

3. See Thomas P. Doherty, *Cold War, Cool Medium: Television, McCarthyism and American Culture* (New York: Columbia University Press, 2003), for an analysis of 1950s television that argues against the received wisdom of the conventionality of its programming.

4. Charles and Louise Samuels, *Night Fell on Georgia* (New York: Dell, 1956); and Harry Golden, *A Little Girl Is Dead* (Cleveland: World Publishing Co., 1965).

Chapter 3. John M. Slaton as a Profile in Courage

1. The critical quotation about the "islands" of Saudek's work comes from Cecil Smith, "Series to 'Profile' Kennedy Work," *Los Angeles Times*, March 16, 1964, C18. See Robert M. Thomas Jr., "Robert Saudek Is Dead at 85; a Pioneer of Culture on TV," *New York Times*, March 17, 1997, B9, for an account of Saudek's many accomplishments.

2. "Kennedy Speaks Words He Didn't Get to Tape," *Los Angeles Times*, December 18, 1964, D22; Robert Saudek to Theodore C. Sorensen, February 6, 1961, box 309, PIC Letters File, 1961, Robert A. Saudek Papers, Wesleyan Cinema Archive, Middletown, Connecticut (hereafter "Saudek Collection"). Saudek mentions the Kennedy Center fundraiser in his unpublished memoir, PIC-2, courtesy of the Saudek family. The standard study of Kennedy-era American television is Mary Ann Watson, *The Expanding Vista: American Television in the Kennedy Years* (New York: Oxford University Press, 1985). See also Michael Curtin, *Redeeming the Wasteland: Television Documentary and Cold War Politics* (New Brunswick, N.J.: Rutgers University Press, 1995).

3. The PIC Letters File, 1961, in box 309, Saudek Collection, contains all the negotiations between Saudek and the White House. See, for example, Robert Saudek to President John F. Kennedy, March 17, 1961; and Myer Feldman, Deputy Special Counsel to the President, to Robert Saudek, April 8, 1961. See also Murray Schumach, "Episodes Added to TV 'Profiles': Series Based on Kennedy's Book Also Plans Deletions," *New York Times*, March 13, 1964, 41; Val Adams, "TV Aids Kennedy Library," *New York Times*, May 2, 1965, 15; "Lesson of History," *Newsweek*, February 15, 1965, 58.

4. Saudek's comment on figures dealing with identical problems comes from Bob Lardine, "Profile of TV's 'Profiles in Courage,'" *Sunday Daily News*, May 10, 1964, in Clippings File, box 310, Saudek Collection. The other Saudek quotations appear in Cecil Smith, "The TV Scene: Series to 'Profile' Kennedy Work," *Los Angeles Times*, March 16, 1964, C18. Names of people considered as possible episode subjects can be found in various letters in the PIC Letters File, 1961, box 309. See, for example, Robert Saudek to Theodore Sorensen, February 6, 1961. One of Saudek's original ideas was to have President Kennedy introduce each episode or have hosts chosen from "among people who have themselves shown personal courage."

5. Saudek, unpublished memoirs, PIC-1, courtesy of the Saudek family.

6. Telephone interview with Theodore C. Sorensen, September 27, 2005; John F. Kennedy, "Three Women of Courage," *McCall's*, January 1958, 36–37; Daniel Marcus, "*Profiles in Courage*: Televisual History on the New Frontier," in *Television Histories: Shaping Collective Memory in the Media Age*, ed. Gary R. Edgerton and Peter C. Rollins (Lexington: University of Kentucky Press, 2001), 93, reprinted from *Film and History* 30, no. 1 (2000): 38–49. The *New York Times* front page for June 10, 1963 — which announced that Saudek would produce the *Profiles in Courage* television series — also featured an article reporting Martin Luther King Jr.'s impatience with the Kennedy administration's slow progress on civil rights, JFK's speech to the nation's mayors on the subject, and a photo of Alabama's National Guard troops alighting from helicopters to be stationed at the defiantly segregated University of Alabama accompanying Claude Sitton's article, "Alabama Guardsmen in Tuscaloosa as Wallace Plans to Defy U.S. Court."

7. John Slaton's name does not appear in Robert Saudek's letter to Theodore C. Sorensen dated February 6, 1961, but it does show up on the "Approved Subject List," August 7, 1963, both in PIC Letters File, 1961, box 309, Saudek Collection.

8. Theodore C. Sorensen to Robert Saudek, January 30, 1964, Slaton Research File, box 246, Saudek Collection. For the record, Sorensen was not always as satisfied with the series scripts as he was with the Slaton script. See, for example, Theodore C. Sorensen to Mary V. Ahern, March 19, 1964: "The Wilson-Brandeis script is the worst you have sent. It is wholly unacceptable, and in my review, incapable of rehabilitation," in Theodore C. Sorensen Correspondence, 1963–64 File, box 310, Saudek Collection. Saudek's writers were able to revise the script to Sorensen's satisfaction.

9. Kennedy's preface to *Profiles in Courage*, "Memorial Edition" (New York: Harper and Row, 1964), p. xiv, notes that "the greatest debt is owed to my research associate, Theodore C. Sorensen, for his invaluable assistance in the as-

sembly and preparation of the material upon which this book is based." The columnist, writing in 1956, was Drew Pearson. Sorensen has consistently denied the allegation. See also Marcus, "*Profiles in Courage*," 86, for some discussion of Sorensen's role in the series.

10. Schumach, "Episodes Added to TV 'Profiles,'" 41; Marcus, "*Profiles in Courage*," 86, 93; Robert Saudek to Myer Feldman, July 15, 1963, PIC Correspondence—Important, April 1963 File, box 310, Saudek Collection.

11. Schumach, "Episodes Added to TV 'Profiles,'" 41. See, for example, a background piece for the inaugural Oscar Underwood episode (airdate November 8, 1964) that boasted: "This episode is historically accurate. All speeches you will hear in the 1924 Democratic National Convention are taken verbatim from the convention record itself. All balloting and voting on the minority plank and on candidates are exactly in accordance with the facts in every detail. Al Smith's conditional offer to Underwood is factual" (box 309, Saudek Collection).

12. Producer's letter, October 26, 1964, box 309; and Saudek to Victor Jory, March 20, 1964, PIC Correspondence—Important, April 1963 File, box 310, Saudek Collection.

13. See Robert C. Allen and Douglas Gomery, *Film History: Theory and Practice* (New York: McGraw-Hill, 1985), 229–38, for an account of the liberal ethos informing public affairs programming in the late 1950s and early 1960s. See Marcus, "*Profiles in Courage*," 84–85, for a discussion of the series's relationship to Minow's famous decree.

14. Paul Gardner, "Pulitzer 'Profiles' Get Video Face-lifting," *New York Times*, October 25, 1964, 17.

15. Gordon Oliver's comments appear in Terry Turner, "Kennedy 'Profiles' Ambitious Project," *Los Angeles Times*, June 12, 1964, D14. Also see Dora Jane Hamblin, "Profiles That Cast Long Shadows," *Life*, January 22, 1965, 8.

16. Robert Saudek's comments on Walter Kerr, Mary Ahern, and Michael Ritchie come from his unpublished memoir, courtesy of the Saudek family. On the credit sequence, see Robert Saudek to Ted Kennedy, July 23, 1964, PIC Correspondence—Important, April 1963 File, box 310, Saudek Collection. JFK apparently quoted the lyrics to "The Boys of Wexford" in his address to the Irish Parliament in June 1963.

17. Saudek's interest in major playwrights is evident from several letters in the Material for California 2-20-64 File, box 309, Saudek Collection; see, for example, Robert Saudek to Robert Bolt, December 3, 1963.

18. Marcus, "*Profiles in Courage*," 86, 93. In her letter to Ross Donaldson (director of Program Services, NBC), February 24, 1964, Mary V. Ahern protested an NBC West Coast executive's dictum that Walter Bernstein was "unacceptable" as

a writer. She pointed out that Bernstein had completed an outline of the Richard T. Ely episode and was now completing the script and that the Saudek team had presented his name three months earlier with no comment from NBC; Michael Ritchie, undated memo, Profiles Ideas File, box 310, Saudek Collection.

19. According to Hal Humphrey's account in the *Washington Post*, Steve McQueen was approached for a role but was not pursued when he demanded $400,000 for his appearance, one hundred times the typical salary for a lead in the series. See "'Profiles in Courage' Delay Was Decided by Kennedy," *Washington Post*, November 2, 1964, B10. On Michael Ritchie, see Charles Champlin, "Film Director Got His Start on Free Pass," *Los Angeles Times*, July 17, 1969, D1.

20. Val Adams, "TV Aids Kennedy Library," *New York Times*, May 2, 1965, 15. NBC paid Robert Saudek Associates $3,510,000 to produce the twenty-six episodes. Budget planning for the series allocated $410,000 for scripts; $13,500 per episode for Kennedy's payments; $5,000 for stars and $12,000 for the cast; $3,000 for directors; and below-the-line costs of $55,000 per episode (see RSA Interoffice Correspondence (PIC) File, box 309, Saudek Collection). That budget was on the low end for popular television series of the period as compared with, for example, the *Alfred Hitchcock Hour* at $152,000 and *Ben Casey* episodes at $143,000; but close to *Disney's Wonderful World of Color* ($136,000). A January 1965 memo estimated the actual average cost per episode at $132,931. See Richard Thomas, memo to Robert Saudek, January 13, 1965, in the same file, box 309. The Slaton episode cost $131,730. Gordon Oliver's production plan was to have finalized scripts in hand three weeks before shooting and then to shoot each episode within an average of six days. The production team would work for a month on four episodes, take a week off, and then shoot another four, with all principal photography completed by the end of October 1964. Michael Ritchie, memo to Robert Saudek re meeting with Gordon Oliver at RSA, September 26, 1963, Material for California 2-20-64 File, box 309, Saudek Collection. Part of Robert Saudek's elation at the rushes of the Oscar Underwood episode arose from the fact that shooting had been completed in five days.

21. When Kennedy was assassinated, Saudek also already had several scripts on hand. In his December 2, 1963, letter to Sorenson, Saudek added: "I want you to know that four of our writers have called to say how they have renewed their own strength by turning back to their scripts at this difficult time and have tried to rewrite in order to make their contributions greater" (Robert Saudek to Theodore C. Sorensen, December 2, 1963, Theodore C. Sorensen Correspondence, 1963–64 File, box 310, Saudek Collection). Sorensen clarified JFK's approval of additional subjects and his own authority to approve additional subjects in a letter to Saudek dated February 12, 1964, Material for California 2-20-64 File,

box 309, Saudek Collection. Saudek's comments on his understanding of why NBC tried to stop the series are in his unpublished memoir, PIC-2, courtesy of the Saudek family.

22. Marcus discusses the scheduling of the series in "*Profiles in Courage*," 86. Also see Humphrey, "'Profiles in Courage' Delay," B10; and Lawrence Laurent, "A Best Bet That Won't Be Back," *Los Angeles Times*, February 18, 1965, C14. I found only one indication that the series was rebroadcast close to its initial run—by KTTV of Los Angeles in May 1965. See "KTTV to Rerun NBC's Profiles in Courage," *Los Angeles Times*, May 29, 1965, B3. The Aluminum, Ltd. company of Canada renewed its sponsorship through late March in January 1965; T. E. Covel (J. Walter Thompson Agency) to Robert Saudek, January 11, 1965, "PIC Aluminum, Ltd., Inc." File, box 309, Saudek Collection.

23. Cecil Smith, "The TV Scene: 'Profiles' Display Kennedy Spirit," *Los Angeles Times*, November 9, 1964, V20; quoted in Marcus, "*Profiles in Courage*," 95.

24. John E. Drewry, Dean, Henry W. Grady School of Journalism, to Robert Saudek, March 25, 1965, PIC Awards File, box 309, Saudek Collection. Other awards included citations from the National School Public Relations Association in August 1965, the American Baptist Convention, and the National Association for Better Radio and Television; *Fame* magazine's Annual Critics' Poll Award for Best Network Television Program; the National Conference of Christians and Jews Brotherhood Award for Best Network Dramatic Program; McDermott's Critics' Poll Award for Best Series of Season; and an unprecedented special citation from the National Council for the Social Studies. The Aluminum Company of Canada received a *Saturday Review* Citation for Distinguished Television Achievement in the Public Interest for sponsoring the series. Marcus, "*Profiles in Courage*," 95. For an announcement of the Peabody Award, see the *Christian Science Monitor*, May 7, 1965, 6; for the Silver Gavel Award, see the *Washington Post*, July 13, 1965, A18. Minow wrote to Saudek: "You really deserved the Peabody Award and I was delighted to write that citation" (Newton N. Minow to Robert Saudek, May 4, 1965, PIC Encyclopedia Britannica Films File, box 310, Saudek Collection). Minow had worked for Encyclopedia Britannica Films since retiring from the FCC and hoped to gain the rights to the *Profiles* series to distribute it around the country to schools and libraries. By April 1965 Saudek had decided to venture into distribution himself. See, in the same file, Robert Saudek to Newton Minow, April 9, 1965.

25. Theodore C. Sorensen, handwritten note to Robert Saudek, date-stamped November 30, 1964, Theodore C. Sorensen Correspondence, 1963–64 File, box 310, Saudek Collection. Writing of the first two episodes (Oscar Underwood and Mary McDowell), Sorensen commented: «I thought they were both *excellent*—

the second even better than the first. Scoring, photography, particularly the acting, everything *first-rate*." The series teaching guides also earned a Superior Merit Brotherhood Award of the National Conference of Christians and Jews. See Robert Saudek to Robert F. Kennedy, April 20, 1964, PIC Correspondence—Important, April 1963 File, box 310, Saudek Collection.

26. Herm., [*sic*] "Profiles in Courage," *Variety*, November 4, 1964. The *Hollywood Reporter* was less enthusiastic about the series. See "'Profiles in Courage' Bows with Story that Suffers from Pedestrian Pacing," *Hollywood Reporter*, November 10, 1964, 9; Marcus, "*Profiles in Courage*," 95. NBC might have comforted itself with the fact that the small audience percentage for *Profiles in Courage* comprised highly educated, upper-middle-class viewers. For a discussion of NBC's attention to demographic breakdowns of NBC audience research (in pursuit of a more youthful audience), see Mark Alvey, "'Too Many Kids and Old Ladies': Quality Demographics and 1960s U.S. Television," in *Television: The Critical View*, 7th ed., ed. Horace Newcomb (New York: Oxford University Press, 2007), 15–36. For correspondence concerning the paperback book from the series, see "Carmen," memo to Mr. Saudek, August 3, 1966, PIC Approvals File, box 309, Saudek Collection.

27. James Reston, "What Was Killed Was Not Only the President but the Promise," *New York Times Sunday Magazine*, November 15, 1964, 24. See the ad in the *New York Times* (November 8, 1964), 14, for the first episode; also Bob Lardine, "Profile of TV's 'Profiles in Courage,'" *Sunday Daily News*, May 10, 1964, Clippings File, box 309, Saudek Collection.

28. See "Bibliography of Governor Slaton and the Leo Frank Case," Slaton Research File, box 246, Saudek Collection; Charles and Louise Samuels, *Night Fell on Georgia* (New York: Dell, 1956). This bibliography included books I discuss in this chapter as well as many 1915 articles on the case from *Outlook* and *Forum* magazines, an abstract of the trial, Georgia court records for 1913, and "Material from the Anti-defamation League File on Leo Frank."

29. Bernard Weinraub, memo to Don Mankiewicz ("Re: John M. Slaton, campaign for the Senate, 1914"), October 17, 1963; Weinraub to Mankiewicz, September 18, 1963; and Bernard Weinraub to Mary [V. Ahern], "Re: Don Mankiewicz John M. Slaton, first draft," n.d., PIC Governor John M. Slaton (hereafter GJMS) Correspondence VP 110 File, box 246, Saudek Collection.

30. See Matthew Bernstein, *Walter Wanger, Hollywood Independent* (Minneapolis: University of Minnesota Press, 2000), 317–39, for an account of the production, development, and reception of *I Want to Live!* that focuses on Mankiewicz's work on the film. For a profile of Mankiewicz from the 1950s, see "Just Name on Books: Don Mankiewicz Wants No Career in Celluloid Jungle,"

Los Angeles Times, February 27, 1955, D1. Mankiewicz wrote six additional episodes for *Profiles in Courage* and would later write the pilots and many scripts for popular series such as *Ironsides* (1967–75) and *Marcus Welby, M.D.* (1969–76). Mankiewicz was paid $5,000 for his work on the Slaton episode, the most paid to any screenwriter for the series; Walter Matthau, by comparison, received $4,000 plus $1,000 for expenses. See "Free Lance Contract, March 18, 1964 between Robert Saudek and Walcar Corp," PIC GJMS Correspondence File VP 110, box 246, Saudek Collection.

31. Matthau would earn Oscar nominations twice more, for the Jack Lemmon-directed family dramedy *Kotch* (1971) and for his role opposite George Burns in the 1975 film adaptation of Neil Simon's comedy *The Sunshine Boys*.

32. The Saudek quotation is from Robert Saudek to Andrew K. Lewis, April 21, 1964, PIC Correspondence—Important, April 1963 File, box 310, Saudek Collection. Daniel Marcus quotes it in "*Profiles in Courage*," 87.

33. Marcus attributes Kennedy's policy for consensus and middle ground to Arthur Schlesinger Jr.'s 1949 study of American politics, *The Vital Ground*. See Marcus, "*Profiles in Courage*," 82–85; the quotation is from p. 88.

34. Sallie Slaton is quoted ("let's commute") in Steve Oney, *And the Dead Shall Rise: The Murder of Mary Phagan and the Lynching of Leo Frank* (New York: Pantheon Books, 2003), 512. Powell recounts the anecdote of Sallie Slaton's "brave man" versus "coward" statement in Arthur G. Powell, *I Can Go Home Again* (Chapel Hill: University of North Carolina Press, 1943), 291–92. Samuel A. Boorstin wrote to Slaton on September 1, 1953, asking Slaton if Sallie truly made that statement. The copy of Slaton's affirmative reply appears in John M. Slaton to Samuel A. Boorstin, September 3, 1953, PIC GJMS Correspondence VP 110 File, box 246, Saudek Collection.

35. John M. Slaton, *Atlanta Constitution*, June 22, 1915, 4.

36. Allan Nevins to Don M. Mankiewicz, December 10, 1963, PIC GJMS Correspondence VP 110 File, box 246, Saudek Collection.

37. See Oney, *And the Dead Shall Rise*, 512, for an account of Slaton's whereabouts immediately after he stepped down as governor. Slaton's comments to the California Civic League were reported in "Mob Hanging Better than Judicial Murder Says John M. Slaton," *Atlanta Constitution*, August 18, 1915, 1.

38. "Mob Hanging Better than Judicial Murder Says John M. Slaton."

39. Slaton's assessment that Georgia's legal community admired him appears in Samuel A. Boorstin, "Memo of facts and conversation had by Samuel A. Boorstin in Atlanta, Ga. on October 12, 1953, including conference with Governor John M. Slaton who commuted sentence of Leo M. Frank," *Profiles in Courage* Research File, box 246, Saudek Collection. For more on Slaton, see

Tammy H. Galloway, "John M. Slaton," *New Georgia Encyclopedia*, http:—www.georgiaencyclopedia.org-nge-Article.jsp?path=-GovernmentPolitics-Politics-PoliticalFigures&id=h-2137, accessed March 22, 2008. See "Slaton Dies at 88," *Atlanta Constitution*, January 12, 1955; the same issue featured an editorial on his death: "Gov Slaton's Courage Ended Political Career," in Clippings File, box 246, Saudek Collection.

40. Mankiewicz, first draft script.

41. G.O. and M.R. [Gordon Oliver and Michael Ritchie], memo to Robert Saudek on stylization in the Slaton script, December 17, 1963, Interoffice Correspondence File, box 309, Saudek Collection.

42. G.O. and M.R., memo to Robert Saudek, January 8, 1964, reviews the procedures by which NBC was to be consulted on series episodes. Maurie Goodman (editor, NBC Broadcast Standards, Pacific Division) to Gordon Oliver, February 7, 1964, Slaton—Master Script File, box 283, Saudek Collection; Mary Ahern, memo to Gordon Oliver, February 11, 1964, Profiles Ideas File, box 310, Saudek Collection. In response to one NBC inquiry, inspired by concern over giving religious offense, Ahern quoted the *Outlook* article, June 30, 1915, which cited a story in the *New York Evening Sun* describing a marching mob that was chanting, "We want John M. Slaton, King of the Jews and Traitor Governor of Georgia."

43. Don M. Mankiewicz, final script draft, February 7, 1964, Slaton (outline and first draft) PIC Mankiewicz, box 309; Maurie Goodman (editor, NBC, Broadcast Standards), memo to Gordon Oliver, February 17, 1964, Slaton—Master Script File, box 283; Maurie Goodman to Gordon Oliver, May 8 and May 14, 1964, Slaton—Master Script File, box 283, all in Saudek Collection.

44. On the matter of the pencil factory's cleanliness, the Samuelses note in *Night Fell on Georgia*, 11, that the plant "was almost incredibly filthy" and that "in the seven years the company had occupied the premises the place had not once been thoroughly cleaned." For Conley's third affidavit that detailed his actions with Frank in disposing of Phagan's body, see Oney, *And the Dead Shall Rise*, 139. Stuart Sprague, Robert Saudek's attorney, obtained a transcript of Conley's testimony at the trial from an Atlanta firm for the Saudek team to consult as Mankiewicz revised the script. See Granger Hansell to Stuart Sprague, January 24, 1964, PIC GJMS Correspondence VP 110 File, box 246, Saudek Collection.

45. Oney, *And the Dead Shall Rise*, 497. The trial transcript excerpts supplied to Saudek Associates also included testimony from police and others about the blood found near the lathe that was initially thought to be Mary Phagan's, and Mankiewicz drew on that material for the factory scene.

46. Oney analyzes Slaton's statement announcing his commutation of sentence in *And the Dead Shall Rise*, 499–502.

47. Mankiewicz, first draft outline.

48. Don M. Mankiewicz, outline for "Governor John M. Slaton," November 1, 1963, PIC GJMS Correspondence VP 110 File, box 246, Saudek Collection; Powell, *I Can Go Home Again*, 288. Neither Leonard Dinnerstein nor Steve Oney, for example, mentions Powell's account of Roan's statement. Powell's book seems trustworthy, although there are errors that do raise the question of how accurate his memories were. For one thing, he misspells Mary Phagan's name (287) and he claims that Frank was lynched "a few nights" after being taken to Milledgeville (291). Also, Powell's prose reflects his friendship and admiration for the Slatons: "Jack Slaton is and always has been a man of unflinching physical and moral courage. In this matter he was put to the test. . . . He knew that unless he let Frank be hanged he would forfeit all his political popularity and ambitions. He commuted the sentence to life imprisonment and told friends privately that he would have granted a full pardon, if he had not believed that in a very short while the truth would come out and the very men who were clamoring for Frank's life would be demanding a pardon for him" (289). Slaton knew of other evidence of Roan's doubts about Conley's honesty, and before his death in 1955 composed a memorandum for private consumption that reviewed his decision in the case; see Stephen J. Goldfarb, "The Slaton Memorandum: A Governor Looks Back at His Decision to Commute the Death Sentence of Leo Frank," *American Jewish History* 88, no. 3 (2000): 325–39.

49. Allen Lumpkin Henson, *Confessions of a Criminal Lawyer* (New York: Vantage Press, 1959), 61–66; see also William B. Hartsfield to Kellam de Forest of de Forest Research, May 26, 1964, PIC GJMS Correspondence File VP 110, box 246, Saudek Collection.

50. Oney, *And the Dead Shall Rise*, 499.

51. For the change in William Smith's assessment of Conley's and Frank's guilt and innocence, see Oney's chapter in *And the Dead Shall Rise*, "A Change of Heart," 423–43. Oney's book is unprecedented in the attention it gives to Smith's life and involvement in the Phagan-Frank case.

52. This overview of the reasons why the Frank team appealed to Slaton rather than Harris comes from Oney's discussion in *And the Dead Shall Rise*, 471–73, which draws in part on Leonard Dinnerstein, *The Leo Frank Case* (New York: Columbia University Press, 1968), 117; the *New York Times*, November 28, 1914; and the *New York Tribune*, May 23, 1915. The John M. Slaton and Nat Harris quotations come from Oney, *And the Dead Shall Rise*, 472.

53. Samuel A. Boorstin, memo of facts and conversation. C. Vann Woodward, *Tom Watson, Agarian Rebel* (New York: Oxford University Press, 1938), 440, cites a letter from John M. Slaton to Thomas W. Loyless, August 27, 1915, printed

in the *Augusta Chronicle*, November 25, 1915. Watson, in turn, had claimed in his monthly/weekly *Tom Watson's Magazine* that Slaton had sought his support for his run for the U.S. Senate before Watson offered his political support (*Watson's*, October 1915); also quoted in Woodward, 440. Bernard M. Weinraub, "John M. Slaton and the Leo Frank Case—Chronology," September 30, 1963, PIC GJMS Correspondence VP 110 File, box 246, Saudek Collection.

54. The Watson quotation is from the *Jeffersonian*, June 10, 1915, and is quoted in Oney, *And the Dead Shall Rise*, 479.

55. Mark K. Bauman, "Factionalism and Ethnic Politics in Atlanta: The German Jews from the Civil War through the Progressive Era," *Georgia Historical Quarterly* 82, no. 3 (1998): 556.

56. Weinraub, "John M. Slaton and the Leo Frank Case—Chronology"; copy of letter from J. M. Slaton to Bishop Warren A. Candler, August 30, 1915; "PIC Scripts and Research, Norris, Ross, Slaton, Taft," PIC GJMS File, box 246, Saudek Collection. See also Mankiewicz, "Governor John M. Slaton," first draft outline, box 293, Saudek Collection; and Bernard M. Weinraub to Don Mankiewicz, September 18, 1963, PIC GJMS Correspondence VP 110 File, box 246, Saudek Collection.

57. Robert Saudek to Robert Kasmire, January 11, 1965, PIC, Complaints, Legal Action File, box 309, Saudek Collection. Weinraub would have agreed with historian Stephen Goldfarb's more recent assessment: "Given all that is known about him, both by his contemporaries and by historians, it is highly doubtful that Slaton would allow his relationship with Rosser to color his judgment about commuting Frank's death sentence, though doubts remain in the minds of some to this day" (Goldfarb, "The Slaton Memorandum," 329).

58. Oney, *And the Dead Shall Rise*, 504.

59. Ibid., 510.

60. The *Atlanta Constitution* reported that one man attempted to climb on the running board of Slaton's car while pointing at Slaton but was apprehended by the militia. See "Great Crowd Sees Harris Sworn in as Head of State," *Atlanta Constitution*, June 27, 1915, 1.

61. Powell, *I Can Go Home Again*, 290. Slaton's nephew, John M. Slaton Jr., recounted a similar story to Bernard Weinraub when the two met to discuss his uncle. Weinraub's notes from the interview are in PIC GJMS File, box 246, Saudek Collection.

62. Henson, *Confessions of a Criminal Lawyer*, 68, 72. Henson describes disobeying Slaton's order not to call in the Georgia National Guard. Oney, *And the Dead Shall Rise*, 504, discusses Slaton's decision to call in the state militia.

63. The Georgia National Guard reports of Slaton's response to the men arrested at Wingfield is quoted in Oney, *And the Dead Shall Rise*, 510.

64. Powell, *I Can Go Home Again*, 291.

65. Kennedy, *Profiles in Courage*, 266; "Kennedy Speaks Words He Didn't Get to Tape," *Los Angeles Times*, December 18, 1964, D22. As this article explains, Kennedy's reading of the final paragraph from his book had been previously recorded for the *Omnibus* series episode Kennedy narrated in 1957. After Kennedy's assassination, Saudek stumbled on the old recording while rescreening "Call It Courage" just before the start of work on the new series.

66. Don M. Mankiewicz notes, October 17, 1963, PIC GJMS File, box 246, Saudek Collection.

67. Don M. Mankeiwicz, first draft script, November 21, 1963, and January 6, 1964, comments (likely from Gordon Oliver), PIC GJMS Correspondence VP 110 File, box 246, Saudek Collection.

68. Allan Nevins to Mankiewicz: John M. Slaton, December 10, 1963, PIC GJMS Correspondence VP 110 File, box 246, Saudek Collection.

69. Theodore C. Sorensen to Robert Saudek, January 30, 1964, Slaton Research File PIC GJMS, box 246, Saudek Collection.

70. Walter Kerr, handwritten comments, November 26, 1963, Early Draft File; and November 8, 1963, comments on Mankiewicz's first draft. Theodore Sorensen made a similar observation: "The nature of the crime, the roles played by Frank, the girl, and Conley, etc., ought to be made much clearer in the first act. The reference on page II-29 is too hurried and confused. It would also be helpful to show Frank himself or at least his picture in the papers early in the first act and in the Prologue" (Theodore Sorensen to Robert Saudek, January 30, 1964, PIC GJMS Correspondence VP 110 File, box 246, Saudek Collection).

71. Gordon Oliver, handwritten, undated memo to Michael Ritchie, Material for California, 2-20-64 File, box 309, Saudek Collection; G.O. and M.R., memo to Robert Saudek on Stylization in the Slaton script, December 17, 1963, RSA Interoffice Correspondence (PIC) File, box 310, Saudek Collection.

72. First draft, November 21, 1963, received in New York, Slaton (Outline and First Draft) PIC Mankiewicz File, box 246, Saudek Collection.

73. John M. Slaton Jr. to Mary V. Ahern, March 26, 1965, John M. Slaton Research File, box 246, Saudek Collection.

74. Robert D. Kasmire (vice president, NBC Corporate Information) to Robert Saudek, March 15, 1965, PIC, Complaints, Legal Action File, box 309, Saudek Collection.

75. Thomas Watson Brown to Robert G. Kintner (president, NBC), March 10, 1965, PIC, Complaints, Legal Action File, box 309. Brown's father (Tom Watson's grandson) had already exchanged letters with Kintner in December and January.

76. Bernard Weinraub to Mary [V. Ahern].

77. Thomas Watson Brown to Robert G. Kintner (president, NBC), March 10, 1965.

78. Robert Louis Shayon, "Order vs. Liberty," *Saturday Review*, December 26, 1964, 22.

79. William B. Hartsfield to Kellam de Forest, May 26, 1964, PIC GJMS Correspondence VP 110 File, box 246, Saudek Collection. See also Robert Saudek to Robert Kasmire, January 11, 1965; Corydon B. Dunham Jr., assistant general attorney, to Tom Watson Brown, Esq., March 22, 1965; and Tom Watson Brown to Corydon B. Dunham Jr., March 31, 1965, all in PIC, Complaints, Legal Action File, box 309, Saudek Collection.

80. See Harold C. Bailey to "Profiles in Courage," c/o NBC, December 6, 1964, PIC Misc File, box 310, Saudek Collection. No reply to this comment appears in the *Profiles in Courage* File, likely because—though powerfully voiced—it was clearly a minority view.

81. Saudek's public comments on the series's relevance appear in Gardner, "Pulitzer 'Profiles' Get Video Face-lifting," 17; Robert Saudek to Theodore C. Sorensen, March 23, 1964, Profiles Letter and Contract File, box 310, Saudek Collection.

82. Jack Gould, "TV: 'Profiles in Courage,'" 67. For a similar point, see Herm., [*sic*], "Profiles in Courage," *Variety*, November 4, 1963; John Marshall Cuno, "Profile in Courage," *Christian Science Monitor*, March 17, 1965, 4.

83. Apparently, Robert Saudek Associates received several letters about the episode, but the company sent them to an associate of Justice Felix Frankfurter. See Liza Molodovsky (secretary to Robert Saudek) to Professor Max Isenbergh, January 15, 1965, PIC Important Corrrespondence File, box 310, Saudek Collection; Dick Gray, "Georgia's Gov. Slaton Hero of 'Profiles' Today," *Atlanta Journal and Constitution*, December 20, 1964, 10D.

Chapter 4. The "Full" Treatment

1. Frank Ritter, Jerry Thompson, and Robert Sherborne, "An Innocent Man Was Lynched," *Nashville Tennessean*, March 7, 1982, 1.

2. Mann's comments about the mob appear in Steve Oney, "The Lynching of Leo Frank," *Esquire*, September 1985, 104. Quotations from the *Tennessean* ap-

pear in Ritter, "An Innocent Man Was Lynched," 1. The *Tennessean* compared the Frank case with a more recent headline-grabbing Atlanta case: "No other [Atlanta] trial even comes close, except perhaps that of Wayne Williams, convicted a week ago in the deaths of two young Atlanta blacks and suspected of being the mass murderer who terrorized Atlanta for months."

3. Steve Oney, "The Lynching of Leo Frank," 93, and Oney, *And the Dead Shall Rise: The Murder of Mary Phagan and the Lynching of Leo Frank* (New York: Pantheon Books, 2003), 93, 644–49.

4. The Oney quotation is from "The Lynching of Leo Frank," 104. The Leonard Dinnerstein quotation is from his "Leo Frank Case," *New Georgia Encyclopedia*, http://www.georgiaencyclopedia.org/nge/Article.jsp?id=h-906&hl=y, accessed June 3, 2007. See also Robert Seitz Frey and Nancy Thompson-Frey, *The Silent and the Damned: The Murder of Mary Phagan and the Lynching of Leo Frank* (New York: Madison Books, 1988); Mary Phagan-Kean, *The Murder of Little Mary Phagan* (Far Hills, N.J.: New Horizon Press, 1987).

5. See the Christopher Awards Web site for an explanation of the award's history and guiding principles: http://www.christophers.org/awardsmm.html.

6. "Column Items," "Profiles in Courage," NBC Publicity, 3, Clippings File, Television Clipping Files, USC Cinema-Television Collection. Viewers of the miniseries will note that the first end credit after George Stevens's is a thank-you to Dan Petrie, who took over shooting when Hale became ill.

7. Eleanor Blau, "Jack Lemmon Returns to Television Drama," *New York Times*, January 23, 1988, 50.

8. Much of this production history of *The Murder of Mary Phagan* comes from my telephone interviews with George Stevens Jr. on August 16 and 23, 2005. Unless otherwise noted, all quotations from Stevens come from these conversations. Stevens makes some similar points in Blau, "Jack Lemmon," 50.

9. Harry Golden, *A Little Girl Is Dead* (New York: World Publishing Co., 1965). For an example of the critics' relative weighting of Golden's book versus Capote's, see, for example, Anthony Boucher, "Criminals at Large," *New York Times*, January 2, 1966, 203.

10. "Harry Golden Settles Suit over 'A Little Girl Is Dead,'" *New York Times*, December 14, 1968, 22.

11. Unless otherwise noted, all quotations from Jeffrey Lane come from an interview with the author in New York City on Thursday, September 8, 2005. Stevens had not seen *They Won't Forget* but might have seen the *Profiles in Courage* episode on John Slaton. Lane saw the LeRoy film only after *The Murder of Mary Phagan* aired, when it was shown on Turner Classic Movies; neither man had seen the Oscar Micheaux film. Stevens recalled, "I don't want to see some-

thing like that, because images get in your head and you want to live with your own imaginative view of what it looked like." In addition, since Golden did not use citations in his book, Stevens and Land had to find sources for their story.

12. McMurtry went on to write the script for the 1994 miniseries adaptation of his novel *Lonesome Dove* and coauthor the Oscar-winning screenplay for *Brokeback Mountain* (2005).

13. In 2005, Lane authored the book for the hit Broadway musical production of *Dirty Rotten Scoundrels*. See Michael Buckley, "Channeling Theatre: A Chat with TV Writer and *Dirty Rotten Scoundrels*' Jeffrey Lane," *Playbill*, August 29, 2004, http://www.playbill.com/features/article/88116.html (accessed March 4, 2008).

14. See, for example, Blau, "Jack Lemmon," 50; Clarke Taylor, "Leo Frank Case on Screen: 1913 'Mob Law' Murder Comes to Life," *Los Angeles Times*, July 10, 1987, sect. 6, p. 24. The article puts the cost of the series at $7 million.

15. See "Column Items," "Costumes Galore," *The Murder of Mary Phagan* press release, 5; and "Historic Steps," NBC Special Mailer, *The Murder of Mary Phagan*, Television Clipping Files, USC Cinema-Television Collection.

16. These comments on the background of the production design for the miniseries derive from my telephone interview with Veronica Hadfield, June 3, 2005. All quotations from her are from this interview.

17. Taylor, "Leo Frank Case on Screen," sect. 6, pp. 2, 4; and W. MacD. [sic], "George Stevens, Jr.; A Filmmaker's Journey to Virginia," *Hollywood Reporter*, October 25, 1988, S-8.

18. Given that cotton was no longer grown in Virginia, Hadfield and her crew took advice from Georgia's Department of Agriculture and planted cotton seed six weeks in advance of the shoot.

19. Interview with Nic Knowland, June 23, 2005, London.

20. Frank Ritter, "Terrified Boy Feared for His Life," *Nashville Tennessean*, March, 7, 1982, 3.

21. Oney, *And the Dead Shall Rise*, 311; Golden, *A Little Girl Is Dead*, 93, 173.

22. Nancy MacLean, "The Leo Frank Case Reconsidered: Gender and Sexual Politics in the Making of Reactionary Populism," *Journal of American History* 78, no. 3 (1991): 930.

23. Ritter, "Terrified Boy," 3.

24. Golden, *A Little Girl Is Dead*, 3.

25. Ritter, "Terrified Boy," 3. Mann described this encounter as taking place under a factory staircase where Conley sat asking passersby for money; this was the spot where Conley alleged that he acted as Frank's lookout.

26. Oney, "The Lynching of Leo Frank," 104.

27. Oney, *And the Dead Shall Rise*, 70.

28. Dorsey's dialogue here references a scandal in which the Atlanta police were caught looking the other way while downtown houses of prostitution were operating; the recently appointed police chief, Beavers, had worked to address this issue and clean up the department. Ibid., 53–59.

29. C. Vann Woodward, *Tom Watson: Agrarian Rebel* (New York: Oxford University Press, 1963), 439.

30. *Jeffersonian*, April 14, May 27, 1915, quoted in Woodward, *Tom Watson*, 438.

31. The miniseries quickly suggests that Watson's understanding of poor Georgians arises from his own financial troubles. When he insists Slaton come to Mary Phagan's funeral, Watson begins by asking Slaton for financial help "for one of my boys" from Slaton's "New York banker friends." Later, when Lucille Frank tells Watson they can meet his price for defending Leo ("The money is there"), Watson declines the offer, noting that such wealth will count against Leo Frank. Watson will take a northern loan in private but will not accept generous pay in public. He shares Georgians' resentment at needing help of any kind from the North.

32. Woodward, *Tom Watson*, 347.

33. Ibid., 431.

34. Ibid., 433–34.

35. Jeffrey Lane recalled that the script originally envisioned Dorsey and Slaton as childhood friends, but that idea became untenable when Jack Lemmon was cast as Slaton, given that Lemmon was significantly older than Richard Jordan.

36. See Oney, *And the Dead Shall Rise*, 91, for an account of Dorsey's takeover of the Frank case investigation and prosecution.

37. See ibid., 94–95, for an account of Dorsey's troubled reputation at the time of Mary Phagan's murder.

38. Leonard Dinnerstein, *The Leo Frank Case* (New York: Columbia University Press, 1968), 59, taken from DeWitt H. Roberts, "Anti-Semitism and the Leo M. Frank Case," unpublished essay in possession of the Anti-defamation League in New York City.

39. Mann's statement accords with his 1982 comment to the *Nashville Tennessean*: "In all the time I worked for him, I never saw Frank put his hand on a girl, never saw him have a conversation with one, never had one to come in his office and stand over or lean over his desk" (Frank Ritter, "Terrified Boy," 3). Dinnerstein discusses the defense's flaws in *Leo Frank Case*, 57–59.

40. Oney, *And the Dead Shall Rise*, 308–9.

41. Ibid., 309.

42. Ibid., 293.

43. Golden, *A Little Girl Is Dead*, 137: "Conley's general bad character was attested to by a score of defense witnesses, members of his own race who had known him all of his life. . . . The State . . . . [was not] able to find one witness who would say a kind word for Conley's credibility."

44. See Oney, *And the Dead Shall Rise*, 141–44, for an account of Conley's guided tour of the factory and its impact on Atlanta police.

45. Conley quoted in ibid., 141.

46. Ibid., 247–48, has an account of Rosser's cross-examination of Conley. Jeffrey Lane recalled, "I believe there was some discussion [of using the 'n' word], but it was absolutely necessary [to use it in dialogue]. Neither George nor I would use it lightly. It wasn't thrown around." Oney, *And the Dead Shall Rise*, discusses white Atlanta's assumptions about blacks' deceitfulness on p. 141.

47. Ibid., 496.

48. The working title for the miniseries was "The Ballad of Mary Phagan." Stevens explained that using Leo Frank in the title would make it "too literal," while NBC speculated that "Ballad" would be too vague for a mass audience. Murder in the title would of course attract more viewers.

49. W. MacD. [*sic*], "George Stevens, Jr.," S-8.

50. Oney, *And the Dead Shall Rise*, 385–87, 407–11.

51. Ibid., 397–403.

52. See R. S. Carraway, "Georgians in the Metropolis," *Atlanta Constitution*, April 27, 1913, A11, for an account of the 1913 Memorial Day festivities; see MacLean, "The Leo Frank Case Reconsidered," 927, for a discussion of child labor in Georgia in 1913.

53. See Oney, *And the Dead Shall Rise*, 470–74, for a discussion of Frank's legal team's strategies after the U.S. Supreme Court rejected his appeal.

54. The scene in part 2 depicting national protest in favor of mercy for Frank evokes a detail in C. Vann Woodward's biography of Tom Watson: Eugene Foss, the former governor of Massachussetts, personally visited the state to plead for Frank's life (Woodward, *Tom Watson*, 436).

55. Ibid., 444.

56. See Oney, *And the Dead Shall Rise*, 488, on Slaton's accomplishments as governor and his likely feelings about having to rule on the Frank appeal; pp. 487, 491, on the crowds gathering outside government buildings to agitate for Frank's execution.

57. See ibid., 490–91, on the Marietta delegation's statements at Slaton's hearing; p. 470 on Frank's appeals team's strategy; and pp. 488–98 for a full account of Slaton's hearing sessions regarding Frank's appeal.

58. Jeffrey Lane interview. "Everybody has his reasons" is a celebrated line of dialogue from Jean Renoir's classic film *The Rules of the Game* (1939).

59. Oney, *And the Dead Shall Rise*, 248.

60. See ibid., 510–11, for a description of Harris's inauguration and the attempt on Slaton's life.

61. Ibid., 498; "Three of Georgia's Six Ex-Governors in Politics, Franklin Nix," *Atlanta Constitution*, September 6, 1953, in Clippings File, box 246, Robert A. Saudek Collection, Wesleyan Cinema Archives, Wesleyan University, Middletown, Connecticut (hereafter Saudek Collection). Dinnerstein describes Slaton's deliberations in *Leo Frank Case*, 122–29.

62. Oney, *And the Dead Shall Rise*, 424–33.

63. See ibid., 499, for a discussion of William Smith's visit to Wingfield, and pp. 97–100, on the *Atlanta Georgian*'s shifting stance on the case.

64. Conley's letters are quoted in ibid., 390, 391.

65. Recall that in *Murder in Harlem*, the white employer Brisbane had to spell "night witch" for Lem Hawkins for the murder notes. Micheaux gave his Leo Frank character definite knowledge of the night witch legend.

66. Oney, *And the Dead Shall Rise*, 254.

67. Slaton's comments to the press are quoted in ibid., 503, and recorded in the *Atlanta Journal*, June 21, 1915.

68. See "Great Crowd Sees Harris Sworn in as Head of State," *Atlanta Constitution*, June 27, 1915, 1, 4, for a contemporary account of the ceremony and the crowd's behavior.

69. Oney, *And the Dead Shall Rise*, 509.

70. The "lynch law" and "no law" quotation comes from the *Jeffersonian*, June 24, 1915, quoted in Oney, *And the Dead Shall Rise*, 508; the "next Jew" comment is quoted in Woodward, *Tom Watson*, 443, from the August 12, 1915, issue of the *Jeffersonian*.

71. *Jeffersonian*, June 24, 1915, quoted in Woodward, *Tom Watson*, 441.

72. Oney, *And the Dead Shall Rise*, 513, 543–44, provides extensive documentation to prove that the Georgia Prison Commission and prison officials knew in advance that the "Knights" planned to abduct and lynch Frank and allowed it to happen. Of course, this revelation postdates the miniseries. Oney mentions that the lynching group informed Frank he would not need his clothes; see ibid., 562. In the series, Lund tells the lynchers Frank can take his shoes with him—a nice detail, because Lund originally appeared at the factory door to retrieve his own shoes after he had been fired.

73. See ibid., 563–64, for an account of Frank's final ride.

74. See ibid., 564–65, for an account of Frank's lynching.

75. See ibid., 555–70, for an account of the crowd's behavior after Frank was lynched.

76. Although scenes of mothers/wives hearing the sad news of a son's/husband's death are legion, the impact of this scene is comparable to *Saving Private Ryan* (1997) when the Ryan matriarch sees the military officials approach her farmhouse to report that three of her four sons are dead and sinks in silent devastation on her front porch.

77. Oney, *And the Dead Shall Rise*, 646–47.

78. Robert Sherborne, "Old Man Looks Back with Misty Eyes," *Nashville Tennessean*, March 7, 1982, 4.

79. Telephone interview with George Stevens Jr., August 23, 2005. As of this writing, no archival collection exists with production documentation that would shed light on the process by which Slaton's conflict of interest was left out or judged unessential to the story.

80. *The Murder of Mary Phagan*, publicity, "Jack Lemmon Stars," 2, Television Clippings File, USC Cinema-Television Library.

81. The comparison to the Dreyfus affair comes from "George Stevens Jr. Miniseries, 'The Murder of Mary Phagan,' to Air on NBC," Publicity, Television Clippings File, USC Cinema-Television Library; Stevens's comments on Slaton appeared in Arthur Ungar, "Producer Stevens Tells What Drew Him to Story of Mary Phagan," *Christian Science Monitor*, January 22, 1988, 21; Jack Lemmon's comments appeared in "Jack Lemmon Returns to Network Television in Gripping NBC Miniseries, 'The Murder of Mary Phagan,' 2; all of these items can be found in the Television Clippings File, USC Cinema-Television Library.

82. Michael E. Hill, "'Mary Phagan'; A Yankee, a Jew, and Above All an Outsider," *Washington Post*, January 24, 1988, TV8. See also Yardena Arar, "Lemmon Restrained—but Not Reluctant," *Los Angeles Daily News*, January 24, 1988, L.A. Life Section, 18, Television Clippings File, USC Cinema-Television Library.

83. "Dramatic Quality of Slaton's Dilemma Too Good to Turn Down,' Says Jack Lemmon of Role in 'The Murder of Mary Phagan,'" NBC Special Mailer, *The Murder of Mary Phagan*, Television Clippings File, USC Cinema-Television Library. See also Blau, "Jack Lemmon," 50: "There has been an incredible erosion of morals and ethics in this country from the time I was a very young man." Clarke Taylor, "Leo Frank Case on Screen; 1913 'Mob Law' Murder Comes to Life," *Los Angeles Times*, July 10, 1987, sect. 6, p. 24.

84. Stevens's and Lemmon's comments on the cast appear in a press release by Orion Television and George Stevens Jr. Productions: "Jack Lemmon Stars in 'The Murder of Mary Phagan,' Dramatic Fact-based Miniseries on NBC," Television

Clippings File, USC Cinema-Television Library. Stevens's comments on his father and the audience appear in "George Stevens, Jr. Miniseries, 'The Murder of Mary Phagan,' to Air on NBC," 1, Television Clippings File, USC Cinema-Television Library.

85. Lemmon's comments on Frank's guilt appear in Hill, "Mary Phagan," TV8; Stevens's claims that the series was not polemical appear in Ungar, "Producer Stevens," 21; also see "Taylor, "Leo Frank Case on Screen," 24.

86. Phil Kloer, "Miniseries Stirs Phagan Controversy," *Atlanta Constitution*, January 7, 1988, D1.

87. Morris B. Abram, "They Lynched an Innocent Man—as the Governor Tried to Save Him," TV *Guide*, January 23, 1988, 32–35.

88. Hill, "Mary Phagan," 12. For simplicity's sake, I list here the reviews of *The Murder of Mary Phagan* that I discuss in the following pages: Yardena Arar, "Television: 'Phagan' a Complex, Bold Study," *Los Angeles Daily News*, January 24, 1988, 19; Martha Bayliss, "A 1913 Child Murder Case," *Wall Street Journal*, January 25, 1988, 29; John Carmody, "The TV Column," *Washington Post*, January 27, 1988, D8; Kyle Counts, "TV Review: 'Murder of Mary Phagan,'" *Hollywood Reporter*, January 22, 1988, 8; David Gritten, "'Murder Most Proper: Even Lemmon Can't Save It," *Los Angeles Herald Examiner*, January 23, 1988, B1; Jeff Jarvis, "People Picks & Pans," *People*, January 25, 1988, 9; John Leonard, "Broadcast Views," *New York*, January 25, 1988, 68; John J. O'Connor, "TV Weekend: 'Murder of Mary Phagan,' on NBC," *New York Times*, January 22, 1988, C30; Tom Shales, "TV Preview: 'Murder' Most Compelling," *Washington Post*, January 23, 1988, G1, G8; Laurie Stone, "Georgia Breach," *Village Voice*, January 26, 1988, 41; "Tone, 'Murder of Mary Phagan,'" *Variety* February 3, 1988, 139; Arthur Ungar, "Worth Noting on TV," *Christian Science Monitor*, January 21, 1988, 21; Kyle Counts, "TV Review: 'Murder of Mary Phagan,'" *Hollywood Reporter*, January 22, 1988, 8.

89. In an April 17, 2007, conversation at the Fox Theater in Atlanta, Dutton recounted to the author that when he took the role of Conley, certain civil rights activists expressed concern over the possibly untoward consequences of his portrayal of Jim Conley and the debate over his innocence or guilt in Mary Phagan's murder.

90. Reviewers often revealed varied knowledge of the case. John J. O'Connor at the *New York Times* understandably assumed that Alonzo Mann's confessions had settled the case once and for all; *Variety*'s reviewer thought Frank had been lynched in his own front yard. The *Hollywood Reporter*'s critic, Kyle Counts, missed the boat most often: he cited the William J. Burns subplot as one of the "extraneous elements" because it bore "little fruit"—forgetting that Burns had a historical

role in the case and that he contributes decisively to Slaton's deliberations in the miniseries. Counts also wished "that Frank's story had been given more attention (as written, he is strangely passive and not particularly sympathetic), and that the story didn't leave the viewer with so many unanswered questions"—but of course Frank's unlikable features and the case's ambiguity were part of the miniseries's portrayal of the historical Frank and the uncertainty about his guilt.

91. Carmody, "The TV Column," D8; "ABC Wins Top Series Emmys," *New York Times*, August 30, 1988, C18; NBC Media Relations press release, "'The Murder of Mary Phagan' Honored with Peabody Award," April 17, 1989.

92. Lifetime Learning Systems, poster, 1988, Anti-defamation League (ADL), made possible by NBC. The ADL poster is in the Peabody Collection, folder 88108ENT, Hargret Rare Book and Manuscript Library, University of Georgia, Athens. Thanks to media archivists Margaret Compton, Nelson Hargett, and Melissa Bush for providing me with a copy of this document. Certain television critics compared *The Murder of Mary Phagan* with similar TV shows. Like John J. O'Connor, the *Village Voice*'s Laurie Stone mentioned ABC's January 1988 TV *Evil in Clear River*, about an actual Canadian neo-Nazi and Holocaust-denying schoolteacher. HBO's *Into the Homeland* looks at American neo-Nazi groups. Stone quipped, "In December Christians get cheery Christmas specials. In January, Jews are getting reminded how much they're hated"; see her "Georgia Breach."

93. Phil Kloer, "'Mary Phagan' Still Compelling; Historians May Carp, but Show Rewards Viewers," *Atlanta Constitution*, January 22, 1988, C1; Katie Long, "Mary Phagan's Great-Niece Says Miniseries Isn't History," *Atlanta Constitution*, January 26, 1988, C2; Celestine Sibley, "'Mary Phagan' Film Left Many Questions," *Atlanta Constitution*, January 29, 1988, C1. These debates continued with the Atlanta premiere of Alfred Uhry's musical *Parade*. See Dan Hulbert, "Mixed Emotions Greet Uhry's 'Parade,'" *Atlanta Constitution*, November 1, 1998, L4; and Yolanda Rodriguez, "'A Renewed Commitment': Ceremony Remembers Lynching," *Atlanta Constitution*, August 18, 2005, C3.

Conclusion

1. See Robert C. Allen's excellent discussion of liberal philosophy as it relates to 1950s and 1960s American documentary filmmaking in his and Douglas Gomery's *Film History: Theory and Practice* (New York: McGraw-Hill, 1985), 233–36.

2. Author's interview with Jeffrey Lane, New York City, September 8, 2005.

3. To take just one example of a current controversy surrounding a convicted killer facing execution as well as reasonable doubt, see Brendan Lowe's article about

Troy Anthony Davis, "Will Georgia Execute an Innocent Man," *Time* online, posted July 13, 2007, at http://www.time.com/time/nation/article/0,8599,1643384,00.html?cnn=yes, accessed March 3, 2008. As an example of the continuing pertinence of the factors that informed the Frank case one can point to the debate surrounding the presidential candidacy of Barack Obama in 2008.

Index

Andy Griffin in *They Won't Forget* (1937), 62–69, 82–83, 85, 86, 88, 100, 101, 105, 258; portrayed in *Profiles in Courage:* "Governor John M. Slaton" (1964), 146, 258; portrayed in *The Murder of Mary Phagan* (1988), 175, 184, 187, 192, 196–97, 200–204, 207–8, 221, 227–28, 238–41, 258

Douglass, Frederick W., 161

Dray, Philip, *At the Hands of Persons Unknown: The Lynching of Black America,* 290n59

Dreyfus affair, 15, 73, 214

drug abuse portrayed in film and television, 120

DuBois, W. E. B., 28

Dutton, Charles, 179, 247, 313n89

Early, Kermit, 58–59

Edgerton, Gary, *Television Histories: Shaping Collective Memory in the Media Age,* 273–74n30

Eight Great Americans (NBC), 134

Einfeld, Charles, 110

Emperor Jones (1933), 31

Engle, Dorothy van, 36, 58

Epps, George, 12; portrayed as Joe Turner in *They Won't Forget* (1937), 62, 89–90, 95–96, 104; portrayed in *Murder in Harlem* (1936), 37–38, 46–47, 55

Esmond, Irwin, 94

Evers, Medgar, 168

Everton, Paul, 68

Exile, The (1931), 35

Farrar, Geraldine, 19–20

Faulkner, William, 119

Federal Communications Commission (FCC), 120

Ferguson, Otis, 114

Ferrer, Mel, 81

Five Star Final (1931), 74, 92, 101–2

Fool's Errand, A (Glory), 47, 180n30

Foote, Horton, 130

Foreman, Carl, 131

Forged Note: A Romance of the Darker Races (Micheaux), 26, 32, 277n14

Foster, Donald, 137, 149

Frank, Leo M., 3, 5–7, 271n21; guilt or innocence of, 10–13, 16, 219, 226–29, 243, 274n31; portrayed as Anthony Brisbane in *Murder in Harlem* (1936), 33, 35, 37, 42, 45–47, 278n16; portrayed as Robert Hale in *They Won't Forget* (1937), 63–69, 90–92, 95–97, 104, 257; portrayed as sexual predator, 3, 13–14, 58–59, 147, 174, 187–90, 196, 198, 206, 309n39; in *Profiles in Courage:* "Governor John M. Slaton" (1964), 257; in *The Murder of Mary Phagan* (1988), 179–80, 186–90, 205, 207, 209, 226, 236, 240, 257

Frank, Lucille, 6–7, 11–12, 15, 69, 135, 177; portrayed as Sybil Hale in *They Won't Forget* (1937), 64, 68–69, 90–92, 99–102, 238; in *The Murder of Mary Phagan* (1988), 180–81, 184, 197, 199, 202–3, 207–9, 217, 225, 236–39, 257

Frank, Rae, 17, 67

Frank Case, The (1915), 19

Frazer, E. Franklin, 50

Freeman, Bee, 50, 58

Frey, Robert Seitz, *The Silent and the Damned: The Murder of Mary Phagan and the Lynching of Leo Frank,* 286n25

Sack, Lester, 55
Sampson, Henry T., *Blacks in Black and White: A Source Book on Black Films* (2d ed.), 273n27
Samuels, Charles, *Night Fell on Georgia*, 295n4
Saudek, Robert, 123–24, 127, 156, 169, 256
Saudek Collection (Robert A. Saudek Papers), 295nn2–3
Schiffman, Franklin, 55, 281n45
Schlesinger, Arthur, 143
Schurz, Carl, 229–30
Schutt, Deborah, 181
Schwerner, Michael, 121, 168
Scottsboro Nine, 46, 58, 80, 99, 115, 248, 255
sectionalism, 9, 13, 61, 64–67, 72–73, 102–6, 290n60; and *Profiles in Courage*: "Governor John M. Slaton" (1964), 162–63, 166; and *The Murder of Mary Phagan* (1988), 195–96, 309n31
September 11, 2001, terrorist attacks, 24
sexuality and homosexuality in film and television, 120
Shales, Tom, 245–47
Sherman, Vincent (né Abraham Orovitz), 20–21; *Studio Affairs: My Life as a Film Director*, 273n28
Shoemaker, Ann, 68
Shogun (1988), 174
Shurlock, Geoffrey, 79
Sibley, Celestine, 249
Sidney, Sylvia, 92
Simmons, William J., 15
Simpson, O. J., trial of, 16
Slaton, John M., 10, 16–17, 140, 215–16; and commutation of death sentence, 9–11, 219–20, 231, 271–72, 303n48; conflicts of

interest, 155–56, 304n57; portrayed as Governor Mountford in *They Won't Forget* (1937), 28, 68–69, 105, 214, 221; portrayed in *Profiles in Courage*: "Governor John M. Slaton" (1964), 117–18, 122, 126, 148–70, 221, 230, 258; in *The Murder of Mary Phagan* (1988), 171, 176, 178, 191–92, 201, 207–8, 214–36, 240–41, 258; threats against, 156–59, 224–25, 232
Slaton, John M., Jr., 135, 166
Slaton, Sallie, 68, 140; portrayed as Mrs. Mountford in *They Won't Forget* (1937), 68; portrayed in *Profiles in Courage*: "Governor John M. Slaton" (1964), 137–40, 157, 158; portrayed in *The Murder of Mary Phagan* (1988), 179, 217–18, 229–32
Smith, William, 67–68, 150, 224, 240; in *Profiles in Courage*: "Governor John M. Slaton" (1964), 138, 143, 147–51
Sobchack, Vivian, *The Persistence of History: Cinema, Television, and the Modern Event*, 273–74n30
social consciousness and commentary in film and television, 118–21, 174
Sorensen, Theodore C., 125–27, 132–33, 141, 164, 169, 296nn8–9, 299n25, 305n70
Soubier, Clifford, 65, 86
Southern Politics in State and Nation (Key), 162
Spacey, Kevin, 179
Stam, Robert, *A Companion to Literature and Film*, 273n30
Standards and Practices Department (NBC), 144, 174
Stanton, Elizabeth Cady, 125
Star Reporters and Thirty-four of